The Impeachment of Andrew Johnson

The Impeachment of Andrew Johnson

by
CHESTER G. HEARN

McFarland & Company, Inc., Publishers
Jefferson, North Carolina, and London

ALSO BY CHESTER G. HEARN

Mobile Bay and the Mobile Campaign:
The Last Great Battles of the Civil War
(McFarland, 1993)

Frontispiece: Andrew Johnson (Massachusetts Commandery Military
Order of the Loyal Legion and the U.S. Army Military History Institute)

ISBN 0-7864-0863-4 (illustrated case binding : 50# alkaline paper) ∞

Library of Congress cataloguing data are available

British Library cataloguing data are available

Manufactured in the United States of America

McFarland & Company, Inc., Publishers
  Box 611, Jefferson, North Carolina 28640
    www.mcfarlandpub.com

To Ann, Chet and the
beloved memory of Wendy

Acknowledgments

Many individuals have contributed to this book, among them Rebecca Livingston at the National Archives, John Hutson and his staff at the Library of Congress, Linda Stanley at the Historical Society of Pennsylvania, Kendra Hinkle at the Andrew Johnson Historical Site, and Evelyn Wesman, who gathered an immense amount of information and research for me through the Erie County Public Library. My thanks to them all. Also, my gratitude goes to the library staff members at Columbia University, Huntington Library at Harvard University, Indiana State Historical Society, New York Historical Society, New York Public Library, Tennessee State Library and Archives, Cleveland Public Library, and to the staff of John Slonaker and Michael Winey at the United States Military History Institute.

I ask forgiveness for not remembering and mentioning the names of all the people who have assisted in some way with this work. To all, I give my warmest thanks.

Table of Contents

Preface

The study of Andrew Johnson and the Radicals has been a subject of my interest for a number of years, though I had never thought of condensing it into a book until another presidential impeachment — that of William Jefferson Clinton — began to take form as early as 1996. This work started many months before impeachment proceedings began against Clinton, using documents, manuscripts, and other works collected, catalogued, and maintained for many years.

What attracted me to writing this book was the search for a deeper understanding of how the impeachment process works, what motivates such action on the part of politicians, and in Andrew Johnson's instance, why he was impeached at all. The book is not about William Jefferson Clinton, but those who followed his trial in the Senate will observe both similarities and differences in the process as it applied to Johnson.

In Johnson's trial, the prosecution called twenty-five witnesses, the defense sixteen. In the Clinton trial, no witnesses were called to testify before the Senate, which tainted the process. In the Johnson trial, there never was any evidence against the president for high crimes or misdemeanors, but Republican Radicals did not like him and believed that since impeachment was a political rather than a criminal process, they could oust the president and replace him with one of their own. In the Clinton trial, there was a mountain of circumstantial and condemning evidence that could have been supported by witness testimony, but weak Senate leadership failed to demand it. The consequences of the Senate's failure, in both instances, to conduct a proper impeachment has established precedents that will make it almost impossible to impeach future presidents for certain forms of criminal behavior.

Andrew Johnson was impeached because he attempted to prevent Congress from usurping executive authority and overriding the Constitution of the United States. William Jefferson Clinton was impeached for perjurious action before a court of law and for abusing presidential powers. Both men were acquitted, but with different consequences for the country. Johnson's acquittal upheld the balance of power provided to the president by the Constitution and prevented Congress from taking over the government. Clinton's acquittal enlarged the powers of the executive in a malfeasant way, and the Senate, by its compromising and superficial actions during the proceedings against Clinton, diminished its own congressional power to restrain or impeach a future president who breaks the law.

It is important for the American

1

public to understand what impeachment is and is not. Andrew Johnson's battle with the Radicals adds a necessary chapter to this understanding. It reveals the evils and corruption of a political system that has grown since the Civil War to dominate and influence the moral fiber of this nation.

Introduction

As youngsters, Andrew Johnson and Abraham Lincoln had much in common. Both were born in southern states, Johnson in Tennessee and Lincoln in Kentucky, the former forty-five days before the latter. Both grew up in poverty, and as lads, neither received much in the way of an education. Both gravitated toward politics, but Johnson had a head start, having by 1831 been twice elected alderman and twice mayor. Lincoln, in the same year, had just returned from a flatboat journey to New Orleans and taken a clerk's job in Denton Offutt's New Salem store. While Johnson served his last term as mayor, Lincoln announced his candidacy for the Illinois state legislature, lost the election, and became a captain in the bloodless Black Hawk War. During the last year of Johnson's term as mayor, Lincoln successfully won election to the Illinois legislature and remained there until 1842. In 1847 Lincoln came to Congress and served a single term while Johnson served his fourth. During Lincoln's two years in the House, he and Johnson became well acquainted, and it would not be the end of the relationship.[1]

Besides enduring hardship in youth, Johnson and Lincoln shared other similarities. Both men opposed the agitation of northern abolitionists because it divided the country. They sought methods of compromise that would eventually bring an end to the "peculiar institution," and both believed that slave holders deserved compensation for liberating their so-called property. Lincoln would be remembered for preserving the Union. Johnson would not be remembered for having tried, though in a speech before the House in 1850 he declared, "The preservation of the Union is paramount to all other considerations." He loved the Union with the same ardor as Lincoln, but Johnson would be mostly remembered as the first president to be impeached by Congress.[2]

Lincoln, in 1862, used more defining words when he said, "If I could save the Union without freeing any slave, I would do it; if I could save it by freeing all the slaves, I would do it. And if I could by freeing some and leaving others alone I would also do that. What I do about slavery and the colored race I do because I believe it helps to save the Union, and what I forbear, I forbear because I believe it would help save the Union." These were words that Andrew Johnson could applaud, but they were words that Charles Sumner, Benjamin Wade, Thaddeus Stevens, Wendell Phillips, Henry Winter Davis, and other fanatical abolitionists could not accept. From this group of influential Republican legislators emerged one of the strongest coalitions ever formed in Congress — the Radicals.[3]

There were also differences between Johnson and Lincoln, the former being a Jacksonian Democrat and the latter a Whig. Johnson owned slaves, whom he used as personal servants, while Lincoln owned none. Lincoln also opposed the Mexican War. Johnson supported it. As president, Lincoln used exceptional tact when imposing his wishes on Congress. Johnson lacked the personal and persuasive skills of his predecessor. But Lincoln had an extraordinary advantage by being able to exercise executive war powers during his disagreements with Congress — a special privilege denied Johnson after the rebellion ended.[4]

While Johnson and Lincoln struggled to rise from poverty and obscurity, handsome and independently wealthy Charles Sumner enjoyed the grand society of the fashionable city of Boston. Three years younger than Johnson, Sumner received the best education money could buy and in 1833 graduated from Harvard Law School. He envisioned himself a scholar but better fit the characterization of prig or pedant. As a lawyer he had style and gracious manners, but no clients, so he granted himself a sabbatical to study in Europe. Like many wealthy men who succeed at nothing, Sumner turned to politics and joined with the abolitionists of the day. A vain, egotistical, arrogant, and opinionated elitist, Sumner would never find common ground with an ex-tailor like Johnson.

Lincoln understood Sumner's personality better than Johnson and played on the latter's weakness for flattery. Because of exposure to the British form of government, Sumner envisioned the Senate as a body of parliamentarians and not as constitutionalists. Lincoln understood the nature of Sumner's political philosophy and turned it to advantage. Johnson ignored Sumner's quirks and repeatedly shoved the Constitution in his face. Sumner lacked breadth in his conception of statesmanship, and though talented, sincere, and patriotic, he practiced both true and false philanthropy without the ability to distinguish between the two. In the practice of great good, he zealously advocated the immediate end of slavery, but after setting slaves free he demanded that they be legislatively elevated above their former masters. Though Sumner loved the Negro in the abstract, he avoided fellowship with him. Having owned slaves, Johnson believed blacks must be educated before obtaining the right to vote, and that the decision for enfranchising ex-slaves belonged to the individual states and not to the federal government. On this issue the philosophies of Johnson and Sumner would irreconcilably collide.[5]

Though an extraordinary man of many talents and a crusader of self-spun causes, Sumner could not lead or manage men. His marvelous gift for eloquence suffered because he failed to comprehend the importance of psychology when dealing with associates. At an early age he narrowed his interests so sharply that he never developed a sense of humor. He comported himself as a snob, remaining aloof from commoners. He won few friends, and though a handsome man, his narcissist nature turned away the opposite sex. A sense of humor may have saved him, but a fellow senator recalled, "His egotism was such as to make it impossible for him to admit that he had an equal in either House of Congress." Henry Adams thought of him as a "pathological study," a person who had "reached the calm of water which receives and reflects images without absorbing them: it contained nothing but itself." Like Thaddeus Stevens, who ruled the House, Sumner was not a constructive statesman, though he thought himself so. Having an absolute disregard for constitutional restraints, Sumner would not find compatibility with a man like Andrew Johnson.[6]

Benjamin F. Wade, born in Massachusetts in 1800, moved to Ohio in 1820. After experimenting with different careers, he studied law and in 1827 passed the bar. He began the practice of law in Jefferson, Ohio. Four years later he formed a partnership with Joshua Giddings, an abolitionist and one of the ablest political leaders in the state. Wade soon joined Giddings in the antislavery movement, attached himself to the emerging Whig Party, and won a seat in the Ohio senate, where he remained until 1843. During his years as a state senator, Wade developed into an outspoken opponent of the fugitive slave laws. In 1847, he became presiding judge of the Third Judicial District. Four years later Ohio elected him to the United States Senate. Salmon P. Chase, who also became a factor in the Andrew Johnson impeachment drama, was then the senior senator from Ohio. Wade's rise to political prominence was not without difficulty, for he could not speak to crowds without feeling intense uneasiness.[7]

After Lincoln's assassination, Johnson became president. Because the office of vice president had been vacated, Wade hoped to oust a Senate colleague and become the next person in succession should Johnson not be able to fulfill Lincoln's second term in office. Wade's ambition to occupy the office became a significant factor during the trial of Andrew Johnson. Because the Radicals were determined to control the government, they backed Wade's ascension to the presidency though many moderate Republicans did not like him. One historian wrote of the senator as "a rough, domineering man of evident vulgarity, with crudely carved features, and an insolent expression — Ben Wade, possessing all of Sumner's vices and none of his attributes." Wade did not like Sumner, disapproving of the senator's "suspicion of arrogance, the flavor of sham," but to wage war against Andrew Johnson, they would need each other.[8]

Clubfooted Thaddeus Stevens hated Andrew Johnson. As an ultra Radical, he became the most powerful member of the House of Representatives. Born in 1792 in Danville, Vermont, Stevens shuffled through his first thirty-nine years of life — not because of his disability, but because people did not seem to like him. After graduating from Dartmouth College in 1815, he settled in York, Pennsylvania, taught school, and studied law. When denied admission to the bar, he moved to Gettysburg and tried again. The legal minds of Adams County liked him no better, so Stevens looked for a cause to which he could attach himself. Destructive opposition fit his personality better than constructive service, so in 1831 he joined the campaign against the Masons. He mounted such bitter attacks against Freemasonry with his vitriolic remarks that supporters elected him to the September Anti-Masonic Convention meeting in Baltimore. Nobody could stir up hate faster than Stevens. Though some questioned his sincerity of purpose, his efforts were enough to get him elected to the

Pennsylvania legislature as an anti–Mason.[9]

Now comfortably ensconced in politics, Stevens moved to Lancaster, where he soon fell out of favor with the Whigs and the Democrats. Through crafty political maneuvering and currying favor, the Whigs nominated him for Congress in 1848, and he won. When the anti–Masonry movement died, Stevens attached himself to the abolitionists. He soon became the most bitter and vituperative enemy of slavery in the House. His malice toward the southern slave holder became the passion of his life. He hated Andrew Jackson, and fairly frothed with rage against Jacksonian Democracy. His indecorous and vilifying speeches infuriated southern moderates. They played into his hands, because Stevens believed the only solution to the slave problem was war. He retired from Congress in 1852, helped launch the Republican Party in 1855, and three years later, at the age of sixty-six, returned to the House.

Stevens cherished having a platform from which hate could be espoused. When war came, he got his wish. After Confederates burned his iron works during the invasion of Pennsylvania in 1863, he hardened against the south with unrelenting malevolence. To get rich had been one of the great objects of his life. With his iron works destroyed, he sought retribution through the confiscation of southern wealth. When John Wilkes Booth assassinated Lincoln — a president distrusted by the Radicals — Stevens, who had become one of the most radical of the group, grasped an opportunity to punish the south in a manner Lincoln would have resisted. But with Andrew Johnson in office, who was not well known in the north nor elected by popular vote, Stevens believed the House and the Senate had the votes to overthrow President Johnson and make their task easier when enacting punitive reconstruction laws. Stevens soon learned that Andy Johnson was a much tougher opponent than any Radical anticipated.[10]

A look at Stevens through the eyes of his contemporaries gives a vivid picture of the man. He was a bachelor, James G. Blaine recalled, and "had the reputation of being somewhat unscrupulous as to his political methods, somewhat careless in his personal conduct, somewhat lax in his personal morals." In corroboration of the latter, another acquaintance once told Stevens: "In every part of the United States people believe that your personal life has been one prolonged sin; that your lips have been defiled with blasphemy; your body with women! A man at Newburyport ... told me three weeks since that he had at the card table heard from your mouth language fit only for an ordinary brothel, and such is the general belief." Stevens seemed to enjoy making himself offensive. "His policy," one of his kinder biographers admits, "was to bring not peace but the sword." Jeremiah S. Black, a distinguished attorney, characterized Stevens' mind as "a howling wilderness, so far as his sense of his obligation to God was concerned." Stevens admitted that "he had been all his life a scoffer at religion and a reviler of sacred things."[11]

In 1865, at the age of seventy-three, Stevens reached the pinnacle of power in the House of Representatives. His dissipation marked him, leaving his countenance cadaverous, his face long and pallid with shaggy "beetling brows," an "underlip defiantly protruding," a "hollow voice devoid of music," and a grim smile that radiated joy only when broadcasting his gospel of hatred. One observer recalled Stevens' mouth as "of unexampled cruelty," his deep-set eyes a pair of "livid coals of fire." He was immensely cunning and did not conceal it. Reproached for an "outrageous" parliamentary trick by a colleague, Stevens simply replied, "You rascal, if you allowed me to have my rights, I would not have been compelled to make a corrupt bargain in order to get them."

Stevens despised hypocrisy and would not deny his own trickery. His worst enemies admired and respected him for his frankness, however cynical and offensive his convictions might be, for he had the courage to express them without a qualm. A journalist who often disagreed with him once wrote that Stevens had "opinions of his own, and a will of his own, and he never flinched from the duty of asserting them." As one historian observed, had Stevens "lived in France in the days of the Terror, he would have pushed one of the triumvirate desperately for his place, have risen rapidly to the top through his genius and audacity and will, and probably have died on the guillotine with a sardonic smile on his face." No other person, not Sumner, Wade, or dozens of others gave Johnson more agitation and grief than Stevens, who dispensed hatred upon the president and his policies with a vengeance.[12]

Edwin M. Stanton developed an adversarial relationship with Johnson while serving as his secretary of war. Stanton entered President James Buchanan's cabinet as attorney general in the waning days of the latter's administration. Born on December 18, 1814, in Steubenville, Ohio, Stanton became a distinguished lawyer. He sought power and seemed willing to compromise his principles to obtain it. He maintained an ambivalent stance against abolition, depending upon the persuasion of his audience. Once when running for election to a minor post in Ohio, he stopped Salmon P. Chase on the streets of Columbus to emphasize complete concurrence with the latter's antislavery views. Stanton cared little about the slavery issue — he cared most about winning the forthcoming election.[13]

To those in power, Stanton comported himself deferentially and obsequiously. Yet he had an amazing ability to convince men holding extreme and opposite views that he was their advocate. To others not so influential or politically out of favor, Stanton could be a heavy-handed bully — insolent, rude, and violent. In 1856, when Stanton invited Lincoln to help litigate the McCormick Harvester Company case, he changed his mind after meeting the gangling country lawyer from Illinois. Lincoln did not understand the snub until overhearing Stanton say that "he would not associate with such a damned, gawky, long-armed ape as that." Lincoln ignored the remark and in 1862 made Stanton his secretary of war. Stanton would not be so forgiving when, in 1867, he became involved in the Radicals' power struggle to oust Johnson.[14]

The differences between Johnson and the Radicals manifested themselves in many ways, but to understand the rupture between Congress and the president requires an understanding of the political philosophies of the personalities involved. The Radicals intended to create a political environment capable of maintaining them in absolute and infinite power in all branches of government. Johnson wanted to restore the south much like it had been before the war but without slavery. If Johnson succeeded, Democrats would return to Congress from the restored states and upset the controlling Republican majority. Hatred toward the south dominated the actions of many in Congress, and Radicals envisioned Johnson as being what he was — a southern Democrat who had been brought into the Republican party during the war because of his fidelity to the Union.

Most moderate Republicans fell into line behind the leaders. Their attitude toward such measures as impeachment were mainly passive, but they thought of themselves as members of the party which had saved the nation. The only way to keep it safe, they believed, was by keeping Republicans in power. They felt that Democrats, especially those in the south, were still disloyal, and with help from Andrew Johnson would undo the work of war. Years later, when looking back on Johnson's administration, Senator Justin S. Morrill admitted the fear "now seems ridiculous," but at the time it "affected even intelligent men."[15]

Johnson held strong beliefs that bred both strengths and weaknesses.

Though he and Jefferson Davis had many differences, they came to know each other when serving together in the prewar Senate. Captured while attempting to flee the country in 1865, Davis spent the next three years in prison at Fort Monroe. Dr. John J. Craven, the prison physician, became one of Davis' few visitors. One day they discussed Johnson's personality. Perhaps no one ever described Johnson better than Davis, who admired the president's honesty of character, justice, kindliness and generosity. But, he admitted, Johnson "was eminently faithful to his word and possessed a courage which took the form of angry resistance if urged to do or not to do anything which might clash with his conviction of duty. He was indifferent to money, and careless of praise or censure, when satisfied on the necessity of any line of action." Davis recalled that Johnson's habits "were marked by temperance, industry, courage, and unswerving perseverance; also by inveterate prejudices or preconceptions on certain points, and these no arguments could change."[16]

The Radicals would try to change him and fail, and a clash of uncompromising personalities became inevitable.

1

The Rise from Poverty

Born in the frontier settlement of Raleigh, North Carolina, on December 29, 1808, Andrew Johnson spent all of his youth in poverty. The town contained a courthouse, two hotels, a number of wooden stores, and a small academy the youngster could not afford to attend. When Andrew reached the age of three, his father, Jacob Johnson, died suddenly, leaving his mother, Mary Mc-Donough Johnson, without a cent and two boys to feed. To make ends meet, she took in laundry and worked as a seamstress. The locals called her "Polly the Weaver," and she adopted the nickname. Polly could not read or write, and neither Andrew nor older brother William ever received an hour's education from their mother. Polly soon married another poor white, Turner Doughtry, another ignorant handyman without a stitch of education.[1]

When William reached the age of ten, Polly apprenticed him to James J. Selby, the local tailor. Andrew followed four years later, and his first opportunity for elementary learning came at the age of ten in Selby's tailor shop. There a local philanthropist, Dr. William Hill, routinely visited the shop and spent hours reading worthy books aloud. He entertained the apprentices with orations of famous American and British statesmen printed in the *American Speaker*. From these classics of forensic art, Andrew laboriously learned to read, and the experience whetted his appetite and stimulated his resolve to become more than just a tailor. Realizing the importance of an education, he began collecting discarded copies of periodicals and took them home to memorize.[2]

At the age of fifteen his apprenticeship ended abruptly when a boyish prank backfired. With his brother and two accomplices, he fled Raleigh and walked fifty miles to Carthage, in Moore County. Still too close to the town of his mischief, Andrew decided to leave the state and hiked into Laurens, South Carolina. He had no influential friends, but he now had a trade and an ambition to advance in life. For two years he worked as a journeyman tailor. There he fell in love with Mary Wood but received a snub from the lady, who mirthfully scoffed at his poverty. There would be snubs of many kinds during Andrew's life. Though the first one struck like an arrow piercing his heart, he healed, and the experience infused him with a determination to surmount his own grim prospects.[3]

For several months he wandered about the Carolinas and Tennessee, working as a tailor and looking for a place to settle. In May 1826, problems at home compelled him to return to

Raleigh, but he could not stay without the risk of being apprehended by Selby for deserting his indentureship. Hurriedly packing the family's scant belongings on a two-wheel cart drawn by a blind pony, he carried his mother, stepfather, and a young tailor named A. D. February to Greeneville, the county seat for Greene County in east Tennessee, and a town of five hundred inhabitants. As the family rolled into Greeneville, a group of girls standing by the road giggled as the dilapidated, dust-laden cart creaked by. Andrew looked away, but one of the girls, seventeen-year-old Eliza McCardle, an attractive lass and daughter of the local shoemaker, caught the young man's eye. According to legend, Eliza turned to her friends and confessed love at first sight, vowing to marry the lad. But Johnson did not intend to remain in Greeneville and presently moved on to seek work in Rutledge, the county seat of Grainger County. Unable to shake from his mind the coy advances of Miss McCardle, he returned to Greeneville. On May 17, 1827, Mordicai Lincoln, a magistrate and kinsman of Abraham Lincoln, married eighteen-year-old Andrew and Eliza.[4]

Johnson rented a house on Main Street, where he established living quarters in the rear for the family and used the front room as his tailor shop. During the quiet hours in the shop, Eliza taught him to write and to perform simple arithmetic computations. Many years would pass before Johnson could write with ease, but those hours spent in the tailor shop under his wife's tutelage marked the beginning of a new career.[5]

Though excluded from socializing with Greeneville's aristocracy, Johnson spent his evenings expanding his knowledge of the country and its politics. In 1828, when Eliza gave birth to Martha, their first child, Johnson now had another mouth to feed. Amid moments of both work and happiness, he continued to be coached by his wife and grew in mental stature. As his business prospered, so did his investments, and by 1831 he owned a home and two town lots with two dwellings and a smith's shop on the corner of College and Depot Streets — the present location of the Andrew Johnson National Historical Site. He continued to purchase property, including a farm not far from town where he settled his mother in comfort. Not until 1851 did he buy the large two-story brick home on Main Street, the site of the present Johnson House.[6]

The tailor shop became a meeting place for the working class of Greeneville. They came to socialize, but they also came to hear Johnson's views on the 1824 election. Andrew Jackson, the political potentate of Tennessee, had won the popular vote for president. The election had been thrown into the House of Representatives, however, and John Quincy Adams emerged the winner. Furious, Jackson began fusing together the elements of the Democratic party and mobilizing his supporters to prepare for the 1828 election. The tailor shop buzzed with opinion, its visitors often debating on local and national issues late into the night. When Greeneville College organized a debating society, Johnson joined it. He found the activity so stimulating and enjoyable that he attached himself to the debating society at Tusculum College and walked once a week four miles each way to participate and learn. Students quickly adopted Johnson, one writing many years later of his "fascinating manners, his natural talent for oratory," and "his capacity to draw the students around him and make all of them his warm friends." Students from the college soon joined the often heated discussions occurring daily in Johnson's crowded tailor shop.[7]

Greeneville's small aristocracy owned slaves and looked down on folks forced to toil for a livelihood. They ran the town and all around it. In 1829, at the age of twenty, Johnson decided that the time had come for change and won the nomination for alderman. By then, he had become a Jacksonian Democrat — what might be called today a person who appealed to the populist sentiments in the electorate. Andy Jackson swept the national election for president in 1828. In 1829, Andy Johnson, with the support of the working class, won the local election for alderman. At the time, a northern contemporary by the name of Charles Sumner was still an undergraduate at Harvard.[8]

After Johnson finished his first term as alderman, the voters returned him for a second term. Neighbors and friends began to feel his power. Nobody seemed to be concerned about his lack of education when in 1834 the Greene County court appointed him a trustee of Rhea Academy. Later that year, though but twenty-five years old, Johnson became Greeneville's mayor, and the voters reelected him twice.[9]

As Johnson's prominence grew, so did his family. Eliza no longer found time nor need to coach her husband. At two-year intervals came three more additions — Charles in 1830, Mary in 1832, and Robert in 1834. The family increase added to Johnson's responsibilities. He still labored at the tailor shop, ran the town, and in 1834 worked diligently to secure the adoption of a new state constitution for Tennessee. It would elimi-

nate many restrictive property qualifications for holding office and expand the right to vote by abridging the influence of large landowners. Johnson stumped the district in support of the new constitution and enjoyed the satisfaction of seeing it passed by more than a seventy percent majority.[10]

In 1835, while mayor of Greeneville, Johnson announced his candidacy for a new seat in the state House of Representatives for the district of Washington and Greene counties. Johnson, a Democrat, found himself pitted against Major Matthew Stevenson, a Whig, and Major James Britton, a friend who had been active in the local debating team. Stevenson had been a member of the recent constitutional convention and had locally earned the reputation of being an able administrator. For a forthcoming debate on Stevenson's home ground, Johnson researched his opponent's political record and exposed it in such a way to garner the support he needed to win the election. He attempted to resign his post as mayor, but the town failed to act on his request. In 1835, at the age of twenty-six, the tailor-mayor became a member of the state legislature. As the House was scheduled to convene, Johnson leased his tailor shop to his apprentices and made arrangements to travel to Nashville. Seven times he had run for office and seven times he had won. Eliza McCardle had every reason to be proud of her pupil.[11]

Greeneville lay in east Tennessee at the foothills of the Great Smoky Mountains, and the people who inhabited the area became the Tennessee mountaineers of fame and fable. They were a tough class of independent fighters and thinkers, and Johnson belonged to these people. He had become their intellectual superior, but because he thought as they did, and would fight for them, the people pushed him forward as their spokesman.

In Washington and Greene counties the farms were small but many and best suited for raising grain and livestock. The region's agriculture did not lend itself to slave labor, and only about one in fourteen were slaves. The broad and fertile valleys of central and west Tennessee attracted slave labor, and the blacks nearly numbered as many as the whites. Johnson had not yet become influenced by the abolitionist movement in New England, though Benjamin Lundy, who hailed from east Tennessee, had been among the first to denounce the evils of slavery. Johnson recognized the plight of those in bondage and viewed slavery with disdain, but like many southerners of the time, he thought of the race as inferior to whites.[12]

On October 6, 1835, Johnson took his seat in the Tennessee legislature. He stood five feet, ten inches in height and possessed a sturdy, muscular frame. He had a dark complexion and smooth face, and he always wore a perfectly fitted black suit. Though he spent several days in session before participating in a debate, an observer wrote that Johnson's "marked and expressive features presented him well and engaged attention when he rose to speak. He made more than the ordinary impression of a new member. He was punctual, laborious, and not unduly forward." He spoke with a natural charm and brilliant forensic style, his voice clear and mellow. Johnson could not decide whether to be a Democrat or a Whig. Though he revered Andy Jackson, he acted independently during the session and attached himself to no organized party.[13]

The freshman legislator fought hard

to defeat a public works bill that promised to become a "system of wholesale fraud." After the bill passed, Johnson continued to denounce it. His persistent opposition to a passed bill led to narrow defeat for reelection in 1837, but when his predictions came true, voters returned him to the state legislature in 1839. In the meantime, he served once again as mayor of Greeneville, dividing his time between public service and the expansion of his tailoring business.[14]

After attempting but failing to defeat Martin Van Buren in the 1836 presidential election, Johnson altered his course during the 1840 campaign and stumped for the president's renomination. Van Buren, a New Yorker with Andrew Jackson's support, lost the election to William Henry Harrison, but Johnson's reputation as a capable political combatant rose to a higher level of recognition within the state. No longer satisfied with Whigs and having no wish to remain independent, Johnson attached himself to the Democrats. Greene and Washington counties moved right along with him, the majority becoming Democrats themselves. In 1840 the Democratic State Convention at Nashville named him as one of the two presidential electors at large, opening the way for him to obtain visibility throughout the state. So much so that in 1841, running from Greene and Hawkins counties, he won nomination and election to the state senate by a majority of two thousand.[15]

Johnson served but two years in the state senate, where he proposed the basis for representation in Tennessee be determined by the census of white voters only. Because slaves had been counted on a three-fifths basis, this would reduce the political power of large slave holders. The measure appealed to the public at large. The mountaineers of the 1st Congressional District liked their man and nominated him for the United States House of Representatives. His opponent, John A. Askin, was an able Jonesboro Democrat, lawyer, and former state representative who had won the support of the Whigs partly because he supported the United States Bank and other conservative causes. During the campaign, Johnson also collided with Parson William G. Brownlow of Jonesboro, a Whig who had frequently opposed Johnson during battles in the Tennessee legislature. Andy Jackson hated the bank and during his term as president had been censured by Congress for attempting to close it. Johnson supported Jackson's policies, as did most Tennesseans, so he stumped his way through the campaign, riding with Askin from village to village on horseback. They joked along the way and became good friends, but in 1843 Johnson, at the age of thirty-four, won by a narrow margin his first congressional seat.[16]

On December 4, 1843, Johnson became a member of the 28th Congress. For ten years he held his seat, and each year he grew in stature. During those years he identified himself with certain policies that became his guiding principles. Having ascended from a life of deep poverty, Johnson fought for the rights of the poor — the laboring class, tradesmen, and the small dirt farmers — against what he characterized as an imperious aristocracy. As a Jacksonian Democrat he opposed protective tariffs and wanton government spending. His stand troubled New Englanders; many of his future enemies resided there.

Few subjects caused more concern to northerners than Congress tampering with high protective tariffs, yet Johnson believed they should be lowered to benefit the majority of Americans. As a southerner and a devout patriot, he accepted slavery as an economic attribute and believed passionately in white supremacy. Nonetheless, he demanded free land for the landless whether the recipient be white or black, and ideas such as those encouraged the aristocracy to unite to thwart him. Though his concepts had been developed in Tennessee, where he advocated a system of free, tax-supported public schools, they did not crystalize and solidify until he came to Washington. As one biographer observed, "Johnson, all his life, had operated as an outsider." His views remained constant, and though the times would change, Johnson remained the product of east Tennessee and stubbornly adhered to his principles both in politics and in public life.[17]

Few men in Congress understood the Constitution better than Johnson. He made the document his personal Bible. Though he affiliated with no church, he put his beliefs in writing: "So far as the doctrines of the Bible are concerned, or the great scheme of salvation, as founded and taught by Jesus Christ, I never did entertain a solitary doubt." So when religious liberty for Catholics became threatened by a mainly Protestant Congress, the freshman legislator from Tennessee defended Catholicism on constitutional principles with such effectiveness that the House dropped the matter. Johnson became intolerant of intolerance and believed like Thomas Jefferson that injustice and tyranny of any sort should not interfere with freedom of conscience. His constituency in east Tennessee, being mainly Protestant mountaineers, might have objected to his position on religion, but their faith in

Johnson never faltered, and they sent him back to Congress in the next election.[18]

When Texas applied for statehood, Whigs north of the Mason-Dixon Line feared the entry of another slave holding state. Admitting Texas would offend the growing number of abolitionists and unbalance the voting ratio between the proslavery and antislavery factions in Congress. For nearly four years both Whigs and Democrats avoided the problem, but in January 1845, Johnson took the floor and delivered a speech favoring annexation. Johnson, however, viewed Texas as a free state — a place where slaves purchased out of bondage could be sent to "colonize." Lincoln proposed much the same idea, but not necessarily in Texas. Neither slave holding interests nor abolitionists approved of the idea, but Johnson recognized a festering domestic problem and presented a compromise. In 1846 his Homestead Bill offered "every poor man in the United States who is the head of a family, to enter one hundred and sixty acres of the public domain, 'without money and without price.'" The only condition was that recipients live upon it and cultivate it for a period of five years. Southerners did not favor the bill, nor did most northerners. As debate over slavery began to consume every session of Congress, Johnson tried repeatedly to revive his Homestead Bill, and the greatest resistance continued to come from the south.[19]

During ten years in the House, Johnson often found himself in opposition to both sides of the aisle — mainly because he studied issues before the legislature and tried to interpret their affect upon the country in constitutional terms. Others spent their time drafting legislation that would diminish the power of the executive or judicial branches of government, thereby enhancing the power of Congress. In 1849 the Free Soil party emerged, marking the beginning of some of the most controversial congressional sessions ever held. Johnson believed so strongly in slavery and the Union that he frustrated both Democrats and Whigs. In Tennessee the Whigs attempted to eliminate him from public life. Their scheme failed, but they eventually succeeded in getting control of the Tennessee legislature and redrew Johnson's district to include more Whigs and exclude his Democratic supporters. Johnson remained a step ahead of the plot, frustrating Parson Brownlow and other Whigs by securing the Democratic nomination for governor of Tennessee. By winning, he broke the tenuous foothold Whigs had established in the state. "When I feel I have got the truth on my side," he once told a colleague, "when I know I have got facts and arguments that cannot be answered, I never inquire as to the difference of ability and experience between myself and those with whom I have to contend." A doctrine such as this, though heroic, can become a minefield of trouble in politics.[20]

Whigs across the country began to fracture and separate into, among other groups, the "Know-Nothings" — mainly Protestant Whigs who wanted to purify themselves by barring Catholics from their brotherhood. They called themselves by an unlikely name — the American Party — and what they espoused was as un–American as a party could be.

During Johnson's first term as governor, another political crisis came to a head in 1854 with the repeal of the Missouri Compromise and the passage of the

Kansas-Nebraska Bill. Stephen A. Douglas championed the bill, which left the question of slavery to the emigrants who settled in the territories. The south envisioned an opportunity to extend slavery — at least to Kansas — and approved the bill. Johnson supported it as did most southerners, but its passage created strange bedfellows in the north. Groups such as Free Soilers, Know-Nothings, and antislavery Democrats bonded in 1856 with disillusioned Whigs and formed the Republican party.

In 1848 nine Free Soilers won election to the House of Representatives. They represented the abolitionist wing of what became the Republican party. George W. Julian of Indiana and Joshua Giddings of Ohio were among them. Thaddeus Stevens entered the House the same year, but as a Whig. The Senate also received its first two Free Soilers, Salmon P. Chase of Ohio and William H. Seward of New York. Two years later Charles Sumner of Massachusetts and Benjamin F. Wade of Ohio entered the Senate. With the exception of Seward, the Free Soilers bonded together and attracted new members. This group formed the nucleus which eventually dominated the radical element of the Republican party.[21]

In 1855, amid national turmoil, Johnson ran again for governor. The Whig-Americans, alias Know-Nothings, had just the man to defeat him, Meredith P. Gentry, a gifted speaker and veteran politician whom they believed would appeal to the large Protestant population of Tennessee. Johnson, however, never backed down from his beliefs. He supported religious freedom, as he had in the House. He stood behind Senator Stephen Douglas of Illinois and the Kansas-Nebraska Bill, which had not yet manifested its many defects. To Tennessee, he claimed his place as a "Democrat east, west, north or south or anywhere else" and "as good a Southern man as anyone who lives within the borders of the South." Johnson's reelection all but destroyed Know-Nothingism in Tennessee.[22]

During both of his terms as governor, Johnson championed improvements in education. Remembrances of the struggles he endured as a youth kept the creation of more and better schools at the top of his political agenda. But his vision always extended beyond the borders of Tennessee. He continued to lobby for the Homestead Bill, which since 1846 had been delayed by opposition from the Whigs. He also saw a need to limit the printing of paper money by state banks. Issues such as these could not be resolved as governor, so on October 8, 1857, the state legislature elected him to the Senate of the United States.[23]

Johnson could not envision where this election might lead. For four years he had been away from Washington, and he seemed pleased to be back. In a speech before the Senate, he said, "I have reached the summit of my ambition. The acme of all my hopes has been attained, and I would not give the position I occupy today for any other in the United States." For Johnson, the zenith and nadir of his political career lay in the future.[24]

The Senate radiated a more imperious atmosphere than the House, its members being among the most distinguished men of the times, if not the most contentious. Stephen Douglas of Illinois and William H. Seward of New York each coveted the 1860 presidential nomination. John Bell, the senior senator from Tennessee, also had presidential aspirations, as well as support from Johnson. New England placed their economic interests in the capable hands of William Pitt Fessenden of Maine and Charles Sumner of Massachusetts. The latter remained at home, still recovering from a recent caning delivered by Preston Brooks on the Senate floor. Pennsylvania looked to the powerful Simon Cameron and his political machine for favors, and Michigan put their faith in Zachariah Chandler. The south's agenda, which included the retention and expansion of their "peculiar institution," received constant attention from advocates such as Jefferson Davis of Mississippi, Clement C. Clay of Alabama, Sam Houston of Texas, Robert A. Toombs of Georgia, James M. Mason of Virginia, and John Slidell and Judah Benjamin of Louisiana. The landed gentry and those of great wealth ran things in the Senate. Self made men like Andrew Johnson received token acceptance. The Senate, once a meeting place for statesmen, no longer had John C. Calhoun, Henry Clay, or Daniel Webster, all of whom had passed away with their reputations immortalized in history.[25]

The junior senator wasted no time making himself known. After failing to garner support for the Homestead Bill in the House, he put it on the floor of the Senate with a vigor, logic, and brashness that astounded older members. Senators from the slave states envisioned their sacred property staking out tracts of public land through funds raised by abolitionists. Johnson believed that freedmen could prosper in the new territories, but his southern counterparts abhorred the thought. Johnson's argument, however, appealed to some of his antislavery colleagues. His proposal died on the floor of the Senate as it had in the House.[26]

In the late 1850s, neither President James Buchanan nor his cabinet, the House of Representatives, or the Senate contained men worthy of the title statesman. They bickered over sectional differences without mitigating the problem. Johnson tried to solve problems as he perceived them. By looking into the future to prepare for it, he recognized how a Homestead Bill could begin to ease the slave problem, and he vigorously pursued that belief in the face of obstinate opposition. Though unacceptable to the Senate, the bill eventually became essential for the country. While Johnson's efforts marked him as a potential statesman, it also created a host of new enemies. How one deals with his enemies very much determines his credentials as a statesman. Johnson still had much to learn. Fellow Tennessean James Knox Polk described him as "very vindictive and perverse in his temper" when opposed. Jefferson Davis referred to Johnson's "intense, almost morbidly sensitive pride," which a psychologist might attribute to the senator's struggle from poverty.[27]

During the four years Johnson spent in the governor's mansion, he missed the fierce debates in Congress on the slavery issue. The only moderates came from border states. From 1840, through Johnson's ten years in the House and his entry into the Senate in 1857, men like William Lloyd Garrison and Wendell Phillips spoke of a higher law and kindled a fierce hatred of the slave owner. If abolishing slavery resulted in overthrowing the Constitution, they were ready to do it. To demonstrate their resolve, they set the document on fire on the streets of Boston.

Sumner expectorated his scorching venom on the floor of the Senate, casting slurs upon South Carolina's Senator Andrew Butler. Preston Brooks, a member of the House and kinsman of Butler, retaliated with his cane, breaking it on Sumner's head. In Massachusetts, Sumner became a martyr. In the south, Brooks became a hero.[28]

No wonder when, in a speech delivered at Rochester, New York, on October 25, 1858, Senator Seward aptly stated that the quarrel between proslavery and antislavery "fanatical agitators" was leading the country toward an "irrepressible conflict."[29]

Sumner recovered from Brooks's attack to become the leader of the Radicals in the Senate. Viperous Thaddeus Stevens, always seeking to throw fuel onto a fire built on hatred, began to dominate the antislavery cause in the House. The Radicals, however, had not quite organized themselves at the time Johnson entered the Senate. But it did not take either Sumner or Stevens long to recognize that the junior senator from Tennessee was not one of them.

Two years before the outbreak of the Civil War, Johnson recognized that Sumner, Stevens, and all their supporters were more than abolitionists. They were disunionists, as anxious to break up the nation as were southern nullifiers and secessionists. In speeches before the Senate, he spoke condemningly of those who favored the dissolution of the Union, whether they be Republicans or Democrats from the north or the south. Men like Sumner and Stevens, each coming from vastly different backgrounds, united in their fanaticism before the Civil War, during it, and afterwards. They had long memories for the likes of the senator from Tennessee. In 1858, Johnson became no more than a minor player in the Senate and even less of an influence in directing the course of the nation. But Johnson had a voice, and it embittered the Radicals.[30]

On April 23, 1860, the Democratic Convention met in Charleston, South Carolina, a state which had already distinguished itself as a hotbed of political dissension. Northern and southern delegates could not agree on a platform, nor on a candidate for president. On sectional issues, northern delegates outvoted their counterparts, so southern delegates packed their bags and on June 18 held their own convention in Baltimore. On June 23, Stephen Douglas received the nomination for president by the splintered group of northern Democrats. In the meantime, southern bolters nominated John C. Breckinridge of Kentucky. During the debates, Tennessee's twelve delegates voted thirty-six times for Andrew Johnson. Their favorite son, however, withdrew his name and endorsed Breckinridge, whom he believed would be the best Democratic candidate to hold the Union together.[31]

While the drama in Charleston and Baltimore ebbed and flowed, the Republicans held their convention in Chicago's "Wigwam," a building constructed for the purpose. After much wheeling and dealing, they rejected William H. Seward, the front-runner, and Salmon P. Chase of Ohio, swinging the nomination on the third ballot to the more obscure candidate from Illinois, Abraham Lincoln. To give the ticket balance, they chose Hannibal Hamlin of Maine for vice president.

The sad state of affairs in the United States prompted the Constitutional Union party to nominate their own presidential candidate, John Bell of Tennessee, a former Whig. Though Bell and Johnson were both Unionists, the latter still supported the Democratic party and held no delegates to swing to Bell.

Four presidential candidates complicated the outcome of the national election. Bell captured a few votes from both parties, Douglas and Breckinridge split the Democratic vote, and Lincoln won the election. The south despised the Republican party because of its opposition to slavery. Had southerners paid more attention to Lincoln's speeches, they might have discovered that the president-elect was not an abolitionist.[32]

South Carolina used Lincoln's election as an excuse to secede and did so on December 20, 1860. Of all the voices in the Senate from the south that could speak against secession, only Andrew Johnson took the floor and spoke "On the Constitutionality and Rightfulness of Secession." He refused to walk out of the Union and implored Congress "to make some effort to save the country from impending dissolution." He made his case on constitutional grounds and appealed equally to all his colleagues — north and south. But with secession set in motion by South Carolina, six more states from the Deep South followed in rapid order, and another three joined the rebellion during the spring of 1861. Much to Johnson's dismay, Tennessee, hemmed in on three sides by southern states, seceded on June 8.[33]

His efforts to preserve the Union received no help from President Buchanan or his cabinet. If Buchanan understood the Constitution, he failed to demonstrate it in any consistent manner, always vacillating when pressed for a decision. He held secession unconstitutional but asserted the executive's inability to do anything about it.[34]

Buchanan made his situation worse by surrounding himself with a cabinet composed of flatterers and secessionists. Of all the characters in Buchanan's cabinet, one of them played a significant role in Johnson's life. Edwin M. Stanton, a trial-hardened lawyer, entered the cabinet as attorney general on December 20, 1860, seventy-two days before Buchanan's administration ended. By curious coincidence, it was the same day South Carolina seceded. Stanton replaced Judge Jeremiah S. Black, whom Buchanan had raised to the post of secretary of state. Unlike some members of the cabinet, Stanton claimed to disassociate himself from abolitionists because of "their hypocrisy, their corruption, their enmity to the Constitution, and their lawless disregard for the rights of states and individuals." But Stanton was not his own man. On issues of momentous importance he behaved with deference to the president and offered no constitutional guidance. He also presented no obstacle to other members of the cabinet, who were mainly sympathetic to the south.[35]

Though Stanton condemned abolitionists, in 1851 he met and established a friendship with Charles Sumner. Sumner did not bond with people who did not accept his abolitionist views, and the influence he exerted over Stanton built slowly but steadily over the years. At times they met privately, even surreptitiously, and Stanton's penchant for conspiracy found a willing confederate in Sumner.[36]

In January 1861, Andrew Johnson found himself in the unenviable position of being scorned by southerners like Jefferson Davis and northerners like Charles Sumner, two of the most powerful politicians in a nation dividing. Undisturbed by opposition, Johnson delivered some of his greatest speeches during the days between South Carolina's secession and Lincoln's inauguration on March 4, 1861. Almost single-handedly, Johnson kept Tennessee in the Union. When Lincoln called for troops after South Carolina's militia forced the surrender of Fort Sumter, Isham G. Harris, Tennessee's governor, decided to side with the proslavery faction of his state. To Lincoln's call, Harris replied, "Tennessee will not furnish a single man for coercion, but fifty thousand if necessary, for the defense of our rights and those of our Southern brothers." In June, after Tennessee seceded, Johnson remained a defender of the Union — his principles on that subject were inviolable.[37]

Referring to the secession states in his inaugural address, Lincoln said, "I hold that in contemplation of universal law and of the Constitution the Union of these states is perpetual." He also said, "I have no purpose directly or indirectly to interfere with the institution of slavery. I believe I have no lawful right to do so and I have no inclination to do so."[38]

Anybody comparing Johnson's speeches with Lincoln's inaugural would observe that the guiding principles of the two men moved in concert.

Abolition, however, set the stage for the Civil War, and secession raised the curtain. Before the fighting reached its end, Johnson would be center stage, and his enemies, the Radicals, would marshal all their power in an effort to overthrow him. But first he must go home to face his fellow Tennesseans. Of twenty-two southern senators, twenty-one joined the secession movement. One had not. Andy Johnson would not secede. He still believed in Tennessee, and he would fight with all his diminished power to see it restored to the Union.

A few days after Lincoln's inaugural, Johnson started home. When the train stopped at Lynchburg, Virginia, a crowd loitering at the station learned the senator was on board. As legend has it, a group of men grabbed him by the nose, dragged him from the car, spat in his face, knocked him down, strapped him in a halter, and led him to a tree. As they prepared to hang him, an old man stepped forward and shouted above the noise, "His neighbors in Greeneville have made arrangements to hang their senator on his arrival. Virginians have no right to deprive them of the privilege." The mob cut Johnson loose and ushered him back to the train, satisfied that the Tennessean would get his reckoning at home.[39]

Crowds at Nashville, Knoxville, Memphis, and elsewhere in the south swung Johnson's effigy from ropes or used it for target practice. Among secessionists, the mere mention of his name induced exclamations of profanity. But Johnson still had friends where he lived. East Tennessee never accepted the Confederate government. Surrounded by secessionists, they remained defiant with the same stubbornness as their fearless senator.

Weeks before Tennessee officially exited the Union, Johnson waged war against secession publicly, risking his life as he traveled through east Tennessee stumping for the Union. Governor Harris dispatched persuasive Confederate sympathizers to speak against Johnson, and east Tennessee became a battleground of fiery debate. Wherever Johnson went, crowds followed, and no address concluded without fights erupting between soldiers and civilians. With sentiment weighted against him, only a brave or foolish man would risk his life to stump for the Union in the face of such fierce opposition.[40]

On June 8 Tennesseans went to the polls and by an overwhelming majority voted for secession. Only in east Tennessee did voters roll up a majority for the Union. On June 24 Governor Harris committed Tennessee — the last of eleven states in rebellion — to the Confederacy.[41]

Disgusted but not beaten, Johnson packed his bags and made his way back to Washington. Though rejected by Tennessee, he returned to his seat in the Senate to renew his fight. Fifty-two years had passed since Johnson began his rise from poverty. Having seen his wealth increase in lockstep with his reputation, he now seemed to have reached the end of the line, being a man without a state. However, Johnson's valiant acts did not go unnoticed by Lincoln, and the senator's life would never again be the same.

2

The War Years

For Abraham Lincoln, the first battle of the Civil War ended in a rout of the Union army. Brigadier General Irwin McDowell took 35,000 Union troops to Manassas, Virginia, and at Bull Run collided with 22,000 grayclads under Brigadier General Pierre G. T. Beauregard, the man who had started the fighting by firing on Fort Sumter. Congress wanted to witness the defeat of the Confederates, so passes were printed enabling privileged spectators to ride to the scene of the expected battle. Ben Wade made the trip with other members of the Senate. The climax occurred on the oppressively hot day of July 21, 1861, when Brigadier General Thomas J. Jackson stopped the federal attack and exposed the Union flank. The rout began, but not according to McDowell's plans. Federal soldiers fled down the hill — a disorderly mass running for their lives and surging through parked carriages of shocked sightseers. Caught in the swell, Wade made his way back to Washington to report the disaster.[1]

Edwin Stanton, who witnessed the aftermath of the crisis from his home in Washington, wrote ex–President Buchanan, "The dreadful disaster of Sunday can scarcely be mentioned. The imbecility of the administration culminated in that catastrophe; the irretrievable misfortune and national disgrace never to be forgotten are to be added to the ruin of all peaceful pursuits, and national bankruptcy is the result of Lincoln's running the machine for five months."[2]

To his fellow senators, Johnson delivered a spirited defense of Lincoln. The disaster at Bull Run provoked a debate and forced other issues to the table. Without congressional approval Lincoln had suspended the habeas corpus act. During the Fort Sumter crisis Congress had not been in session and the president had responded by calling for 75,000 volunteers and proclaiming a blockade of southern ports. Johnson asked for a joint resolution approving of Lincoln's actions. Senator Breckinridge of Kentucky, who had not yet resigned from the Senate to take up arms against the Union, argued that such a resolution would give the president powers of a dictator. Johnson, who supported Breckinridge's nomination for president at the Democratic convention, now regretted being so misled. He took the Senate floor in Lincoln's defense, arguing the nature of executive war powers and used constitutional precedents to make his case. Though not a lawyer, Johnson had worked assiduously at preparing his comments, and his vehement support of the President's policies attracted Lincoln's notice.[3]

Paying fealty to his former boss,

Abraham Lincoln. (Massachusetts Commandery Military Order of the Loyal Legion and the U.S. Army Military History Institute.)

Edwin Stanton continued to criticize the Lincoln administration by reporting his thoughts to Buchanan. The source of Stanton's information came from personal friends in the government, among them Charles Sumner. Stanton added his own opinions to the profuse amount of inside information collected. One might ask why Stanton continued to report on the progress of secession to a former president whose cabinet had been composed of southern sympathizers.[4]

One might also ask why Lincoln eventually chose Stanton to become his secretary of war. The choice must have come as quite a surprise to both Buchanan and Stanton. The reason, however, had more to do with the need to remove Simon Cameron of Pennsylvania from the post. Cameron's corruption preceded him, followed him into office, contributed to his ineptness in the cabinet, and finally his censure by Congress. His presence in the cabinet had been arranged without the president's knowledge by his campaign managers. In January 1862, Lincoln gently shoved him aside, naming him Minister to Russia.[5]

On January 13, 1862, when Stanton learned that Lincoln would nominate him for secretary of war, he replied, "Tell the President I will accept if no other pledge than to throttle treason shall be exacted." Stanton's scruples were such that he found no difficulty in accepting the trust from one whom he secretly condemned. Stanton may have lobbied to displace Cameron. The two men had been in close conversation over legal issues confronting the war department. Both knew Cameron faced ejection, and if Stanton suspected that Lincoln intended to make a change, he certainly had the connections to make his interest in the post known to others. He also included Chase in his network of advocates, who boosted Stanton as the best man to replace Cameron. Senator Sumner lobbied for Stanton's immediate confirmation. Some argued that the nominee's loyalty should first be investigated. No one had seen Stanton's letters to Buchanan, so on January 15 the Senate confirmed him.[6]

Secretary of the Navy Gideon Welles, who assessed people with keen insight, considered Stanton "more violent than vigorous ... more vain than wise ... rude, arrogant and domineering toward those in subordinate positions if they submit to his rudeness, but ... a sycophant and dissembler in deportment with those whom he fear." Others who could stand aside and judge the man would agree with Welles, but during the war years Stanton displayed a devotion to the cause and a virtue for "hard work, financial integrity, and merciless energy against the rascal contractors." Lincoln kept him under control using methods too subtle for a personality like Stanton's to understand. One of Lincoln's earlier biographers summed up the situation best when he wrote, "Mr. Lincoln was the only ruler known to history who could have cooperated for years with such a minister." By 1867, Andrew Johnson would agree.[7]

Next to Virginia, no state suffered more battles, skirmishes, invasions, and countermarches than Tennessee, and much of the fighting occurred in the eastern section of the state. As early as November 1861, the mountaineers sought reinstatement with the federal government. Because of this action, Confederate agents swept the area early in the war, confiscated crops, plundered the area, and forcibly conscripted men into the army. This attack on his people did not escape the notice of Andrew Johnson.[8]

He found the abuses especially painful. While he lived in comfort in Washington, his invalid wife endured ejection from her home, which the Army converted to a barracks. His sons had been imprisoned and his son-in-law driven into the mountains to be "hunted and pursued like beasts of the forest by the secession and disunion hordes.... Helpless children and innocent females are murdered in cold blood. Our men are hung and their bodies left upon the gib-

bet." "For what?" Johnson asked. "Because I stand by the Constitution."[9]

The president understood Johnson's plight, but he also saw an opportunity to secure a portion of Tennessee. Lincoln intended that Brigadier General Don Carlos Buell move a force into east Tennessee and hold the Cumberland Water Gap. Buell moved too slowly and lost the opportunity, but in February 1862, Major General Ulysses S. Grant captured Fort Henry on the Tennessee River and Fort Donelson on the Cumberland River, thereby forcing the Confederates to abandon portions of west and central Tennessee. On February 22 Grant placed the occupied area under martial law, forcing the governor to move operations from Nashville to Memphis.[10]

Grant's success in Tennessee opened the door for Lincoln to take the first step toward restoration of the south. The president understood there were many loyal citizens in the state, and he did not wish to burden Grant with the administration of captured territory. On March 4, 1862, he named Johnson Military Governor of Tennessee with the rank of brigadier general of volunteers. Johnson promptly accepted the appointment knowing it would be dangerous and at times disagreeable. He also realized his term in the Senate would expire in another year and there would be no legislature to reelect him. He chose to remain politically viable. Something better might come along. Besides, who else understood Tennessee and the needs of its people better than the man the majority of the inhabitants now claimed to hate?[11]

Lincoln's action produced peculiar consequences. Though the Senate approved Johnson's appointment, the House questioned whether the president had the constitutional authority to create a military governorship. The problem whetted Thaddeus Stevens' curiosity. He began to develop the doctrine that seceded states no longer belonged to the Union. If so, the Constitution no longer applied to them. Stevens' explorations bothered Lincoln not at all, but the pit bull of the House had found a bone to gnaw on for the remainder of his life.[12]

In the early days of the republic, Congress measured its actions by the Constitution. Johnson zealously adhered to the same practice. When the rebellion began, Stevens scouted the worthiness of the Constitution. "The laws of war," he growled, "not the Constitution. Who pleads the Constitution?" he angrily asked. Answering his own question, he replied, "It is the advocates of the rebels." Then, when colleagues hesitated to accept the proposition to arm slaves and turn them against their masters, he scoffed at their reluctance and said, "I for one shall be ready for it — arming the blacks — horrifying to gentlemen as it may appear." In time, such views as those expressed by Stevens would clash with those of Johnson, who for the moment had a war to fight.[13]

As Johnson packed for the trip to his home state, he received a letter from General Buell in Nashville; "You must not expect to be received with enthusiasm but rather the reverse." From Nashville, Brigadier General William Nelson warned Chase to not "send Andy Johnson here in any official capacity. He represents a party! Let him come as Senator if he wants to. He is too much embittered to entrust with a mission as delicate as the direction of a people under the present circumstances." There may have been some merit to Nelson's warn-

ing. A month earlier Johnson had spoken in the Senate and said, "I am a Democrat now. I have been one all my life; I expect to live and die one, and the cornerstone of my Democracy rests upon the enduring basis of the Union." Instead, Johnson experienced more narrow escapes traveling to Nashville than when he arrived. All along the twisted route angry crowds gathered at train stops and attempted to storm his car.[14]

Reaching Nashville on March 13, he found the public less interested in killing him and more curious to hear what he had to say. That evening an enormous crowd assembled outside the St. Cloud Hotel and demanded he speak. In a short address, he assured the public that they could voice their concerns freely and rebuild their lives without fear. Four days later he elaborated further, advising them that they would be protected by the federal government. Tennessee, he said, along with other states occupied by federal troops, would be returned to the constitutionally guaranteed republican form of government as soon as the present crisis ended. Until then, he would be their military governor and friend, and, as quickly as possible, restore "government to the same condition as before the existing rebellion." He blamed the war on the slave issue, but stressed that traitors must be punished and treason crushed. The military governorship of Tennessee had begun.[15]

Johnson wasted little time warring against traitors. On March 17 he ordered the provost marshal to seize the Bank of Tennessee and all court records left behind by the departed state government. On March 27 he took steps to reorganize Nashville's city government. When the mayor and city council refused to take the oath of allegiance, Johnson filled their places with loyal citizens. When secessionist presses continued to operate against the government, he closed them. When six ministers came before him charged with preaching treason, he asked them to take the oath of allegiance. When they refused, he arrested five and paroled the sixth because of poor health.[16]

Johnson found governing Nashville far less difficult than defending it against attack. Major General Henry W. Halleck pulled Buell's troops away from the city and ordered them to report to Grant at Shiloh. Though Buell assured Johnson that the regiments withdrawn would be replaced, Halleck assumed command of Grant's troops after the battle of Shiloh and retained part of Buell's army for other operations. In the meantime, cavalry detachments from the commands of Nathan Bedford Forrest and John Hunt Morgan staged raids, cut rail lines, and blew up bridges. In July, Forrest's horsemen swept through outlying towns and surrounded Nashville. Johnson screamed for reinforcements. By the end of the month he could no longer communicate with the north and supplies could not be obtained from outside. Johnson poured heart and soul into the defense of Nashville. The small garrison rounded up a thousand slaves from secessionists and put them to work building fortifications. When Buell worked his way back to Nashville and declared the city at risk, Johnson said to him, "I am no military man, but anyone who talks of surrendering I will shoot."[17]

Morgan's raids emanated out of Kentucky and often fell upon the Louisville and Nashville Railroad. Buell remained reluctant to expose his force to the raiders. Johnson became livid when he heard that Buell might surrender Nashville, so he appealed directly to the president. Lincoln suggested that Johnson communicate with General Halleck, whose promotion to general in chief was about to bring him to Washington. Halleck did nothing, and the governor continued to fight his battles with whatever help he could raise.[18]

In August, ignoring Johnson's threat to shoot anyone who "talks of surrendering," Buell suggested evacuating the city. Johnson replied, "I'll be damned if Nashville shall be surrendered." On August 31 he again wrote Lincoln. Referring to Buell, he declared, "May God save my country from some of the generals that have been conducting this war." In the latter part of 1862 a court of inquiry reviewed Buell's failure to defend Nashville and all the credit for saving the capital went to Johnson. Finally, on October 24, Major General William S. Rosecrans relieved Buell.[19]

Johnson learned that a Confederate court had labeled him an "alien enemy," sequestered all the "property, rights, and credits belonging to him," and ordered that they be sold at auction. He had no time to worry about his possessions. His first concern was the safety of Nashville, and on that matter he found Rosecrans no more cooperative than Buell. Because Rosecrans held a higher rank, he wanted control over Johnson and the district's civil authority. When Stanton learned of the dispute over conflicting jurisdictions, he instructed Halleck to direct Rosecrans to keep his hands off civil authority and suggested that Johnson be given command of the troops at Nashville. Rosecrans replied that Nashville was too important to trust to a nonmilitary man, but he would consider some arrangement providing Johnson reported to him. Halleck served Rosecrans with a severe rebuke, reminding him that Johnson was no ordinary brigadier general but the governor of the state with full powers of that office. Rosecrans apologized and equanimity was restored.[20]

On September 22, when Lincoln issued his preliminary Emancipation Proclamation, Johnson's eye caught what he considered the main message — "that hereafter and heretofore the war will be prosecuted for the object of practically restoring the constitutional relation between the United States and each of the states … in which … the relation is … suspended or disturbed." Though the divided country had been at war for eighteen months, Lincoln still stood ready to provide pecuniary aid to southern states agreeing to abolish slavery. The proclamation provided that on January 1, 1863, "all persons held as slaves" within any state then in rebellion "shall be thence, thereafter and forever free." At Johnson's request, Lincoln did not include Tennessee among those states listed as disloyal, and the omission worked to Johnson's advantage in trying to draw the state back into the Union.[21]

One year earlier Thad Stevens had seeded the ground for emancipation, allowing it to propagate in a field of sectional hate fertilized from his own lips. Using every opportunity to fulminate against the south, he espoused his policy of hatred; hang the leaders — crush the rebellion — arm the blacks — confiscate the land. Lincoln's mild policies infuriated him, but for the moment he could do little to change them — so he chose to bide his time, watching and waiting.[22]

On political matters, the minds of Lincoln and Johnson operated in parallel. In his speech on July 4, delivered in Nashville, Johnson said, "I am for this Government above all earthly possessions, and if it perish, I do not want to survive it. I am for it, though slavery should be struck from existence and … swept from the balance of the world … give me my Government and let the negro go!"[23]

On occasion, Johnson's attitude toward the slave issue lacked consistency. For most of his life he defended the "peculiar institution," convinced that blacks were inferior to whites and ought to be treated that way. When the war began he insisted that slavery would be secure only if the Union was preserved. When a general suggested that northern antislavery advocates opposed slavery because it was unjust, Johnson replied, somewhat heatedly, "D — n the negroes; I am fighting these traitorous aristocrats, their masters." The statement illustrates two of Johnson's lifelong biases; one toward the landed gentry whose snubs he had endured for much of his life, and the other toward blacks, whom he classed as decidedly inferior. These biases never changed.[24]

In November 1862, Rosecrans lifted the siege of Nashville, and on January 2, 1863, he checked General Braxton Bragg's Confederate army at the Battle of Stone's River. But elsewhere in Tennessee the war continued with no decisive end in sight. Johnson believed that if *all* the rebels could be expelled, especially from east Tennessee, that restoration of the state by a decided majority would follow. On December 10 he issued a proclamation to hold congressional elections in the 9th and 10th districts at year end. General Forrest got wind of the election, sent his cavalry into the area, and most of the voters stayed home. Johnson thanked Forrest for the intrusion because it prevented the election of anti-Union congressmen.[25]

Never satisfied with cooperation

from the army, Johnson began to raise his own regiments. Authority to recruit a home guard had been granted upon his arrival in Nashville, but the governor wanted more men, more arms, and more equipment to deal with the recurring cavalry raids. During the crisis in July 1862, he obtained permission to add more cavalry. When Rosecrans seemed unable to occupy east Tennessee, Johnson obtained permission to recruit regiments for a term of three years. On March 1863, he asked for and obtained orders to raise ten regiments of infantry with a corresponding number of artillery and cavalry units. To his surprise, Johnson received a message from Lincoln encouraging him to form "a negro military force. In my opinion the country now needs no specific thing so much as some man of your ability, and position, to go to this work." Lincoln's advice gave Johnson something to think about, and when federal money became available to purchase slaves for $300 each, Johnson took advantage of it and enrolled the freedmen. He eventually organized twenty-five mainly white regiments, recruiting a small number of them from other states, but the war department never provided him with enough arms and equipage for his regiments to become a viable fighting force. Johnson's military activities caused conflicts with generals operating in the field — most of whom he did not like — and the results did not always justify the means. But Johnson was determined to recover east Tennessee and needed men to do it. Not until late 1863 did Eliza Johnson make it through the lines to Nashville, and her life had been one of intense suffering at the hands of secessionists.[26]

During the early months of 1863, federal forces expanded their grip on central Tennessee, but the eastern section of the state — and Johnson's hometown — remained in Confederate control. On June 1 Governor Harris, whose state government in rebellion had been driven from one town to another, attempted to nominate candidates for the Confederate congress. The convention met, only to be disrupted by the advance of federal forces.

For Johnson, political matters went much better. A Unionist convention meeting in Nashville on July 1 passed a resolution approving Lincoln's appointment of Johnson as military governor and praised the latter's administration. The delegates also voided all actions of the Harris convention. Unionists asked Johnson to issue writs of election for the first week of August, but he declined, preferring to wait until guerrillas had been driven from east Tennessee so the entire state could participate in an election.[27]

In mid-August Major General Ambrose E. Burnside marched his army from Kentucky into east Tennessee. Simultaneously, Rosecrans advanced on General Braxton Bragg at Chattanooga, forcing the latter to draw reserves from Burnside's line of march. On September 2, 1863, Burnside occupied Knoxville, and on the 9th, Rosecrans forced Bragg out of Chattanooga and into northern Georgia. In east Tennessee the mountaineers gave three cheers for the Union and three more for Andy Johnson. For them, the day of reconciliation had come.[28]

Lincoln reacted quickly to the good news and on September 11 telegraphed Johnson:

> All Tennessee is now clear of armed insurrectionists. You need not be reminded that it is the nick of time for re-inaugurating a loyal State

government. Not a moment should be lost. You and the co-operating friends there can better judge of the ways and means, than can be judged by any here.... The whole struggle for Tennessee will be profitless to both State and Nation, if it so ends that Gov. Johnson is put down, and Gov. Harris is put up. It must not be so. You must make it otherwise. Let the reconstruction be the work of such men only as can be trusted for the Union. Exclude all others, and trust that your government, so organized, will be recognized here, as being the one republican form, to be guaranteed to the state, and to be protected against invasion and domestic violence.

I see that you have declared in favor of emancipation in Tennessee, for which, may God bless you. Get emancipation into your new State ... Constitution ... and there shall be no such word as fail for your case.[29]

Johnson and his supporters took to the highways and byways, canvassing Tennessee and preparing for the upcoming elections. Once again military setbacks postponed elections. General Bragg turned Rosecrans back into Tennessee, and only Major General George H. Thomas's stand at Chickamauga prevented the Confederates from rolling over the Union army. Stanton recalled Rosecrans and put Thomas in charge of the Army of the Cumberland. On October 23 General Grant arrived and ordered Major General William Tecumseh Sherman up from Vicksburg. One month later Grant's army captured Lookout Mountain and Missionary Ridge, eliminating the threat to Chattanooga. While Grant dealt with Bragg, Lieutenant General James Longstreet, who had been detached from General Robert E. Lee's army of northern Virginia to support

Bragg, attempted to retake Knoxville. Burnside held the Knoxville line, compelling Longstreet to withdraw on the night of December 4 to Russellville, a few miles northwest of Johnson's home town of Greeneville.[30]

While waiting for the army to clear the state of enemy troops, Johnson went about the business of his office. Lincoln gave him free rein, and so did Stanton. Johnson always wanted more railroads in Tennessee, so during the summer of 1863 he began building the Nashville and Northwestern Railway and completed it in May 1864. The Union army subsisted off the railroad, but the responsibility of guarding it against guerrilla attacks fell to Johnson.[31]

Swamped at times with administrative matters and by mountains of paperwork, Johnson withstood the demands on his time and remained patient. A breakthrough came on December 8, 1863, when Lincoln issued his Amnesty Proclamation to accelerate restoration of the states. Eighteen days passed while Tennesseans digested the message. The proclamation drew a positive reaction. By taking an oath of allegiance, a mere ten percent of the number voting in 1860 could initiate the restoration of a state government. The problem remained east Tennessee, which would not be cleared for another year. On December 26 the citizens of Memphis met and petitioned for a reestablishment of civil government in accordance with the proclamation's terms. On New Year's Day a meeting of Unionists at Nashville declared that Tennessee had committed suicide as a state and asked for restoration in compliance with Lincoln's offer. A few days later Johnson spoke for emancipation — all of his slaves had been confiscated but two who escaped to Nashville and now worked for him for wages.

On January 21 Johnson spoke again of his plan for restoration. With his hand to guide them, a large gathering met in the House of Representatives to condemn slavery and pass the requisite resolutions. Five days later the governor issued his own proclamation, calling on legal voters to elect their representatives. Tennesseans took the oath and on March 5th, 1864, Johnson held the first state election. Citizens cast only fifty thousand votes, enough to fill public offices in about two-thirds of the counties of the state.[32]

To explain the poor turnout at the polls Johnson needed to look no further than his own proclamation. He irritated many of the Conservative Unionists when he inserted an amendment to Lincoln's December 8 proclamation by adding language intended to antagonize his old personal enemies — secessionists and plantation owners. The Unionists resented having to take the same oath as secessionists, arguing that they had never "sinned against the Government." Lincoln wanted no misunderstanding when he issued his restoration plan. It gave substance to a point he made in his first inaugural address when he said, "no state upon its own mere motion can lawfully get out of the Union." On July 4, 1861, in a special message to Congress he reaffirmed this guiding principle, stating that all states had "their status in the Union" and could "have no other legal status." His Amnesty Proclamation paved the way for reunification with a minimum of strings attached. Johnson discussed the amendment with Lincoln, who unfortunately did not understand the temperament of loyal Tennesseans. After a cursory examination, and anxious to get Tennessee restored to the Union, he approved it. Johnson should have put his biases aside and not tampered with Lincoln's carefully crafted language.[33]

Johnson's proclamation split the Conservatives away from the unconditional Unionists. He had not intended to do this. It obstructed the main object of his appointment as military governor — to create a new free state. Instead of bringing people together, he created enemies, including two old rivals, Parson William Brownlow and Daniel C. Trewhitt. During a mass meeting at Knoxville to call a state convention to nominate a governor, Johnson defended his proclamation with the consequence that members walked out, some thoroughly polarized. Johnson finally succeeded in creating a new state government, but not until 1865. Had he set aside old prejudices, nine months might have been saved.[34]

For the restoration of states Lincoln recited his constitutional power to grant reprieves, pardons, and amnesty "to persons who may have participated in the existing rebellion." On taking the oath to "support, protect and defend the Constitution, all rights of property would be restored with the exception of slaves, which would be freed. The proclamation also provided for elections to be held in all states of the south where the votes cast equaled or exceeded ten percent of the votes cast in the 1860 presidential election. Thereafter, qualifying states would be protected by the United States, protected from invasion and domestic violence, and guaranteed the privileges of a republican form of government. Only those persons, however, who accepted the Emancipation Proclamation would be entitled to pardons and qualified to establish a state government.[35]

Lincoln's proclamation issued during the latter days of 1863 was pure, simple, and consistent with everything he had ever said on the subject. By the exigencies of war, slavery would end. Except for this and the men and money expended to put down the rebellion, there would be no punishment of the south because of its attempt to secede.

Although Lincoln did sometimes stretch his executive power as a matter of necessity, he keenly understood what powers the Constitution granted Congress. The proclamation's last paragraph clarified that "whether members sent to Congress from any state shall be admitted to seats constitutionally rests exclusively with the respective Houses and not to any extent with the Executive." This affirmation of the separation of powers should have stifled questions emanating from the legislative branch accusing the president of exceeding his executive power, but men like Sumner in the Senate and Stevens in the House would never be satisfied with letting the south down easy.[36]

Having come from a border state, and having the brothers of his wife fighting and dying for the Confederacy, Lincoln understood the south much better than his adversaries in Congress. He also understood human nature better than his military governor of Tennessee. Before the war he had met and admired many congressmen from the south. He knew most of them as men of honor who could be trusted, and if defeated, would accept their fate like gentlemen. As early as March 6, 1862, Lincoln obtained from Congress a resolution in favor of gradual reconstruction and urged the south to adopt it. Nine months later, in his annual message to Congress on December 1, 1862, he advocated a constitutional amendment providing for gradual compensated emancipation. The message also

spoke to the south, and he urged them to accept it. The south did not listen, and neither did Congress. This did not change Lincoln's position on reconstruction, and the message came one month before the promulgation of the Emancipation Proclamation.[37]

Sumner and Stevens trusted no southerner and conveniently forgot that eight months earlier Congress had agreed as a body to gradual reconstruction. As the war dragged into years, the radical element became even more vindictive. Sumner had already stated his position in 1861 when he said "any vote of secession becomes a practical abdication of all rights under the Constitution ... so from that time forward the territory falls under the exclusive jurisdiction of Congress ... and the state ... ceases to exist." Later, Stevens adopted the same theme, saying, "I would lay a tax wherever I can, upon the conquered provinces, just as all nations levy them upon provinces and nations they conquer." Stevens went a step further than Sumner, adding that Congress "must treat those states now outside of the Union as conquered provinces, and settle them with new men, and drive the present rebels as exiles from this country."[38]

When Lincoln issued his reconstruction policies, Stevens flew into a rage, and the growing number of Radicals in Congress began to rally around their leaders. Bitten by hatred of the south, nothing would satisfy them short of dispossessing the landowners, confiscating the remnants of their greatly diminished wealth, and driving them from the country. With Sumner and Stevens at the wheel, statesmanship in the Senate and House diminished to acts of pure vindictiveness. The sharp division between the Radicals' program of punishment and Lincoln's policy of "malice toward none and charity for all" formed a new rift between the president and Congress.[39]

In an effort to find a way to undermine Lincoln's restoration plan, Stevens organized a special committee to study it. He designated Henry Winter Davis of Maryland, a former "Know Nothing," as chairman. Davis, a bright, cocky, egotistical, and opinionated legislator, did not like Lincoln. Under Stevens' influence, he became an outspoken Radical. On January 18, 1864, Davis presented his bill to Congress embodying the Radical scheme for reconstruction. Portions of the measure openly conflicted with Lincoln's views. Davis treated the eleven states in rebellion as territories and advocated reparations for all the blood and treasure expended by the north in prosecuting the war. The bill went further, directing each "territory" to design new constitutions along lines formulated by Congress. Davis' bill demanded the immediate abolishment of slavery, an act Lincoln recognized could only be achieved through an amendment to the Constitution.[40]

The central issue promoted by Stevens in the House and Wade in the Senate came down to jurisdiction over reconstruction. Was it to be congressional or executive? If the states were still members of the Union, as Lincoln claimed, then Congress could not interfere in their laws and constitutions. If they were not part of the Union, Lincoln believed that Congress would have no more right to dictate their laws than if they were Canada or Mexico. Lincoln understood the motives of the Radicals and willfully resolved to thwart a hidden conspiracy to spoliate the south.

Stevens reviewed Davis's bill and decided it was not harsh enough. It did not fulfill Stevens' dream of conquered provinces where an influx of carpetbaggers could sequester the property of the south and enjoy the stolen wealth. Davis revised the bill, inserting his own changes. "The bill takes for granted," he explained, "that the President may partially interfere in the civil administration not as a conqueror but as President of the United States. It seems to me to take away the chance of the confiscation of property of the rebels.... When we come to enforce the rights of conquest we should be justified in insisting upon the extreme rights of war."[41]

No amount of debate, though many tried, could keep the Radicals from pushing the Davis Bill through the House, and on May 4, 1864, it passed. The bill went over to the Senate and into the hands of Ben Wade. There a committee less outrageous than the one in the House mulled over the wordage. They modified Stevens' pet confiscation plans and proposed the passage of a Thirteenth Amendment, abolishing slavery. In the meantime, the Republican Convention met in Baltimore and nominated Lincoln for president and Johnson for vice president. Both Davis and Wade had unsuccessfully done all in their power to prevent that from happening. Having failed, Wade took special pleasure on June 30 when he sponsored the Wade-Davis Bill and informed the Senate that "The executive ought not to be permitted to handle this great question to his liking." The bill passed the Senate on July 1 and reached the president two days later. Its revisions had as much to do with rebuking Lincoln as punishing the south.[42]

One day later, July 4, Congress adjourned. Lincoln knew the contents and purpose of the Wade-Davis Bill and laid it aside. Feeling some anxiety over the fate of the bill, Charles Sumner, Zachariah Chandler, and George S. Boutwell called upon the president urging that he sign it. Lincoln put them off, suggesting that Congress had usurped its authority. When Lincoln pocket vetoed the bill, it died. Four days later he issued a proclamation explaining why he chose not to sign the bill. Ben Wade and Winter Davis read the proclamation and envisioned a disintegration of all their plans. Stevens vowed to yet thrust the radical form of justice upon the president. Wade turned to his powerful friend, Horace Greeley, and used the *New York Tribune* to extol the virtues of the bill by publishing the "Wade-Davis Manifesto," which, among other inflammatory declarations, chastised the president for his "indignant

Proclamation." The lines between the president's executive power and those of Congress were now drawn. The fight would go on, but without Henry Winter Davis, who lost his seat in the 1864 election because of his opposition to Lincoln.[43]

Lincoln did not live to see his hopes and plans for restoration of the country implemented. Those chores of office fell upon the shoulders of a man as equally committed to moderate and gradual reconstruction as Lincoln himself. But could Johnson, or any man of the times, including Lincoln, handle the festering hatred oozing from the black hearts of the Radicals in Congress? And did Johnson really support Lincoln's policy or just parts of it? Where would the latent prejudices of the vice president take him should he become president?

3

The Emergence
of the Radicals

Early in 1864 Lincoln expressed doubts about becoming a second-term president. The war continued to drag indecisively and enlistments to fill federal losses in the field declined sharply, bolstered mainly by recruitment of black regiments and unemployed immigrants. Tennessee made its own decision on the 1864 election. In a state convention at Nashville on May 30 it recommended Lincoln's renomination with Andy Johnson as vice president. Satisfied they had picked the right slate, delegates traveled to Baltimore for the Republican Convention scheduled to convene on June 7. Hoping to attract as many Democrats as possible, the Republicans called themselves the Union party, and selecting a former Democrat as the president's running mate became a distinct possibility. Many, however, doubted whether Lincoln should run again.[1]

Contenders included Salmon P. Chase, Lincoln's secretary of the treasury, who before and since entering the cabinet had never abandoned his ambition to become president. As the convention date drew near, Chase accelerated his criticism of Lincoln. To those pressing the president to remove Chase, Lincoln charitably replied, "Mr. Chase makes a good secretary and I shall keep him where he is. If he becomes President, all right. I hope we may never have a worse man." Lord Charnwood, one of Lincoln's many biographers, wrote of Chase, "This dignified and righteous person was unhappily a sneak." Lincoln's characterization of his troublesome secretary fit Chase best. "He is a very able man ... a very ambitious man, and I think on the subject of the presidency a little insane."[2]

The Radicals, all of whom were Republicans, remained so dissatisfied with Lincoln's stand on the war and his mild reconstruction policies that they attempted to postpone the convention until September. They were united in number and most forcible when intimidating others to accept their views. There were conservative and moderate Republicans in both chambers of Congress, but Radicals occupied all the powerful committee chairmanships and dominated the agenda. In the House, Galusha A. Grow held the speakers post and Thaddeus Stevens the ways and means committee. The latter contained such influential members as Owen Lovejoy, Joshua Giddings, and George W. Julian. In the Senate, Charles Sumner, Henry Wilson, Benjamin Wade, John P. Hale, and

Zachariah Chandler all occupied chairmanships. Lincoln even tolerated two Radicals in his cabinet, Chase and Stanton. Outside the Capitol, Radicals recruited the support of friendly New England papers and Horace Greeley's *New York Tribune* in an effort to postpone the convention, but on June 7 the delegates met on schedule in Baltimore.[3]

Among the delegates were Stevens and Grow, as were men from the recently reorganized states of Tennessee, Arkansas, Louisiana, and West Virginia. Stevens tried to oust the southern delegates but failed, though he succeeded in denying West Virginia a vote. Missouri cast its first ballots for Grant. When all the other ballots went to Lincoln, Missouri delegates added theirs to make it unanimous.[4]

The most contentious issue involved the selection of a vice president. Hannibal Hamlin of Maine had served for four years under Lincoln. His distinguished record included three terms in the House, two in the Senate, and two as governor. Hamlin possessed all the credentials for renomination. He had served Lincoln capably, but the Republican party had the reputation of being a sectional party and many delegates believed the time had come for a change. To what extent Lincoln meddled in the selection of his vice president is not clear, but the delegates decided the nominee should be chosen from the south. No individual had so distinguished himself as Andy Johnson. On the first vote Johnson captured the plurality but not the majority, and Hamlin ran a strong second. When the outcome became unclear, delegates sought the president's advice. Lincoln's two secretaries, John Hay and John G. Nicolay, stated that the president refused to interfere with the nominations, but did he?[5]

Lincoln often got his way without ostensibly asking for it, and he certainly saw the political advantage of having Johnson as his running mate. This view is supported by Alexander K. McClure, a frequent visitor at the White House. On the subject of Johnson's selection, he wrote: "He [Lincoln] was guided in what he did, or what he did not, in planning the great campaign of his life, that he believed involved the destiny of the country itself, by the single purpose of making success as nearly certain as possible." Into that equation, Johnson fit better than Hamlin.[6]

Secretary of State Seward also played a role in Johnson's nomination. Though he personally preferred Hamlin, he took several delegates into his confidence and said, "While the President wishes to take no part in the nomination for vice-president, yet he favors Mr. Johnson." Seward may have been speaking for himself. He did so quite often.[7]

Stevens and Cameron also sought the president's advice. Lincoln asked, "Why would Johnson not be a good man to nominate?" Stevens bluntly replied, "Mr. President, Andrew Johnson is a rash demagogue, and I suspect a damned scoundrel." Though Stevens voted for Johnson's nomination, he did not like him. At one point during the convention he addressed the delegates and said, "Can't you find a candidate for Vice-President in the United States without going down to one of those damned rebel provinces to pick one up?"[8]

Stevens failed in his efforts to prevent Johnson's nomination. On the final ballot the Tennessean amassed 494 votes, Hamlin 17, and Charles Dickinson 9, after which the vote became unanimous for Johnson. On June 9, 1864, the editorial page of the *New York World* scoffed at the Republican ticket, declaring, "The age of statesmen is gone; the age of rail splitters and tailors, of buffoons, boors, and fanatics has succeeded…. Such nominations … are an insult to the common sense of the people. God save the Republic!" But Lincoln still doubted whether he could win a second term, and the *New York Herald* questioned the constitutionality of selecting a candidate from Tennessee.[9]

On August 29, Democrats held their convention and nominated Major General George B. McClellan, who pronounced the war a failure and promised to end it. The Democratic platform read "that after four years of failure to restore the Union by the experiment of war … justice, humanity, liberty and the public welfare demand that immediate efforts be made for a cessation of hostilities."[10]

At the time of the Baltimore convention, Lincoln's popularity had so declined that many Republicans doubted if he could win a second term. Some Radicals welcomed the notion of shedding Lincoln, so much so that Wendell Phillips, one of Stevens' staunch supporters, met with his own convention of delegates, attempted to establish a third party, and nominated John C. Frémont for president. Frémont had no hope of becoming president, having tried before, but his position on total emancipation appealed to the splinter group of Radicals. One plank in the platform could have been written by Stevens, though the credit went to Phillips. It stipulated that "the question of the reconstruction of the rebellious states belongs to the people through their representatives in Congress and not to the executive." The plank never became a part of the Republican platform, but the Radicals adopted it among themselves. Three years

later the consequences of doing so would have a telling affect on Johnson's ability to work with Congress on reunifying the country.[11]

Johnson's nomination received a warm reception by the Unionists of Tennessee. On accepting the nomination, he gave his local constituency a rousing speech, pledging to put down "this Rebellion because it is a war against democracy." At the time, he did not know that the third plank in the Republican platform urged a Thirteenth Amendment to the Constitution, one to "terminate and forever prohibit the existence of slavery within the limits and jurisdiction of the United States," an action Johnson would enthusiastically endorse. He blamed the war on southern aristocrats, and he directed his message as much to them as to anyone. "Let me say to you Tennesseans and men from the Northern states that slavery is dead. It was not murdered by me. I told you long ago what the result would be if you endeavored to go out of the Union to save slavery, and that the result would be bloodshed. I am for emancipation … because it is right … and because in the emancipation of the slaves we break down an odious and dangerous aristocracy." Johnson's vigorous support of the party platform gave the Radicals a measure of comfort in their nominee.[12]

In late June, Johnson learned of the language in the Wade-Davis Bill. He strongly objected to the congressional scheme of restoration, which implied that state governments of the south organized under Lincoln's ten percent formula were invalid. Among other conditions, the bill demanded that elections be held for delegates to a state constitutional convention *only after a majority of the registered voters had taken the oath of*

Wendell Phillips, outspoken abolitionist, who stumped for Johnson's impeachment. (Library of Congress.)

allegiance to the Union. The bill also disqualified all high-placed civil officials and military officers from holding political office while forbidding former Confederate officeholders from swearing the oath. Johnson did not like the bill, and fearing it might pass, he wrote Lincoln asking that Tennessee be exempted should the measure become law.[13]

When Lincoln pocketed the Wade-Davis Bill, the Radicals stepped up their efforts to remove both him and Johnson from the ticket. To get the ball rolling, Horace Greeley spoke through the *New York Tribune,* writing, "Mr. Lincoln is already beaten. He cannot be elected. And we must have another ticket to save us from utter overthrow." On the heels of Greeley's editorial, a committee of Radicals met in New York and decided to issue a circular letter enclosing a petition for a new convention to be held on

September 28 in Cincinnati. Possible candidates discussed included secretary of the treasury Salmon P. Chase and Major General Benjamin F. Butler. Sumner stayed away from the meeting but added his comments by letter, writing, "I see no way of meeting the difficulties from the candidacy of Mr. Lincoln unless he withdraws patriotically ... so as to leave no breach in the party."[14]

The defeat of the Wade-Davis Bill mobilized the Radical zealots, and they sought the president's destruction. Had the statements in the "Wade-Davis Manifesto"—published by Greeley on August 5 in the *Tribune*—been true, the Radicals would have had enough tinder to spark impeachment hearings. But they did not want to impeach their own president when other means seemed to be at hand. They conspired to oust him by public acclamation, hold a new Republican convention, and select a fresh candidate. When Lincoln explained his pocket veto of the bill, Stevens replied with a sneer, "What an infamous proclamation." Wade and Davis informed Lincoln that congressional authority was paramount, and if he wished Radical support, he should confine himself to executing the laws and not interfere with the making of them. His business was "to suppress by arms, armed rebellion and leave political reorganization to Congress."[15]

The conspiracy, however, met with an irretrievable reverse when on August 5 Rear Admiral David Glasgow Farragut captured Mobile Bay, and on September 1 Major General Sherman captured Atlanta. An outburst of revived patriotism swept the nation. Fourteen days later Major General Philip H. Sheridan whipped Major General Jubal A. Early's army at Fisher Hill, Virginia, and one month later again at Cedar Creek. For the first time in four years it appeared that Lincoln had been right all along. The Union would be preserved. The Democratic platform collapsed with McClellan on it, and Lincoln's reelection now seemed certain. On September 13 a friend advised Frémont to withdraw, sinisterly writing, "Something tells me that Lincoln will never fill a second term. If I am right, Johnson will be the President, a man who I have loved since [eighteen] sixty-one. I have no doubt he will do you and your friends justice." And despite the sponsorship of men like Wendell Phillips, Charles Sumner, and Winter Davis, Frémont wisely abandoned his presidential aspirations.[16]

On November 8, 1864, the Lincoln-Johnson ticket won the election with a plurality of 494,000 popular votes. If the Radicals did not like their leader, the public did, but would this be enough to snuff the ambitions of the Radicals to upset the president's program for restoration?[17]

Though Lincoln maintained great confidence in Chase's ability to run the treasury department, he had grown tired of the antics of his politically untrustworthy financial czar. When Chief Justice Roger B. Taney died on October 12, 1864, Lincoln nominated Chase to fill the vacancy. The Senate confirmed it, and four days later Chase took the oath of office. When hearing of his nomination, Chase wrote Lincoln, "I cannot sleep before I thank [you] for this mark of your confidence, and especially for the manner in which the nomination was made. I shall never forget either and trust that you will never repent either. Be assured that I prize your confidence and good will more than nomination or office."[18]

To his diary, Welles questioned the

Horace Greeley, publisher of the *New York Tribune,* the most widely read Radical press in the United States. (Library of Congress.)

wisdom of Chase's nomination, writing, "I hope this selection may prove a good one. I would not have advised it…. He will be likely to use the place for political advancement and thereby endanger confidence in the court. He, though selfishly stubborn, sometimes wants moral courage and frankness, is fond of adulation, and, with superiors, is a sycophant. I hope the president may have no occasion to regret this selection." Neither Welles nor Lincoln could have envisioned that Chase would preside over the most important trial in the nation's history.[19]

On December 6, 1864, Lincoln delivered his fourth and last annual message to Congress. With war hastening to an end, he reiterated his own program for mild reconstruction. He also encouraged the passage of the proposed Thirteenth Amendment abolishing slavery, which the Senate had passed in April. With Lincoln pushing the amendment, along with help from the Radicals, the measure passed in the House on January 13, 1865, by the slim margin of three votes.[20]

With the amendment on the way to the states for ratification, the House Radicals decided to revisit the Wade-Davis Bill. James Ashley of Ohio presented a new version, just as invidious as the original bill. The same cast of characters — Stevens, Davis, and company — once again renewed their nefarious efforts to diminish the power of the president in order to get their own way. When Ashley's bill failed to pass in the House, he merely said that he hoped when the new Congress convened it would "pass even a better bill."[21]

In the 1864 elections Winter Davis lost his seat in the House, and his lame duck status only made him meaner. Major General Jacob D. Cox happened to be in Washington and attended a dinner given by Major General James A. Garfield. Davis attended the affair with ex-Major General Robert C. Schenck, one of the Union's inept political generals who had resigned his commission to run for Congress. Cox never forgot that evening. "The berating of Lincoln by [Davis and Schenck] was something to take one's breath away.... [Lincoln] was charged with all the folly, stupidity and semi-treason that could be imagined." According to Cox, the evening accented the growing division between the Radicals and the administration.[22]

On February 3, 1865, Lincoln and Seward attended a peace conference at Hampton Roads, where they met with Alexander H. Stephens, Robert M. T. Hunter, and Judge John A. Campbell. Lincoln and Stephens were old friends, but the commissioners asked for concessions the president would not grant. Lincoln demanded that the south disband its army and permit a reunited national government to resume its normal functions, a request the Confederate commissioners had no power to grant. Seward assured them that Lincoln would "exercise the powers of the Executive with the utmost liberality," but the commissioners understood the changing attitudes in Congress and feared the dilution of presidential power.[23]

Jefferson Davis summed up the situation accurately when on March 13, 1865, in reference to the Radicals, he wrote:

> There remains then, for us no choice but to continue the contest to a final issue, for the people of the Confederacy can be but little known to him who supposes it possible that they would ever consent to purchase at the cost of degradation and slavery, permission to live in a country garrisoned by their own negroes and governed by officers sent by the conquerors to work over them.[24]

Thaddeus Stevens impatiently waited to hear what new concessions the president had granted the rebels. To his inquiry, Lincoln replied in five words: "The conference ended without result." Nor could it have ended differently. Southern statesmen feared the vindictive and vicious disenfranchisements of the "Wade-Davis Manifesto" and the rejected Ashley bill. They, too, had read the words spoken by Winter Davis in the House when he said, "Treat those who hold power in the South as rebels and not as governors or legislators; disperse them from the halls of legislation; expel them from executive mansions, strip them of the emblems of authority." So on went the war, staining the country with more American blood.[25]

The war in Tennessee reached its climax on December 15, 1864, when Major General George H. Thomas shattered Confederate forces under Lieutenant General John Bell Hood. The vice president-elect witnessed the battle, writing Parson Brownlow, "This is the most crushing blow which has been given since the inauguration of the rebellion. Thomas has immortalized himself and stands equal, if not superior, to any military chieftain of the times." At long last, Andrew Johnson could begin his work of restoration. The Tennessee Convention met at Nashville on January 9, 1865, and on the 12th Johnson made his first appearance. He knew exactly what needed to be done. The delegates abolished slavery, repealed the ordinance of secession, submitted the amended constitution to the people, and nominated Brownlow for governor.[26]

On January 13 Johnson wrote Lincoln, "All is now working well, and if Tennessee is now left alone will soon resume all the functions of a state according to the genius and theory of the government." The message contained two key words — "left alone" — because Johnson was not ignorant of the president's growing difficulties with the Radicals. On February 22 the people went to the polls. Though the turnout was light, the public approved the amended state constitution by a vote of 25,293 to 48.[27]

Nearly two years had elapsed since Johnson returned to Tennessee as military governor. Now worn down by his labors and weakened by typhoid, he asked the president for permission to remain in Nashville on March 4 to see the

Henry Winter Davis, representative from Maryland, co-author of the Wade-Davis Bill, and an outspoken political enemy of Johnson. (Library of Congress.)

state government seated. The date conflicted with the presidential inauguration, and Lincoln wanted his running mate back in Washington. "While we fully appreciate your wish to remain in Tennessee," Lincoln replied, "it is our unanimous conclusion that it is unsafe for you to not be here on the 4th of March. Be sure to reach here by that time." Johnson sought precedents that might enable him to remain in Tennessee until after the inauguration, but John W. Forney, a devoted friend, encouraged him to get to Washington and be on hand to represent the War Democrats. So on February 25 Johnson packed his bags and boarded a train for Washington.[28]

The battle between Lincoln's use of war powers and those of Congress received another test when Louisiana applied for readmission to the Union. Two representatives from Louisiana, Michael Hahn and Benjamin F. Flanders, had already been seated in the House. Because this occurred as a singular incident in 1863, Radicals had not mobilized their efforts to contest Lincoln's plans for the future. In 1864 Hahn became governor and delegates met in New Orleans to develop the state constitution. In September the voters adopted a constitution abolishing slavery. It restricted suffrage to white males, but following Lincoln's advice, it also empowered the legislature to decide when to confer the franchise on blacks. To Johnson's way of thinking, Louisiana acted properly in withholding black suffrage until ex-slaves obtained enough education to vote responsibly.[29]

For more than two years Hahn and Flanders had worked with diligence in the House of Representatives to gain Louisiana's readmission to the Union. But when the issue came before the Senate in February 1865, Sumner espoused the Radical cause by voicing a vicious protest. "The pretended state government of Louisiana is utterly indefensible whether you look at its origin or its character," he stormed. "To describe it I must use plain language. It is a mere seven months' abortion, begotten by the bayonet in criminal conjunction with the spirit of caste, and born before its time, rickety, unformed, unfinished — whose continued existence will be a burden, a reproach and a wrong." Sumner certainly knew that the "begetter" was not the bayonet but Lincoln.[30]

Ben Wade agreed with Sumner, declaring, "When the foundation of this government is sought to be swept away by executive usurpation it will not do…. If the President can initiate a state gov-

ernment and bring it here and force us … to receive as associates on this floor these mere mockeries … your republic is at an end…. A more absurd monarchical and anti-American principle was never announced on God's earth." The Radicals won the debate, and the resolution recognizing Louisiana failed to pass the Senate.[31]

The next issue before the joint chambers concerned the electoral vote. Both Louisiana and Tennessee had submitted theirs. The Radicals now applied a new logic to the question. If Louisiana could not qualify as a state, how could Congress accept its votes? And since Tennessee shared the same status, then its votes should not be counted either. On February 8 Vice President Hamlin informed both chambers that he held the returns from Louisiana and Tennessee, and his duty required that he not present them. Repudiating Tennessee's votes after nominating and electing Johnson vice president demonstrated the degree to which Radicals would go to gain power over the president and defeat his restoration plans.[32]

On the heels of Radical actions in Congress, Johnson arrived in Washington. On March 3 he tendered his resignation as military governor and brigadier general to Secretary of War Stanton, who replied by graciously expressing his admiration and gratitude for services rendered. That night Johnson met with John Forney for supper. In an effort to dull the effect of his illness, he consumed too many glasses of whiskey. Exhausted by the trip, and ill, he went to bed early. He trusted Lincoln to look after the conflict with Congress. It must have been some satisfaction to Johnson to know that as vice president, he would chair the Senate.[33]

On March 4, 1865, Lincoln delivered his second inaugural address. He voiced great hope for reunification:

> With malice toward none, with charity for all, with firmness in the right as God gives us to see the right, let us strive on to finish the work we are in, to bind up the nation's wounds, to care for him who shall have borne the battle and for his widow and his orphan, to do all which may achieve and cherish a just and lasting peace among ourselves and with all nations.[34]

At noon Andrew Johnson entered the Senate to be inaugurated as vice president. The spacious galleries provided a mass of rain-soaked spectators with standing room only. Vice President Hamlin occupied the chair for the last time. Next to him in the clerk's chair sat Johnson. Official witnesses to the ceremony included members of the cabinet, distinguished officers of the army and navy, the diplomatic corps, foreign attachés, the officers of the Senate, and all its members.[35]

Hamlin introduced the vice president-elect, who looked very much like a man recovering from a bad night on the town. The formality required a seven minute speech from the outgoing and incoming vice presidents. Hamlin did not like Johnson and limited his valedictory to two hundred fifty words. Then Johnson took the rostrum. He did not have command of himself and dismayed his audience. His voice slurred, the message sputtered in hoarse, rambling tones, and the gallery soon surmised that their vice president was either sick, drunk, or both. Having been ill for the past several days, Johnson had sipped brandy as an astringent during his trip to Washington. Before the ceremony, Hamlin provided him with a flask of whiskey. Johnson drank too much, and when delivering his speech, he wobbled precariously and could not command his voice. He seemed to forget what he wanted to say and kept repeating himself, mumbling to various members of chamber, "You got your power from the people, whose creatures you are!" Most observers attributed Johnson's pathetic appearance to drunkenness. But Hamlin, had he wanted, could have restrained Johnson's drinking until after the ceremony.[36]

In a display of overt shame, Charles Sumner covered his face with his hands and lowered his head to his desk. Actions such as this did not go unnoticed by the press. The vice president had "not proceeded far," reported the *New York World*, "when Senators on the Republican side began to hide their faces." Hamlin took advantage of a pause in Johnson's address to hurriedly administer the oath. On the way out of the chamber Lincoln turned to one of the marshalls and said, "Do not let Johnson speak outside!" The vice president's shoddy performance played directly into the hands of the Radicals.[37]

Lincoln knew Johnson drank in moderation. In a passing statement to Hugh McCulloch, who had become secretary of the treasury, he said, "I have known Andy Johnson for many years; he made a bad slip the other day, but you need not be scared; Andy ain't a drunkard." Responding to another inquiry, he admitted, "It has been a severe lesson for Andy, but I do not think he will do it again." As time passed, Colonel William H. Crook, the president's bodyguard, confirmed Lincoln's prediction. While the White House was always stocked with fine wines and liquors, Johnson "never drank to excess." Said Crook, "I saw him probably every day ... and I never saw him once under the influence of alcohol."[38]

During Johnson's lifetime struggle against adversity, nothing blemished him more than those fifteen minutes when he spoke before the Senate. An outraged Charles Sumner thought the vice president should be immediately impeached. Because the House was not in session, he settled for assembling the Senate Republican caucus to discuss a resolution demanding that Johnson resign. His colleagues disagreed, arguing that nobody would have paid much attention to the vice president if Sumner had not been "so exquisite about it." They defeated Sumner's motion, but the Radicals would never let Johnson forget the incident. Were it not for the catastrophic events of the next four years, history may have treated the "bad slip" with more gentleness. But on March 4, 1865, the greatest tragedy of the war, and the one that would change Andrew Johnson's life forever, waited to strike like a silent specter. Lincoln had but forty-one days to live.[39]

4

Lincoln's Legacy

Abe Lincoln had a marvelous way of ignoring the Radicals while creating the policies he believed would bring the Union back together in a magnanimous and harmonious manner. Few contemporary politicians shared his vision of the future. Even fewer could keep stride with him because Lincoln made the rules as he went along. His close friends and ardent supporters did not always agree with him — often because he did not exercise prudent political caution and carelessly provoked the Radicals.

On April 2 Grant broke through General Lee's defenses at Petersburg and began driving the Confederate army westward across Virginia. Government officials and military personnel spilled out of Richmond, and by daylight on March 3 most of them had vanished, leaving sections of the city smoldering in ashes. Lincoln, having gone to City Point, Virginia, on March 24 to be with Grant, decided on April 4 to visit the Confederate capital. With a small guard he walked the streets of the evacuated city, followed by a group of blacks who instantly recognized him. Lincoln met with Major General Godfrey Weitzel, the local commander, and on April 5 returned to City Point. After mulling over the conditions he had just observed, Lincoln wrote Weitzel suggesting that the general permit "the gentlemen who have acted as the Legislature of Virginia … may now desire to assemble at Richmond, and take measures to withdraw the Virginia troops, and other support from resistance to the General government. If they attempt it, give them permission and protection…" unless they commit some hostile action against the United States.[1]

Lincoln asked Weitzel to keep the matter confidential, but by the time the president reached Washington, Stanton, Wade, and Welles had all learned of the request and greeted him with strong opposition. Each had different reasons for their objections. Stanton thought the action rash, and Wade believed that the president had once again overstepped his executive authority. When Welles expressed concern that the Virginians might be inclined to "conspire against us," Lincoln replied that he "had no fear of that. They were too badly beaten, and too much exhausted." He added that "the members of the legislature comprising the prominent and influential men of their respective counties better come together and undo their work." On April 11 he rescinded permission for the Virginia legislature to meet, writing, "I cannot go forward with everybody opposed to me." For Lincoln time was running short, and his compassionate views on reconstruction were beginning to drive the Radicals to acts of desperation.[2]

On April 9 the Army of the Potomac surrounded the remnants of the Army of Northern Virginia at Appomattox, Virginia, and General Lee surrendered to General Grant. Soldiers mingled together, shared rations, and exchanged expressions of mutual respect. Union officers paroled the ragged grayclads and sent them home — "Not to be disturbed by United States authority." Thad Stevens and his followers probably never read Grant's "not to be disturbed" terms of parole, and had they done so, it would not have made a bit of difference.[3]

News of Lee's surrender reached Washington on the morning of the 10th. At daylight the celebration began — bells tolled, cannon roared, flags fluttered from every building, and jubilant crowds swarmed the streets. An evening serenade at the White House brought Lincoln to a window. He joined the mood of the crowd and had a little fun. Seeing the band at hand, he treated them to a chorus of "Dixie," followed by "Yankee Doodle." It had been a daylong celebration, but Lincoln had more on his mind.[4]

On April 11 he addressed the public because he wanted to once again explain his position on reconstruction. With the war's end in sight, he had won the public's confidence, and now he needed their support during the forthcoming skirmishes with the Radicals. Lincoln wanted every southern state to adopt the same formula for reunification as had Louisiana and Tennessee, a simple methodology unacceptable to the Radicals. In a private letter, Chief Justice Chase advised Lincoln that Congress might be more receptive to accepting Louisiana's constitution if it provided stronger guarantees for the "safety and justice to colored citizens through the extension to loyal colored men of the right of suffrage."

Chase still did not see the whole picture, but Lincoln did. The president knew that imposing instantaneous black suffrage on the south would not mend the country. Though Chase had aligned himself with the Radicals over the issue of abolition, he remained moderate. Unlike Sumner, Stevens, and Wade, Chase did not believe justice would be served by turning the defeated south into territories to be plucked of their wealth by northern carpetbaggers.[5]

Lincoln used his public address on April 12 to draw a distinct line between himself and the Radicals, and he had confidence in his ability to get his way. Charles Sumner saw the battle coming, writing, "The President's speech and other things augur confusion and uncertainty in the future, with hot controversy. Alas! Alas!" Three days later, during his final cabinet meeting on April 14, Lincoln reaffirmed his intentions. "There is too much desire on the part of some of our very good friends to be masters, to interfere with and dictate to those states, to treat the people not as fellow citizens; there is too little respect for their rights. I do not sympathize in these feelings."[6]

That evening Lincoln and his wife attended a performance of "Our American Cousin" at Ford's Theater. The presidential party arrived late. When Lincoln entered his box the actors paused, the audience cheered, and the orchestra played "Hail to the Chief." Lincoln settled into his chair and relaxed. John Wilkes Booth, himself an actor though not in the play, stole into the box, pointed a Derringer at Lincoln's head, and pulled the trigger. The ball entered the president's brain, inflicting a mortal wound. At 7:22 A.M., April 15, 1865, Lincoln died.[7]

Booth's action involved others.

On the same evening, April 14, George Atzerodt drew the assignment of killing Andrew Johnson while Louis Paine was to murder William H. Seward. On the day of the crime, one of Booth's cards mysteriously turned up at Johnson's hotel. Later, Radicals would use the incident to suggest that Johnson conspired with Booth to assassinate Lincoln. Booth also targeted General Grant, but the Grants, who had been invited by Mary Lincoln to join them for the performance at Ford's Theater, had departed from the city to visit their son. Atzerodt lost his courage while waiting to kill Johnson, but Paine forged ahead. The latter entered Seward's home, brutally stabbed the secretary and his son, but failed to kill either man. Booth escaped after shooting Lincoln but broke his leg when jumping from the presidential box to the stage. By the morning of April 15 the entire country lapsed into mourning, and Stanton began a nationwide manhunt for the assassins.[8]

Shortly after Lincoln died, Johnson received a note from the cabinet: "The emergency demands that you should immediately qualify according to the requirements of the Constitution and enter upon the duties of the President of the United States." At 10:00 A.M. on April 15, Chief Justice Chase and William P. Mellen entered Johnson's quarters at the Kirkwood House. Secretary of the treasury Hugh McCulloch, attorney general James Speed, Frank and Montgomery Blair, and several members of Congress arrived later. Chase found Johnson "calm but very grave" and at 11:00 A.M. administered the oath. Johnson replied, "I do solemnly swear that I will faithfully execute the office of President of the United States, and will do the best of my ability to preserve, protect and defend the Constitution of the United States." For Johnson, defending the Constitution had been his life's work. With emotion and sincere earnestness, Chase took Johnson's hand and said, "May God support, guide, and bless you in your arduous duties!" Johnson thanked his guests and made a brief, dignified address. He admitted being deeply saddened by the late events and felt unprepared to perform the duties of an office so important as the presidency. All signs of his illness had vanished, and, according to the press, he looked in remarkably good health.[9]

At the age of fifty-seven, with most of those years spent in public service, Johnson became the seventeenth president of the United States. It could not have happened at a worse time. He had endured all the storms of politics since beginning his career as a small town alderman in Greeneville. Few public officials ever experienced the new president's breadth of training or the adversity he overcame to achieve such distinction. To be vaulted into the presidency under so disheartening circumstances had never entered his thoughts. After taking the oath he turned to witnesses in the room and said, "I have been almost overwhelmed by the announcement of the sad event which has so recently occurred." When asked what he intended to do, Johnson replied, "The only assurance that I can now give of the future is reference to the past." He did not want to make a statement at this time, but he asked the cabinet to meet at noon at the treasury department, where a temporary office had been provided until the White House became available. Seward, who had been assaulted, could not attend the meeting. Stanton recommended that William Hunter, chief clerk of the state department, be appointed ad

Andrew Johnson taking the oath of office. (Library of Congress, from Leslie's *Illustrated Weekly*.)

interim secretary of state and Johnson agreed. Members of the cabinet asked Johnson about his views on reconstruction. Without hesitation he replied, "In all essentials it would be the same as that of the late president." But Johnson had not been given time to think about policy or what impact his statements might have on the issue.[10]

In addition to Lincoln's political adversaries, Johnson inherited the president's cabinet. Some of the occupants were new, having been appointed during the past year. Others, like Seward and Welles, had been with Lincoln since the beginning of his first term. Stanton joined the cabinet in 1862, entrenched himself in the position, and now with Lincoln gone, he felt less constrained to flex his muscle by a higher authority.

At the height of the crisis caused by

Lincoln's death, the most able cabinet member, sixty-four-year-old William H. Seward, lay in bed. Nine days before Paine's attempted assassination, Seward had been thrown from his carriage and severely injured. On the night of April 14 he lay in bed with his neck in a cast. When Paine entered the bed chamber, drew his knife, and slashed at Seward's neck, the very injury that disabled the secretary saved his life.[11]

In 1820 Seward graduated from Union College and two years later became a member of the bar. His career in politics began at the age of twenty-nine, when elected as a Whig to the New York senate. At thirty-seven he became New York's governor and eleven years later, a United States senator. Quite early in his career Seward met Thurlow Weed, who became a commanding influence in state politics. In Seward, Weed observed a bright young man pliable enough to shape as his own political front man. In Weed, Seward beheld an influential force that could mold his political career. Despite this raw political relationship, the two men became great friends, though not always did they agree.[12]

Seward spent four of his eleven years in the Senate in fellowship with Johnson. He supported Johnson's Homestead Bill, believing that the slave issue could be alleviated by the opening and settlement of new territories. He also respected Johnson's fidelity to the Union, when in 1861 Tennessee seceded.[13]

After joining the Senate, Seward's presidential aspirations evolved with strong backing from Weed. At the time, Lincoln was a virtual unknown as a political force. On March 11, 1850, Seward delivered his first speech before the Senate. He aroused the country by arguing against the expansion of slavery in the new territories and advocated "a higher law than the Constitution." Eight years later he delivered a speech in Rochester, predicting the emergence of "an irrepressible conflict," meaning "that the United States must, and will sooner or later, become either entirely a slave holding nation or entirely a free labor nation." During May 1860, while the Republicans met in Chicago to nominate a president, Lincoln wrote: "I agree with Seward in his 'irrepressible conflict,' but I do not endorse his 'higher law doctrine.'"[14]

Seward's greatest setback in life occurred when he lost the presidential nomination to Lincoln. He had been too closely connected with Thurlow Weed

William H. Seward, secretary of state under both Lincoln and Johnson. (Massachusetts Commandery Military Order of the Loyal Legion and the U.S. Army Military History Institute.)

and too much hated by Horace Greeley, who used his personal influence and the *New York Tribune* to destroy Seward's candidacy. When Seward lost, Weed shed tears. Seward, however, took the disappointment as a gentleman and in the months ahead stumped through New York and the northwest in support of Lincoln.[15]

Lincoln recognized Seward's administrative skills and in December 1860 offered him the post of secretary of state. Seward accepted, but after Lincoln named Salmon P. Chase for the treasury, with whom Seward held political differences, the latter withdrew his acceptance. Lincoln persuaded him to reconsider, and on March 5, 1861, Seward became the number one man in Lincoln's cabinet.[16]

For many Republicans who had doubts of Lincoln's ability to run the government, Seward became "the master spirit of the administration." Seward thought so, too, and on April 1 made the egregious error of submitting his "Thoughts for the President's Consideration," recommending a general war with Great Britain, France, Spain, and Russia as a means of reunifying the country. He then took a step further and offered to direct it, adding, "I neither seek to evade nor assume responsibility." Lincoln fully understood Seward's motives and replied that whatever must be done, "I must do it." Lincoln kept the matter private, but he made it crystal clear that Seward would be no "premier" and that the government would be run by the president. Lincoln let Seward down easily, and three months later the secretary confided to his wife, "The President is the best of all of us.... There is but one vote in the cabinet and that is cast by the president."[17]

Seward's appreciation of Lincoln's skills rapidly grew, and he became the most trusted and reliable member of the cabinet. His statesmanship in foreign affairs kept Great Britain and France out of the war. He also adopted Lincoln's conservative policies, giving balance to a cabinet containing two fledgling Radicals — Chase and Stanton. Because of Seward's fidelity to Lincoln, the Radical senators, with surreptitious help from Stanton, tried to drive him out of the cabinet. Lincoln outmaneuvered the Radicals and Seward stayed.[18]

Through the darkest days of the war, Seward provided Lincoln with something the latter very badly needed — a friend, someone to talk with who could be both thoughtful and entertaining. Unlike Stanton, Seward possessed amiable and genial manners, scholarly insight, eloquence, and personal charm. With Seward, Lincoln could relax. But during the days following Lincoln's assassination, the sixty-three-year-old secretary lay in bed fighting for his life. The most important person in the cabinet would not for many weeks be available to give counsel to Andrew Johnson, who had been thrust into one of the most important moments in the history of the United States by an act of great wickedness.[19]

While Seward lay disabled, fifty-year-old Edwin McMasters Stanton flexed his muscles and took matters into his own hands. He had held the office of secretary of war since January 15, 1862, and during his tenure grabbed as much power as Lincoln would give him. He owed his position to Seward, without whose recommendation Lincoln may have chosen another. Welles summed up Stanton's character, writing, "[He] is by nature an intriguer, courts favor, is not faithful in his friendships, [and] is given to secret underhand combinations. His obligations to Seward are great but would not deter him from raising a breeze against Seward to favor himself."[20]

During Johnson's term as military governor of Tennessee, he enjoyed a compatible working relationship with Stanton. Despite differences, both were patriots and devoted all their energies to winning the war and reuniting the country. The two men, however, did not share the same thoughts on reconstruction. What made matters worse, Stanton did not have the respect for Johnson that he held for Lincoln, and when Johnson became president, Stanton became less trustworthy.

Having served under Lincoln throughout the war, sixty-two-year-old Gideon Welles provided stability, consistency, and competency in running the navy. He kept out of matters that did not concern his office, partly because he had no navy at the beginning of the war and building one consumed all of his time. Though a keen observer of human nature, he confided most of his opinions to his *Diary* and rarely gave advice unless asked. Before joining the cabinet, Welles had been editor of the *Hartford Times,* a Democratic member of the Connecticut house of representatives, state comptroller, and Hartford postmaster. During the Mexican War he headed the bureau of provisions and clothing for the navy department. The Kansas-Nebraska struggle in the 1850s aroused his antislavery sentiments and he joined the Republican party. Lincoln thoroughly trusted Welles. Whenever he needed a balanced opinion during a cabinet debate, he would turn to "Father Neptune," as he affectionately called Welles, to ask his thoughts. Welles contributed immensely to the war effort by blockading and capturing the important ports of the south. Unlike Stanton, Welles had a "singular sagacity in judging men" and consistently chose his best captains to lead squadrons while the war department blundered through the first two years of the war trying to find a general.[21]

Welles's unfavorable opinion of Stanton grew out of the latter's cunning quest for personal power. During one phase of the war Stanton demanded that the navy take orders from the army, but Lincoln refused to consider the request.

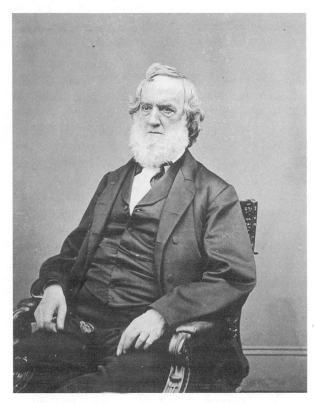

Gideon Welles, secretary of the navy under both Lincoln and Johnson and an admirer of both. (National Archives, 11-B-5821.)

Stanton learned to behave under Lincoln, but how would he behave under Johnson?[22]

After Salmon Chase resigned, William Pitt Fessenden accepted temporarily the post of secretary of the treasury. In March 1865 he returned to the Senate, and fifty-six-year-old Hugh McCulloch replaced him. McCulloch had been in the treasury post for less than six weeks when Johnson became president. Though a lawyer, McCulloch associated himself with the State Bank of Indiana and remained in the financial sector until called to Washington. An excellent administrator with exceptional fiduciary instincts, McCulloch won praise from Welles, a laurel which never came easily. "Though

Edwin M. Stanton, secretary of war under both Lincoln and Johnson and one of the key figures in Johnson's impeachment. (Massachusetts Commandery Military Order of the Loyal Legion and the U.S. Army Military History Institute.)

the office of secretary of the interior for five weeks prior to Lincoln's assassination. He had been the president of Ohio Wesleyan University at the age of thirty-three and elected to the Senate at the age of thirty-five. Postmaster General Dennison had long been connected with the Radicals. When Lincoln made the appointment, he did so to pay off a political debt to the Radicals. Dennison had the skills to run the department, but his aristocratic and pompous behavior did not win him many friends outside the circle of his associates. Attorney general James Speed, a former Whig, was the brother of one of Lincoln's oldest and most trusted friends from Springfield, Joshua Speed. It had been Joshua who had helped Lincoln establish a law practice and later introduced him to Mary Todd. When making the appointment, Lincoln would never have guessed that under Johnson, Speed would turn Radical.[24]

Johnson knew few of the men of his cabinet. He had met Seward in the Senate, but the secretary could be of no help until he healed. During the war Johnson's relations with Stanton had been cordial and professional, but at the time Stanton had been Johnson's superior. With the relationship reversed, Johnson did not have the benefit of insight into Stanton's character. He respected Welles, though he did not know him well. McCulloch, Harlan, Dennison, and Speed were all new personalities met during the first week of March. The days following Lincoln's assassination were

not trained in public office or an experienced politician," Welles considered him "the most reliable and sensible man in the Cabinet."[23]

Other new members included forty-five-year-old James Harlan of Illinois, forty-nine-year-old William Dennison of Ohio, and fifty-three-year-old James Speed from Kentucky. Harlan had held filled with tension, both inside and outside of the cabinet. Johnson's poor performance at the inaugural did not help him establish a fast, openhearted, and trusting relationship with his cabinet. They did not know quite what to think of him — or he of them. So while the country mourned, Johnson attempted to take hold of his new responsibilities. One of his first mistakes was inviting the cabinet to retain their offices, but under the circumstances, he had little choice.[25]

Lincoln's death gave the Radicals new hope for their mandate of pursuing retribution from "conquered provinces." In Johnson they saw a man who had risen from poverty and who had been shunned by the landed aristocracy of Tennessee. Why would he not want their property confiscated and given to those who had fought for the Union? After all, it was Johnson who in 1861 spoke to the Senate and said, "Were I the President of the United States, I would do as Thomas Jefferson did in 1806 with Aaron Burr, who was charged with treason; I would have them arrested and tried for treason, and if convicted by the Eternal God they should suffer the penalty of the law at the hands of the executioner. Sir, treason must be punished."[26]

Knowing something of Johnson's views during the war, conservatives wondered where he stood on reconstruction. Some recalled that when Johnson became military governor, he announced that "while it may be necessary to punish conscious treason in high places, no merely retaliatory or vindictive policy will be adopted" in Tennessee.[27]

During the first week of his presidency, Johnson became inundated by visits from Radicals and conservatives, each trying to divine the president's intentions while lobbying support for their own initiatives. On the day the president died, George W. Julian, one of the House's outspoken Radicals, recalled spending the afternoon in a political caucus held for the purpose of determining whether they should confront Johnson and demand a new cabinet less conciliatory than the one selected by Lincoln. "While everybody was shocked by his murder," Julian wrote, "the feeling was nearly universal that the accession of Johnson ... would prove a godsend to the country. Aside from Mr. Lincoln's known policy of tenderness to the Rebels ... his well-known views upon the subject of reconstruction were as distasteful as possible to Radical Republicans."[28]

Pressure on Johnson to punish the south did not come solely from Radicals in Congress. Voices from the pulpit clamored for retribution, and the northeastern press, using equal amounts of threat and flattery, urged Johnson to accept the doctrine of revenge. Radicals blamed Lincoln's death on a conspiracy organized by southern leaders, and they had Stanton in the cabinet to promote their theory. With so much propaganda engulfing the public, even they turned circumspect. General Joseph E. Johnston, the last Confederate general who still commanded an organized army in the field, voiced the sentiments of the south when he wrote, "The loss was most serious to the people ... who had begun to realize that Mr. Lincoln was the best friend the South had."[29]

In the minds of Radicals, the question of reconstruction remained unanswered. On April 15, after Johnson delivered his inaugural address, conservatives and Radicals studied it for answers. The only clue to Johnson's intentions lay in one obscure statement:

The only assurance that I can now give of the future is reference to the past. The course which I have taken in the past in connection with this rebellion must be regarded as a guaranty of the future. My past public life, which has been long and laborious, has been founded, as I in good conscious believe, upon a great principle of right, which lies at the basis of all things.

Johnson did not clarify what he meant by placing the future in reference to the past or exactly what he meant by the "great principle of right." Nor was it clear to anyone but Johnson what he meant when he referred to his past "connection with this rebellion ... as a guaranty of the future."[30]

Johnson was simply buying something he badly needed — time. For the next few weeks, conservatives and Radicals continued to be baffled by his ambiguous statements. George Julian summed up the political dilemma, writing:

> The question of reconstruction had found no logical solution, and all was confusing respecting it. The question of negro suffrage was slowly coming to the front, and could not much longer be evaded. The adequate punishment of the Rebel leaders was the demand of the hour. What would the new president do? He had suddenly become the central figure of American politics, and both Radicals and Conservatives were as curious to know what line of policy he would follow as they were anxious to point the way.[31]

Charles Sumner represented a good share of Radical curiosity in the Senate and on April 15 called upon Johnson at the Kirkwood House. Though using a diplomatic matter as an excuse for the visit, Sumner turned the conversation to his real concern — Johnson's policy toward the south. The senator found the president "careful in what he said but very determined." On the 16th Sumner returned to the Kirkwood House, this time with Chase, to probe deeper into Johnson's thoughts on the matter of enfranchising the blacks. The president's draft of a proclamation for declaring the war at an end in Virginia and North Carolina made no mention of the matter. Sumner voiced his unwillingness to discuss reconstruction unless "the blackman had his rights." After a protracted conversation, Johnson announced "There is no difference between us; you and I are alike." Sumner departed happily convinced that his ideas and Johnson's were in accord. To friends, he wrote, "In the question of colored suffrage the President is with us."

Sumner continued to call on Johnson, and on all important issues such as the timing and methodology of reconstruction, the two men continued to be in agreement. Sumner even got Johnson to admit that "no state can be *precipitated* into the Union; that rebel States must go through a term of *probation*." They even agreed that leading Confederates should be exiled instead of executed. There can be no division in the Union party, Johnson told Sumner. "I mean to keep you all together." When the Senate adjourned in May, Sumner returned to Boston gladdened that Lincoln had been replaced by a man who shared his views. In his eagerness for support of his own policies, Sumner misread Johnson, but two weeks would elapse before the first blow came.[32]

According to chief justice Chase, Johnson had not formulated his plans when speaking with Sumner. On April 29

Chase approached the president offering a rough draft of an address on "the reorganization of the rebel states." It incorporated Sumner's plan for the "recognition of loyal colored men as citizens entitled to the right of suffrage." Chase read it to Johnson twice before the president replied, "I agree to all you say, but I don't see how I can issue such a document now. I am new and untried and cannot venture on what I please."[33]

In the meantime, Johnson sent word to Mrs. Lincoln that she could remain in the White House as long as she wished. Sam Hooper, a member of the House, opened his home on the corner of Fourteenth and H Streets to the president, and for the moment, Johnson seemed content to live with the Hoopers and work out of the room adjacent to McCulloch's office in the treasury department.[34]

McCulloch observed Johnson's habits and left the following record. "He arrived at his office every morning before nine o'clock and he rarely left before five. There was no liquor in his room. It was open to everybody. His luncheon, when he had one, was like mine: a cup of tea and a cracker.... For nearly four hours I had daily intercourse with him frequently at night, and I never saw him when under the influence of liquor. I have no hesitation in saying that whatever may have been his faults, intemperance was not among them."[35]

McCulloch learned more about Johnson's reconstruction plans from those four-hour conversations than the president thought wise to share with Stanton, Sumner, or Congress. When a conservative delegation from McCulloch's home state of Indiana met with the president in late April, he told them essentially what he had confided to McCulloch.

"Upon this idea of destroying states," he said, "my position has been heretofore well known, and I see no cause to change it now. Some are satisfied with the idea that the states are to be lost in territorial and other divisions; are to lose their character as states in the possession and enjoyment of a republican form of government.... In putting the government on its legs again, I think the progress of this work must pass into the hands of its friends, not smothered by its enemies."[36]

Johnson fostered a concept rather than a plan, and he kept his own counsel. It adhered to the principles of reconstruction articulated by Lincoln during the last weeks of his life. But could Johnson do it, and would the Radicals let him? Lincoln recognized that his restoration policies were wartime measures. Once the fighting stopped, certain unilateral prerogatives to act without the advice and consent of Congress would also end. Johnson became president during the Confederacy's final collapse. What Lincoln would have done under peacetime conditions remains an unanswered question. His approach to reconstruction might have changed, though he would have exerted every effort to work with Congress to achieve reconciliation and total reunification of all eleven southern states. In his last public address, he openly advocated limited black suffrage, perhaps to demonstrate to Congress that both branches could work together in restoring the south.[37]

Johnson and Lincoln differed in many ways but none more so than on the slave issue. Each had a different vision of the future. Johnson accepted emancipation without fully shedding his racial prejudices. Lincoln, who once considered exporting freedmen, came to accept the possibilities of black development in the

United States as an economic asset. Where Johnson seemed content to leave freedmen to the management of their former masters, Lincoln would certainly have advocated a policy providing some form of protection and civil rights.

Both men adhered to their own fundamental principles, but on issues requiring compromise, Johnson manifested an unrelenting stubbornness on constitutional issues. Lincoln dealt with political resistance subtly and pliantly, never losing sight of his objective. Johnson took the Jacksonian approach, flexing executive muscle to get his way. He dealt with adversaries more harshly, more obstinately, and created enemies. He understood Lincoln's restoration policies as they existed during the war. He had little or no insight into what Lincoln intended after the war, and unfortunately, the president's sudden assassination left Johnson with many unclarified assumptions.[38]

Johnson's indecision on precisely how to work with Congress in guiding the reconstruction effort would result in confusion when Republicans attempted to pass the first bill after Lincoln's death. When influential members of Congress had pressed him for statements of policy during the early days of his administration, he misled them, though perhaps not intentionally. Having been thrust into the presidency so unexpectedly, his thoughts had not crystallized, but he sowed seeds of distrust that would soon germinate into sharp differences. Because of his long absence from Washington, Johnson did not fully understand the mood of Congress. At the moment Booth's Derringer ended the life of Abraham Lincoln, the president was less the leader of his party than Thad Stevens, whose frank indifference to the morals of his personal political strategy made him a most dangerous foe for Andrew Johnson.

5

Johnson Takes Charge

Like Lincoln, Johnson received daily visits from swarms of people wanting favors or special privileges, but the most annoying demands came from impatient politicians. Having been many years in politics, Johnson had mastered the skill of double talk — making a statement that could be interpreted one way or another or not at all. During the war the Radicals had formed the Joint Committee on the Conduct of the War, and Johnson had once been a member. The committee acted in an oversight capacity to investigate the management of the war. Under the leadership of the Radicals it became a coalition to bring pressure on Lincoln to remove Democratic generals, such as George B. McClellan, or cabinet members, such as William Seward and Montgomery Blair. Led by Benjamin Wade, Zachariah Chandler, and George Julian, the committee created an annoyance but seldom got their way with Lincoln. On Sunday, April 16, they called by appointment on President Johnson. Once again, Wade had cabinet removals in mind and intended to ask Johnson to replace Seward, Welles, and Dennison with Butler as secretary of state, Henry G. Stebbins as secretary of the navy, and Congressman John Covode of Pennsylvania as postmaster general.[1]

Wade acted as spokesman for the committee and opened the discussion by saying, "Johnson, we have faith in you. By the Gods, there will be no trouble now in running the government." Johnson made no commitments, but his reply gave the Radicals unintended encouragement when he said, "I hold that robbery is a crime; rape is a crime; murder is a crime; *treason* is a crime and must be punished. The law provides for it; the courts are open. Treason must be made infamous, and traitors must be impoverished." Johnson's statement might have applied to John Wilkes Booth and his gang of assassins, or perhaps to Jefferson Davis and his government of rebels, but not to a policy for restoring the south. The Radicals, however, departed somewhat cheered by Johnson's remarks.

After giving the president's comments more thought, they returned the following day to clarify some points. Johnson soothed the committee's concerns by convincing at least one member, George Julian, who wrote, "although I had some misgivings, the general feeling was one of unbounded confidence in his sincerity and firmness, and that he would act upon the advice of General Butler by inaugurating a policy of his own, instead of administering on the political estate of his predecessor."[2]

Why Johnson would agree to follow the advice of Ben Butler was a question the Radicals failed to ask themselves.

Lincoln had removed Butler from the military administration of Louisiana for corrupt practices, and General Grant had demanded his removal from the Army of the James for incapacity as a military commander. Despite his poor record during the war, Butler remained a popular and powerful politician from Massachusetts with a shrewd legalistic mind — a fact well known to Johnson when he made it clear to Wade's committee that no changes would be made in his cabinet.[3]

On the matter of punishing the leading rebels, Wade suggested forcing them into exile or hanging ten or twelve of the worst offenders to set an example. Johnson thought it would be difficult to select so small a number. Wade misinterpreted Johnson's reply and, fearing that the president might overreact, warned that executing too many Confederates might go against the public. But exactly what Johnson meant during his meeting with the committee still remained obscure. Referring to John Wilkes Booth in a speech, Johnson said, "Is he alone guilty? The American people must be taught — if they do not already feel — that treason is a crime and must be punished; that the Government will not always bear with its enemies; that it is strong not only to protect but to punish." Was this an indictment of the south or of Booth? The message could be read either way, and at this stage of Johnson's administration, he may have wanted it that way. Wade departed thinking that Johnson would take no action inconsistent with the wishes of Congress.[4]

With Johnson, however, the Radicals took few chances and wasted little time. They became well organized and equally determined. Twice they had been successful in thwarting Lincoln's restoration plans for Louisiana and Tennessee. They did not stop to ask Johnson what he thought of their actions. So they plunged ahead, convinced that Johnson would happily join their conspiracy and persecute his own people. Had they studied Johnson's speech more thoroughly, a more insightful person might have asked the president to clarify what he meant when he said, "When the question of exercising mercy comes before me it will be considered calmly, judicially, remembering that I am the Executive of the nation." On the subject of amnesty and pardons, was Johnson nominating himself as judge to the exclusion of Congress? The Radicals also began to wonder where private conversations between the president and conservative Democrats might be leading.[5]

After the second meeting with Johnson ended, Wade recruited Stanton, who accepted the assignment of meeting privately at the war department with Sumner and his friends from the Senate. Welles happened to be in Stanton's office when Sumner's coterie arrived. He soon surmised that nobody wanted him there, but he stayed long enough to ascertain the purpose of the meeting. Sumner wanted Stanton's support for the Radical platform and asked him to encourage Johnson to accelerate plans for negro suffrage. Welles retired from the meeting before hearing Stanton agree. With Lincoln out of the picture, the secretary of war faithlessly yielded to the schemes of those who had opposed his former chief.[6]

The persistency of the Radicals operated at all levels of government and created grave concerns among the loyal men of the south. In late April a deputation called on Johnson to ask how he intended to administer his trust. He replied, "Mercy and clemency have been pretty large ingredients in my composition, having been the Executive of a state, and thereby placed in a position in which it was necessary to exercise clemency and mercy." Had Ben Wade's committee been a party to this conversation, they might have paused to reflect on the president's previous remarks.[7]

Johnson hesitated to make a clear public policy statement until the national hatred evoked by Lincoln's murder subsided. "This man we have seen revered and loved," Johnson declared, "one who if he erred at all erred ever on the side of clemency and mercy — that man we have seen Treason strike." For that, the traitors should pay with their lives. But, he asked, "What should be done with him or them who have raised impious hands to take away the life of a nation composed of thirty millions of people? What should be the reply to that question?"[8]

To "that question" the Radicals had an answer — make them pay for treason, disenfranchise them, impoverish them, divide their land among the blacks! But the country, and especially the south, waited for clear answers from Johnson. For Jefferson Davis and the political leaders of the Confederacy, Johnson understood why the public expected some form of stern justice — but what about the people? For them Johnson made a case for "amnesty, conciliation, clemency and mercy to the thousands of our countrymen whom you and I know have been deceived or driven into this infernal rebellion.... I intend to ... bring back peace to our distracted country."[9]

Johnson's dissimilarities with the Radicals were as distinctly different as those drawn between two distinguished brothers, Senator John Sherman of Ohio, a Radical, and Major General William T. Sherman, whose army had marched across Georgia and South Carolina and on April 17, 1865, forced the surrender of General Joseph E. Johnston's Confederate army in North Carolina. "There should now be literally no terms granted," the senator declared. "We should not only brand the leading rebels with infamy, but the whole rebellion should wear the badge of the penitentiary, so that for this generation at least no man who has taken part in it would dare to justify or palliate it." The general replied, "The mass of the people south will never trouble us again. They have suffered terrifically, and I now feel disposed to befriend them, — of course not the leaders and lawyers, but the armies who have fought and manifested their sincerity, though misled." The general realized that his brother had been insulated from the war by the walls of the Senate, and a few days later he restated his position, writing, "The South is broken and ruined and appeals to our pity. To ride the people down with persecutions and military exactions would be like slashing away at the crew of a sinking ship. I will fight as long as the enemy shows fight, but when he gives up and asks for quarter I cannot go further. This state of things appeals to our better nature."[10]

With the possible exception of the president, General Sherman understood the pain and anguish of the beaten Confederate soldier better than anyone else in Washington. When General Johnston surrendered on April 17, Sherman granted the defeated army terms that included a number of political concessions, such as the recognition of existing Confederate state governments, guarantees of property rights, and universal amnesty. Nothing in the document supported emancipation of slaves or their rights as freedmen.

Johnson called a special cabinet meeting to discuss the matter and revoked the agreement. He dispatched Grant to North Carolina to meet with Sherman and Johnston, restructure the agreement, and delete the political terms. Stanton published his disapproval of Sherman's action in the newspapers and antagonized the general to the point where the latter would not speak to the secretary. Johnson, however, won a few points with the Radicals by promptly shelving Sherman's original armistice agreement and a few days later salved the general's wound by expressing his personal good will.[11]

General Sherman could not comprehend as a soldier what his brother as a politician saw clearly. The fighting Sherman witnessed the devastation of war Confederate politicians had inflicted on their countrymen. Senator Sherman and the Radicals envisioned the huge block of Republican votes to be derived from black suffrage. Before the war, the secession states cast 923,000 white ballots. With the addition of 672,000 black votes, Republicans envisioned endless control of the government. The Radicals knew if left to the whims of the individual southern states, years might pass before blacks would be given the right to vote. But what if the government forced them to do it now? Would the north really care if the same legislation did not apply to northern blacks? Only six states of the north enfranchised blacks, and for those that had, many demanded conditions of property ownership — a requirement that did not apply to whites. When General Sherman heard of the scheme he warned Chase that giving "all loyal negroes the same polit-

ical status as white voters will revive the war."[12]

Welles watched as Radicals intensified their pressure on the president. He agreed with General Sherman's assessment of sentiment in the south. But on May 9, he still remained uncertain of the president's intentions when he wrote:

> There is fanaticism on the subject with some who persuade themselves that the cause of liberty and the Union is with the negro, and not the white man.... Sumner is riding this one idea at top speed. There are others less sincere pressing the question for party purposes.... No one can claim that the blacks, in the slave states especially, can exercise the elective franchise intelligently.... Is it politic and wise or right even, when trying to restore peace and reconcile differences to make so radical a change — provided we have authority which I deny — to elevate the ignorant negro who has been enslaved mentally as well as physically, to the discharge of the highest duties of citizenship, especially when our free states will not permit the few negroes to vote?
>
> It was never intended by the founders of the Union that the Federal government should prescribe suffrage to the states. We shall get rid of slavery by constitutional means. While [the president] can exclude traitors [from the right of holding office or of voting], can he legitimately confer on the blacks ... the right to vote? I do not see how this can be done by him or by Congress.
>
> Stanton has changed his position, has been converted, and is now for negro suffrage. These were not his views a short time since. But aspiring politicians will as the current now sets generally take that road.[13]

On May 22, 1865, one might wonder about Johnson's thoughts as he watched

65,000 of Sherman's hardy veterans march by the reviewing stand in front of the White House. With him stood Grant, the cabinet, and scores of other dignitaries. People from around the country crowded the streets, admiring the battle-scarred volunteers as they made their final march. But for those of the impoverished south, Sherman's punishing wreckage and desolation of Georgia and the Carolinas created a vast despondency among the people. "War is Hell!" Sherman once said. Now it was over. But was it? Stevens, Sumner, Wade, and the Radicals contemplated a different kind of invasion, one with politicians carrying carpetbags into captured "territories" to be filled with southern wealth. Lincoln had stubbornly resisted the threat, but could Johnson? Time had come for him to speak out.[14]

Pressed by southerners requesting pardons, petty politicians seeking patronage, Union soldiers attempting to escape punishment for desertion, and a constant parade of curiosity seekers who wished to shake his hand, kept Johnson busy day and night. A *New York Herald* correspondent wrote, "if the pressure of the last few weeks is kept up it is doubtful whether he will be able to stand it." Welles agreed, worrying to his diary that "if some means are not devised of protecting him from personal interviews with ... busybodies of both sexes, they will make an end of him." During a summer heat wave Johnson grew pale and languid, and Welles feared the president would be smitten by a stroke.[15]

On May 29 Johnson acted on the first of many problems. He issued a Reconstruction Proclamation that adopted the mild course advocated by his predecessor. For forty-four days he had weighed the consequences, knowing the opposition would rise up in a fury to obstruct his course. His was an act of courage and perhaps a little foolish — a step that could bring him great grief. Having neither the popularity of Lincoln nor the public's full confidence, Johnson relied solely on himself and his executive powers. Through his own rightful acts he hoped to garner the support of others. After referring to two of Lincoln's earlier proclamations, Johnson showed his colors:

> To the end ... that the authority of the Government of the United States may be restored and that peace, order, and freedom may be established, I, Andrew Johnson ... do proclaim and declare that I hereby grant to all persons who have, directly or indirectly, participated in the existing rebellion, except as hereinafter excepted, amnesty and pardon, with restoration of all rights of property, except as to slaves and except in cases where legal proceedings under the laws of the United States providing for the confiscation of property of persons engaged in the rebellion have been instituted; but upon the condition, nevertheless, that every such person shall take and subscribe the ... oath and thenceforward keep and maintain such oath inviolate.[16]

Johnson listed fourteen exceptions to grants of pardon and amnesty. However, those exclusions provided that "special application may be made to the president for pardon by any person belonging to the excepted classes, and such clemency will be liberally extended as may be consistent with the facts of the case and the peace and dignity of the United States." He understood his constitutional power to grant "reprieves and pardons," and he intended to use that power to defy acts passed by Radicals with which he disagreed. Lincoln had done so when necessary, but with war powers. Johnson intended to do so, but without war powers. Much of the language in Johnson's proclamation paraphrased Lincoln's December 8, 1863, proclamation. Nothing Johnson wrote was any longer nebulous.[17]

Because Seward had recently returned to the duties of his office, Radicals who believed that Johnson had reversed his policy blamed the secretary for masterminding the proclamation. Seward denied all claims of authorship and rightly so. Johnson's opinions on constitutional questions were well understood long before his election as vice president. He welcomed the return of Seward, who could be relied upon for good advice, and unlike some members of the cabinet, had no hidden agenda.[18]

On May 29 Johnson issued a second proclamation, this one concerning the restoration of North Carolina, but the president had no intention of stopping there. He wanted to pave the way for reestablishing a republican form of government "whereby justice may be established, domestic tranquillity insured and loyal citizens protected in all their rights of life, liberty and property." To get the process started, he appointed William W. Holden provisional governor of the state. With few exceptions, Johnson followed the same formula promulgated by Lincoln for reinstituting the state governments of Louisiana and Tennessee. To choose delegates to the state convention, a qualified voter must take the oath of amnesty and be qualified "as prescribed by the Constitution, and laws of the state of North Carolina in force immediately before the 20th day of May,

A.D. 1861, the date of the so-called ordinance of secession."[19]

What nettled the Radicals most came next. "The said convention when convened, or the legislature that may be thereafter assembled will prescribe the qualification of electors and the eligibility of persons to hold office under the constitution and laws of the state — a power the people of the several states composing the Federal union have rightfully exercised from the origin of the government to the present time." The message contained no edict demanding that blacks be enfranchised. It clearly gave that authority to the state, not the United States Congress. On that issue, Johnson adhered to the Constitution and rearticulated the plan proposed by Lincoln. To put force behind his words, he directed the army to assist the provisional government "in carrying into effect this proclamation" and "to abstain from in any way hindering, impeding or discouraging the loyal people from the organization of a state government as herein authorized." Every word of the proclamation recognized North Carolina as a state. Johnson meant the proclamation to be a starting point for the south. When Sumner read the details, he could not believe that Johnson excluded blacks from the polls. Nor could Sumner admit that he had allowed his own hopes to deceive him as to Johnson's policy.[20]

On May 23, 1865, Mary Lincoln departed from Washington, and two weeks later Eliza, though confined to a wheelchair, arrived from Tennessee to join her husband in the White House. With her came Martha, the oldest daughter, who took over the social chores for her father. Her husband, David T. Patterson, had just been elected a senator from

Tennessee. Because Congress was not in session, Johnson used the time to press forward his program. He remembered a statement Lincoln made on the day before his death. "I think it is providential that this great rebellion is crushed out just as Congress has adjourned and there are none of the disturbing elements of that body to embarrass us. If we are wise and discreet we shall reanimate the states and get their governments in successful operation, with order prevailing and the Union reestablished before Congress comes together in December." Johnson lost but six weeks settling into his new responsibilities before casting lot with his mentor.[21]

The clock began to run. For Johnson there could be no turning back. Aware that Sumner, Stevens, Wade, and their followers had once discussed the impeachment of Lincoln, could Johnson expect much less? Chief Justice Chase believed that reconstruction should be initiated only in Louisiana and Florida because both states had abolished slavery and seemed to be making progress toward black enfranchisement. Moreover, the Radicals had mustered strength, capitalizing on public hysteria after Lincoln's assassination. Stanton's methods in the pursuit and capture of Booth's confederates gave the tragedy the appearance of a southern conspiracy. Only through alacrity could Johnson hope to thwart the dogmatic demands of the Radicals.[22]

He acted with speed. On June 13 he issued a proclamation granting Mississippi the same terms as North Carolina and appointed William L. Sharkey its provisional governor. In another document issued the same day he declared "the insurrection, so far as it relates to and within the State of Tennessee as reorganized and constituted under their recently adopted constitution ... is suppressed." Four days later two more proclamations emanated from the White House announcing the same terms for Georgia and Texas. Another proclamation, dated June 21, granted the same privileges to Alabama, followed nine days later by South Carolina, and on July 14, Florida. Virginia he handled differently. Because a state government already existed in western Virginia, Johnson expanded the responsibilities of Governor Francis H. Pierpont and instructed him to extend the "administration of the State Government throughout the geographical lines" of greater Virginia. Johnson also recognized Lincoln's reconstructed governments of Louisiana and Arkansas.[23]

By mid-summer Johnson completed the first stage of what he envisioned as Lincoln's reconstruction program, and the wheels of progress began to spin as the Radicals indignantly watched. Angered by betrayal, Sumner attributed Johnson's sudden turnabout to political pressure, blaming men like Seward for plying the president's mind with apostasy. Still holding to a frail hope, Sumner wrote Chase, "He is our President, and we must keep him ours unless he makes it impossible to go with him." But he encouraged Wade and other Radical colleagues to make speeches that would mobilize public opinion against Johnson's proclamations. In September Sumner presided over the Massachusetts Republican Convention and mustered all his oratorical skills in an attack on the president's program by denouncing Johnson's claim that reconstruction was a function of the executive branch of government. Rather, argued Sumner, Congress held "plenary powers over the whole subject."[24]

Encouraged by Johnson to act quickly, the provisional governors of the southern states went to work organizing their delegations. Mississippi held its convention on August 14, Alabama followed on September 12, South Carolina on September 13, North Carolina on October 2, and Georgia and Florida on October 24. Texas missed the mark and did not meet until March 1866. By November 8 every state but South Carolina and Mississippi had repudiated debts incurred in the furtherance of the rebellion. By the end of 1865 every state but Mississippi and Texas had ratified the Thirteenth Amendment to the Constitution and abolished slavery.[25]

With the work of reconstruction vigorously underway, leaders and citizens of the south — upwards of fourteen thousand of them — came forward seeking the personal pardon of the president. Lincoln's conception of restoration occurred so swiftly that Johnson, on October 15, declared, "We are making very rapid progress — so rapid I sometimes cannot realize it. It appears like a dream!"[26]

After all the doubts raised by his regrettable inaugural address, Johnson found his image restored. The *New York Herald* called him "the proper man for the crisis," but the press also warned that "we may expect from the Republican Radicals of the Sumner school and of the Chief Justice Chase school, too, as well as from Wendell Phillips and his school a lively movement and a stirring agitation of negro suffrage, henceforward if necessary to the next Presidential election. We are content with the reconstruction policy proclaimed by President Johnson. It is a practical program ... [and] it will be supported by the country."[27]

The entire cabinet, including Stanton, endorsed the proclamations. Stanton's support, however, was curiously disingenuous. In the privacy of his office he quietly divided the south into eighteen military departments and assigned to them a multitude of generals. When postmaster general Dennison asked Stanton a direct question on the subject, the latter attempted to shift the blame to Grant. Welles noted that Stanton replied with "a sneer and insolence in a manner more offensive even than the words." Dennison confided to Welles that he had known Stanton for twenty-five years and always considered him a "charlatan" who cleverly manipulated people to create differences between them.[28]

Hearing that certain Radical leaders brooded at home during the recess, McCulloch on August 22 wrote Sumner, "The policy which is now being tried is, I believe, approved by a large majority of the Union men at the North." State conventions held during the summer also endorsed Johnson's program. This unexpected and unwanted support did not make the Radicals happy. The only condemnation of Johnson's actions came from Pennsylvania and Massachusetts, where Thad Stevens and Charles Sumner pulled the strings. Welles noted with no surprise that the Pennsylvania state convention passed a resolution "endorsing Mr. Stanton by name but no other member of the Cabinet."[29]

Welles also observed Sumner's machinations, writing on August 19 that "extensive operations are on foot for an organization hostile to the Administration.... It is the old radical anti-Lincoln movement of Wade and Winter Davis with recruits. Sumner bewails the unanimity of the Cabinet: says there is unexpected unanimity in New England against the policy of the Administration; thinks I ought to resign; says Wade and Fessenden are intending to make vigorous opposition against it." Others watching the activities of the state conventions must also have noticed that "There is an apparent determination among those who are ingrained Abolitionists to compel the government to impose conditions on the Rebel states that are wholly unwarranted."[30]

The statement applied to Wendell Phillips, one of Sumner's Massachusetts henchmen. Four days after Johnson's May 29 proclamation, the *New York Herald* declared, "Wendell Phillips is a man whose mission is to oppose everything. He first opposed slavery, then the Union, then the rebellion, and now he opposes President Johnson. Among other things he occasionally opposes himself.... He [states] that President Johnson's plan for reconstruction was a practical fraud upon the North. He denounced the President as a robber and a 'Jeff Davis' sycophant." As erratic as Phillips appeared to the editor of the *Herald*, the Radicals used him as front man for their divisive tactics. In October at the Boston Music Hall, Phillips accelerated his attack, charging that, "The President has put a rebel in every spot, he has put a bayonet in front of every Southern claim, he has spiked every Northern cannon.... Andy Johnson may not be a traitor but he is an enemy.... You cannot trust Andy Johnson."[31]

A tirade here and there against Johnson did little to change the public's favorable opinion. A few members of Sumner's coalition began to defect. "If something is not done," Stevens warned Sumner, "the President will be crowned king before Congress meets." In August, Stevens wrote again, "The danger is that so much success will reconcile the people to almost everything." Ben Wade added his concerns, writing Sumner on July 29 that Johnson was handing the Union and the Republican party over to the very same "rebels we have so lately conquered in the field and their copperhead allies in the North.... To me all appears gloomy."[32]

During the summer of 1865, with urging from the Radicals, Chase sallied forth on a tour through the south. Sumner confided to an English friend, "The chief justice started yesterday on a visit ... and will on his way touch the necessary strings, so far as he can. I anticipate much from this journey." With him traveled Whitelaw Reid, a clever young journalist to chronicle Chase's observations. Every city, town, and plantation wore the scars of war and destitution, but Chase looked beyond the shattered lives of the people. He had come to investigate the status of freedmen and expressed surprise when he learned that ex-slaves refused to work. He found them lolling in the streets and living idly in squalor, but he did not ask why. Everywhere he went the local gentry greeted him with courtesy, but this did not impress him any more than the bouquets of fragrant flowers or the proffered hospitality. Southerners were reconciled but not bitter, but they quietly understood the purpose of Chase's visit and felt threatened by black suffrage.[33]

Union League Clubs of the north had already paved the way for Chase's journey into the "captured territories." Black delegations from local clubs sought Chase at every stop and urged him to give them a voice in government. Chase heard what he wanted wherever he went. Though surprised that freedmen refused to take work, he failed to encourage them to change their ways. Instead he held mass meetings, and, behaving much like a presidential candidate stumping for votes, said, "If all the people feel as I do, you will not have to wait long for equal rights at the ballot box; no longer than it would take to pass the necessary law." To black rallies Chase appeared as Moses promising to deliver his people from bondage, and the fealty worked on the chief justice as a tonic spiked with hallucinates.[34]

Meanwhile, southerners fought for the preservation of a civilization. If blacks would not work, plantations could not produce. At night ex-slaves warded off idleness by prowling the highways and byways pillaging farms. Fed and clothed by federal funds, freedmen clung to the illusion planted in their minds by Radical demagogues that their economic status would be reversed by the redistribution of land. For this notion blacks had no farther to look than Stevens, who during a meeting at Lancaster laid out the plan for the seizure of every estate worth ten thousand dollars and containing at least two hundred acres. Stevens calculated that 394,000,000 acres would be subject to confiscation, dispossessing 70,000 southerners. By granting forty acres to every adult black, some 40,000,000 acres would be allocated. A residue of 354,000,000 acres could then be sold at ten dollars an acre and the proceeds divided to pay off the national debt and to compensate pensioners disabled by the war. A slice would also go to loyal men for losses caused by the war — such as Stevens himself, whose foundry had been burned by rebel invaders. "What loyal man," Stevens declared, "can object to that?" When someone questioned the wisdom of punishing innocent American women and children, Stevens coldheartedly replied, "That is the result of the necessary laws of war."[35]

But Chase dwelt on the political opportunities from garnering the black vote without troubling himself with the problems of economic restoration or the humanitarian needs of southern whites. He revealed his real mission when writing Sumner that Johnson had made a "great mistake in refusing to recognize the colored citizens as part of the people." He suggested that if the president continued on his course, it might become necessary for Congress to propose another amendment beyond the Thirteenth. Having received the very advise he wanted, Sumner urged Chase to return to Washington where he could help rally resistance to the president's policy. Sumner grumbled that Johnson was "dividing the party" and giving the nation over to the "peace" Democrats.[36]

If the Radicals felt "gloomy," they had good reason. Being in recess they could correspond with each other but not take legislative action. Many claimed the president had deceived them, though few were really surprised. They also resented Johnson's unexpected popularity, making their work doubly difficult. What amazed the Radical leaders was the rapidity with which Johnson restored the states of the south. But December was fast approaching and soon the schemers would be together again.

When a group of black soldiers called upon Johnson in October, he gave them friendly advice. He warned against the evils of idleness and reminded them that liberty did not mean lawlessness. He urged them to adopt a life of morality and impressed upon them the sanctity of marriage, the importance of controlling their passions, and encouraged them to develop their intellect while applying their muscle to the industrial needs of the country. The Radicals objected to

Johnson's advice, not because it was bad advice but because it undermined their program to make the blacks obligated to Congress.[37]

Being apart from Washington had not rendered the Radicals idle. Johnson had enjoyed a good run, and by doing so, placed the Radicals in a position of jeopardy. Of 50 senators from the 25 non-seceding states, 39 were classed as Republicans and 11 as Democrats. Of 184 members of the House, 141 were classed as Republicans and 43 as Democrats, giving the Republicans more than a 75 percent margin in both houses. Should the 22 senators and 58 representatives from the eleven reconstructed states be admitted, the nominal majority of the Republicans in the Senate would be reduced from 28 to 6, and the nominal majority of the House from 98 to 40, assuming that all southerners would vote with Democrats. Faced with the threat of legislators from the south filling the long-vacant seats of Congress and disrupting their comfortable majority, the Radicals conceived a plan, and President Johnson would not like it.[38]

6

The Radicals Organize

On December 1, 1865, members of Congress began filing into Washington. For four years the Republicans had enjoyed a modicum of serenity without interference from legislators of the south. The only obstacle had been President Lincoln. Now as the Radicals looked about, they observed a stream of familiar faces not seen in Congress since early 1861. It appalled and horrified them. Here were the "damned rebels," back again in force. But why should anyone be surprised? Would not electors want experienced politicians to represent their interests?

Of the two senators from Georgia, Alexander H. Stephens had been the vice president of the Confederacy and Herschel V. Johnson a member of the Confederate senate. With them came William A. Graham of North Carolina, another ex-Confederate senator; Benjamin F. Perry, a judge from South Carolina; and John L. Manning, a volunteer aid to General Beauregard.

The House of Representatives also received its share of well known figures. From Alabama came Cullen A. Battle, an ex-Confederate general, and Thomas J. Foster, a member of the Confederate house. Georgia sent Philip Cook and William T. Wofford, both Confederate generals. Mississippi elected two Confederate colonels, Arthur E. Reynolds and R. A. Pinson, along with a Confed-

erate congressman, James T. Harrison. The Carolinas and other states of the south followed suit. The Radicals found themselves staring into the faces of their former enemies, and they did not like it.[1]

With Congress convening, the public at large wondered what the Radicals would do with the president's recently consummated work of reconstruction. The new additions from the south all enjoyed presidential pardons. They came in good faith with their credentials of election, but would they be seated? Ben Wade and Charles Sumner ran the Senate, and though Schuyler Colfax held the speaker's seat, Thad Stevens ruled the House. With his customary smile, Colfax delivered a prepared speech which was dutifully printed by the press and labeled by the *National Intelligencer* as being in bad taste. Welles read it and wrote, "It is the offspring of an intrigue, and one that is pretty extensive. The whole proceeding was premeditated." Had Welles been able to read Sumner's recent correspondence to Ben Wade and Carl Schurz, he would have found ample evidence to support his opinion.[2]

On December 3, the day before Congress convened, members of both chambers caucused to consider the readmission of elected representatives from states recently in rebellion. The caucus appointed Stevens to present the study.

In this arrangement, Welles noted, "there was something bad." Referring to Stevens's attitude toward the south, Samuel S. Cox thought the "intensity of his hatred was almost next to infernal," and when he handed down his decrees, woe to the colleague who rejected them.[3]

The "bad" manifested itself when Congress convened on the following day. Edward McPherson, clerk of the House of Representatives, obliged Stevens and called the role, omitting the names of members from the south. The law required McPherson to read the entire role, but Stevens would not allow it. Horace Maynard of Tennessee protested, and William E. Niblack of Indiana offered a resolution asking that the south's elected representatives be entitled to the privileges of the floor. But Stevens orchestrated a motion to adjourn and stopped further discussion on the issue. Before adjourning, however, the House reelected Colfax as speaker.[4]

During the debate on the floor, James Brooks of New York argued against seating Maynard, adding, "If Tennessee is not in the Union, the President of the United States must be a foreigner and a usurper." In the 39th Congress, Brooks's choice of words — "foreigner" and "usurper" — would echo often and with growing crescendo in both chambers.[5]

Knowing that Stevens carried a resolution in his pocket that had been drafted by the caucus, Brooks asked him to present it. The scenario about to be played out in the House had all the trimmings of a carefully organized conspiracy. Under normal circumstances, Congress would wait to hear the president's annual message before drafting new legislation. But for the first session of the 39th Congress, Stevens devised a different

plan. Congress would announce its position on the president's recent proclamations before permitting Johnson to explain them. Stevens extracted the document from his pocket and introduced it. As one biographer aptly stated, "It was a declaration of war against Andrew Johnson." The resolution provided for a joint committee of fifteen on reconstruction consisting of nine representatives and six senators. They were to inquire into the condition of the southern states and "report whether they or any of them are entitled to be represented in either House of Congress." Until the committee made its report, no person would be received "in either House from any of the so-called Confederate States." Stevens knew he had the votes and whipped the resolution through the lower chamber. Who best to chair the House committee but Stevens himself, and he salted it with some of his most radical cronies, John A. Bingham of Ohio, George Boutwell of Massachusetts, and Justin S. Morrill of Vermont.[6]

The Senate forged ahead with its own manifesto. Sumner made certain that his system of reconstruction repudiated all the constructive work begun by Johnson. His resolutions redefined the duties of Congress, subverted the policies of Lincoln and Johnson, and placed limitations on the power of the executive. Sumner demanded "the complete suppression of all oligarchical pretensions," and though many of the state conventions of the north had denied negro suffrage as "heavy and premature," Sumner demanded the immediate enfranchisement of blacks. He also demanded that no secession state be permitted to resume its relations with the government until fully complying with the conditions specified in his resolution.

Charles Sumner, senator from Massachusetts and a leading Radical in the Republican Party. (Massachusetts Commandery Military Order of the Loyal Legion and the U.S. Army Military History Institute.)

Sumner and Stevens had communicated often during the summer and reached agreement months ago. Stevens summed up the arrangement succinctly, writing, "Get the rebel states into territorial condition, and it can be easily dealt with. That I think should be our great aim. Then Congress can manage it."[7]

On December 2, two days before the 39th Congress convened, Sumner went to the White House to encourage the president to change his course. He did not expect to succeed and anticipated, even welcomed, a rupture between the president and the Republican party. He preferred that Johnson initiate the break in relations over the issue of reconstruction, but the president anticipated the clash and intended to provoke Sumner into forcing the split. Each man warily circled the issue, waiting for the other to make a fatal slip. Both were equally culpable, Sumner for allowing Johnson to proceed with reconstruction without calling a special session of Congress, and Johnson for advocating black suffrage and then permitting every southern state to reorganize on the basis of white supremacy. After more than two hours of verbal fencing, both men found their differences irreconcilable. Sumner implied that Congress would war against the president, and on the opening day of the session, he reported his conversation to the Senate. He did not wait to hear what Johnson had to say in his annual message. He took the floor and introduced a flurry of resolutions, bills, and constitutional amendments outlining a program of reconstruction consistent with his own philosophy and contrary to the president's. There is no evidence that the joint committee seriously considered adopting any of Sumner's proposals.[8]

On December 5 Andrew Johnson sent his first annual message as president of the United States to Congress. The optimistic, statesmanlike language pointed to the future of the united country. "To express gratitude to God in the name of the people for preservation of the United States," Johnson declared, "is my first duty in addressing you." With sadness he remembered the death of Lincoln, and in his own way, he reached out to Congress:

> His [Lincoln's] removal cast upon me a heavier weight of cares than ever devolved upon any one of his predecessors. To fulfill my trust I need the support and confidence of all who are associated with me in the various departments of Government and the support and confidence of the people. There is but one way in which I can hope to gain their necessary aid. It is to state with frankness the principles which guide my conduct, and their application to the present state of affairs, well aware that the efficiency of my labors will in a great measure depend on your and their undivided approbation.[9]

Johnson talked about the Constitution, how it guaranteed the perpetuity of the states, of their mutual relation to each other, and why, in the nation's political system, they were indissoluble. "The whole cannot exist without the parts, nor the parts without the whole. So long as the Constitution of the United States endures, the States will endure.... It has been my steadfast object to derive a healing policy from the fundamental and unchanging principles of the Constitution." He then gave his reasons for treating the south with gentleness and forgiveness, reasons that territorialists like Sumner and Stevens did not want to hear. "Besides," Johnson continued, "the policy of military rule over a conquered territory would have implied that the states whose inhabitants may have taken part in the rebellion had by the act of those inhabitants ceased to exist. But the true theory is that all pretended acts of secession were from the beginning null and void."[10]

During the congressional recess, Johnson had reestablished customhouses, post offices, federal courts, and reopened southern ports. He now asked, "And is it not happy for us all that the restoration of each one of these functions of the General Government brings with it a blessing to the States over which they are extended?" Johnson anticipated repercussions from the Radicals and added, "I know very well that this policy is attended with some risk; that for its success it requires at least the acquiescence of the States which it concerns.... But it is a risk that must be taken. In the choice of difficulties it is the smallest risk: and to diminish and if possible to remove all danger, I have felt it incumbent upon me to assert one other power of the General Government — the power of pardon."

Johnson invited the nation to abolish slavery by ratifying the Thirteenth Amendment. "The adoption of this amendment reunites us beyond all power of disruption; it heals the wound that is imperfectly closed; it removes slavery ... which has so long perplexed and divided the country; it makes of us once more a united people, renewed and strengthened, bound more than ever to mutual affection and support. The amendment to the Constitution being adopted, it would remain for the States whose powers have been so long in abeyance to resume their places in the two branches of the National Legislature, and thereby complete the work of restoration. Here it is for you, fellow-citizens of the Senate, and for you, fellow-citizens of the House of Representatives, to judge, each of you for yourselves, of the elections, returns, and qualifications of your own members." As Congress listened to a reading of Johnson's message, Georgia's legislature ratified the Thirteenth Amendment. Before the year ended, all the southern states had done so but Texas and Mississippi.[11]

The president then discussed black suffrage. "On the propriety of attempting to make the freedmen electors by proclamation of the executive," Johnson declared, "I took for my counsel the Constitution itself.... When, at the first movement towards independence, the Congress of the United States instructed the several States to institute governments of their own, they left each state to decide for itself the conditions for the enjoyment of the elective franchise."

Johnson knew that while the Radicals wanted the black vote imposed upon the south, they did not want it extended to the north. Using the Radicals' own double standard, he based his argument on a constitutional premise, writing, "a concession of the elective franchise to the freedmen by act of the President of the United States, must have been extended to all colored men wherever found, and so must have established a change of suffrage in the Northern, Middle, and Western States, not less than in the Southern and Southwestern. Such an act would have created a new class of voters, and would have been an assumption of power by the President which nothing in the Constitution or laws of the United States would have warranted. On the other hand, every danger of conflict is avoided when the settlement of the question is referred to the several States."[12]

Johnson understood that freedmen must be given a fair opportunity to become respected citizens of their state, writing:

> But while I have no doubt that now, after the close of the war, it is not competent for the General Government to extend the elective franchise in the several States, it is equally clear that good faith requires the security of the freedmen in their liberty and personal property, their right to labor, and their right to claim the just return of their labor. I cannot too strongly urge a dispassionate treatment of this subject, which should be carefully kept aloof from all party strife. We must equally avoid hasty assumptions of any natural impossibility for the two races to live side by side in a state of mutual benefit and good will. The experiment involves us in no inconsistency; let us, then, go on and make that experiment in good faith, and not be too easily disheartened.[13]

Because the Radicals passed their joint resolutions in an effort to obstruct the president's policies before giving him the customary courtesy of hearing his annual message, they mildly embarrassed themselves. The press heralded and endorsed the president's position, referring to it as a remarkable example of "wisdom" and "sublime statesmanship." If Stevens read the December 6 issue of the *New York Tribune*, he must have winced at the words of Horace Greeley who doubted "whether any former message has contained so much that will be generally and justly approved and so little that will or should provoke dissent."[14]

Because of the statesmanlike character of Johnson's message, his detractors claimed that he could not have written it. Johnson often engaged the help of Seward, but the message incorporated all of his own and his predecessor's fundamental beliefs. Having always been a constitutionalist, and far more knowledgeable on the subject than his legislative obstructionists, Johnson's message achieved the distinction of being a carefully crafted document differentiating between the powers of the executive and the legislative on the issues facing the nation. Seward often received credit for writing Lincoln's addresses, and though he read many of them beforehand, he did little more than suggest changes.

Welles, who came to know Lincoln, Johnson, and Seward intimately, wrote on December 5, "I think the message which went in this P.M. will prove an acceptable document. The views, sentiments and doctrines are the President's, not Seward's. He may have suggested verbal emendations, — nothing except what related to foreign affairs. But the President himself has vigorous common sense and on more than one occasion I have seen him correct Seward's dispatches." Even Welles, whose observing character seldom missed an important detail, failed to discover that the president's message had been prepared by George Bancroft, the noted American historian. Though the thoughts were Johnson's, Bancroft had worked with the president since summer to perfect the document.[15]

Johnson's remarkable document, heartily applauded by the public, baffled but did not deter the Radicals. If they could not make their case one way, they would contrive another.

Lincoln recognized the plight of the freedmen in his December 8, 1863, proclamation, their need of education, and "their present condition as a laboring, landless and homeless class." Knowing all states would have to make arrangements for dealing with the problem, he granted each of them great latitude in devising their own solutions. Then on March 3, 1865, he signed into law an act providing for the temporary relief of freedmen and refugees. Ex-slaves, unable to read and misinformed by those who could, believed that those without work would be granted forty acres and a mule by the federal government. They expected the endowment to occur between Christmas and New Year's Day, and that the land would be divided from their former masters' plantations. Under this misconception, the freedmen of the south refused work and idly wandered about, some sustaining themselves by theft while waiting for their allotment of land.[16]

States such as Mississippi, Louisiana, and South Carolina faced a troubling problem because the black population equaled or exceeded the whites. For many blacks, freedom meant idleness, so southern states needed to create new laws and pass them quickly. In Mississippi, freedmen engaged in labor became apprentices. Restructured civil laws gave many of the rights enjoyed by whites to blacks, but there were extra restrictions placed on trespass, carrying fire arms, assault, and other crimes. For rape of a white woman, blacks suffered death.

Mississippi's legislators tried to address the problems of the state, but Radicals found some of the practices objectionable. In the control of apprentices, the master could apply the same "moderate corporal chastisement as a [parent] ... is allowed to inflict on his or her child." Black children who were orphans or unsupported by their parents would be apprenticed by the court to some "suitable person" until the age of eighteen for women and twenty-one for men. In addition, blacks who would not work at the prescribed wage would be considered vagrants and subject to penalties. Also, freedmen could not hold office, perform jury duty, or vote, but some of those same restrictions still applied to six states of the north.[17]

Nevertheless, the Radicals labeled

the south's enactments as "black codes" and used the term to undermine Johnson's reconstruction plan. They deceptively declared that the south intended to reenslave the blacks. Their motives went beyond the altruistic impression they wished to convey of advocating black equality. Before the war, the stronghold of the Democrats had been the south. A quick assessment of the elected representatives waiting to occupy their seats in Congress verified that nothing had changed. During four years of war, the Republicans had carried the banner of patriotism, branding Democrats traitors or Copperheads. Now southern Democrats were back, claiming seats in both chambers.

The new threat from the south bedeviled Republican leaders because they envisioned their comfortable margin dwindling in both Houses. Equally worrisome to the Senate were the House resolutions demanding the appointment of a Joint Committee of Fifteen on Reconstruction. Four Republican senators bolted and voted against it, further depleting the Radical majority. Knowing that Johnson, though elected as a Republican, was a philosophical Democrat made the situation even worse. Assuming all new seats would be occupied by southern Democrats, Stevens, Wade, and Sumner quickly calculated that overriding a presidential veto could become difficult, especially if more Republicans defected. Instead, if they could disenfranchise the newly elected legislators from the south, give the vote to the blacks, and train them in Republican ways, the Radicals could control Congress for years to come. To implement the whole scheme, however, required new legislation — something so attractive that it would entice discouraged Republican office

seekers to pack their carpetbags and seek new political careers in a milder climate. There, as they raided the public wealth, they would be protected by Grant's army.[18]

Sumner struck the first blow, declaring that Johnson's "heart was with the ex-rebels ... that by the assassination of Abraham Lincoln the rebels had vaulted into the Presidential chair. Jefferson Davis was then in the casement of Fortress Monroe," the senator declared, "but Andrew Johnson was doing his work." Sumner had no basis for making the statement, and he knew it, but the Radicals realized that if Johnson's reputation could not be scandalized and besmirched, their program could go up in smoke.[19]

Sumner conceived another way to deprecate Johnson — make scurrilous statements about those members of the cabinet who would not align themselves with the Radical doctrine. He never liked Seward, and men such as McCulloch and Welles were too supportive of the president and hard to intimidate. Yet on December 8 he attempted to recruit Welles but received a polite rebuff. The latter recorded much of the conversation, writing that "Sumner's vanity and egotism are great. He assumes that the Administration is wholly wrong, and that he is beyond peradventure right; that Congress has plenary powers, the executive none, on reestablishing the Union. He denounced the policy of the President on the question of organizing the Rebel States as the greatest and most criminal error ever committed by any government."

Sumner also accused Welles, who came from Connecticut, of misrepresenting the good citizens of New England, but he did not stop there. The senator denounced McCulloch for being "imbued with the pernicious folly of Indiana" and chastised Welles and Seward for being "foully, fatally culpable in giving … countenance and support to the President and his policy." Welles probed Sumner, asking if any member of the cabinet opposed the president's policies. Sumner said Stanton. When Welles replied that he was unaware of it, the senator seemed surprised. Sumner's style of attacking those who opposed him makes it easier to understand why Preston Brooks once felt compelled to club the senator with a cane.[20]

Three days later Sumner tipped his hand. Knowing whatever he shared with Welles would be conveyed to Johnson, he sent through the mail a newspaper containing a memorial calling for the president's impeachment. Sumner marked certain passages and made notations in the margins which contained answers to some of the questions Welles had asked during the recent meeting. Though anonymously written, Welles could see Sumner's hand in the work. After discussing the incident with Johnson, Welles wrote, "I think they will not shake him." But here was the first flagrant disclosure — not at all subtle — of the Radicals' malevolent intentions toward the president.

Johnson dismissed the threat as being just another attempt on the part of the Radicals to intimidate him, but he asked Welles for a copy of the memorial and kept it. No president had ever been impeached. He must have pondered over what aspect of the Constitution had been violated that rose to the level of high crimes and misdemeanors? He had broken no laws, committed no crime, or usurped executive authority. Out of necessity he had exerted constitutional powers, but those acts could not be construed

as high crimes and misdemeanors by any court of the land. But Sumner, whatever his motive, put the president on notice, and Johnson became more watchful.[21]

To seriously consider ousting Johnson the Republicans needed to staff the Joint Committee on Reconstruction with senators who would faithfully pursue the Radical agenda. Sumner organized a cabal consisting of two moderate Republicans, William Pitt Fessenden of Maine and James W. Grimes of Iowa; three Radicals, Ira Harris of New York, Jacob M. Howard of Michigan, George H. Williams of Oregon; and one Democrat, Reverdy Johnson of Maryland. Sumner did not chair the committee. That honor went to Fessenden, who remarked that "Mr. Sumner was very anxious for the place, but, standing as he does before the country, and committed to the most ultra views, even his friends declined to support him, and almost to a man fixed upon me."[22]

Thad Stevens' contribution to the committee included himself, Elihu B. Washburne of Maine, Justin S. Morrill of Vermont, John A. Bingham of Ohio, Roscoe Conkling of New York, George S. Boutwell of Massachusetts, Henry T. Blow of Missouri, and two Democrats, Andrew J. Rogers of New Jersey and Henry Grider of Kentucky. After all members had been selected, Fessenden remarked optimistically, "I think I can see my way through, and if Sumner and Stevens and a few other such men do not embroil us with the President, matters can be satisfactorily arranged — satisfactorily, I mean, to the great bulk of Union men throughout the States."[23]

James G. Blaine of Pennsylvania, one of the few Republican senators who did not ally himself with the Radicals, observed that "The contest predestined

On December 16 Sumner again called upon Welles, probing in a determined way to learn whether the memorial on impeachment had altered Johnson's position on reconstruction. Welles described Sumner as "almost beside himself on the policy of the Administration which he denounces with great bitterness." The senator chafed at the president for taking action "without the consent and direction of Congress." Welles stopped him and replied, "There are two lines of policy before us. One is harsh, cold, distant, defiant; the other kind, conciliatory and inviting. Which will soonest make us a united people?" Sumner faltered and changed the subject, closing the conversation with a violent denunciation of Johnson's provisional governors and angrily stating that "the majority of Congress was determined to overthrow the President's policy." Welles replied that "conciliation, not persecution was our policy, and therein we totally disagree."[25]

Thaddeus Stevens, representative from Pennsylvania and a rabid Radical advocating Johnson's impeachment (Massachusetts Commandery Military Order of the Loyal Legion and the U.S. Army Military History Institute.)

and already manifest, between the President and Congress might, unless conducted with great wisdom, so seriously divide the party as to compass its ruin." Blaine foresaw that Stevens, by chairing the Committee of Fifteen on Reconstruction, had made himself an absolute dictator in the early years of the movement by giving himself a devastating power no federal legislator had ever wielded. It marked the end of restoration conceived by Lincoln and the beginning of reconstruction as defined by the Radicals.[24]

Sumner's attempts to justify the Radical doctrine met with another blow. On December 15 General Grant returned from an inspection of the south. He reported the people more loyal and better disposed to reconciliation than he expected and quite ready to become reunified with the Union. Carl Schurz had also made a tour of the south at the behest of Stanton. Schurz suggested that a committee be sent to the south to investigate troublesome conditions, which was exactly what Stanton wanted him to report. Sumner knew of Schurz's observations and asked Johnson for a copy of the report.

Attaching Grant's and Schurz's reports together, Johnson sent both to the Senate, along with a personal message from himself. He declared the rebellion "suppressed" and advised the Senate that "courts of the United States have been restored, post offices reestablished, and steps taken to put into effective operation the revenue laws of the country." He complimented the people of the south for "yielding obedience to the laws and Government of the United States with more willingness and promptitude than under the circumstances could reasonably have been anticipated." He reminded the Senate that most of the south had already ratified the Thirteenth Amendment abolishing slavery, and that state governments were effectively restoring the south by taking the "measures instituted by the Executive."[26]

Sumner experienced another bad day when Grant's report arrived with Schurz's. Grant enjoyed the confidence of the public. Barely anyone knew Schurz. So what could the Radicals do with the Schurz report while Johnson still held a copy of Grant's report? The answer was nothing, except among themselves. Furious at Johnson for outwitting them, they ignored Grant's report and among themselves decided that only the Schurz report deserved attention. Why? Because Schurz argued for the immediate enfranchisement of freedmen and recommended that no state should be readmitted to the Union until blacks were allowed to vote. He backed his argument by alleging that southern whites intended to reduce blacks to "some species of serfdom" by employing devious methods that did not violate their pledge.[27]

Sumner put Grant's report aside and determined to strike back at Johnson through the Schurz report, which he characterized as "a very important document." To support Schurz's allegations, which were eventually printed as an "Executive Document," Sumner encouraged his northern allies to solicit and collect any news clips or letters that supported the Radical position on reconstruction so he could have them read in the Senate. No method existed for monitoring whether the assortment of documents flowing into the Senate contained fact or fiction, but Sumner did not care. He liked in particular a letter claiming that blacks had "no rights" and were "killed and their bodies thrown into ponds or mud holes." The same writer went on to say, "They are mutilated by having their ears and noses cut off." Did such atrocities occur? Perhaps, but Johnson, in a meeting with Sumner, got the latter to admit that on occasion similar crimes also occurred in Massachusetts."[28]

While Sumner badgered the Senate with unvalidated leaflets, Stevens went to work on the House with his "territorial" imperatives. He denounced the south's new state governments as illegally adopted, insisting they must first "learn the principles of freedom and eat the fruit of foul rebellion. Under such governments," Stevens declared, "while electing members to the territorial legislatures, they will mingle with those to whom Congress shall extend the right of suffrage." Though all but three of the southern states had already ratified the Thirteenth Amendment, Stevens ignored good faith and demanded that no "rebel state" be consulted regarding constitutional amendments.[29]

On the same day that Stevens trumpeted his repudiations in the House and Sumner shared his gall with the Senate, Secretary of State Seward certified the Thirteenth Amendment abolishing slavery, writing: "Whereas the whole number of states in the United States is thirty-six, [the twenty-seven states enumerated] constitute three-fourths of the whole number of states in the United States," therefore the amendment is in force. Among the thirty-six states passing the amendment were eight of the south. So much for Stevens' claim that rebel states should not be consulted on constitutional amendments. On this matter, the Stevens cabal remained judiciously silent, but they still wanted their "territories" to ravage.[30]

The Radicals worried as they watched Democrats aligning themselves with Johnson. A growing number of Republicans also inclined toward the president's way of thinking, and Stevens sought ways to curb defections before they became unmanageable. As a stop-gap measure, John A. Bingham moved a resolution which in plain words threat-ened Johnson to comply with the bidding of Congress or act at his own peril. On January 8, though unaware of Bingham's resolution, Welles wrote, "The President and the Radical leaders are not yet in direct conflict, but I see not how it is to be avoided."[31]

Johnson underestimated the will of Thad Stevens — a man whose inability to compromise was both his strength and weakness. The trait made Stevens a leader. As one historian observed, Stevens "held no council, heeded no advice, hearkened to no warning, and with an iron will pushed forward as his instinct bade, defying, if need be, the opinion of his time, and turning it by sheer force to his purpose." And Welles, the consummate observer, awoke to "the dark revolutionary intrigues of Stevens."[32]

The conflict had begun, the lines were drawn, and the opportunity for compromise had vanished.

7

The Battle Begins

Having marshaled their forces in opposition to Johnson, the Radicals sought ways to mount their attack. What better place to start than with the Bureau for the Relief of Freedmen and Refugees, an organization created on March 3, 1865, to operate "for one year thereafter"? Stanton controlled the Freedmen's Bureau, having named Major General Oliver O. Howard as its commander. By May 1865, Howard had opened offices throughout the south. The legislation provided relief to freed slaves, but its welfare extended to thousands of white refugees equally in need of food and clothing.

The measure also created a huge bureaucracy of commissioners and agents who controlled it. Their role included the leasing of abandoned lands under the Homestead Act of 1862, which gave rise to the misconception on the part of many ex-slaves that such land would be provided to them with a mule and at no cost. This encouraged thousands of blacks to quit work, congregate in the cities, live off the Freedmen's Bureau, and wait for their land grant. Brigadier General Joseph S. Fullerton, assistant commissioner in Louisiana, said that the agents sent south came "to foster disunion rather than cure and heal," giving credence to the belief that many of the officers were corrupt, and the agents incompetent and "fanatical persons."[1]

Following his inspection tour of the south, Grant reported that the bureau's affairs had not been conducted "with good judgment or economy." There he observed open conflicts between army officers and agents of the bureau. He warned that blacks would not make contracts for work in 1866 because they expected to receive land divided from the property of their former masters, as told to them by the bureau's own agents. Grant's report suggested something needed to be done to correct the mess. Instead of addressing the issues recommended by Grant, the Radicals envisioned the Freedmen's Bureau as an agency through which they could expand their intrusion into southern affairs. So on January 9, 1866, Senator Lyman Trumbull of Illinois introduced a bill to enlarge the jurisdiction of the bureau.[2]

In the meantime, Fessenden formed a subcommittee of three to call upon Johnson and urge him to "defer all further executive action in regard to reconstruction until the joint committee had taken action on the subject." Johnson replied that "he desired to secure harmony of action between Congress and the Executive, and it was not his intention to do more than had been done for the present." With the two branches on better speaking terms, Fessenden reported the president's amiable response to the Senate.[3]

The new Freedmen's Bureau Bill, however, went well beyond the original intention of providing welfare. It divided the south into districts, districts into subdistricts, and provided for an abundance of assistant commissioners, agents, and clerks recruited from military and civilian positions. The bill also abolished laws enacted by the states, provided a new list of punishable offenses, and set fines and penalties, including imprisonment, for a variety of new violations. To complicate matters, it would not be courts but commissioners and agents of the bureau who would rule on violations and determine the penalties. The bill also interfered with a state's jurisdiction to govern freedmen and transferred that power to the bureau. One historian agreed the act was nothing more than an attempt by the Radicals "to set aside the state governments whose reconstruction Lincoln planned and Johnson carried out." Another historian wrote, "Thus in one stroke all the Southern laws were to be abrogated by Congress, not by the Supreme Court of the United States!"[4]

The bill created a storm of concern among friends of the administration and some members of the cabinet. On January 10 ex-postmaster Montgomery Blair stopped by Welles' office to warn that Stanton "is intriguing" and that a "cloud" exists between the secretary and the president. So untrustworthy had Stanton become that Welles replied, "It would be well if there was a wall between them."[5]

Two days later Sumner called at the navy department to entice Welles' support for the bill. The senator minced no words with the secretary, pontificating that the president was "the greatest enemy of the South that she ever had, worse than Jeff Davis, and the evil which he had inflicted upon the country was incalculable. All this was to be done over again and done right." Sumner kept referring to the "conquered people" of the south, eliciting a reply from Welles that "were this assumption true, and they a foreign conquered people, instead of our own countrymen, still they had their rights, were amenable to our laws and entitled to their protection; modern civilization would not permit of their enslavement."[6]

Sumner wanted the bill signed by the president, and in his demanding demeanor told Welles that "Congress ... was becoming of one mind, and while they would commence no war upon the President, he must change his course, abandon his policy." Sumner's statement was disingenuous because he and Stevens had already declared war upon Johnson. In a final dig at Welles, Sumner said, "The President, in his atrocious wrong, is sustained by three of his Cabinet. Seward is as thick-and-thin a supporter of the whole monstrous error as you or McCulloch." To Sumner's suggestion that three members of the cabinet sided with the Radicals, Welles questioned the senator on his source of information. Sumner replied, "Why, one of them has advised and urged me to prepare and bring in a bill which should control the action of the President and wipe out his policy. It has got to be done. Half of the Cabinet, as well as an overwhelming majority of ... Congress, are for it, and the President must change his whole course." If not, Sumner warned, "Congress would." Who in the cabinet would collude with Sumner to overthrow the president's policies but Stanton? No pending legislation could overthrow the president's policies faster than the Freedmen's Bureau Bill.[7]

On January 25 the Senate passed

the bill and on February 10 sent it to the White House. After five days elapsed with no response from Johnson, Sumner once again strolled over to the navy department to court support from Welles. He now claimed that four — not three cabinet members — supported the bill. Welles probed the matter further, searching to discover who those members were. Sumner remained evasive, and Welles concluded that nothing had changed apart from Stanton's collusion. Later in the day Welles spoke with the president, who remained firm in his stated policy of reconstruction. Of those trying days, one historian wrote, "had [Johnson] been willing to 'abandon' the policy of Lincoln, he would have had Sumner, Wade and Stevens fawning upon him, and he would have received the plaudits of historians who praise them."[8]

Johnson's life had been marked by difficult challenges from its very beginning. He did not pretend to be a clever man. Rather, he had always moved ahead on a straight line and brushed away opposition when it confronted him. Nothing, however, had ever imposed a more powerful threat to his political existence than the Radicals.

For many years men like Sumner, Stevens, Phillips, Stanton, and Wade had insulated themselves from the south. Since being caned on the Senate floor, Sumner hated all southerners. Stevens hated them for burning his iron works. Phillips hated them for holding slaves. Wade hated them for political reasons. Should Lafayette Foster resign as president pro tempore of the Senate, Wade would be in line to fill the post. If so, he would become president upon Johnson's

Benjamin F. Wade, senator from Ohio and leading Radical, who stood in line to be president upon Johnson's conviction. (Library of Congress.)

removal from office. Stanton, who did not like Johnson and should have resigned, aligned himself with the Radicals and remained in the cabinet to spy on the president. As a group of five they did not understand the culture or the honorable nature of most southerners, and they cared less. From Sumner's perspective, "Massachusetts could govern Georgia better than Georgia could govern herself."[9]

Sumner would not listen to Grant any more than Senator John Sherman listened to his brother. General Sherman knew his foe and respected them. Writing from St. Louis on February 11 he encouraged the senator to not "shove the South back as territories, and all steps to that end must fail for many reasons, if for no other than ... it compels the people already there to assume a hostile attitude. The well-disposed of the South must again be trusted — we cannot help it. You are classed universally as one of the rising statesmen, above mere party rules. And whilst you should not separate from your party, you can moderate the severity of their counsels." The general appeared to understand statesmanship better than his brother, but the bill had already passed the Senate and been delivered to the president.[10]

When Johnson read the Freedmen's Bureau Bill, he found features inconsistent with his conversation with Fessenden. Later, meeting with Welles, he referred to an "extraordinary intrigue ... going on in Congress having nothing short of a subversion or change in the structure of government in view. The unmistakable design of Thad Stevens and his associates was to take the government into their own hands ... and to get rid of him by declaring Tennessee out of the Union."[11]

On February 16, after it became apparent that Johnson would veto the bill, Fessenden's subcommittee came to him with a proposition. If Johnson would sign the bill, Congress would seat the representation from Tennessee. Sumner did not approve of the deal, nor did Johnson, but each for opposite reasons. Sumner wanted no southerners in Congress, and Johnson would not bend his scruples for a deal to remodel the Constitution.[12]

On February 19, before releasing his veto message, Johnson met with the cabinet. Seward, Dennison, McCulloch, and Welles agreed with the president. Speed, Harlan, and Stanton thought the bill should be signed but made no rational proposals or any emendations to the president's veto message. "The effect of his veto," wrote Welles, "will probably be an open rupture between the President and a portion of the Republican members of Congress." In rallying votes to override the veto, Welles predicted that the Radicals would "be active as well as cunning."[13]

After the cabinet meeting Johnson sent his veto message to the Senate. He wrote, "There is no immediate necessity for the proposed measure. I share with Congress the strongest desire to secure to the freedmen the full enjoyment of their freedom and property and their entire independence and equality in making contracts for their labor, but the bill before me contains provisions which in my opinion are not warranted by the Constitution and are not well suited to accomplish the end in view." On constitutional grounds, he rejected the idea that bureau agents and military personnel could strip state courts of their power to adjudicate civil actions involving the rights of blacks. The bill clearly called for "negro rule through white men abetted by bayonets." Johnson also examined the other side of the bill. Knowing that he controlled the military and the department of the interior, he explained why the "power that would thus be placed in the hands of the President is such as in time of peace certainly ought never to be intrusted to any one man." In arguing against military courts Johnson reminded the Senate that the country no longer engaged in war, and such a tribunal within a state could not be lawfully justified.[14]

Johnson might have expressed fewer objections to the Freedmen's Bureau Bill — or perhaps reached for a compromise — if the Radicals had not inserted their pet scheme of confiscation. To the so-called statesmen in the Senate, he replied, "The bill proposes to take away land from its former owners without any legal proceedings ... contrary to that provision of the Constitution which declares that no person shall be 'deprived of life, liberty or property without due process of law.'" The president recognized that freedmen needed to be protected by civil authorities, and if left alone, he believed that blacks and whites would work together in achieving a balanced relationship. He also believed that interference from the federal government as proposed in the bill would only make conditions worse.[15]

Three days after the veto of the Freedmen's Bureau Bill, the city paused to celebrate Washington's birthday. The Radicals arranged ceremonies at the Capitol in memory of Henry Winter Davis, who had insulted Lincoln with the Wade-Davis Manifesto and Johnson in a letter to *The Nation*. Welles believed the proceedings were "intended to belittle the memory of Lincoln and his policy as much as to exalt Davis, who opposed it." But at Grover's Theater a gathering of supporters spoke in favor of Johnson's veto. After speeches by Montgomery Blair, Samuel S. Cox, and others, the crowd proposed a serenade for the president, and the procession marched to the White House.[16]

Using the occasion to speak on behalf of his veto, Johnson emerged from the north door and faced a surging crowd of wildly enthusiastic partisans. Having no prepared speech, and promising McCulloch that he would merely make acknowledgments, Johnson threw caution to the wind. He attacked the Committee of Fifteen as "an irresponsible central directory" which had unto themselves assumed all the powers of Congress. He had another point to make, and it materialized part way through his speech. "The rebellion," Johnson declared, "is put down by the strong arm of the government in the field. But is this the only way we can have rebellions? I am opposed to the Davises, the Toombses, the Slidells and the long list of such. But when I perceive on the other hand, men I care not by what name you call them — still opposed to the Union ... I am still for the preservation of these states, I am free to say to you that I am still in the field."[17]

Voices from the crowd began shouting, "Call them off!" "Call them traitors — give us their names!"

Johnson asked himself — should he do it? Had the time come to lay the issues before the public? Throughout his life he had always been faithful to his constituency, and they had preserved him as their representative in government. Now the people — though a different set of people — demanded the truth. "The gentleman asks for three names," Johnson replied. Still he paused and deliberated. Then raising his voice, he shouted, "Suppose I should name to you those whom I look upon as being opposed to the fundamental principles of this government, and as now laboring to destroy them. I say Thaddeus Stevens of Pennsylvania; I say Charles Sumner of Massachusetts; I say Wendell Phillips of Massachusetts." Johnson could have listed a dozen more, but three were enough to give notice to his adversaries. Knowing the press would report his comments, he then gave his reasons for opposing the Freedmen's Bill and made a public appeal for support, ending the impromptu message with: "Let us stand by the principles of our fathers though the heavens fall. I intend to stand by the Constitution as the chief ark of our safety, as the palladium of our civil and religious liberty. Yes, let us cling to it as the mariner clings to the last plank, when the night and the tempest close around him." The president might well have kept his opinions to himself. His foolish and intemperate remarks played into Sumner's hands and vindicated some of the senator's frequent outbursts of temper.[18]

What irritated Johnson most was Stevens' and Sumner's ploy of forming the Committee of Fifteen on Reconstruction to obstruct elected southern representatives from taking their seats in Congress. This prevented the southern states from being heard. The president lashed back at the Senate, writing, "The Constitution imperatively declares ... that each state shall have at least one Representative.... It also provides that the Senate of the United States *shall* be composed of two Senators from each state and adds with peculiar force 'that no state without its consent shall be deprived of its equal suffrage in the Senate.'" He challenged Congress to do their constitutional duty and seat its southern members, adding, "As eleven States are not at this time represented in either branch of Congress, it would seem to be [the president's] duty to present their just claims to Congress."[19]

In the Senate both applause and hisses greeted the reading of Johnson's veto message, causing a stoppage while major portions of the galleries were cleared. The Radicals did not want a lesson in constitutional law from a tailor. Outraged by the president's dignified reply, Sumner demanded an immediate vote to override the veto. Others wanted to wait a day. On February 20 the Senate called the vote. Six Republicans bolted and the required two-thirds failed by two

votes. Sumner became livid, and once again a disturbance in the galleries caused them to be emptied. Stevens became vindictive and announced that he had planned to seat the Tennesseans, but because the president vetoed the bill, the House would not now consent. Stevens then passed a resolution declaring that "the Union is divided, that the States which were in rebellion should not now have their constitutional right of representation." On March 2 the Senate adopted the same resolution.[20]

Johnson had his own biases. While he understood white southerners well, he completely misjudged the character of northern politics by underestimating the bonds of principle and economic interest which unified Republicans, even when in heated disagreement. His message, which he intended as a catalyst to drive a wedge between the leading Radicals and the Republican moderates, thereby driving the likes of Sumner, Stevens, and Wade out of the party, created the opposite affect. Republicans resolutely closed ranks and vowed to overrule the president on the next test of strength. To flex their collective muscle, they now reconsidered the vote taken in December and agreed that no congressman from a southern state would be seated until both the House and the Senate consented to readmission.[21]

After ten months as president, Johnson's fragile working relationship with Congress came to an end. George Julian declared, "The President stands squarely against Congress and the people." Wendell Phillips joined a growing number of members in the House threatening to impeach the president. Sumner added his voice, proclaiming that "by the assassination of Lincoln, the Rebellion had vaulted into the presidential chair."[22]

General Sherman, always willing to pester his brother on matters before the Senate, wrote; "The political aspect now is interesting to a looker-on. Sumner and Stevens would have made another civil war inevitably — the President's antagonistic position saves us war save of words, and as I am a peace man I go for Johnson and the Veto. I recollect that Congress is but one of three co-ordinate branches of the Government. I want to hear the Supreme Court manifest itself, and then can guess at the conclusion…. Let Johnson fight it out with Sumner, who, though sincere, represents an antagonism as ultra as of [Jefferson] Davis himself…. The Republican party has lost forever the best chance they can ever expect of gaining recruits from the great middle class who want peace and industry."[23]

John Sherman could straddle both sides of an issue. During a speech before the Senate he resonated some of his brother's advice and reminded his fellow senators that Johnson had every right to follow in the footsteps of Lincoln and resist the blusterings of Sumner's partisans. He also reminded them that Johnson had been "fighting all the days of his life; the very courage with which he resists opponents whenever they present themselves, we commended five years ago as the highest virtue of Andrew Johnson's life." He is "a man who never turned his back upon a foe, personal or political, a man whose great virtue has been his combative propensity; as a man who repelled insults here on the very spot where I now stand, when they came from traitors arming themselves for the fight; can you ask him, because he is President, to submit to insult?" Then on the subject of the Tennesseans waiting to be seated, Sherman said, they "are as true and loyal as any of your Senators without exception." But Sherman went on to say, "I do most deeply regret [Johnson's] speech of the 22nd of February. I think there is no true friend of Andrew Johnson who would not be willing to wipe out that speech from the pages of history. It is impossible to conceive a more humiliating spectacle than the President of the United States invoking the wild passions of a mob around him with the utterance of such sentiments as he uttered on that day." It was all right, however, for certain members of Congress to use their resources to do the same.[24]

Contrary to Sherman's rebuke, the *New York Herald* backed Johnson, reporting, "A desperate effort was made here last night by the Radicals to create the impression that the President had made an outrageous speech. Dispatches were sent all over the country to this affect for the purpose of prejudicing the minds of the party leaders…. Numerous dispatches of approval received from leading Republicans from all directions this morning prove that the false stories sent from here have accomplished nothing against the speech." The *New York Times* agreed with the *Herald,* and the *Chicago Times* reported that the time had come to dissolve the "Rump Congress" and arrest Sumner, Stevens, and Phillips for the "crime of treason." But the day of factional hate had only begun.[25]

While the Senate and House bemoaned Johnson's speech, and the conservative press condoned it, Seward went to New York and spoke to a huge crowd at Cooper Union in defense of the president's veto. Later he telegraphed the White House: "The Union is restored and the country saved. The President's speech is triumphant." Henry J. Raymond of the *New York Times* agreed, writing, "Any section with men in it fit to live would become exasperated and goaded into rebellion within one year after such a policy [as the Radicals'] had been inaugurated."[26]

But the day of Radical partisans had only begun. They collectively vowed with as much determination to implement their doctrine as Johnson pledged to destroy it. With every passing day it became obvious to the Radicals that Johnson was a much tougher customer than they anticipated. Fierce, stubborn, and righteously defiant, the president began to pull the public into the emerging battle with Congress.

On February 25 Ohio Governor Samuel S. Cox called at the White House, afterwards writing, "If you could meet his straightforward honest look and hear the hearty tone of his voice, as I did, I am well assured you would believe with me, that although he may not receive personal assaults with the equanimity and forbearance Mr. Lincoln used to show, there is no need to fear that Andrew Johnson is not hearty and sincere in his adhesion to the principles upon which he was elected."[27]

After the ratification of the Thirteenth Amendment, Johnson did not want the Constitution further amended until the south recovered from the war. The black population needed to be economically integrated, plantations needed to be restored, commerce and trade reestablished, and military rule permanently removed. Johnson did not want to stir up hatreds that would last another century, but the powers in Congress did not see the future in the same way. True statesmanship requires vision. A psychological understanding of humankind helps, and a perception of the future is essential, but the Radicals were shifting their focus to one object, the removal of the president of the United States.[28]

On February 22, the birthday of one of our first distinguished statesmen, Welles noted that "Stevens and his secret joint committee or directory have taken into their hands the government and the administration of affairs. It is an incipient conspiracy. Congress, in both branches, or the majority of Congress, are but puppets in the hands of the directory and do little but sanction and obey the orders of the committee." Sumner, Wade, and Stevens wanted it that way. They were not interested in statesmanship. They were not interested in protecting and preserving the Constitution. They were only interested in having their own way. To do it meant eliminating Andrew Johnson.[29]

8

Force Bills and Riots

Johnson expressed his opposition to the Radicals in clear terms when he vetoed the Freedmen's Bureau Bill. His position on not wanting further constitutional amendments emanated from knowledge that Lyman Trumbull of Illinois had begun work on a Civil Rights Bill, one claiming "to protect all persons in their civil rights and furnish their means for vindication." The bill provided against discrimination in civil rights or immunities rising from race, color, or previous condition of servitude. A debate ensued in the Senate over constitutional power, involving whether Congress could pass laws for the ordinary administration of justice in the states.

Trumbull's language adopted the machinery of the Fugitive Slave Law, the last clause authorizing the use of land and naval forces in the enforcement of the act. The opposition objected to the use of federal forces, but Trumbull claimed he had conferred with Johnson on the measure, and in the absence of contradictory evidence, the Senate passed the bill on February 2, 1866. Conservatives in the House raised the same questions, and Stevens could not whip it through until March 13. The measure reached the White House five days later, and the Radicals hoped that the criticism heaped upon the president during the past weeks for vetoing the Freedmen's

Bureau Bill might nudge him into accepting the milder Civil Rights Bill.[1]

When Johnson did not immediately sign the bill, Sumner and Fessenden anticipated a veto and began looking about the Senate for votes. A new member, Democrat John P. Stockton of New Jersey, had been seated on December 4, 1865. In January Radical members protested his election, claiming technical irregularities. A two week inquiry followed and on January 30 investigators declared him elected. Sumner clearly wanted Stockton ejected. On March 22, four days after the Civil Rights Bill went to the president, Sumner again tried to have him removed. By a 21 to 20 vote, Stockton retained his seat.

Sumner, whose moral senses were never keen where his prejudices were concerned, devised another way to oust Stockton. William Wright, also of New Jersey, was absent due to illness, and Lott M. Morrill of Maine held Wright's vote. Morrill, by gentlemen's agreement, promised not to use Wright's ballot until the latter returned to the Senate. Sumner and Fessenden impelled Morrill to break the agreement and a tie resulted. Because of Morrill's breach of faith, Stockton demanded his right to vote, which was allowed, and he held his seat. Three days later Sumner moved to strike Stockton's vote. The motion carried and Stockton was expelled. The following day, March 27, 1866, Johnson vetoed the Civil Rights Bill.[2]

When explaining his veto, Johnson attempted to elucidate the public on the underlying motives of the Radicals. His argument accused Congress of passing discriminatory laws by refusing representation to the eleven southern states most affected by the legislation. If Congress wished to "make the entire colored population ... citizens of the United States," should not they give persons of foreign birth the same privilege? The bill also contained certain measures from the now defunct Freedmen's Bureau Bill, such as prohibiting a state from passing laws not in accordance with the Civil Rights Bill. These measures rendered state lawmakers and judges subordinate to "commissioners who are to be charged with the performance of quasi-judicial duties," and made them subject "to fine and imprisonment for the performance of the duties such state laws might impose." Johnson accurately predicted that "This extraordinary power is to be conferred upon agents irresponsible to the Government and to the people, to whose number the discretion of the commissioners is the only limit, and in whose hands such authority might be made a terrible engine of wrong, oppression and fraud."[3]

Johnson predicted that the bill would "frustrate" the adjustment between races, arguing that commissioners and agents would use the bill to "foment discord between the two races." He understood the southern mind and its economy better than the Radicals, whose main object remained constant — to gain black suffrage and retain power in government. "In all our history," Johnson lamented, "no such system as that con-

templated by the details of this bill has ever before been proposed or adopted. They establish for the security of the colored race safeguards which go infinitely beyond any that the General Government has ever provided for the white race." Once again Johnson warned that the passage of the bill would "resuscitate the spirit of rebellion and ... arrest those influences which are more closely drawing around the States the bonds of union and peace." Johnson closed his message by expressing a willingness to approve any bill that placed both races on equal footing. He promised to protect the civil rights of the freedmen, as well as those of all other classes, but "by judicial process, under equal and impartial laws, in conformity with the provisions of the Federal Constitution."[4]

With the bill vetoed, the Radicals rushed to override it before two ill senators, William Wright of New Jersey and James Dixon of Connecticut, returned to sustain Johnson's veto. On April 5, the day of the vote, Edgar Cowan of Pennsylvania moved for postponement until the absent senators returned. Ben Wade bolted to his feet, demanded the floor, and furiously objected. "If the President of the United States can ... by a veto compel Congress to submit to his dictation he is an emperor and a despot. Because I believe the great question of congressional power and authority is at stake here I yield to no importunities on the other side ... but I will tell the President and everybody else that if God Almighty has stricken a member of this body so that he cannot be here to uphold the dictation of a despot, I thank him for it and I will take every advantage of it."[5]

The Senate voted the following day. Edwin D. Morgan of New York confided to Welles that he would sustain the veto, but Radicals coerced him into voting against Johnson. The aspiring William M. Stewart of Nevada decided that his political future lay with the Radicals and voted for the bill. Wright hobbled into the Senate and cast his vote in support of the veto, but his colleague, Stockton, had been expelled. The final vote — 15 in favor and 33 against the president — gave a bare two-thirds majority to the Radicals. Had Sumner and his colleagues failed to unseat Stockton or to convert Morgan and Stewart, Johnson's veto would have been sustained. On April 9 the House overturned the president's veto by a margin of 122 to 41. Speaker Colfax joyously cast his vote proclaiming himself among the majority, and the Civil Rights Bill became the law.[6]

Friends of Johnson noticed that during the recent debate Stanton had been surreptitiously active in securing the passage of the bill in the Senate. Those who voted to sustain the veto remarked that their influence had been frittered away to some degree by the meddling of the secretary. Cabinet members began urging the president to dismiss Stanton, but Johnson replied, "I am breasting the storm," and he promised to be ready to act at the proper time.[7]

House Radicals had the votes to override any veto, but Sumner recognized a need to unify Senate Republicans in order to be successful against future presidential vetoes. They needed a safety net because the seats of Stockton, Wright, and James Dixon would be filled one way or another. No help could be expected from the south, so the Radicals looked west. Colorado's population on May 6, 1866, though a mere 30,000, attracted Sumner's attention. If admitted to the Union, Colorado would give the Senate two more seats, and if done with care,

those seats could be filled by Republicans. Because Colorado's constitution limited suffrage to whites, Sumner rejected the admission of the state without extending the franchise to the ninety blacks who resided in the territory. The bill for Colorado statehood passed the Senate, but Sumner, Fessenden, and Grimes vowed to sustain a presidential veto. The Republicans were furious with Sumner, whose obsession with equal rights at all costs acted in all matters before the Senate as both attribute and curse.[8]

To the Senate Radicals two more votes meant more than just overriding presidential vetoes. They needed absolute control of a two-thirds majority to overthrow Johnson if impeached by the House. Collusion between the House and Senate went smoothly, and the bill to admit Colorado to the Union landed on Johnson's desk. The president knew exactly the purpose of the bill and on May 15 sent it back to the Senate vetoed.

In his veto message Johnson cited the paucity of population as not justifying "the establishment of a State government." Further, there had been no interest expressed on the part of the "majority" of Colorado residents to exchange their territorial government for a state government. Johnson did not believe the time had come to admit a territory with no more than 30,000 inhabitants when New York claimed a population of four million and most other states counted at least a million. Johnson also reminded the Senate that in 1864, when the only legal Colorado election addressed the subject of statehood, a majority of 3,152 voted against it. If admitted, Colorado would have one representative in the House and two in the Senate. Johnson believed that Colorado's admission would create a proportionate disadvantage to all other states should Colorado be admitted. He then reminded the Senate that "Eleven of the old states have been for some time and still remain unrepresented in Congress" and that "no new state should be prematurely and unnecessarily admitted" until Congress accepted and seated elected representatives of the south. Johnson's argument made so much sense that the Radicals could not muster the votes to override the veto.[9]

Having failed to admit Colorado, the Radicals returned to their pet project — black suffrage. They needed to create a Republican political platform for the 1866 elections while simultaneously convincing the public that the south deserved to be punished. To accomplish this goal, Stevens conceived the Fourteenth Amendment.[10] One historian wrote: "Of all the contrasts history affords, none is more depressing than that between the statesmen who convened in Philadelphia in 1787, through conciliation and wise counsel to form a more perfect Union, and the men who sat in Washington in 1866 plotting to change the Constitution of the founders." Elihu Root summed up the situation by writing, "the grave error of reconstruction legislation which went on the theory that by merely giving a vote to the negro he would be made competent to govern." Black suffrage had not been an issue of the war, nor had a musket been fired to achieve it.[11]

The plot produced a transparency that fooled few people. What motivated discussions leading to the Fourteenth Amendment involved a change in the basis for representation that would reduce the power of the south in Congress. James G. Blaine introduced an amendment that provided for representation based upon the whole population of the

state "except those whose political rights or privileges are denied or abridged by the Constitution of any state on account of race or color." In other words, a state's representation would be reduced if it disenfranchised any of its voters, black or white. Because Blaine's amendment returned the matter of determining suffrage to the individual states, Sumner denounced it, demanding immediate and unconditional enfranchisement of blacks.[12]

While the Senate debated Blaine's amendment, Stevens' Joint Committee on Reconstruction sought to create legislation enabling the north to dictate indefinitely to the south. They approved of Blaine's apportionment provisions but with reservations. Through a separate bill they added a coercive condition — that until the southern states ratified the Fourteen Amendment, their senators and representatives would not be admitted to Congress. "In other words," one historian wrote, "until the South surrendered its constitutional right to reject a proposed amendment, — one especially designed to humiliate, injure and degrade her — the states would be denied all rights to statehood." When finally drafted, the bill disqualified any southerner from holding office or becoming a presidential elector if they had participated in the rebellion. This clause stripped all the leading men of the south of power and disqualified most of the representatives recently elected but not seated in Congress. It also compelled the south, as provided in the Blaine amendment, to give her ex-slaves the vote or suffer a proportionate loss in representation.

The measure did not pass during the first session of Congress, but Stevens intended to revisit the matter during the next session. In the interim, he submitted a majority report placing the "conquered rebels" at the mercy of the "conquerors." He stipulated that "Confederate states are not at present entitled to representation in the Congress of the United States."[13]

Not all members agreed with Stevens' majority report. Reverdy Johnson of Maryland, in the minority discourse, pointed to constitutional inconsistencies. "States unequal," said he, "are not known to the Constitution." To submit to the southern states an amendment admits that they "are and never ceased to be states of the Union." He argued against Stevens' intended coercion because it degraded the south. "To consent to it will be to consent to their own dishonor." In keeping with the rules, the House published both reports.[14]

Welles read the bill and predicted that Stevens' plan would keep the country divided for "four years longer at least. No one can read the propositions submitted without seeing that the whole scheme is one for party ascendancy." Welles also predicted that the result of the bill would be "a struggle perhaps of years" and "the ultimate overwhelming and disgraceful defeat of the authors and their party."[15]

The president clearly understood the machinations of Congress. The Radicals demanded the exclusive right to determine the policy of reconstruction. Johnson characterized the propositions to tinker with the Constitution as being "as numerous as preambles and resolutions at town meetings called to consider the most ordinary questions connected with the administration of local affairs." What annoyed him most were the carefully crafted words in the third section of the bill that granted Congress, by two-thirds vote, to set aside any presidential pardon.[16]

Having fewer supporters, the Radicals in the Senate encountered opposition to the amendment, resulting in several weeks of debate. Meanwhile, Irish police in Memphis bolstered the Radical cause when in April boisterous and drunken black soldiers, recently disbanded but quartered in the city, provoked a riot that lasted two days. Whites joined with the police in an attack on the black population of the city. When the shooting ended forty-six blacks lay dead, and twelve black schoolhouses and four churches lay in ashes. The Senate blamed the incident on the leniency of Johnson's policies.[17]

Not until June 13 did the amendment pass both chambers. Two days later Seward transmitted the Fourteenth Amendment to the governors for consideration in their state legislatures, including all the states of the south. On constitutional amendments, the president performs no function, but he sent a message to Congress protesting amendments as long as the south remained unrepresented. Concerned that the public would misunderstand his position on the matter, Johnson explained that while amendments must be sent to the states for consideration, doing so did not imply that he approved or recommended an adoption of the amendment.[18]

Perhaps the most despicable example of coercion in passing the amendment occurred not in a northern state but in Tennessee. Since being elected governor with the help of Johnson, Parson Brownlow witnessed the power struggle in Washington and began connecting himself with the Radicals. This he did notwithstanding a poor showing on the part of the Radicals in recent state elections.

Despite the Memphis riot, Stevens already had his eye on the state, writing in his majority report that "perhaps ... Tennessee has placed itself in a condition to resume its political relations with the Union."[19]

Three days after receiving the amendment, Brownlow issued a proclamation convening on July 4 a special session of the state legislature. When a quorum could not be obtained, Brownlow waited another ten days. Still short the required number, he asked General George H. Thomas for assistance in rounding up the delinquent legislators. Thomas thought not and wired Stanton for advice. Stanton dallied for three days before bringing the matter before Johnson. The president replied that the army was "not to meddle with local parties and politics." Meanwhile, the state's senate ratified the amendment, and Brownlow waited upon the house, which still lacked the necessary quorum. Out of patience, he located two members, ordered their arrest, and dragged them into the chamber. Both men refused to vote, arguing that the measure had not been placed before the public. They obtained a writ of habeas corpus and presented their case before Judge Thomas Frazier, an appointee of Andrew Johnson.[20]

The House did not wait for a decision from the judge. On July 19 police forcibly escorted both men into one of the rooms off the floor. A roll call still showed two members short, but the House voted anyway — forty-three for and eleven against the proposed amendment. Having no quorum, the speaker disqualified the vote, but the members present overruled him. On the evening of the 19th, Brownlow proudly reported to the secretary of the United States Senate that the amendment had passed. "We

have fought the battle and won it," Brownlow declared. "Give my respects to the dead dog in the White House." The following day Judge Frazier declared the arrest of the two House members illegal. Irritated by Frazier's decision, the Radicals got even. They impeached the judge for "high crimes and misdemeanors" and removed him from office. Tennessee became the third state to ratify the Fourteenth Amendment, preceded only by Connecticut and New Hampshire.[21]

On the heels of Brownlow's illegal actions, the Radicals rejoiced. Three days later both chambers adopted a joint resolution declaring that Tennessee, having ratified both the Thirteenth and Fourteenth Amendments, was "hereby restored to her former practical relation to the Union, and is again entitled to be represented by Senators and Representatives in Congress."[22]

As badly as Johnson wanted his home state restored to its proper place in Congress, he did not approve of it being done improperly. In a message to the House on July 24 he stated that the joint resolution "comprises no legislation, nor does it confer any power which is binding upon the respective Houses, the Executive, or the States." Nonetheless, in an effort to demonstrate compromise, Johnson signed the resolution, reminding the House that his approval "is not to be construed as an acknowledgment of the right of Congress to pass laws preliminary to the admission of duly qualified Representatives from any of the states." He encouraged Congress to act with speed in admitting "all other states to a fair and equal participation in national legislation when they present themselves in the persons of loyal Senators and Representatives who can comply with the requirements of the Constitution."[23]

After seating Tennessee's elected members, the Radicals formed misgivings. Of eight representatives, four were Republicans and four Democrats, not enough to threaten the Radical balance of power in the House. The two Senators presented a more troublesome problem. The Radicals believed that Joseph Fowler would vote with them and quickly awarded his seat, though in time they would learn otherwise. Because the other senator, David D. Patterson, was Johnson's son-in-law, Radicals accused him of disloyalty and attempted to force his removal. Patterson's wife acted as mistress of the White House, and this added to the Senate's dilemma. Too many members vouched for Patterson, creating such a ruckus that on July 25 the Senate reluctantly seated him.[24]

With the congressional session scheduled to end on July 28, Radicals rushed through two more bills, each designed to strengthen their political advantage. Having failed to override the president's veto on the Freedmen's Bureau Bill, they designed another. And because the territory of Nebraska would bolster the Radical majority in the Senate, they believed that statehood could be justified.[25]

The new Freedmen's Bureau Bill contained all the objectionable conditions of the defeated bill. Johnson vetoed it on July 16 and sent the bill back to the House, referring to all the reasons he had given for rejecting the first bill. He specifically objected to the power it granted to Secretary of War Stanton, writing, "The only ground upon which this kind of legislation can be justified is that of the war-making power." The original bureau, created in March 1865, for no more than one year "from the cessation of hostilities and the declaration of peace" still remained in operation. Congress had extended the original act by refusing to seat representatives from the south because another clause of the same act provided that military tribunals would remain in place until each "State shall be fully restored in its constitutional relations to the Government and shall be duly represented in the Congress of the United States." While the Radicals sought to expand the jurisdiction of the military through the new bill, Johnson attempted to limit military interference by sustaining the act of March 1865, at least until Congress reconvened in December.[26]

The Radicals anticipated Johnson's veto. When it arrived on July 16, the House overrode it by a margin of three-to-one, and the Senate by a bare margin of two-thirds. Their ace in the hole was Stanton, to whom the bill gave unprecedented authority. Johnson predicted that the Freedmen's Bureau would create enormous friction between the whites of the south and the federal government. One clause stipulated that the army would provide protection to the freedmen "under such rules and regulations as the President *through* the Secretary of War shall prescribe." Johnson could have challenged the constitutionality of the act, but he viewed Chief Justice Chase as friendly toward the Radicals and withheld a challenge.[27]

Unable to override Johnson's veto on the admission of Colorado, Ben Wade, in the closing hours of the session, introduced a bill to admit Nebraska. Sumner balked because Nebraska's constitution confined the vote to white males. Nevertheless, both chambers passed the measure on Friday, July 27, one day before adjournment. Johnson did not sign the bill, and it failed.[28]

Ben Wade wanted Nebraska admitted to the Union for personal reasons. As a first step, the Radicals would elevate him to the post of president of the Senate, thereby putting him in line to replace Johnson. As step two, the House would impeach Johnson, after which the Senate would try and convict him. Wade would then become president, and the Radicals would enjoy full control of the government. To ensure a two-thirds majority for conviction, the Senate wanted the extra insurance of having two Republican senators from Nebraska. With Wade as president, Radicals believed they could continue to exclude southern representatives from seats in Congress and deny the south's participation in the next presidential election.

The Radicals suffered a setback when, in mid-July, three of their supporters in the cabinet honorably resigned—Speed, Harlan, and Dennison. Stanton, the president's arch nemesis, did not resign, though common knowledge prevailed that he supported the Radicals and not Johnson. Of Lincoln's original cabinet, only Seward, Welles, and McCulloch supported the president. Why Stanton did not resign puzzled Johnson as much as it did later historians. The reasons included the Radical chieftains, who wanted Stanton to remain in office, and Stanton himself, who had hardened against Johnson and supported his impeachment. The less obvious reason involved Sumner, who believed a parliamentary form of government more manageable than an impeachment trial. With Stanton acting as a trusted minister, Congress could simply poll a vote of "noconfidence" among its members and unburden themselves of an uncooperative executive. But Sumner did not have such a system at his disposal, though sometimes he liked to think of it as such. One historian claimed that the Radicals conspired to "rob the President of his constitutional prerogatives, to change the form of government from the presidential system to the parliamentary system of administration. It is difficult to find any sufficient defense for Mr. Stanton's course."[29]

Johnson did not trust Stanton and failing to remove him from the cabinet was a mistake. He knew Stanton communicated on a regular basis with Radicals and had spies operating throughout the administration. But the secretary could be cleverly servile, and at the time Johnson probably felt that filling three cabinet posts with supporters might pull Stanton back into line.[30]

Johnson acted quickly to fill the vacancies, and he did so without referring the matter to the remaining members. To replace Attorney General Speed, he chose sixty-three-year-old Henry Stanbery, a distinguished lawyer from Ohio. For postmaster general, he replaced Dennison with former Wisconsin governor Alexander Randall, a forty-seven-year-old diplomat whose credentials included service as judge of the Milwaukee Circuit Court. For Harlan's role as secretary of the interior, Johnson named Orville Hickman Browning, one of Lincoln's oldest and most trusted friends. In 1860, Browning worked for Lincoln's nomination and election. A year later, after Stephen Douglas died, he took the latter's seat in the Senate. All three additions supported Johnson and bolstered the cabinet with strong and honorable counsel. But Stanton remained in power, and spies roaming the hallways of Government remained as active as ever.[31]

An incident occurring in New Orleans in late July—two days after

Congress adjourned — should have induced Johnson to cashier Stanton. Pardoned leaders of the Confederacy occupied every office of state government but the governorship, held by J. Madison Wells. The state Constitution, adopted in 1864 under Lincoln's administration, did not provide for black suffrage. The Radicals in the state, encouraged by friends in Washington, decided to take control of the state government through the medium of black suffrage. To do this meant amending the state constitution, so they attempted to illegally assemble a convention using members who had finished their work and adjourned two years earlier. Mayor John T. Monroe, a rebel pardoned by Johnson, warned Major General Absalom Baird that if the now defunct delegates attempted to assemble, they would be arrested and indicted by the grand jury. Baird did not know what action to take and wired Stanton asking for instructions *from the president.* "Please," said Baird, "instruct me at once by telegraph." Stanton received the message on July 29, but he said nothing to the president for ten days.[32]

Meanwhile, Louisiana Radicals encouraged the blacks to demand suffrage and, if necessary, to fight for it. From the steps of city hall one rabble-rouser fervently addressed the mob and encouraged them to take action if any delegates were arrested. "If interfered with," he shouted, "the streets will run with blood."[33]

Johnson only learned through Louisiana's lieutenant governor, Albert Voorhies, and the attorney-general, A. J. Herron, that the proposed convention was before a grand jury. If delegates attempted to assemble, there might be an incident. Johnson replied, "The military will be expected to sustain, and not interfere with, the proceedings of the court." He also wired Governor Wells, demanding to know why the convention had been called. Wells replied that he had not called a convention, only an election.[34]

Because Stanton failed to properly apprise Johnson of the seriousness of the problem, preparations for July 30 were not in place when an enormous procession of blacks took to the streets that morning. Many carried arms, and during the march someone in their group fired a shot. Other shots followed, and the police appeared on the streets. They rushed into Mechanics' Institute firing their weapons and killed the black leaders. Before the ensuing riot ended, two hundred men lay dead or wounded, most of them black. By the time the army reached the scene, the trouble had ended.[35]

Radicals blamed Johnson for the riot, claiming that he had intentionally let it happen. Stanton said nothing, except to blame Louisiana's attorney general and Mayor Monroe, referring to them as "pardoned rebels who had instigated the murder of the people in the streets of the city" and caused the "terrible blood-shedding." A congressional committee formed to investigate the causes of the riot filed a report charging Johnson as an accomplice in the crime. The northern press did not bother to check any details when editing the report for the public, and all the political repercussions fell upon Johnson. Welles, however, would not be fooled. He believed that Stanton had intentionally misled the president about the seriousness of the threat, and that the whole affair had been orchestrated by Radicals in Congress. "There is a determination to involve the country in civil war," Welles wrote, "if necessary, to secure negro suffrage in the states and radical ascendancy in the General Government."[36]

Though Stanton participated as a silent conspirator in the New Orleans riot, no one could prove it. The secretary laid the matter at Baird's feet, claiming the general had given no reason for alarm. Stanton knew exactly what the president would do if given the message — quash the convention without waiting for a ju-dicial decision — and the secretary did not want this to happen. Why the president put up with Stanton baffled Welles. It also puzzled many historians who had the benefit of hindsight because Stanton no longer attempted to hide his radicalism but flouted it. By doing nothing, Johnson imposed a problem upon himself which would become infinitely more difficult to overcome later.[37]

9

A "Swing Around the Circle"

During the summer of 1866 the rupture between Johnson and Congress so enlivened politics that four national conventions were held, an unprecedented number for an off year election. On August 14 the Philadelphia convention in support of Johnson met first, drawing both Republicans and Democrats from the north and the south. So unified was this gathering that delegates from the north paired themselves with ex-Confederates and entered the building arm in arm. Of cabinet members, only Stanton balked at supporting the convention and offered no help.[1]

The delegates shared a common purpose — to preserve the Union and protect it from a new form of destruction. Fresh talk of war pervaded the huge convention center on the corner of 20th Street and Girard Avenue. Twelve thousand men and women squeezed into the wigwam, many content with standing room only. Senator James R. Doolittle of Wisconsin brought the convention to order and read a telegram from President Johnson: "The people must be trusted and the country will be restored." Hats flew in the air and a new round of cheering thundered out the openings and onto the street.[2]

Welles discounted murmurs of war, blaming the problem on a weakness of intellect in Congress whose members were being led "into rashness and error by a few designing leaders, who move and control the party machinery. There is no individuality," he mused, "and very little statesmanship.... The war on the President and on the Constitution as well as on the whole people of the South is revolutionary."[3]

The delegates supported Welles' view, adopting resolutions and declaring that "no state or combination of states has the right to withdraw from the Union, or to exclude, through their action in Congress or otherwise, any other state or states from the Union. The Union of states is perpetual." The resolution praised the president for his steadfast "devotion to the Constitution, the laws and interests of his country ... and in the principles of free government." In him they recognized "a Chief Magistrate worthy of the nation, and equal to the great crisis upon which his lot is cast; and we tender him in the discharge of his high and responsible duties, our profound respect and assurance of our cordial and sincere support."[4]

The accolades showered upon Johnson alarmed the Radicals almost as much as the resolutions so adroitly fashioned to upset their plans for confiscation and military rule. The composition of the delegates also worried the Radicals, giving the convention an appearance that "Democrats were the party of peace and reunion, while the Republicans were in favor of a continuation of the hostile status." Sumner expressed dismay at the outcome of the convention. Referring to his favorite theme of black suffrage, he wrote a friend, "All this might have been easily established had the President gone with Congress. Now we have before us terrible strife and perhaps war again." Some of Sumner's statements breathed spasms of paranoia. When writing John Bright in England, he said, "Before the adjournment of Congress, many persons were satisfied that the President contemplated a coup d'état." Closing his letter on the subject of the recent riot in New Orleans, he added, "Stanton confessed to me that [Johnson] was its author." Sumner's frequent correspondence to Bright illustrates how inadequately the senator understood the motives of Stanton and the altruistic efforts of the president.[5]

When the convention adjourned on August 16, members of the cabinet hurried back to Washington to warn Johnson that Stanton must be removed. Two days later the president met with one hundred delegates from states north and south who collectively urged him to stay the course but remove Stanton. Speaking on behalf of one delegation, Reverdy Johnson castigated the Radicals and implied that Stanton, whom the president had omitted from the meeting, be discharged. Grant and Welles attended the session, the latter writing, "There comes, I see, a strong pressure against Stanton

from Philadelphia. Whether it will have an effect upon him or the President is doubtful. The latter cannot need to be undeceived." Welles noticed that many of the delegates had been connected with the rebellion but had accepted their fate with grace and sincerity. "But the Radicals are filled with hatred, acrimony and revenge toward them," he observed, "and would persist in excluding not only them but the whole people of the South from any participation in the government. For four years war was waged to prevent them from going out, now the Radicals wage as fine a war to shut them out."[6]

With such strong support from Philadelphia, Johnson felt inclined to aid the cause by making a "swing around the circle of the Union." Invitations to speak came from Chicago and elsewhere, and he anxiously accepted the opportunity to stump for those Republicans and Democrats who endorsed his policies. No president prior to Johnson had ever campaigned on his own or his party's behalf. Breaking the precedent required caution—not the customary tactics employed when stumping through the mountains of east Tennessee.[7]

As one historian observed, Johnson's oratory was that of the frontier—"elemental, without finesse, graceless, void of humor, overcharged with intensity, but often overpowering in its sincerity, and persuasive in its downright honesty." He had a finely modulated voice, and no man spoke at critical moments with more power and determination. When overwrought, he sometimes stumbled into grammatical errors, but when under control, he became a master of forceful rhetoric. Having confronted mobs in Tennessee, and having stood before crowds who threatened to shoot him, Andy Johnson thought he could deal with any agitators met along the way. Having a passion for knowledge, he packed his speeches with facts, often spending hours haunting the Congressional Library's archives in search of evidence. His speeches were always "packed with substance," never "frothy and unsubstantial things," but advisors warned him to use care on the circuit.[8]

Though many Democrats supported Johnson, they remembered him as a Republican running on the ticket with Lincoln and as a consequence would not fully support him. Ultra Radicals had already resolved to depose him. For Johnson to seed Congress with friends, he must appeal to both parties — an almost hopeless task. He had become a man without a party because he placed the country first. As a consequence, he became a favorite of neither party.[9]

Johnson also needed friends in the offices of government, but unlike his predecessors, he ignored the executive's prerogative to fill the departments under his purview with allies. Yet the Radicals filled every office within their grab with partisans. Stanton's department swarmed with presidential enemies, and McCulloch discovered the same problem existed with treasury positions filled by Chase. "It is lamented," wrote Welles, "that the President permitted the Radicals to remove his friends and substitute their tools ... [and they] contemplate further infringement on Executive rights, provided they can compact their party to that end."[10]

McCulloch referred to Johnson as "a man of unblemished personal integrity," and what baffled the cabinet was why the president put up with the likes of Stanton and his government paid spies. The president believed that persons in positions of honor would behave in an honorable and forthright manner. For this confidence in his fellowman, he would pay a price for his naivete.[11]

Johnson could only win his battle with Congress by carrying the forthcoming elections. On August 28 the presidential entourage departed from Washington for the so-called swing around the circle. Guests included Seward, Welles, and Randall from the cabinet, the Patterson's from the president's family, Admiral David G. Farragut, General Grant, and a half dozen officers from the army and navy. To no one's surprise, Stanton claimed his wife had taken ill and canceled at the last moment. Johnson planned to make dozens of stops, beginning with Baltimore, Philadelphia, and New York City. Then sweeping across the Empire State to Buffalo, the train would swing west through Cleveland, Toledo, Detroit, and Chicago, strike a southerly course to St. Louis, and return to Washington through Indianapolis, Louisville, Cincinnati, Pittsburgh, and Harrisburg, making brief stops at smaller cities along the way.[12]

Trouble lay ahead. Though supporters turned out in great numbers to greet the party, provide entertainment, fire salutes, and hear what the president had to say, the Radicals arranged for operatives spanning more than thirty congressional districts to disrupt the president's stops. Johnson had prepared but one speech, the theme of which he repeated with some variation at each stop. Welles noted that though the press often misreported or misrepresented what Johnson said, "the speech would do him no discredit as a patriot and a statesman."[13]

The reception at New York exceeded Johnson's expectations. A distinguished committee met the train at Jersey City,

Andrew Johnson's reception in New York during the swing around the circle. (Library of Congress, from Leslie's *Illustrated Weekly*.)

and after a short ceremony continued into New York. As the train crossed the river, warships and forts located in the harbor fired salutes. The entourage landed at the Battery, and from there paraded up Broadway to city hall, accompanied by bands, two regiments of cavalry, the city police, and twenty regiments of New York militia. As the carriages carrying Johnson and his party passed along Broadway, flags fluttered from every staff. Banners stretched across open ways praised the president, one reading; "The Constitution — Washington established it, Lincoln defended it, Johnson preserved it." An immense crowd jammed the streets from curbstone to doorway. The *New York Herald* reported "Every window was filled with happy smiling faces, roofs were crowded while every tree and awning post was alive with men and boys."[14]

That evening the reception commit-tee held a sumptuous banquet at Delmonico's, followed by a cast of speakers extolling Johnson's stand against the Radicals. The affair provided a rejuvenating atmosphere for the president. When the moment came for him to speak, thunderous applause filled the banquet hall. He introduced the members of his party, giving special recognition to General Grant and Admiral Farragut, the latter having recently become a popular resident of New York City. After more rousing cheers, Johnson expressed his deep appreciation for secretary of state Seward, another New Yorker who had served his state and country for more than thirty years. Cheering continued, and the hour drew late before Johnson could speak on the theme that brought him to the city.

His Delmonico speech summarized all the contentious issues before the nation. He renewed his attack on the

Radicals, showing how before the war they had denied the south the right to legally secede, but now with war over, they refused states no longer in rebellion the right to be represented in Congress. Should we, Johnson asked, permit those states to "remain as they are, in practical dissolution?" "No, no—never," the crowd replied. Then, speaking in defense of the integrity of his countrymen below the Mason-Dixon Line, Johnson declared, "They are our brethren. They are part of ourselves. They are bone of our bone and flesh of our flesh." The words brought the listeners to their feet, and men cheered themselves hoarse. "Why," asked Johnson, "is a Southern man not to be believed?" And the audience replied, "They are to be believed," and more applause followed with a frantic waving of handkerchiefs.

As the hall gradually fell silent, Johnson said, "While I am a Southern man, I am a Northern man; that is to say I am a citizen of the United States, and I am willing to concede to all other citizens what I claim for myself." He denounced the Radicals for degrading and debasing those Americans who had been in rebellion, for they had thrown down their arms, taken the oath of allegiance, been pardoned by the executive, and welcomed back into the Union by declaration and proclamation. "I want them to come back with all their manhood," Johnson said, and not with "ignominy and contempt."

As he neared the end of his speech, Johnson explained the cause of the war, comparing it to the hammer and the anvil, one being the secessionists of the south, the other being the abolitionists of the north. While the war dissolved the secessionists, those representing the abolitionists were "still trying to give it life

and effect. I fought those in the South who commenced the rebellion," Johnson explained, "and now I oppose those in the North who are trying to break up the Union. I am for the Union. I am against all those who are opposed to the Union … the whole Union and nothing but the Union." Applause reached a new crescendo before Johnson could finish. Finally he closed by saying, "I find the union of these states in peril. If I can now be instrumental in keeping the possession of it in your hands, in the hands of the people; in restoring prosperity and advancement in all that makes a nation great … that I [will] have seen the glory of thy salvation…. I would rather live in history, in the affection of my countrymen as having consummated this great end, than to be President of the United States forty times."

Johnson made a great speech at Delmonico's, one of his finest. New York City heard and agreed with his denunciation of the Radicals and his fierce determination to defy their abasement of the Constitution. "I am proud," he told them, "to find a liberal and a comprehensive view of this whole question on the part of the people of New York. I am proud to find too that here you don't believe that your existence depends upon aggression and destruction; and while you are willing to live you are willing to let others live."[15]

When leaving Manhattan, the swing around the circle portended good prospects for success, but Johnson and his party would have been better advised had they returned to Washington. Surprised by the president's popularity and appeal in New York City, the Radical network intensified their efforts to undermine his appearances. Their vehicle for disruption became the friendly press and a national network of activists. Though large crowds continued to greet him at every stop, reporters misrepresented his speeches and newspapers used artists to present him in caricature. Critics sneered at his grammatical errors and jeered at his penetrating sentences, but there was never a time that the Radicals did not fear his effect upon a gathering of voters. As a defensive measure, they organized mobs to howl him down as he moved from city to city. Despite increased crowd rowdiness, Johnson delivered the same message in each city, usually leaving his audience with: "I leave in your hands the Constitution and the Union, and the glorious flag of your country not with twenty-five but with thirty-six stars."[16]

So physically demanding had the swing become that when the entourage reached Niagara Falls, friends and family became concerned about the president's health. When Welles advised him to get more rest, Johnson replied that "he was performing a service and a duty in his appeals to his countrymen, and desired to address them face to face on the great issues of the country." He had been accustomed to doing the same in Tennessee and believed his methods could be as effective in the north.[17]

On September 3 the presidential train arrived at Cleveland, where Radicals hoped to prevent Johnson from speaking, or if he did, to embarrass him while doing so. An enormous crowd jammed the lakefront station, and every arriving train added to congestion at the depot. Cleveland police fought thousands in an effort to force a pathway from the presidential train to waiting carriages. When Johnson appeared, shouts erupted in a roar for the president and his entourage. The streets from the depot to the Kennard Hotel on the public square

became a solid mass of humanity. Chinese lanterns hung from the hotel, flags flew from every window, and lights from nearby homes illuminated the streets.[18]

Ohioans had been prompted by the friends of Ben Wade — the man who wanted to become president — and the *Cleveland Herald*, a Radical organ, had already begun its campaign to "belch forth every calumny" of the president. The *Herald* distributed circulars branding the president as renegade, traitor, faithless demagogue, and referred to him as the "man made president by John Wilkes Booth." When Johnson stepped onto the balcony of Cleveland's Kennard House, the disrupters were ready with catcalls and hisses. While the vast majority of the crowd remained decent and attentive, it contained a sprinkling of the scum of the community, many of them drunk and planted by Radicals to insult the chief executive. Most of the audience listened with appreciation, but the mood had drastically changed since New York. Johnson reminded the crowd that if Lincoln had lived, the "mendacious press" and the "subsidized gang of hirelings who have not ceased to traduce me" would have poured their "vials of wrath" upon him.[19]

Radical demonstrators put Johnson on the defensive, and his presentation lacked the persuasive punch he enjoyed in Manhattan. When he stepped to the balcony, he had intended to say a few words and retire. Rowdies circulating below the balcony cursed and jostled the crowd. Scuffles erupted, and Johnson would have been better advised to cut short his appearance, but he had never backed away from a skirmish. Shouts of "traitor" only made him madder. Speaking directly to his audience with resolute firmness and harsh logic, he won back their attention. Then he spoke directly to the troublemakers, reminding them that there "is a portion of your countrymen who will always respect their fellow-citizens when they are entitled to respect, and there is a portion of them who have no respect for themselves and consequently have no respect for others." When someone shouted "Traitor," Johnson invited him to come forward into the light, to show himself so that a reply could be made, or remain in the shadows a coward. No one stepped forward.[20]

The press reported Johnson's open debate with the crowd as undignified, and many historians shared this opinion. Senator Doolittle had warned Johnson he would be followed by "reporters of a hundred presses who do nothing but misrepresent." He also advocated prudence, cautioning the president that what is "said extemporaneously in answer to some questions" will be used against him. One historian, however, recognized that Johnson was engaged in the most desperate political struggle since secession. The president needed to get his message out, and if necessary, to engage in hand-to-hand combat with Lincoln's enemies — "with whom conciliation had proved idle, and soft-spoken words an invitation to new assaults." The president should have heeded Doolittle's warning, but he prided himself at being an effective stump speaker. Knowing this, Radical organizations in every city along the president's route turned out battalions of paid agitators.[21]

While the president addressed Clevelanders, the Radicals held a convention in Philadelphia for the express purpose of "bringing the loyal Unionists of the South into conjunctive action with the North." This made good rhetoric, but the true objective was to eradicate the positive effects achieved by Johnson's convention held in the same city of brotherly love twenty days earlier. Another issue concerned the promotion and passage of the Fourteenth Amendment. Republicans intended to make it "the leading feature of the campaign, to enforce it in every party convention, to urge it through the press, to present it on the stump [and] to proclaim it through every authorized exponent of public opinion."[22]

The so-called loyal Unionists represented a smattering of southerners who had not joined their neighbors in rebellion. They came mainly from the mountainous districts in east Tennessee, north Georgia, and North Carolina. They were few in number and not well positioned economically, socially, or influentially. From this small core of "loyal Unionists" the Radicals planned, in conjunction with black suffrage and the help of military tribunals, to create a lasting source of Republican power within the nation. When the "loyal Unionists" arrived at the convention, one observer admitted that they "compared unfavorably in character and ability ... and for the most part were soldiers of political fortune." Northern delegates avoided fraternizing with southerners, and the convention split into two dissimilar groups threaded together by common political interests.[23]

Republicans launched their convention by awarding the permanent chairmanship to James Speed. If they intended to undermine Johnson, what better place to start than having as their chairman the president's former attorney general. Speed, who after spending fifteen months in Johnson's cabinet, set the tone of the convention. For five days he reviled his former chief with a storm of vituperations. He devoted two of the days to the business of the southern "loyalists," who reciprocated by denouncing Johnson's policies as "oppressive and intolerable." The "loyalists" were no defenders of the Constitution. Their resolutions expressed the radical dogma of men like Sumner and Stevens. Referring to the political status of the south, they declared that "the rights of the people of such states are political questions, and are therefore *already within the control of Congress to the exclusion of the independent action of any and every other department of the Government.*" Hence, Congress intended to take over the government, including the Supreme Court as well as Andrew Johnson. Anybody reading the carefully crafted "loyalist" resolution must find Speed's hand in drafting it. Of the nine southern states represented at the convention, only two, Alabama and North Carolina, voted against the resolution. By using "loyalists" to help promote the underlying Radical agenda, the press became a willing tool of the Republicans in deceiving the public. As a consequence, the president experienced an increase of crowd disruptions midway through his swing around the circle.[24]

Beginning with the stop in Cleveland, the Radical press became intensely involved in the campaign to undermine Johnson's efforts to muster support. They reported his back-and-forth banter with the crowd as further proof of presidential intoxication, diminishing his every appearance to that of a low comic drunkenly lurching his way from city to city. Because the press said it, some historians believed it, but one correspondent who accompanied Johnson throughout the tour later wrote that "there was no sign of drunkenness at all on the trip." Denials, however, never carry as much weight as accusations.[25]

On the morning after the Cleveland speech, the train steamed westward, but Grant was not on it. To his wife, the general wrote that the president's free-swinging speeches made him "exceedingly uncomfortable." Black flags greeted the president as the entourage sped by Elyria. After a brief stop at Toledo, the party detrained at Detroit. Johnson noticed Grant's absence. Radicals had hoped that Grant would not waste "political capital" by making the tour with Johnson, but the general felt obligated. Historians who accused Johnson of drunkenness had the wrong man. Only Grant drank heavily during the tour. Admiral Farragut's wife described the general as so "stupidly communicative" that friends at Cleveland put him on a Detroit-bound boat "to conceal his shame." But at stops along the way, Johnson could not help noticing that while agitators hurled insults on him, the same persons clamored for the sight of Grant.[26]

Since the beginning of the tour, Chicago had been the objective. Though local authorities refused to welcome him, Windy City supporters provided a "magnificent" reception. Radicals, however, had prepared for Johnson's arrival. They hired a band to play the "Dead March," draped banners along the way reading "No Welcome to Traitors," and dispensed other demeaning insults.[27]

Johnson stopped briefly at Springfield to visit Lincoln's tomb, only to be condemned by Mary Lincoln for making an unwanted pilgrimage to her husband's resting place. She boycotted the visit, so the president continued on to Alton where thirty-six steamers, each representing a state of the Union, picked up the passengers and carried them to St. Louis. The city extended "unsurpassed" cordiality, but it soon became evident that Radicals lately in Philadelphia were now in St. Louis and dogging the footsteps of the president. They mingled among a crowd gathering outside the city's Southern Hotel and demanded a speech. Johnson had not prepared a speech, but the rowdy crowd threatened to get out of control.

He made the mistake of responding to the call and walked into a trap set by enemies. Once again, instead of quickly extricating himself, he rallied his supporters and fought it out with the hecklers. While doing so, he heartily vociferated against the Radical doctrine. Though there were "Hurrahs for Andy Johnson," the agitators shouted blasphemy when Johnson accused Sumner, Stevens, and Wendell Phillips of comparing themselves to the Savior.

Johnson's fiery impromptu speech poured more fuel into the inferno being prepared for him by his enemies. The mendacious press ridiculed him, and for the second time during the swing around the circle, Johnson made the mistake of becoming controversially embroiled in a public gathering. Even his advisers, who had encouraged him to speak publicly, though briefly, now wished he had not done so.[28]

When Johnson's train pulled into Indianapolis, Radical opposition staged a riot in the public square, killing one man. Placards ringed the depot: "We want nothing to do with traitors." Yet during the war Johnson had often come to Indiana, always to be greeted by enormous gatherings of wildly enthusiastic supporters. The president wisely said nothing and rolled on to Louisville. For several days, Welles noticed "an extreme Radical conspiracy to treat the President with disrespect and indignity" wherever he went.[29]

The tour continued with mixed results. Louisville provided a grand reception, but Seward fell ill with cholera and had to be sent home on a separate train. For Johnson, not having Seward beside him created an emptiness he could not replace. The reliable minister provided the president with the best advice money could buy. At times he sheltered the executive to keep him away from confrontations with Radical ringleaders, many of whom he knew on an intimate basis. During the swing around the circle Seward had made the introductions, usually saying, "Here is Grant. He has done his duty. Here is Farragut, who has done his duty. Here is the President, who has done his duty, and now you men who vote, — you are to do yours." Since the death of Lincoln, Seward had lost his wife and his daughter, but he stayed at his post and faithfully prosecuted the office of state with consummate ability. Johnson could not afford to lose him.[30]

Grant had been wanting an excuse to separate himself from Johnson, and when the steamboat docked at Cincinnati, he temporarily detached himself to visit his father. During the trip he had frequently sought solace in the baggage car, presumably to puff on a cigar. "But," said Welles, "first at Detroit, then at Chicago, St. Louis and Cincinnati, it became obvious that he had begun to listen to the seductive appeals of the Radical conspirators." Grant made no outward gesture suggesting that he resented being dragged around the country as the president's icon, but he confided to his wife that "I have never been so tired of anything before as I have been with the political speeches of Mr. Johnson from Washington to this place. I look upon them as a national disgrace." He cautioned his wife to not share his feelings with anyone, but Welles observed subtle changes in Grant's demeanor. The Radicals were looking down the road to the 1868 elections, and who better to pit against Johnson than Grant.[31]

At Columbus the public seemed more interested in chatting with Grant than listening to Johnson. "Great pains have been taken by partisans to misrepresent the President," Welles observed, "and prejudice the people against him. There is a special vindictiveness and disregard of truth by members of Congress everywhere." The few dignitaries on hand to greet the president did not include the governor.[32]

When the train pulled into Pittsburgh a hostile mob surrounded it. They cheered Grant and Farragut but would not let Johnson speak, so the train moved on to Harrisburg. A small crowd — minus the governor — met them at the station, and the entourage expressed relief at being able to take a carriage, without crowd molestation, into the city for supper. During the meal a messenger came to the table and informed Johnson that Seward lay in a car at the depot unable to be moved and on the verge of death. Welles accompanied the president to the station and watched as Seward feebly grasped Johnson's hand, muttering, "My mind is clear, and I wish at this time to say that your course is right, that I have felt my duty to sustain you in it, and if my life is spared, I shall continue to do so. Pursue it for the sake of the country, it is correct." The words came as a great relief to Johnson. Seward soon rallied and, though worn and noticeably weakened, resumed his post in the cabinet.[33]

On September 15, nineteen days after the swing around the circle commenced, the travelers returned to Washington threadbare and discouraged at the outcome. Johnson expressed the conviction that though the tour fell short of meeting his expectations, it would nonetheless help bolster support for Lincoln's plan of reconstruction. Welles admitted that while Johnson may have garnered some support, the Radical press had diminished the effort, and given time, would nullify it entirely. Senator Doolittle, a staunch supporter of the president, woefully claimed that Johnson's reaction to crowd agitation "lost to our cause" 200,000 votes. One researcher observed that Johnson's speeches went amiss because he never took time to prepare them in detail, which led to blunders and a deficiency of needful diplomacy. The president, however, remained unchagrined. "His manner was absolutely as when he first took upon himself the cares of office," wrote Colonel Crook." He made no reference to the trip, and "there was not an added line in his face."[34]

The president no longer cared about party politics. He would accept support from whomever would give it — Republican, Democrat, or any voter in between. What he needed most for the forthcoming election were endorsements from those who still stood with him on the preservation of the Constitution. Endorsements, however, came in dribbles and too often from former officers of the south. After the war, ex-Lieutenant General Nathan Bedford Forrest became, according to Francis P. Blair, "more powerful than ... any man in West Tennessee." General Howard, chief of the Freedmen's Bureau, believed that Forrest "is disposed to do everything that is fair and right for the Negroes which might be employed." Like most southern generals, Forrest suppressed his resentment at seeing certain privileges denied whites given to blacks. He read newspapers voraciously and learned of the president's plight midway through the tour. During a gathering of former Confederate officers at Memphis, Forrest joined in sending a telegram endorsing the president's efforts to rally support in the next election. The message fell into the hands of the Radicals, thereby bolstering Sumner's charge that Johnson had gone over to the enemy. Senator Blaine declared that no other circumstance so deeply affected northern opinion as the telegram signed by Forrest, whose antecedents included slave peddling and, during the war, the Fort Pillow massacre of federal soldiers.[35]

Johnson mustered support in cities such as New York and Chicago, but not enough to make a difference. The radical propaganda sweep dominated the press. It could not be subdued by truth, honesty, or factual evidence. Try as he may, Johnson could not capture the confidence of the country. One advocate declared, "I thank God that Andrew Johnson is what he is, and not what his assailants wish him to be"—kind words, but only words. Vetoes could no longer quell the tempest roaring across the country—nor could votes.[36]

10

The Elections of 1866

As election day approached, Sumner's impeachment threat issued ten months earlier gathered momentum, swirling across the country and unifying the efforts of Radicals to secure a solid two-thirds majority in both houses. Newspapers and orators borrowed a phrase from Sumner's annual speech, referring to Johnson as the "presidential obstacle." They asked the public if justice could be served by enabling rebels who had killed their fathers, brothers, and sons to be brought back to the seat of government. Fanned by the flames of hatred, prejudice, and passion, the public responded to the Radical propaganda machine and denounced Johnson "as a traitor because he does not repel and persecute the beaten Rebels."[1]

The problem magnified when Radical organs spread outright lies. A Philadelphia paper charged Johnson with asking his attorney general for an opinion on his right to "send a message to 'an illegal and unconstitutional assemblage pretending to be the Congress of the United States.'" According to the *Ledger,* Johnson wanted to know whether his oath of office "required him to enforce those provisions of the Constitution which give to each State an equal right of representation in Congress." The article accused the president of planning a coup d'état — a favorite theme introduced by

Sumner. An obscure retraction printed days later did not alleviate the damage to the president. Such were the nationwide actions of the Radicals.[2]

Radical candidates comprised a cast of characters having questionable credentials — men such as former Major General Benjamin F. Butler, who had used the war to enrich himself; John Morrissey, an ex-boxer and gambler; and James Ashley, Stanton's friend from Toledo. Butler, a Democrat turned Radical, ran for Congress in a district where he did not live. Despite his tarnished war record, the voters of Massachusetts returned their popular general to Congress as a Republican. Ashley brought no credentials. Having been a druggist, he joined the Radicals to dispense his poisons through fellow members of the House. Described as a short, fat man with a clean shaven face and bushy hair, Ashley provided no aptitude for intellectual situations and became "splendid material" for promoting the schemes of Stevens. Having once been caught offering bribes for political favors, Ashley fit nicely into the brood of Radicals.[3]

Butler brought to the House the credentials of an ultra Radical. Over the years he had acquired the reputation of being a shrewd lawyer with sharply honed political skills. After plundering Louisiana in 1862 and embarrassing himself in 1864 as a military commander in Virginia, Butler, at the age of forty-eight, sought redemption by adopting the Radical cause. The idea of raiding all the states of the south while maintaining political dominance through black suffrage appealed to him. Ousting Johnson, however, became an even more tempting challenge. After being stigmatized by a shabby military performance, Butler needed to reassert himself as a political power, and joining the Republicans provided that opportunity. He did not limit his campaign to the district nominating him. He stumped throughout the north, extolling the virtues of the Fourteenth Amendment and denouncing Johnsonism. "Impeach him and remove him now," demanded Butler. "Let the sergeant at arms place him under arrest and tell him that unless he does as told, the boys in blue will make him." By election day the Republicans considered Butler "one of the most valuable spokesmen of their cause."[4]

Never had there been a campaign so mendacious and bitter as the one waged by Republicans in 1866. Aside from loyal cabinet members, Andrew Johnson faced the attacks alone. During the swing around the circle he had placed his case before the people. But the real issues seemed scattered to the wind by a Radical tempest of propaganda and abuse. September election returns from Maine and Vermont boded ill for the president.

October elections in Pennsylvania, Ohio, Indiana, and Iowa gave the Radicals impressive majorities. Johnson did not have to wait for returns from other northern states to know his administration had been defeated. In the Senate, Sumner's fondest hopes materialized when he learned that forty-two Republicans would stand against only eleven

Democrats. In the House, the Radical margin remained overwhelming with 143 Republicans and only 49 Democrats. Johnson fully expected to engage in serious battles with Congress during the next two years, but he did not consider impeachment a serious threat because he had broken no laws. Southerners, however, predicted their doom, one writing to another, "We may read our destiny in the indications just at hand from the Northern elections — utter ruin and abject degradation are our portion."[5]

Welles blamed the failure of Democrats on "equal folly and selfishness ... to install their old party organization in force, regardless of the true interest of the country.... The consequence has been that instead of reinstating themselves they have established the Radicals more strongly in power." Writing from Maine, Fessenden summed up the problem differently. Aside from the swing around the circle, he blamed the president's defeat on Seward's policies, citing allegations that some government posts had been put up for sale by unnamed politicians attached to the administration. Seward's practices were above reproach, but during his long years in politics he gathered many personal enemies. Neither Radicals nor Democrats liked him. To support the president, Democrats wanted recognition through political patronage. Johnson refused to replace Seward, but had he spread patronage among Democrats, he would have gotten their support. But Johnson stuck to the party that had elected him, even though the Republicans no longer wanted him, and he continued to grant appointments to officials who did not support him.[6]

In late November Radical leaders filed back to Washington to organize the agenda for their followers. The objectives remained unchanged — to remove Johnson and install Wade in his place; to disrupt the southern governments; to divide the south into military districts; and to legislate black suffrage and disenfranchise whites. Stevens, growing feebler by the day, became more domineering as he felt his life flickering away. Reflecting on the issues, Welles observed that "If Thad Stevens gets his caucus machinery at work, he will grind out the refractory and make them timid guilty participants.... Afraid of Stevens, they shrink from the avowal of an honest policy.... The threat of impeachment is less loud for the past few days, but the extreme Radicals will press it if they have a shadow of hope that they can succeed." Stevens understood his power. Welles called it "Genius and audacity without wisdom, imagination but not sagacity, cunning but not principle."[7]

In the battle for the blacks, Johnson set aside some of his fundamental prejudices in an effort to convey the impression that Radicals were using freedmen for partisan purposes while he was their true friend. Though he received ex-slaves at the White House, his token gestures lacked the sincerity and will necessary to be convincing.[8]

On December 3, 1866, Andrew Johnson sent his annual message to Congress — a mild report expressing hope that "a restoration of fraternal feeling must be the earnest wish of every patriotic heart," promising that with it "we will have accomplished our grandest national achievement, forgetting the sad events of the past ... [as we] resume our onward career as a free, prosperous, and united people." Much of what Johnson said paraphrased his 1865 message. He restated his annoyance that elected representatives from ten southern states had

not been permitted to take their seats. By denying their admission, Johnson warned Congress that "our relations as one people" will be threatened and "become a serious cause for discontent on the part of the inhabitants of those states" for many years to come. He knew his words would fall on deaf ears, but he made his case prophetically clear and closed by adding, "The interests of the nation are best to be promoted by the revival of fraternal relations, the complete obliteration of our past differences, and the reinauguration of all the pursuits of peace." While a few newspapers praised Johnson for delivering a dignified and statesmanlike message, Horace Greeley's *Tribune* attacked the president as an enemy of the people — an obstructionist who failed to aid Congress in the work of reconstruction. Greeley set the stage for new legislation, writing, "The truth is, there *is* but one question of moment remaining to be settled; and that is Manhood Suffrage. Enfranchise the Blacks, and further rebellions at the South are impossible; and we can have a great National party, which can hopefully contest every State in the Union." The *London Telegraph* took Johnson's side, writing that the United States "may remain a republic in name, but some eight million of the people are subjects, not citizens."[9]

Congress aided its agenda on the opening day of the second session. Through black leaders in Washington, Sumner organized a march to the Capitol in support of suffrage. More than a thousand residents complied. During the parade Sumner introduced a bill for the immediate enfranchisement of blacks in the District of Columbia. Stevens brought the House together to support the measure. Since Congress had the constitutional power to decide who should vote in the District of Columbia, the bill was valid. However, it denied the franchise to persons who had "voluntarily given aid and comfort to the rebels of the late rebellion." To his colleagues Sumner explained the bill as an "opening wedge" to form "an example for the whole country." It was not enough to grant the franchise to just those who could read and write, he declared. By giving to those alone, "you will not secure the new allies which are essential to the national cause!"— new allies being the blacks, and the national cause being the retention of Radical power. When Democrats suggested that women also be granted the franchise, Sumner cast it aside as a "great question for the future"— but not now.[10]

The suffrage bill passed both Houses, and on December 26 — six days after Congress adjourned for Christmas — it arrived at the White House. "There is not a Senator who votes for this bill," Welles observed, "who does not know that it is an abuse and wrong. Most of the negroes of this district are wholly unfit to be electors…. It is pitiable to see how little sense of right, real independence, and what limited comprehension are possessed by our legislators. They are the tame victims and participators of villainous conspirators."[11]

Johnson discussed the bill with the cabinet. All but Stanton, who had come to the meeting with a prepared statement, agreed upon a veto. Stanton said he had read the bill and regarded it constitutionally sound. Grant, who happened to be at the meeting, disagreed with Stanton on the grounds that Congress should not be granting black suffrage in the District of Columbia without first doing so in their own states. In the press

Elizabeth Cady Stanton spoke out on women's rights, asking why intelligent white women of property were not considered as much entitled to a vote as the "semi-barbarous negroes of the islands of Charleston." Women voters were not what the Radicals wanted because they would throw their support to the Democrats.[12]

On January 5, 1867, Johnson vetoed the bill, arguing that the measure had been tested at Washington and Georgetown in 1865 and defeated by more than ninety-nine percent of the voters. With Sumner in mind, he accused the Senate of disregarding the will of the inhabitants of the district. He also made reference to Massachusetts, where "male persons are allowed to vote without regard to color, provided they possess a certain degree of intelligence." He suggested that if Congress wished to extend the franchise to blacks in the District of Columbia, the new voters should follow the same popular right used by citizens of a state or territory, meaning that before new legislation affecting social and economic conditions were imposed on the public, an election should be held. Johnson gave Congress a lesson in civics, explaining that "The exercise of the elective franchise is the highest attribute of the American citizen, and when guided by virtue, intelligence, patriotism, and a proper appreciation of our institutions, constitutes the true basis of a democratic form of government in which the sovereign power is lodged in the body of the people." The Senate ignored the veto and overrode it by a vote of twenty-nine to ten. Before the veto reached the House, Stevens whipped together a two-thirds majority, and the bill passed. The veto, however, sparked another outburst in the House, and Benjamin F. Loan of

Missouri added his voice to the growing clamor for Johnson's impeachment.[13]

Also in December Ben Wade revisited an old issue and offered new bills for the admission of Colorado and Nebraska. Wade might have been less obvious in his quest for the presidency had he not goaded one of his cronies into presenting the bills. He wanted the assurance of more votes in the Senate if Sumner's plans for Johnson's impeachment materialized sooner rather than later. To stimulate interest in the bills, Wade informed the Senate that Colorado and Nebraska were ready to "assist you in carrying out your great principles." Many in the Senate knew what Wade meant by "great principles" and were not so anxious to make him president. Knowing that a comfortable two-thirds majority would be in place with the 40th Congress, some senators wanted the matter dropped. Sumner agreed with the bill, aiding Wade in its passage, and for a second time, both bills went by messenger to the White House.[14]

On January 28, 1867, Johnson vetoed the Colorado bill, and the following day the Nebraska bill. He reiterated all his previous arguments and submitted additional data to support his premise that neither territory had sufficient population to justify representation in Congress. The Senate failed to override the president's veto on the Colorado bill, but Wade won a partial victory when in March 1867, the Senate repassed the Nebraska bill.[15]

While the Senate labored to pass its agenda, Stevens brought the House together on the first day of the session to begin work on one of the most controversial bills ever introduced by either chamber. Operating at light speed, he created the Tenure of Office Bill. He did so without waiting to see what the president proposed in his second annual message. After the bill passed the House, Johnson's message arrived. Stevens contemptuously declared the document too long, but his motion failed to postpone its reading until the following day.[16]

Stanton contributed to Stevens' urgency in passing the bill. During a private meeting with Colfax and Boutwell, Stanton claimed that orders had been issued to the army by the president without the war department's knowledge. He suggested a conspiracy "by the President to reorganize the government by the assembling of Congress in which the members from the seceding states and the Democratic members from the North might attain control through the aid of the Executive." Stanton knew nothing would horrify the Radicals more than a presidential coup d'état, so he outlined a way for Congress to limit executive power. His plan required that Congress make Grant the funnel through which Johnson must send all orders to the army. It specified that the president must not move Grant from Washington without congressional consent. Furthermore, Johnson must disband militias in the south. Colfax and Boutwell departed with the drafted bill and handed it to Stevens. Delighted with a method to handcuff Johnson, Stevens reached beyond Stanton's inspiration to a more insidious concept. Why not make Stanton the sole authority for army communications and limit the president's power to remove him?[17]

Stanton may not have realized — though he probably did — that he had helped set the stage for a new onslaught on Johnson: the isolation of the president from control of the vital elements of his own administration. Stevens' joint committee enhanced Stanton's proposal by drafting the Tenure of Office Bill. The bill specified that every person, except members of the cabinet, "holding any civil office to which he has been appointed by and with the advice and consent of the Senate ... shall be entitled to hold office until a successor shall have been in like manner appointed and duly qualified." In effect, Johnson could no longer remove civil officers whose tenure was not limited by law without the advice and consent of the Senate. On the first day of the session, George H. Williams of Oregon introduced the bill to the Senate. Sumner had nothing to do with framing the bill, but he enthusiastically supported any attempt to restrain Johnson from removing his subordinates, arguing that "the Senate was less liable to become depraved and bad than the president."[18]

For the first eighteen months of his administration, Johnson had made few changes of personnel in civil offices. After his swing around the circle, he removed 1,283 postmasters and weeded out some of Chase's appointees. This caused much rancor among the Radical's constituencies. Secretary of the treasury McCulloch found none of the changes objectionable, writing a friend, "The President desires to make as few changes as possible, and none on political grounds unless it is clear that the interests of the service, or the interests of the administration are to be clearly benefited by them."[19]

Never had a president's authority to hire or fire civil employees been questioned, and only a small class of appointees required the advice and consent of the Senate. While the Constitution is clear on the process of approving the appointments of ambassadors, cabinet members, and "all other officers of the United States whose appointments are not herein otherwise provided for and which shall be established by law," the Constitution is silent on the subject of removal.

James Madison, who authored much of the document, contended with compelling logic that the Constitution gave the president the right, without the advice and consent of the Senate, to remove officers whom he appointed, and the power of removal was incident to the power of appointment. In the final bill, words were added providing for an officer called the Chief Clerk of the Department of Foreign Affairs, who, "*whenever the principal officer* [being the secretary of state] *shall be removed from office by the President ... shall during such vacancy have charge.*" The bill passed and on July 27, 1789, George Washington signed it into law. For seventy-seven years the president's right to remove any person in the executive branch of government had been the law. Now the Radicals wanted to change it with the Tenure of Office Bill.[20]

Fearing that Johnson would choose men opposed to the Radical platform, the Senate blocked appointments for the Supreme Court. In doing so they had in mind the forthcoming Milligan case. Though they had an ally in Chief Justice Chase, four of the justices had been appointed by Lincoln and one each by Buchanan, Polk, Tyler, and Johnson, leaving in May 1865, another vacancy to be filled. The Radicals worried most about the five justices appointed by Lincoln and Johnson. The outcome of the Milligan case threatened to overturn the Freedmen's Bureau and its military tribunals. When Johnson nominated attorney general Stanbery to fill the vacancy on the Supreme Court, the Senate contemptuously refused confirmation. Three months later they passed a law stipulating that no vacancies were to be filled until the number of judges fell to seven.[21]

The Milligan case emanated from the Civil War when a citizen of Indiana by the name of Lambdin P. Milligan, joined the "Knights of the Golden Circle"—an organization of Democrat Copperheads opposed to the war and advocating the formation of a northwestern confederacy. On October 5, 1864, Major General Alvin P. Hovey, military commandant of the district of Indiana, arrested Milligan with several others and charged them with a long list of disloyal activities. Nine days before his scheduled execution on May 19, 1865, Milligan obtained a writ of habeas corpus from the circuit court of Indiana praying that he be tried by a proper civil tribunal or be discharged from custody. He claimed that having never been in military service, he should be tried, if at all, after indictment by a grand jury in courts duly authorized by the state. Thus Milligan, who one historian considered a "worthless scamp," initiated a landmark case that threatened to remove military tribunals where state courts had been established to adjudicate civil crimes.[22]

During the week of March 6, 1866—two months after Congress adopted the Fourteenth Amendment, and at the time when the contest between Johnson and Congress began to polarize beyond reconciliation—the Supreme Court argued the Milligan case. The "worthless scamp" had the benefit of representation from three of the country's distinguished lawyers, Jeremiah Black, James A. Garfield, and David Dudley Field. James Speed and Benjamin F. Butler argued to sustain the military court. Black's learned defense left Speed and Butler outclassed and all but speechless. Chase listened but said little.

On April 3 the Supreme Court announced unanimously that the military court condemning Milligan and his associates had done so without lawful power. When Congress asked the Supreme Court upon what grounds the decision had been made, the judges said they would not reply until next winter. The delay caused concern in Congress and with the president because each held an opposing interest in the ruling. The Freedmen's Bureau Act established military tribunals in the south for the express purpose of superseding state courts on civil rights issues and certain other matters. Johnson called the military tribunals illegal, and now it appeared that the Supreme Court agreed with him. Though warned by moderates to accept the Fourteenth Amendment as the best settlement he could obtain, Johnson did not wait for the court's opinion. Instead, he actively interfered with the ratification of the amendment and ordered a halt to military trials of civilians in the south. His action thrust confusion on civil rights legislation and the Freedmen's Bureau, as well as the war department's regulations regarding the military occupation of the south.[23]

Stanton and Grant found themselves in the awkward position of obeying a presidential proclamation inconsistent with legislation passed by Congress. They collaborated on a solution and issued a secret circular placing bureau commanders in the ambiguous position of complying with the president's proclamation while retaining in reserve the martial authority Congress prescribed in the habeas corpus, Freedmen's Bureau, and Civil Rights acts. The confidential circular stated that Johnson's policy did not remove martial law, but it would not be expedient "to resort to military tribunals where justice can be attained through the medium of civil authority." The wordage of the circular fell short of defining "justice" and left that matter to the "discretion" of each officer.[24]

Eight and a half months later Judge David Davis published the opinion of the court, writing that "martial law can never exist when the courts are open, and in the proper and unobstructed exercises of their jurisdiction. It is also confined to the locality of actual war." The opinion became one of the bulwarks of American liberty and fully vindicated the president's opposition to the military controls imposed by the Freedmen's Bureau Act.[25]

The Radicals excoriated the Supreme Court for the decision and induced Chase to write another opinion. Perhaps the *Cleveland Herald* gave Chase a nudge when it suggested that "Congress will reorganize the court." The chief justice faced a dilemma. After being reminded by Radical friends that judges could also be impeached, Chase worried that the ruling might upset his still cherished hope of becoming president. In response to stimulation from the Senate, Chase collaborated with three judges to produce a second opinion, one that upheld the ruling of the court but allowed, under certain circumstances, that "trial and punishment by military commission, in states where civil courts are open, may be authorized by Congress, as well as arrest and detention." The chief justice appeared to be talking out of both sides of his mouth. He succeeded, however, in accomplishing the intended purpose — leaving matters in the south not much changed from how Radicals wanted them.

Anyone reading Chase's opinion might apply either interpretation they wished.[26]

Stevens, however, anticipated trouble. He denounced the Supreme Court's decision and sought advice from Stanton. After a lengthy discussion, Stevens considered impeaching the justices along with the president, from whom, he said, "all the evils flow." "Evils" seemed to occur anywhere Stevens encountered opposition. He told a reporter that "some stringent measures" would be forthcoming to "protect the country from the evil tendencies of the Supreme Court." The Radical press suggested that the Supreme Court "be swamped by a thorough reorganization" and an increase in the number of judges.[27]

Opinions of the Supreme Court meant little more than a nuisance to Stevens. He had a bigger program underway. On December 17, 1866, the very day Davis issued his opinion in the Milligan case, Ashley introduced a motion supported by Stevens to impeach the president. To the chamber he shouted, "I do impeach Andrew Johnson, *Vice-President and acting President of the United States* for high crimes and misdemeanors. I charge him with a usurpation of power and violation of law: In that he has corruptly used the appointing power; in that he has corruptly used the pardoning power; in that he has corruptly used the veto power…, interfered with elections and committed acts which in contemplation of the Constitution are high crimes and misdemeanors."[28]

By a vote of 108 to 38, the House passed the resolution. Colfax referred the matter to the judiciary committee, asking for an investigation to determine whether Johnson "had been guilty of acts which are designed or calculated to overthrow, subvert or corrupt the government of the United States or any department thereof." The committee worked eleven months trying to formulate answers to questions from its members — What is impeachment? What represents "treason, bribery, or other high crimes and misdemeanors?" Who had the power to make the charge — "The House of Representatives ... shall have the sole power of impeachment" — that is, to make the charge. What court tries impeachment? — "The Senate shall have the sole power to try impeachments." Who presides at the trial? — "When the President is tried, the Chief Justice shall preside." Never had a president been impeached, and the judiciary committee worked with little enthusiasm for the task. At one point Senator Grimes, a moderate from Iowa, declared against the investigation, warning his colleagues that their effort would "establish an example which might result in making ours a sort of South American republic where the ruler is deposed the moment popular sentiment sets against him."[29]

One day after the House acted to investigate the impeachment of the president, they overrode Johnson's argument against the Fourteenth Amendment by a vote of 113 to 38. Now the two-thirds majority in both Houses flexed their muscle with the power to do whatever they wished. If the Constitution became an impediment, they could simply shove it aside by creating new amendments. Nothing could stop them but resistance from new members or refusal by the states to ratify.[30]

Frustrated by the judicial committee's lack of action on impeachment, Stevens eventually transferred the investigation to his own Committee on Reconstruction and began to hold hearings. When several committee members argued that Johnson had committed no crimes or misdemeanors, Stevens became furious. In frustration he said, though insincerely, "I shall never bring up this question of impeachment again," yet he continued to pursue the matter with a vengeance. But for the moment Stevens had a more important matter in mind — the formulation of his own punitive Reconstruction Bill.[31]

11

The Reconstruction Act

On December 4, 1866, one day after the passage of the Tenure of Office Bill, Stevens reappointed the Joint Committee on Reconstruction. The main members — Bingham of Ohio, Boutwell of Massachusetts, Elihu B. Washburne of Illinois, and Justin S. Morrill of Vermont — remained with Stevens on the committee to carry out the anti-Johnson agenda of the Radicals. Once again they decided to deny southerners their seats. Because the committee did not trust the president, it passed a motion to call the 40th Congress into session on March 4, as soon as the 39th adjourned, instead of waiting until December. Stevens had developed his plans thoroughly and looked to incoming members like Ben Butler to help in bringing them to fruition.[1]

Though aware of the momentum building against him in Congress, Johnson stayed his course. On January 8 he met with the cabinet to discuss ways of preventing Stevens from stripping the south of statehood and reverting it to territories. He suggested issuing a proclamation granting a more extended amnesty, much like Lincoln had first done in September 1862. He sought a united opinion of the cabinet on the issues before him, feeling that whatever he did would hold more weight if everyone agreed. "He was pale and calm," Welles observed, "But no one could mistake that he was determined in his purpose."[2]

Every member of the cabinet but Stanton enthusiastically denounced Stevens' concept of territorializing the south. Though he said he agreed with the president, Stanton also claimed he had "communicated his views to no man" but had "assented to and cordially approved every step" taken to rehabilitate the states and "saw no cause to change or depart from it." He went on to say that he had not spoken "with Sumner or anyone else" for a year, and that he did not concur with the view that a state could be "remanded to a territorial condition." These words came from a man who five weeks earlier had met privately with Colfax and Boutwell to express concern that Johnson might take over the government. During that meeting Stanton had drafted language for a bill to protect himself, and a few days later Stevens introduced the Tenure of Office Bill. Could all this be coincidence?[3]

Though for eighteen months both McCulloch and Welles had viewed Stanton as "false and treacherous" and "a steady spy," forty years passed before the relationship between the war secretary and the Radicals irrefutably surfaced. Referring to Stanton, one historian said, "This strange personage, whose amazing record of duplicity strongly suggests the vagaries of an opium eater, assumed now the task of inspiring in Congress the belief that his chief, the President, was a desperate character, bent on overriding the majority by military force." Stevens never expressed any fear that Johnson would attempt a coup d'état, but it worked to his advantage to have his more gullible colleagues believe it. Why Johnson retained Stanton in his cabinet remains a puzzle. It no doubt gives credence to the opinions of many that the secretary possessed the skills of an accomplished "sneak."[4]

Johnson's thoughts on granting further amnesty emanated from two recent rulings of the Supreme Court involving men who had refused to take the oath of allegiance. One, a former member of the Confederate congress named Garland, had been pardoned by Johnson in July 1865. The other, a southern clergyman named Cummings, claimed to have not supported the rebellion. In Cummings' case, Justice Field wrote on January 24 that since the southern states had been reformed, they were no different than any sovereign state under the Constitution. Citizens of such were not required to take oaths of allegiance. Garland's case tested Johnson's power of pardon, and the court ruled that a president's constitutional power was unlimited as to all crimes against the United States, except in cases of impeachment. "This power of the President," wrote Field, "is not subject to legislative control. Congress can neither limit the effect of pardon, nor exclude from its exercise any class of offenders. The benign prerogatives of mercy reposed in him cannot be fettered by any legislative restrictions…. When the pardon is full, it releases the punishment and blots out the existence of the guilt, so that in the eye of the law the offender

is as innocent as if he had never committed the offence."[5]

The two decisions startled the Radicals. While one ruling banished oaths of allegiance, the other opened the door for Johnson to exercise more presidential pardons. According to the Supreme Court, Congress could do nothing short of impeachment to stop him. All the plans of the Radicals would be undermined unless they could get rid of the court right along with the president. However, four of the nine judges had dissented in the case, among them Chief Justice Chase, and since Chase still aspired to the 1868 presidential nomination, the Radicals considered him receptive to a back alley bargain. Instead of approaching Chase directly — but knowing he was listening — Radicals let the press do the work of denouncing the Supreme Court for incompetent decisions in the Cummings and Garland cases.[6]

After hearing Field's opinion on January 24, Benjamin Loan of Missouri again rose in the House to call for Johnson's impeachment. Knowing whatever he said would find its way to the press, he nonsensically accused the president of conspiracy in the assassination of Lincoln. Colfax and Stevens each had an opportunity to squelch Loan's crude attack, but since it served their purpose, they permitted it to continue. Stevens had started the ball rolling on January 7 when he said, "Yes, sir, I think he ought to be impeached, but I am not willing to go into the matter hastily; when it is done, it ought to be done thoroughly and certainly." Such support from Stevens gave men like Loan and Ashley encouragement to keep the matter alive by floating periodic resolutions of impeachment. Ashley, coached by Colfax and Stevens, set about the task of seeking incriminating evidence by either purchase or fabrication. Though such allegations were absurd, Welles feared that Stevens' endorsement of the effort would eventually lead to trouble for the president.[7]

Because of contrary Supreme Court decisions, the Radicals worried about the ratification of the Fourteenth Amendment. After an optimistic start in June and July when Connecticut, New Hampshire, and Tennessee ratified, the year ended with only three more additions — New Jersey, Vermont, and Oregon. Every state of the south rejected the amendment but Louisiana, which had not voted. In January, Kentucky rejected the amendment, but most of the northern states passed it. Though three-fourths of the north approved the amendment, the Radicals still lacked the majority they needed to make it law and sought ways to avert another setback.[8]

The other piece of pending legislation concerned the Tenure of Office Bill, which until January 10 gathered dust on the Senate docket. After the first reading, Timothy O. Howe of Wisconsin moved that the bill apply to cabinet members as well as civil officers, as they, too, required the advice and consent of the Senate. Howe could muster only eight votes for his amendment. Sumner attempted to add a far more drastic section, compelling any head of a department appointed by the president after July 1866, and receiving an annual salary of one thousand dollars or more, be terminated. The amendment, though absurd, gave Sumner the opportunity to cast more invectives on Johnson. "The President," he said scornfully, "has usurped the powers of Congress on a colossal scale, and he has employed these usurped powers in fomenting the rebel

spirit and awakening anew the dying fires of rebellion. He has become a terror to the good and a support to the wicked." Like Howe, Sumner failed to garner support, and the bill went back to the House.[9]

In the meantime Stevens and his conspirators sensed that Stanton may have fallen out of favor in the cabinet. If so, perhaps their original bill should be amended to include restraints on cabinet member removals. By a party vote of 111 to 38, the House amended its bill making cabinet, as well as other officers, not removable by the president without the approval of the Senate.[10]

When the amended Tenure of Office Bill came back to the Senate for debate, Senator John Sherman asked the obvious question — what if "some Cabinet minister under the old administration should hang on to his office. It is hardly a probable supposition ... because I do not see how any gentleman could ... hold an office of that kind against the will of his chief; yet if we were to adopt the amendment ... we compel the President to retain in office ... any man who has not courtesy enough to retire.... I cannot imagine a case where a Cabinet officer would hold onto his place in defiance and against the wishes of his chief, and if such a case should occur I certainly would not by any extraordinary legislation protect him in that office."[11]

Sherman's argument deterred the bill from passage in the Senate, but Sumner liked the idea and would not let the matter drop. He believed that "It was the duty of every patriotic minister to remain in the counsels of a perverted administration as 'a privileged spy.'" During a dinner with friends, Sumner exposed the real reason for the House amendment. When the subject of Stanton came up, he declared, "it should be made impossible for Johnson to remove him."[12]

Resolute in his determination to pass the bill, Sumner returned to the Senate, formed a committee with the House, and had little difficulty working with Williams in grinding out a compromise. The final bill remained much as the House had presented it, but on the issue of the removal of cabinet officers, Sumner amended the bill just enough to satisfy the Republicans who objected to it. The new terminology read that cabinet officers *shall hold their offices respectively for and during the term of the President by whom they may have been appointed, and for one month thereafter, subject to the removal by and the advice and consent of the Senate.*"[13]

Exactly what the new proviso meant puzzled even those who voted for it. The Radicals may have blundered in their efforts to protect Stanton because the secretary had been appointed during Lincoln's first term and never reappointed. Sherman interpreted the clause as meaning that a cabinet officer would hold his office during the life or term of the president who appointed him. If a president dies, said Sherman, the cabinet goes out "so that the government will not be embarrassed by any attempt by a cabinet officer to hold on to his office despite the wish of the President or a change in the Presidency." Whatever the Radicals intended, they inadvertently left Stanton removable by Johnson without the concurrence of the Senate — but did they? They clearly wanted to protect Stanton — and perhaps trap the president — so they added additional language making removal "contrary to the provisions of this act ... high misdemeanors" punishable

by a fine not exceeding ten thousand dollars or by imprisonment not exceeding five years, or both. On February 19 the bill passed both chambers, and Sumner believed he had obstructed the president from removing Stanton.[14]

Johnson discussed the bill with the cabinet, who united in condemning it as a usurpation of executive powers by Congress and more than likely unconstitutional. All agreed that Lincoln's appointees could be removed by the president without the approval of the Senate. Stanton spoke of the measure as "flagrant abuse," declaring that "any man who would retain his seat in the Cabinet when his advice was not wanted was unfit for the place." He would not under any circumstances "remain a moment" longer than wanted. But when Johnson asked for his help in preparing a veto message, Stanton declined, claiming an overload of work. Seward agreed to put together a rebuttal if Stanton would help. Johnson asked them to do so, but later he turned to Welles and in an undertone said, "[You] have given this matter a good deal of thought" and asked for a separate veto message.[15]

When on March 2 Johnson vetoed the bill, he did so believing that no "gentlemen then present" in his cabinet would ever become a cause of future embarrassment. He later admitted that "If any of these gentlemen had then said to me that he would avail himself of the bill in case it became law, I should not have hesitated a moment" to remove him. "I felt," Johnson said, "that if these gentlemen came within the purview of this bill, it was to them a dead letter, and that none of them would ever take refuge under its provisions." Despite their differences, Johnson attributed a full measure of honor to the men of his cabinet, and he felt no compulsion to solidify the working relationship by demanding from them pledges of fidelity. Johnson's veto became a classic rendition of constitutional law, in which he predicted that "the power of removal from office by the Executive will be found indispensable." Fifty-nine years passed before the Supreme Court, delivering a judgment on a similar law, sustained Johnson.[16]

Johnson's distinguished veto message probably went unread by most members of Congress. On the day of its arrival, both House and Senate overrode the president's veto with their omnipotent two-thirds majority.[17]

During the congressional debate over the language of the tenure measure, Stevens never let up on his self-imposed mission to create a Reconstruction Bill — one that would fully engage the services of secretary of war Stanton. Stevens encountered opposition to the bill within his own party, but as one historian observed, "The old man's energy was astonishing. Vindictiveness seemed to animate his frame," and the bill would never have been carried through without his "able and despotic parliamentary leadership."[18]

Despite the Supreme Court's decision in the Milligan case, holding that no military tribunals could judge civil cases while civil courts operated, Stevens pressed forward denouncing the work of Lincoln and Johnson as a "bastard reconstruction." On the House floor he threatened to sponsor the bill as a war measure, conveniently overlooking the south's willing adoption of the Thirteenth Amendment. When he accused the south of still being in a state of rebellion, one of his staunchest supporters cautioned, "If this is not so, then we must abandon the bill." Stevens then softened

his tone, referring to the measure as merely a "police bill." But his concept of reconstruction involved military occupation of the south, authorizing the general of the armies — not the president — to appoint a general officer to command each of the military districts into which the south would be divided and empowered those officers to try civil as well as criminal cases before military commissions. For this concept, he had the full support of Senator George H. Williams, who had reported a similar bill to the Senate.[19]

The bill as first drafted by Stevens repudiated the Supreme Court's decision in the Milligan case and was therefore unconstitutional except during war — which was precisely why Stevens called it a war measure. Francis C. LeBlond of Ohio sharply criticized Stevens for "inaugurating enough here to destroy any government ever founded." Blaine told Stevens to tone down the bill, offering an amendment that enabled the south to reestablish its civil governments by assenting to the Fourteenth Amendment and other more palatable conditions. Stevens flatly refused, declaring that he did not wish to see generosity and benevolence "squandered upon vagabonds and thieves." At one point he threatened to table the bill if he could not get his way. Word of this action reached the White House in late January, giving Johnson hope that the bill would never come to vote in the House.[20]

On February 13, however, Stevens pushed his bill through the House without the Blaine amendment, which he condemned as being a step toward "universal amnesty and universal Andy-Johnsonism." John Sherman took charge of the bill in the Senate and quashed Stevens' elation by putting Blaine's

amendment back into the bill and re-
verted the appointment of commanders
in the five military districts to the president, not the general-in-chief. Stevens
objected to the change, but the Senate
refused to strike the amendments. On
February 19 the House, making only
minor changes, voted on the bill and
passed it.[21]

Stevens, though he voted on the bill,
believed it missed the mark. However,
the first Reconstruction Act declared all
of Johnson's state governments merely
provisional. It divided the south into five
military districts, each commanded by a
general appointed by the president. The
district commander acted as an arbitrary
potentate over civil courts and could rule
as he wished. Only sentences of death
were reviewable by the president. The
bill also stipulated that the affected states
would be readmitted after framing constitutions in conventions elected by universal suffrage. However, the term universal suffrage disfranchised certain ex-
Confederates and enfranchised ex-slaves.

Thirty-five years later historian John
W. Burgess, in an elaborate study of the
bill, wrote: "There was hardly a line in
the entire bill which would stand the test
of the Constitution." To have demanded
of southern states as a condition of admission "their acceptance of things not
yet in the Constitution of the United
States, things not obligatory on the 'states'
already in the Union was tantamount to
the creation of a new sort of union with
another kind of Constitution by an act of
Congress."[22]

On February 22 Johnson called a
meeting of his cabinet to discuss the bill.
Only Stanton urged approval. During
the past ten days Johnson had voiced
suspicions of Stanton's fidelity to the
cabinet. Though the secretary's advice

had often been helpful, a recent incident
troubled him.[23]

Seven weeks ago Congress had asked
the president for facts concerning any
problems occurring in the enforcement
of the Civil Rights Law. All members of
the cabinet submitted their reports on
time but Stanton. Two days after Stevens'
Reconstruction Bill passed the House,
Stanton produced a brief report from
Grant and an extensive report from General Howard, accompanied by 440 news
clippings alleging numerous murders of
ex-slaves, neighborhood strife, and other
accounts that appeared to have been
dredged up with the help of the war department. Most cabinet members believed that unverified accounts of a scandalous and inflammable nature should
not be submitted to Congress, but Stanton "betrayed guilt" when he replied that
he was "as desirous to act in unison with
the President as any one" but felt that the
material seemed proper to both him and
Grant. He stated that "If others wished
to suppress it they could make the attempt, but there was little doubt that
members of Congress had seen this—
likely had copies." When Stanton departed, Stanbery and McCulloch remarked that "here was design and intrigue
in connection with the Radical conspirators at the Capitol."[24]

At the time, the tenure bill had not
been signed, and Johnson could have
removed Stanton without fear of violating the law. Friends of the president
suggested that he act promptly and either oust Stanton or ask for his resignation. Welles warned that "the Administration was coming under the War
department." Of Johnson's ambivalence,
one historian wrote, "It was magnificent
restraint, but it was a mistake." But not
until Stanton urged the president to sign

the Reconstruction Bill did Johnson evince disapproval of the secretary's advice. Welles captured the moment, writing of Johnson, "Few men have stronger feeling; still fewer have the power of restraining themselves when evidently excited."[25]

On March 2 Johnson returned the Reconstruction Bill to the House with his veto. Few in the House read the message, but Johnson's vision of the future of the nation under the bill made it one of the great documents in American history. Had the Radicals listened to Johnson's arguments and reconsidered their actions, there would never have been the "solid south" or the long decades of misunderstanding and strife that reached far into the twentieth century. Nor would there have been the carpetbag regime, or the profits stolen by northern scoundrels sent south to wheedle into positions of political power. Admirers of Stevens rank him high on the list of vanguards for racial justice without crediting him with the consequences of the Reconstruction Act. Nor do they admit that most Radicals cared little for the blacks. They merely intended to use black suffrage as their ticket to retaining permanent political power. As Johnson so deftly observed, "The negroes have not asked for the privilege of voting; the vast majority of them have no idea what it means. The bill not only thrusts it into their hands, but compels them as well as the whites to use it in a particular way."[26]

Johnson argued that the bill "places all the people of the ten States ... under the absolute domination of military rulers; and ... declares that there exists in those States no legal governments and no adequate protection for life or property, and asserts the necessity of enforcing peace and good order within their limits. Is this true as a matter of fact?" he asked. Anyone reading the 440 gossip-ridden newsclips submitted by the war department might answer yes, but Johnson disagreed. Each state, following proclamations issued by the president, had reformed their governments and created the executive, legislative, and judicial branches of a free state. "To pronounce the supreme law-making power of an established state illegal," Johnson declared, "is to say that law itself is illegal." He admitted there had been instances of criminal behavior but found it no different from elsewhere in the country. He emphasized that provisions made by southern governments for the suppression of crime and the redress of private injury were the same as those prevailing in the north. The southern people, he said, "are completely united in the effort to reorganize their society on the basis of peace and to restore their mutual prosperity as rapidly and as completely as their circumstances will permit."[27]

Johnson understood the character of the south much better than Stevens or Sumner. He sincerely believed that the bill would actually retard social and economic reconstruction while imposing serious damage to future relations between the north and the south. He argued against the deployment of a military oligarchy, not only because it exercised domination over state governments, but because it would not be used "for any purpose of order or for the prevention of crime, but solely as a means of coercing the people into the adoption of principles and measures to which it is known they are opposed, and upon which they have an undeniable right to exercise their own judgment."

In 1862 he had watched as General Butler and his cronies raided the occupied sections of Louisiana, and he envisioned it happening all over again. "The power ... given to the commanding officers over all the people of each district," Johnson declared, "is that of a complete monarch. His mere will is to take the place of all law. He alone is permitted to determine what are rights of person or property, and he may protect them in such a way as in his discretion may seem proper" regardless of the existing laws of the state. "It places at his free disposal all the lands and goods in his district, and he may distribute them without let or hindrance to whom he pleases. Being bound by no State law.... He can save his friends from justice and despoil his enemies contrary to justice."[28]

"Our Constitution," Johnson declared, provides "the only system of free government which we can hope to have as a nation. When it ceases to be the rule of our conduct, we may perhaps take our choice between complete anarchy, a consolidated despotism, and a total dissolution of the Union; but national liberty regulated by law will have passed beyond our reach. It is the best frame of government the world ever saw." The war, he said, had been "to punish the gross crime of defying the Constitution and to vindicate its supreme authority.... Shall we now acknowledge that we sacrificed a million of lives and expended billions of treasure to enforce a Constitution which is not worthy of respect and preservation?"

Then, in the frail hope that Congress might yet cast aside the imposition of military tribunals and give the ten southern states representation in Congress, he made a final appeal to the House, writing, "While we are legislating upon subjects which are of great importance to the whole people, and which must affect all parts of the country, not only during the life of the present generation but for all ages to come, we should remember that all men are entitled at least to a hearing in the councils which decide upon the destiny of themselves and their children."[29]

The veto message reached the House on Saturday afternoon, March 2, two days before the dissolution of the 39th Congress. Nobody read it. There would be no "hearing in the councils" of the legislature — not for the south and not for the president. Stevens moved for immediate consideration to quash the veto. Colfax allowed but one minute for members of the opposition. Charles A. Eldridge of Wisconsin condemned the bill as a "dissolution of the Union." William E. Finck of Ohio called it "a monstrous scheme to subvert constitutional government in this country." LeBlond compared the bill to a "death-knell of republican liberty upon this continent." Of the three, Finck came closest to the mark. Stevens mocked the opposition, drawing a snicker from Radicals when he referred to their arguments as merely "melancholy feelings." In a partisan vote of 135 to 48, the House repassed the bill. Acting in collusion with Stevens, Blaine moved to suspend the rules of the Senate. Before the day ended, the Senate repassed the bill by a vote of 38 to 10. James A. Woodburn, one of Stevens' earlier biographers and professor of American history and politics at the University of Indiana, wrote: "It is not improbable that his [Stevens'] determined purpose to punish the South would have wrought something worse than this military bill into the legislation of his country could he have had his way."[30]

The 39th Congress imposed one more measure on Johnson before the session ended, and it emanated from the private meeting Stanton held in early December with Boutwell and Colfax. Stanton's amendment stipulated that the general of the army should be stationed in Washington, that all orders of the President or secretary of war be issued *through* the general of the army, and that all militia in the ten southern states be disbanded. Stanton promoted the amendment under the pretense that Johnson planned to perform some sort of coup d'état. Stevens, as chairman of the Ways and Means Committee, which included appropriations, attached the amendment as a rider to the Military Appropriations Bill. Stanton slyly encouraged the signing of the bill, but the clear treachery of his advice enraged the president.

Because Reverdy Johnson supported the bill, the president felt obliged to sign it, but he protested the language because it violated his constitutional prerogatives as commander in chief of the army. He also objected to the disbandment of state militias, arguing that the rider violated the constitutional right of ten southern states to protect themselves in an emergency. None of his protests made a speck of difference. Because he knew a veto would be useless, he allowed the bill to pass. Tricked by Stanton, Johnson grumbled "I am compelled to defeat these necessary appropriations if I withhold my signature from the act."[31]

During cabinet discussions over the Tenure of Office and Military Appropriations Bills, Jeremiah S. Black, the great constitutional lawyer, sat at the president's table preparing veto messages for both bills. So engrossed had he become that people entered and departed from the office without his notice. Though Johnson signed the appropriations bill, Black prepared messages that argued against both measures. Though considered "masterpieces of political logic, constitutional interpretation, and official style," more than two-thirds of the Senate ignored the messages and repassed the tenure bill. A few days later those same senators observed their names highlighted with black borders in the *New York World*, followed by the comment, "The time is coming when every man in the above list will stand accurst in our history."[32]

The Radicals had marshaled and unified their forces. There would be no letup. The incoming additions to the 40th Congress would enhance their political power, and, they hoped, give them the muscle to impeach and convict the president.

12

The 40th Congress

On March 4, 1867, the 40th Congress convened without including members elected from ten southern states. Representatives from Tennessee, Kentucky, and five northern states were not available because elections had not been held, leaving a third of the states unrepresented. The galleries filled with witnesses to the unprecedented event. Surely, they thought, something urgent and of monumental consequence must be imminent to call the 40th Congress together. Could it be the impeachment of the president?[1]

In a cabinet meeting on March 3 the president appeared calm, but more dejected than Welles had ever remembered him. When Johnson excused himself and left the room, the cabinet privately discussed impeachment. Seward felt the matter would be dropped, but Welles disagreed, pointing to the lack of leadership among the "well-meaning members." The Radicals, said Welles, "had entire control of the whole mass of Republicans." Referring to Stevens, Butler, and Boutwell, Welles declared that a "few violent partisans" led the group and "in revolutionary times such as these … the violent always controlled." Such men would "unquestionably impeach" whether they found good reason or not.[2]

Acting quickly, the House returned Colfax as speaker and reelected Stevens as chairman of the powerful Ways and Means Committee, but the House did not renew the Joint Committee of Fifteen on Reconstruction. So obsessed had Stevens become on destroying Johnson that his declining health did not deter him from demanding and retaining his customary seat of power. Because of the absence of representation from seventeen of the states, Democrats protested the elections, but under the rules, the clerk refused to submit the protest for discussion.[3]

The Senate needed to replace Lafayette S. Foster of Connecticut as pro tem President — the man in succession to become president of the United States should Johnson be impeached. Ben Wade waited anxiously until Foster departed from the chamber. Taking the floor, he reminded the Senate that he was no parliamentarian, but nobody cared. It was Wade's raw craving for the presidency the Senate wanted. As chief executive, Wade made the perfect tool for the Radicals, and he easily won the election. He took the gavel, declared the 39th Congress adjourned, and without leaving his chair proceeded to organize the 40th.[4]

Many newly elected senators were as hostile to the president and as anxious to have him removed as Wade. The aged and corrupt party boss of Pennsylvania, Simon Cameron, replaced Edgar Cowan. Roscoe Conkling of New York, outspoken in his disparagement of moderate Republicans, moved into the seat of Ira Harris. James H. Lane of Indiana, after voting against the civil rights bills in 1866, lost his seat to ex-governor Oliver H. P. T. Morton of Indiana. Morton, a wartime supporter of Lincoln, did not like Johnson or his lenient policies. James Harlan of Iowa, a one-time cabinet member under Johnson, came to the Senate to defeat the policies of his former chief. Three other Radicals joined the Senate, Charles D. Drake of Missouri, Cornelius Cole of California, and Henry W. Corbett of Oregon, all disciples of the Radical cause. Republicans now held a comfortable margin and could pass whatever legislation they wished.[5]

Benjamin F. Butler represented the most conspicuous addition to the House. Stevens had waited anxiously for the general's arrival, aware that the unscrupulous lawyer from Massachusetts possessed certain reprehensible gifts that could bolster the effort to impeach and convict the president. Blaine cautioned that out of more than 1,700 party newspapers, not twenty-five regarded impeachment talk seriously. Stevens scoffed at the comment, castigating Blaine to his face for having said in a private conversation that there would be no impeachment because "we would rather have the President than that scalawag Ben Wade."[6]

After new House members took their seats, Ashley resumed his call for Johnson's impeachment, fingering the president as a drunkard who had turned the White House into a "den of thieves and pardon brokers." Referring to the object of his scorn as "the foulest blot" on "our country's history," Ashley declared that "the nation cried out in its agony to Congress to deliver them from the shame and disgrace the acting President has brought upon them." Some of the Radicals thought Ashley's speech inappropriate and branded the "whole scheme of impeachment as one of consummate folly." They argued that "not one act amounting to a crime or misdemeanor has as yet been proved against the Executive." Nor did they believe that any such proof would be forthcoming. Butler disagreed. He promised the House would favor impeachment once he prepared a final report. High crimes and misdemeanors meant nothing, he said, even evidence was unnecessary. Acts of misconduct would be sufficient to convict. To dispose of a president, he said, was a simple process, and he would lead the way. Reinforced by Butler's confidence, the House decided that the investigation should continue.[7]

After learning of the actions in the House, Johnson met with his cabinet. Browning suggested ways the president might thwart impeachment, but Johnson replied that he intended to do nothing about it. "I am tired of hearing allusions to impeachment," he said. "God Almighty knows I will not turn aside from my public duties to attend to the contemptible assaults which are got up to embarrass the Administration. Let the House go forward and busy themselves in that matter if they wish."[8]

Butler and Johnson shared two naiveties in common—neither of them understood the impeachment process. The only precedent involved not a president but justice Samuel Chase, whose trial before the Senate began on February 4, 1805. It ended with his acquittal on March 1. Butler believed that if a story could be put together against the president, it would force a trial in the Senate. Johnson did not know how to prepare for such a contingency and even contemplated the possibility of being arrested. Because vagueness surrounded the impeachment process, Johnson, in his stubborn way, took little action to protect himself. Welles believed that by ignoring the problem, the president weakened himself in the estimation of the public. "Yet," he wrote, "I know of no man who is more firm when he has once taken a stand."[9]

Johnson's "stand" on impeachment was to wait and do nothing. The decision had merit. The Senate wanted to adjourn and go home. Only the extreme Radicals lobbied to remain in session and press forward with impeachment — the only business still on the table. Sumner thought the Reconstruction Act contained deficiencies, and he intended to use the session to improve the system for registering voters and for holding elections in the south. On March 6 he introduced an elaborate bill so unreasonable and unfair that it appalled most of his colleagues. More shocking were certain of Sumner's proposals on black suffrage — he demanded they also apply to the north. Many in the Senate had grown tired of listening to Sumner's tirades and wanted a short session. The Radicals decided to stay in session, however, and the 40th Congress looked around for new reconstruction bills to enact, but not Sumner's.[10]

With the passage of the Reconstruction Act, Johnson fulfilled the odious requirement of naming five generals to command the military districts of the south. Until the Supreme Court ruled on the constitutionality of the act, Johnson would perform his legally imposed duties. Grant, however, issued the appointments, naming major generals to the five districts; John M. Schofield, Daniel E. Sickles, George H. Thomas, Edward O.

C. Ord, and Philip H. Sheridan. Four days later Grant added Major General John Pope to the Cumberland district, who traded commands with Thomas. Of the six generals, all were professional military men but Sickles, whose political background worried every member of the cabinet but one — Stanton, who seemed delighted with the choice. Welles, the cautious observer, suspected that Grant had been swayed by Radical influence, and wrote, "The slime of the serpent is over them all."[11]

While Ashley and Butler worked on impeachment, Stevens pressed for a supplementary Reconstruction Bill. He demanded that property owned by insurgents be sold at auction to compensate loyalists for their losses. He also demanded that all public lands in the ten states in question be forfeited to the government. He stipulated that the president promptly seize property specified in the second Confiscation Act, thereby enabling the commissioners in each district to distribute, under ten years' trust, forty acres of land among the freedmen. As rationale for his land grab, Stevens declared that in the absence of a conquered government from which to demand reparations, plantation owners must pay the price. Congress rejected Stevens' program but agreed to consider amending the Reconstruction Act.[12]

The supplementary bill passed by Congress on March 19 provided an entirely new procedure for holding elections in the south and new rules for creating state constitutions. It specified methods for district commanders to follow when registering voters and arranging elections. Blacks could vote, but it denied the franchise to any person who had fought for the Confederacy. By directing the commander of each district to appoint boards of registration and superintend elections, the bill attempted to counteract conservative schemes to remain under military rule in preference to accepting black suffrage. Stevens had fallen ill and had little to do with the details of the bill, but the south blamed him for imposing black suffrage and smothered him with letters threatening bodily harm. Some of the changes in the supplementary Reconstruction Bill contained Sumner's demands, but most of the measures were framed by Fessenden, Trumbull, and Sherman. Sumner voiced mild condemnation of the bill, convinced that "we shall regret hereafter that we have not done more."[13]

Four days later Johnson vetoed the bill — not just because it provided for black suffrage but because it denied the vote to the soldiering class of whites. Once again he tried to convince Congress that their methods would cause decades of dissension between the north and the south, but few in Congress had the vision to see beyond the present. After a perfunctory reading of Johnson's veto message, both Houses repassed the bill.[14]

Historians for decades have either praised or denounced the Reconstruction Acts. Professor John W. Burgess witnessed the aftermath of the reconstruction period and called it "one of the 'blunder-crimes' of the century," his point being that in many districts the majority of the electorate would be "negroes and mulattos, about all of whom had been three years before slaves." Having lived through the period, Burgess predicted the fomentation of civil strife for many decades after the military tribunals ended, and he was right.[15]

Having done its work, Congress discussed adjournment, but December lay eight months away. Sumner voiced concern that Congress could not leave the president without oversight for so long a period. "You must not forget," said he, "that the President is a bad man, the author of incalculable woe to this country, and especially to that part which, being most tried by war, most needed kindly care. Search history, and I am sure you will find no elected ruler who during the same short time has done so much mischief to his country. He stands alone in bad eminence." On March 30 Congress moved to adjourn but with the understanding that it would reconvene on July 3 to determine whether the "bad man" in the White House had created by proclamation any more "mischief."[16]

The Senate, however, remained in special session until April 20, the subject being Seward's proposed acquisition from Russia of the territory of Alaska, a land as large as the original thirteen states. Seward had negotiated a purchase price of $7,200,000, which some senators thought too high for this "vast area of rocks and ice" known as "Walrussia." On April 9, after several days of debate, the Senate ratified the treaty with only two opposing votes. Funds could not be appropriated until the following year, and another debate ensued in the House. In need of funds, the Russians spent vast sums bribing various members of the House. Seward claimed that Thad Stevens had for his "sop" taken $10,000. Doing so would have been uncharacteristic of Stevens, especially since he had always been an expansionist and supported the appropriation.[17]

Stevens' Reconstruction Act invoked the wrath of another "bad man," Governor Benjamin G. Humphreys of Mississippi, an ex-Confederate general who had led his brigade through major battles in Virginia, Georgia, and Tennessee. Aware of the decisions in the Milligan, Cummings, and Garland cases, Humphreys believed the Supreme Court should intercede and strike down the abusive law. On April 5 Robert J. Walker, Alexander Garland, and William Sharkey made a motion in the Supreme Court on behalf of Mississippi to enjoin Andrew Johnson ... and his officers and agents," including major general Ord, "from enforcing the Reconstruction Act of 1867."[18]

On April 12 the unprecedented case to prevent a president from carrying out the laws of Congress came before the Supreme Court. Observers witnessing the arguments noted restlessness among the justices and predicted they would shrivel from the pressure. After the ruling in the Milligan case, ultra Radicals had suggested impeaching the Supreme Court along with the president. The threat had been made to keep Chase in line with the Republican cause. Aware of the politics behind the scene, the New York Independent wrote of the Supreme Court: "This tribunal, already suspecting that as now constituted, is regarded as a diseased member of the body politic, will not run the risk of amputation by touching the edged tools of Sharkey and Walker." The Independent hit the bullseye. Three days later the Supreme Court ruled that it had no jurisdiction to enjoin the president from performing "his official duties."[19]

Perplexed by the ruling, Georgia retained Walker, hired Jeremiah Black, and sent both attorneys back to the Supreme Court in an effort to enjoin Stanton from his part in executing the hated acts. Walker challenged the ambiguity of a position which asserted that secession had been originally impossible, but which now enacted laws as if

secession had in fact occurred. He insisted the confusion be clarified. A few days later the court replied, ruling that while it possessed power to rule on civil matters, it could not adjudicate issues having a political character. Disgusted by the cowardice of the court, The Nation expressed contempt by writing that "it is no light matter that the highest court in the land should thus disclaim the power of enquiring into the constitutionality of an act of Congress destroying the government of ten states." Those among the public having the insight to objectively assess the deterioration of the republic, despondently agreed that no longer could any state in the Union rely upon protection from the Supreme Court.[20]

Because the court admitted having jurisdiction to adjudicate the rights of "persons or property," Mississippi amended its petition in an effort to protect the property of the state from seizure by military tribunals. A divided court decision denied the petition, thereby removing all "legal obstacles to reconstruction." In his battle with the Radicals to preserve the Constitution, Johnson now stood alone, and he would not back down.[21]

All the criticism heaped upon the president for granting amnesty did not deter him from following his predecessor's example of issuing pardons. Since May 1865, Jefferson Davis and Clement C. Clay had been imprisoned at Fort Monroe and, among other things, charged with complicity in the assassination of Lincoln. Because of poor health Clay was released in 1866, but not Davis. When Johnson learned that the fort's commander, Brigadier General Nelson A. Miles, kept Davis confined in irons, he ordered Miles mustered out of the service. Stanton removed the general, but retained him in the army as a colonel. Varina Davis still had influence in Washington and appealed to the president to free her husband. Johnson sent Davis to Richmond for trial, where the judge released him on $100,000 bail. In 1869 the court dismissed the case without prosecution.[22]

The release of Davis in May 1867, sparked new attacks on the president by Boutwell, Ashley, and the House Judiciary Committee. The committee performed two roles — the first to determine whether Johnson played a role in the assassination of Lincoln; the second to look for impeachable offenses. The committee found no evidence, and every wild allegation led down a blind alley. With reluctance, the committee voted five to four to adjourn, writing that "from the evidence before them it did not appear that the President was guilty of such high crimes and misdemeanors as called for the impeaching power of the House." Boutwell dissented but went home with the others. Before departing he passed a committee resolution to censure the president, the vote being along strict party lines. Welles called the effort "shameless and disgraceful," recounting the number of times the committee had investigated Johnson's public and private acts, including, "his household affairs, his domestic life, his bank accounts, his social intercourse" and every "act or transaction or expression which would justify or excuse an arraignment of the Chief Executive." No man since the formation of the republic had been subjected to such intense investigation; yet the Radicals could find nothing incriminating.[23]

Johnson remained optimistic. He believed the Supreme Court would eventually strike down the Reconstruction Act, but until they did, he would enforce it. In the meantime the military tribunals

began to flex their muscle. The first crisis erupted in Louisiana, where Major General Sheridan ruled the Fifth Military District. On the eighth day of his administration he removed a judge of the New Orleans Criminal Court, the attorney-general of Louisiana, and Mayor Monroe of New Orleans. On June 3 he dismissed the legislature and deposed the governor. Though the general acted within the authority granted by the Reconstruction Act, Johnson never anticipated such extreme action when he approved Sheridan's assignment to the district.[24]

Having never been a lawyer, Johnson asked Attorney General Stanbery to find some way to alleviate the harsh fate imposed on the south. The cabinet bent their back to the work — all but Stanton, who declared that the act "invested the commanders with absolute power!" He defended the military tribunals, and his reluctance to aid Stanbery suggested to the others that Stanton may have been the "original adviser if not the originator of these laws. He may not have drafted them, but he, and probably [Joseph] Holt in consultation with him, devised the plan." Using laws enacted as far back as Revolutionary days, Stanbery published his opinion on June 12, hoping to mitigate the rule of military despots operating in the south.[25]

Using Stanbery's opinion as a working document, Johnson on June 20 issued through the war department an order to all military commanders. Hereafter all persons offering themselves to be registered as voters must be enfranchised upon taking the oath. Having once taken the oath, no new oath would be required, nor could a board of registry repudiate that oath. Furthermore, participation in the war or in a militia would not disenfranchise a voter until a law or a judicial sentence of some competent authority so ruled. Also, disloyal sentiments or opinions that did not provoke civil strife or rebellion would not disqualify a person from voting. Though his own department issued the orders, Stanton disagreed with them, and once the orders became public, the Radicals reacted with furor. Chase, however, found no cause for panic and said, "I see no ground for thinking that the President has not intended to carry out the Reconstruction Acts in good faith." Sheridan, however, differed with the president and complained to Grant, who replied, "Enforce your own construction of the military bill until ordered to do so otherwise."[26]

On July 3, 1867, the 40th Congress reconvened. Among the first order of business the House by party vote tendered its thanks to Sheridan for the "able and faithful performance of his duties." Such praise was meant to encourage Sheridan to continue with his work of despotism. Ben Butler next introduced another scheme to look into the murder of President Lincoln because he questioned the conclusions of Boutwell's committee — hence, the House formed a new Assassination Committee with Butler as its chairman.[27]

Capitalizing on Sheridan's work in Louisiana, the House developed another supplement to the Reconstruction Act. The bill authorized military tribunals to remove or suspend any person holding office in state governments of the south and to fill vacancies with whomever they wished. Only Grant could review suspensions or removals — not the president.[28]

On July 19 Johnson vetoed the bill, declaring that military authority "is no longer confined to the preservation of public peace, the administration of criminal law, the registration of voters, and the superintendence of elections, but 'in all respects' is asserted to be paramount to the existing civil governments. It is impossible to conceive any state of society more intolerable than this; and yet it is to this condition that 12,000,000 American citizens are reduced by the Congress of the United States..." and have no rights and no protection under the Constitution. The bill also repudiated Stanbery's opinion and included language exempting military commanders from being "bound in his action by any opinion of any civil officer of the United States," which usurped the president's power as commander-in-chief of the armed forces. Johnson explained the separation of powers in great detail, but he also pointed to another flaw, writing that military appointees might very well say, even when their action is in conflict with the Supreme Court, that since the court is composed of civil officers, they are not bound to any opinion from that authority.[29]

Disgusted with being bullied by Congress, Johnson minced few words when he replied, "Whilst I hold the chief executive authority of the United States, whilst the obligation rests upon me to see that all the laws are faithfully executed, I can never willingly surrender that trust or the powers given for its execution. I can never give my assent to be made responsible for the faithful execution of the laws, and at the same time surrender that trust, and the powers that accompany it to any other officer, high or low, or to any number of executive officers." To the Radicals, Johnson's admonishment thundered like war. Both chambers hurriedly repassed the bill.

Boutwell declared that the president's threat "provokes and demands the exercise of the highest and gravest duty of the House" — impeachment.[30]

By mid-July the oppressive heat of Washington exhausted the Radicals, but some still felt the president required constant vigilance. Sumner stirred a debate on the Senate floor, advocating that "we ought to stay in our seats to encounter the evil proceeding from him." There he stands, said Sumner, "a constant impediment to peace and an ally of the Rebellion. And yet knowing these things it is proposed to go home and leave him undisturbed master till winter." The debate continued with Sumner stubbornly arguing that "our president is a public enemy…. His influence is great, ours is greater. If we choose to say so we can master." Sumner still preferred a parliamentary form of government where a vote of no confidence could unseat a prime minister. Many of his speeches suggested that he practiced the British process. Nonetheless, on July 20 Congress voted to adjourn until the 21st of November.[31]

Sumner chose to "master" all, to have everything his way, to govern as he saw fit. He already decided that soon he would be called to "judge the President," remove him, and thrust Ben Wade into the White House. With two branches of the government under the wing of the Senate, he could then deal with the third — Salmon Chase and the Supreme Court — whose most recent decisions on reconstruction indicated a better obedience to the wishes of Congress. Though Sumner lost the fight to remain in session, the Radicals had effectively hamstrung the president with the Reconstruction Acts. Sumner admitted little reason to worry. Besides, Stanton would keep a watchful eye on Johnson during the recess and report any presidential mischief. Sumner did not know, however, that Johnson's patience with his deceptive war minister had finally diminished to the point where the president wondered why a man of honor would "persist on holding onto his place" when his views were in opposition to the administration.[32]

With the passage of the untested Tenure of Office Act, Johnson now had a conundrum. If Stanton would not resign, could he be legally removed? But removed, he must be.

13

The Puzzling Issue of Impeachment

During the month of July, Andrew Johnson no longer knew whom to trust outside of his cabinet, the exception being Stanton, who no longer shielded his sub rosa persona as a spy for the Radicals. Sheridan's insubordination, coupled with Grant's silence, caused Johnson to speculate whether Grant had become a confederate of the Republicans or whether Stanton merely suppressed the general's reports to the war department. Sheridan had recently removed governor James W. Throckmorton of Texas and replaced him with E. M. Pease, a man the governor had beaten six to one in an election held twenty months earlier. Johnson considered removing Sheridan, but he suspected that the problems emanated from Stanton's office would only increase. He pondered the matter for more than a month, using every suggestive method at his disposal to encourage Stanton to resign. The cabinet favored Stanton's removal but expressed concern over the ramifications of the Tenure of Office Act. Johnson warmed to the subject as he listened to the debate. Thoroughly aroused, he said: "If they would impeach me for ordering away an officer who I believe is doing wrong — afflicting and oppressing people instead of protecting and sustaining them — if I am to be impeached for this, I am prepared."[1]

While the president contemplated his options, the wife of Sanford Conover stopped at the White House for a favor. Conover, an ex-informant for the House Impeachment Committee, was now scheduled to serve a postponed sentence in the Albany penitentiary for complicity in Lincoln's murder. Conover had ingratiated himself with Ashley, Boutwell, and Butler during the time when the committee sought unsuccessfully to implicate Johnson in the assassination plot. Conover lied to the committee, and they finally discarded him without granting the promised pardon. Now Mrs. Conover attempted to keep her husband out of jail by supplying documents to the president that exposed Ashley, Boutwell, and Butler as the scoundrels behind the plot to establish a conspiratorial relationship between Johnson, Jefferson Davis, and John Wilkes Booth. Johnson discussed the Conover papers with trusted members of his cabinet and stated that he intended to go "to the fountainhead of mischief," meaning Stanton.[2]

The wily minister refused to be honorably and graciously goaded into surrendering his office. So on August 5,

1867, the president asked for the war secretary's resignation. Welles believed that Stanton would honorably quit his office, as would any other member of the cabinet. Johnson hoped so, admitting at last that Stanton had "been the prolific source" of the administration's difficulties. Johnson reflectively grumbled, "To think that the man whom I trusted was plotting and intriguing against me." When Stanton refused to resign before the next session of Congress, Johnson fumed, confiding in Welles, "it is impossible to get along with such a man in such a position, and I can stand it no longer."[3]

Johnson waited a week, hoping Stanton would change his mind. When nothing happened he decided that Grant would be the best man to replace Stanton and talked to the general privately. Though some members of the cabinet questioned Grant's fidelity to the president, the general seemed amenable to the proposal and simply replied that he always "obeyed orders."[4]

At some point after August 5, Grant sent a private letter to Johnson, writing, "It certainly was the intention of the legislative branch of the government to place Cabinet ministers beyond the power of Executive removal, and it is pretty well understood that ... it was intended specially to protect the Secretary of War in whom the country felt great confidence." Grant's wording of his private letter contained legalese suggestive of help from a practiced lawyer, but his comments failed to contain knowledge of Senator Sherman's unofficial postscript that the bill should not permit the government to "be embarrassed by an attempt by a Cabinet officer to hold on to his office despite the wish of the President." Grant worried that he could not do the job, being unfamiliar with the

duties of the secretary of war. He also worried about being too closely connected with Johnson because Radicals had privately approached him as their nominee for president.[5]

Though unverifiable, the cabinet suspected that Grant had colluded with Stanton in preparing the reply. Welles remarked, "Grant is going over." The president simply replied, "I have no doubt that most of these offensive measures have emanated from the War Department." "Not only that," Welles added, "but almost all the officers of the army have been insidiously alienated from your support by the same influences." Johnson listened and agreed, but at the conclusion of the discussion said that one way or another, he intended to "bring this matter to a conclusion in a few days." Johnson's hesitancy to act quickly was caused by a reluctance to cross Grant because of the general's national popularity, and he wanted to avoid missteps in obtaining Grant's support.[6]

On August 12 Johnson suspended Stanton in strict conformity to the Tenure of Office Act, writing, "By virtue of the power and authority vested in me, as President, by the Constitution and the laws of the United States, you are hereby suspended from the office of Secretary of War, and will cease to exercise any and all functions pertaining to the same." He then named Grant secretary of war ad interim and ordered Stanton to transfer all records and other public property to the general. Using the tenure act for protection, Stanton challenged Johnson's legal authority to remove him without the advice and consent of the Senate. Then, as if to suggest that Johnson conspired to wrest the government from the hands of Congress, Stanton added, "But inasmuch as the General Commanding the armies of the United States has been appointed ad interim, and has notified me that he has accepted the appointment, I have no alternative but to submit, under protest, to superior force."[7]

By appointing Grant as temporary secretary of war, Johnson hoped to attach the general to the cause of the administration. Because Radicals openly courted Grant, Johnson did not know how far the general had succumbed to their advances. When Grant said he always "obeyed orders," Johnson interpreted the statement literally. He expected the general would be a candidate for the presidency in 1868, but which party would attract him remained uncertain. Under the circumstances, one might question why Grant agreed to the cabinet post. By doing so, the general rankled friends, and the Radical press expressed concern that he would be stained by "Johnsonism." The president, however, understood the advantage of having a person of Grant's popularity in his cabinet, and if he could be won over, keeping him there would perplex the Radicals.[8]

Grant, however, proved to be an expedient measure and not a solution. He did not understand civil law, and Radicals had convinced him that the presidency occupied a position subordinate to Congress. Nor did he understand that Johnson, in the execution of presidential powers, was perfectly within his right to choose between his oath to the Constitution and his duty to support laws deemed to be in conflict with the Constitution. One day Grant came forward and asked Welles directly, "Was not Congress superior to the President?" "It pained me," said Welles, "to see how little he understood of the fundamental principles and structure of our government and of the Constitution itself." Welles called Grant "a political ignoramus" who "needs instruction." But a popular chap like Grant would make a wonderful tool for the Radicals, and the general did not hide his political aspirations.[9]

Conflict with Grant began on August 17 when the president issued orders to transfer Sheridan from Louisiana to the department of Missouri. At New Orleans Sheridan had precipitously removed twenty-two aldermen and the city's treasurer, chief of police, and attorney. He then reached into the parish and disposed of justices, sheriffs, and other local officers, replacing all with his own appointees. Ignoring objections from Grant — a personal wartime friend of Sheridan's — Johnson ordered mild-mannered Major General George H. Thomas into the Fifth Military District of Texas and Louisiana. Because of poor health Thomas asked to remain in Nashville. Johnson did not want Sheridan in the deep south, so he replaced him with Major General Winfield S. Hancock. Grant argued both decisions, stating that Sheridan was merely following explicit orders and should be invited to Washington for a conference. When Johnson denied the request, Grant grumbled that the president's orders conflicted with his own orders. "While I have no wish to come in conflict with anyone," Grant said, "I have a duty to perform. I must see the Reconstruction law executed." Johnson calmly replied, "General Grant will understand it is my duty to see the laws are executed, and also that when I assign officers to their duty my orders must be obeyed. I have made this arrangement and performed this work deliberately, and it will go with as little delay as possible."[10]

Grant fell silent. Later, during the same meeting, he confessed to not being a politician and "preferred not being mixed up in political questions. He wished, therefore, not to attend cabinet consultations and pass opinions on the subjects which came up for consideration and decision." Johnson told the general that he could do as he wished. Grant asked permission and withdrew from the meeting. Though Grant merely acted as secretary of war ad interim, one might wonder why a person who wanted to be the eighteenth president of the United States would not avail himself of the political education he admittedly needed to manage the country.[11]

Even Chief Justice Chase appealed to Johnson, pleading that he not antagonize Congress further, but the president remained adamant. As Chase predicted, the Radicals fumed over Sheridan's transfer, and Grant began to get unsolicited advice from those in power. When General Sickles attempted to obstruct the courts of the Carolinas using the premise that they "would soon pass on the Reconstruction acts and pronounce them unconstitutional," Grant countermanded that portion of Sickles' order that applied to federal courts. In the meantime Radicals got to Grant, and the general rescinded his order. To explain his action, Grant told the cabinet that Congress had put in his hands the enforcement of this law, and "he intended to see it was executed." Johnson had seen enough of Sickles and relieved him of command. The secretary of the navy observed Grant's actions and assessed them with a shudder. "Radical advice and intimacy," Welles noted, "had overcome his own better judgment. Grant is an insincere man ... very ambitious, has low cunning, and is unreliable, perhaps untruth-

ful.... Grant has power and position without the knowledge of how to use them properly."[12]

Johnson began to have misgivings about his selection of Grant and looked for ways to test him. Knowing Radicals would adhere to their definition of the tenure act, Johnson sought Grant's interpretation. For obvious reasons, Radicals did not want the act put before the Supreme Court. When a situation involving a corrupt governor in Idaho came to Johnson's attention, he asked the cabinet what might happen if he appointed a new governor, but the incumbent invoked the tenure act and refused to leave office. McCulloch suggested that the army remove the governor. All looked to Grant, who said, "In that case the military would not respond. They would sustain the Tenure-of-Office bill, which Congress has enacted, until the judges said it was unconstitutional." In other words, if the president asked him to remove a corrupt governor, Grant, who always "obeyed orders," would not do it.[13]

Grant had spoken, and no member of the cabinet wished to argue with his explanation. But the general's reply produced a hypothetical question — What if the Senate reinstated Stanton and Johnson should resist? Would Congress call in soldiers to enforce their directive or would such a decision lead to an orderly review of the tenure act by the court? Worse, did Congress now control the army by virtue of the Reconstruction Act, or did the Executive? The unknown answer placed Grant squarely in the position of deciding.

Johnson broached the question with Grant, who replied that he "should expect to obey orders." This did not answer Johnson's question, but Grant finally agreed that if asked by Congress to arrest

Johnson, he "would advise the President in season, that he might have time to make arrangements." Days later Boutwell disavowed any intention of arresting Johnson, declaring that he did not favor "the scheme of Stevens to that purpose." For those who had watched as the impeachment conspiracy unfolded, most believed that Grant had informed Boutwell that he would take no part in such an act.[14]

Radicals continued to court Grant, and as the elections of 1867 approached, they realized the importance of not losing him to Democrats. They feared Johnson's impressionable influence on the general because the president no longer held the views of most Republicans and could be friendly and persuasive.[15]

The first returns from fall elections alarmed them even more. Pennsylvania went Democratic, giving Stevens a mild jolt when the Democrats carried his hometown. Stricken with "dropsy of the chest" and thought to be dying, Stevens looked out upon the political wreckage and said, "Impeach now!"[16]

Ohio elected Rutherford B. Hayes governor and gave him a Democratic legislature. Worse, Ohio voters struck down an amendment to the state constitution that provided for black suffrage. Four more states went to the Democrats; New York, Connecticut, New Jersey, and California. Throughout the country Republican majorities diminished. Senator Sherman of Ohio confided to his brother, who had predicted Republican losses due to Radical legislation, that "the mistakes of Republicans may drift the Democratic party into power. If so the rebellion is triumphant and no man active in suppressing it will be trusted and honored." In 1868, the Republicans must have Grant if they hoped to hold power.[17]

The Radicals, however, had already laid the groundwork to offset their losses, but they needed time. They expected help to come from carpetbaggers. On December 3 Virginia held the first of the newly imposed state conventions — the majority of its members being transplants from New York, Pennsylvania, Ohio, Maine, Vermont, Connecticut, Maryland, the District of Columbia, Ireland, Scotland, Nova Scotia, Canada, and England. Only 35 whites and 24 blacks came from the Old Dominion. Officers of the convention were foreigners or blacks. Few members understood parliamentary order, and those who did understood their Radical mission.[18]

Some Radicals blamed the poor returns on their failure to impeach Johnson. Others believed the conservative and Democratic gains in Congress would end the impeachment effort. But what incensed Radicals was Johnson's removal of Stanton, Sickles, and Sheridan. Reflecting on the subject of impeachment, Speaker Colfax declared "It must come," and he promised the "most exciting scenes." William Pitt Fessendon agreed, writing McCulloch on September 2, "With regard to political matters, I see that the D[evi]l will be to pay when Congress meets."[19]

Congress reconvened on November 21, 1867, to face new problems. They had slightly more than three months before the newly elected Democrats filed into Washington to claim their seats. Ben Wade confronted an especially unpleasant problem. His term expired on March 4, 1869, and the Democrats who now controlled the Ohio legislature would surely oust him. His one hope of political survival depended upon the impeachment and conviction of Andrew Johnson. Thad Stevens, pale and hopelessly emaciated, tottered unsteadily to his seat, his eyes burning with fervor.

During the summer and throughout the fall, Radicals had combed the streets and back alleys in search of information to incriminate Johnson. They talked to felons and perjurers, deposed ninety-five witnesses, and once more investigated the president's household and personal records. What they found filled twelve hundred octavo pages of questionable testimony. The investigators submitted their report on November 25 with the resolution that Andrew Johnson be impeached for high crimes and misdemeanors, though they failed to specify what crimes or misdemeanors the president had committed.[20]

The report of the Radical wing of the committee, written by Thomas Williams of Pennsylvania, accused Johnson of a "usurpation of power." It alleged that he had pursued "one great overshadowing purpose of reconstructing the shattered governments of the rebel states in accordance with his own will in the interests of the great criminals who carried them into rebellion." Williams reiterated the familiar Radical theme without providing substance for his claims. Two Republican members, James F. Wilson of Iowa and Frederick E. Woodbridge of Vermont, analyzed the report, tore every charge to shreds, and in a second report recommended that the impeachment proceedings be dropped. Committee Democrats agreed with Wilson and Woodbridge, but the Radicals prevailed. By a 5 to 4 vote they closed their findings recommending that Johnson be impeached, stating blandly that though "the case fails upon the law and the testimony, from a political standpoint it is a success."[21]

On November 21 Johnson learned of the Judiciary Committee's decision. To his confidential secretary he calmly replied, "If it be so, let it be," but he could not suppress the agitation welling inside. If impeachment went forward, the question of whether he would be suspended during the trial phase, as Stevens wished, constantly nagged him. Numerous friends, Democrats, and Confederate veterans offered to provide him with armed resistance — to raise an army if necessary — to keep him out of the hands of the Radicals. Johnson appreciated the gesture of support, but his weapon would be the Constitution, not muskets and sabers.[22]

On November 30 Johnson met with the cabinet to discuss his forthcoming annual message. Towards the close of the meeting he broached the subject of Stevens' bill to suspend him. He believed that his constitutional duty compelled him to resist suspension, but he wanted the opinion of others. All agreed, including Grant, that no such law could be binding without an amendment to the Constitution. They unanimously supported Johnson's position. Stevens' bill, however, died in the House, much to the relief of all.[23]

On December 3 Johnson sent his Third Annual Message to Congress. He predicted the destruction of the Constitution and the calamities that could follow. Without obedience to its principles, Johnson warned, "we can look forward only to continual outrages upon individual rights, incessant breaches of the public peace, national weakness, financial dishonor, the total loss of our prosperity, the general corruption of morals, and the final extinction of popular freedom." He urged Congress to avoid those problems. "To me," he said, "the process of restoration seems perfectly plain and simple. It consists merely in a faithful application of the Constitution and laws. The execution of the laws is not now obstructed or opposed by physical force. There is no military or other necessity, real or pretended, which can prevent obedience to the Constitution, either North or South." Johnson chastised Congress for creating "the only obstacle ... to a perfect union of all the States" by the excessive use of legislative power. He warned that by denying constitutional liberty to the south, Congress threatened to dissolve the Union and repeal the Constitution. "That is a power," Johnson said, "which does not belong to any department of this Government, or to all of them united."[24]

Again he condemned Congress for denying a republican form of government to ten states of the south — the right to habeas corpus, trial by jury, personal freedom, and security without the fear of prejudice or "rapacity of the ruler." Johnson agreed that the freedmen deserved equal rights and equal protection, but he refuted the notion that they should rule the white race, and make and administer new laws. "Would such a trust and power be safe in such hands?" he asked.[25]

The president's message struck hard at the core beliefs of Radicals. Sumner, Stevens, Wade, Butler, Boutwell, Colfax, and all the others felt the barbs penetrate, and it only made them madder. But Johnson had not finished. He gave them something to think about, adding: "How far the duty of the President 'to preserve, protect, and defend the Constitution' requires him to go in opposing unconstitutional acts of Congress is a very serious question." Johnson suggested that "Where an act has been passed according to the forms of the Constitu-

tion... Executive resistance to it, especially in times of high party excitement, would be likely to produce violent collision between the respective adherents of the two branches of the Government. This would be simply civil war, and civil war must be resorted to only as a last remedy for the worst evils. Whatever might tend to provoke it should be most carefully avoided" as long as peaceable solutions remain open to the executive and his constituents. Johnson warned that if compelled to stand on his rights, he would do so regardless of the consequences. As an example, he said:[26]

> If Congress should pass an act which is not only in palpable conflict with the Constitution but will certainly, if carried out, produce immediate and irreparable injury to the organic structure of the Government, and if there be neither judicial remedy for the wrongs it inflicts nor power in the people to protect themselves without the official aid of their elected defender, — if, for instance, the legislative department should pass an act through all the forms of law to abolish a coordinate department of the Government, — in such a case the President must take the high responsibilities of his office and save the life of the nation at all hazards.[27]

Johnson admitted that while he considered the Reconstruction Acts unconstitutional, they did not fall "within the class last mentioned." But did the Boutwell-Stanton measure or the Tenure of Office Act apply? The president's message put the Radicals on notice. Come what may, he would fight them to the end and use every legal means at his disposal to beat them.[28]

Johnson's defiant protection of the Constitution won the praise of Democrats and appealed to a broad range of reflective Republicans. Sumner, however, raged against the message "as an incendiary document calculated to stimulate the rebellion once more and to provoke civil war." Now, he gloated, we have "evidence of a direct coalition between the President and the former rebels." But before the Senate could try Johnson, the House must first vote to impeach.[29]

For four days the House wrangled over the Judiciary Committee's recommendation. Midway through the debate James A. Garfield of Ohio took the floor, declaring that he had read all the testimony and concluded there was no case. "I shall therefore vote against the measure," said he, though "It may and probably will cost me my political life." By voting against impeachment, Garfield admitted that he would be going against the efforts of Wade, his fellow Ohioan, to become president and whose "late defeat makes this his only great chance life can offer." Republicans like James Blaine declared they would never vote for impeachment because they did not want any of Ben Wade's "Shellywaggers" around the White House. Forty-two Republicans joined with sixty-six Democrats to defeat the impeachment resolution, and Johnson escaped another crisis by a crushing 108 to 57 vote. Garfield, however, had a little political explaining to do. A few weeks later he did so, saying, "I voted against it not because I did not believe that his conduct deserved the severest condemnation, but because I did not believe the attempt was likely to be successful."[30]

The lopsided vote against impeachment reinforced Johnson's aggressive stand against the Radicals, but this did not deter the latter from investigating other channels. As a next step, they ques-

Ulysses S. Grant, general of the army, who practiced duplicity in the imbroglio between Congress and Johnson over the War Department. (From *Personal Memoirs of U.S. Grant.* New York: Charles H. Webster, 1886.)

tioned whether Johnson violated the Tenure of Office Act by removing Stanton. If so, all the other investigations could be dropped. For the Radicals, here was a fresh bone to chew.[31]

The tenure act required that the president give reasons for Stanton's suspension within twenty days after Congress reconvened. Stanbery urged Johnson to meet the deadline and both prepared drafts. Using Stanton's own condemnation of the act as unconstitutional and his subsequent failure to respond to General Baird's request for orders during the New Orleans riot, Stanbery justified the president's actions in a most favorable light. Johnson informed the Senate that Lincoln's mild reconstruction plan for the south had been prepared by Stanton and that he was merely carrying out the policy of his predecessor. "There is perhaps no act of my Administration," wrote Johnson, "for which I have been more denounced than this. It was not originated by me but I shrink from no responsibility on that account, for the plan approved itself to my own judgment and I did not hesitate to carry it into execution." Though Grant's close connection with the Republicans had become worrisome, Welles knew that Radicals would not want to oust the man they wished to make president, so he suggested that a section be added praising the general's able performance as secretary ad interim.[32]

On December 12 the Senate reviewed the president's justification for the war secretary's suspension. Stanton wrote a reply to Johnson's report, but he never sent it to the Senate. Because the impeachment resolution in the House had failed, and the nation responded favorably to Johnson's suspension message, Stanton saw no point in sending a rejoinder that would merely provoke another squabble between himself and

the president. Instead, he handed a copy of his rebuttal to Senator William A. Howard of Michigan, who leaked it to the press, enabling Stanton to get all his views before the public without initiating a personal exchange between himself and the president. Though characteristically sneaky, the document received sufficient attention in the Senate to keep the impeachment pot simmering.[33]

The Stanton-Grant situation gave the Senate trouble. Democrats and Republicans both courted Grant. The Senate would not reinstate Stanton if Grant wished to remain in the cabinet, nor would they anger the general by asking him to resign. John Binney, a New York political observer, wrote Senator Fessenden warning that Grant should not give his views on reconstruction prematurely because "his enemies would endeavor to destroy him as a Presidential candidate. Besides," Binney added, "in his present position as General of the Armies and Secretary of War, it is better that he interfere in politics as little as possible."[34]

Sumner, Wade, Stevens, and their associates looked about for a solution to the problem. Soon they would find one.

14

A Crisis in
the War Department

On Christmas Eve, Edwin M. Stanton returned to Washington, not to enjoy the holiday but to collaborate with his supporters. General Grant made overtures of friendship, and a few days later the *Intelligencer* reported the general in secret meetings with Stanton, Senator Howard, and several Republican congressmen. To some observers the conferences suggested a new power play on the part of Radicals. To reinstate Stanton, Grant must agree to resign as secretary ad interim, and the switch had to be accomplished with dignity and decorum so as not to tarnish the future president's image. The only reason why Stanton would want reinstatement would be to vindicate his removal, yet it was he who said that "any man who would retain his seat in the cabinet as an adviser when his advice was not wanted was unfit for the place." Grant, unwilling to expose himself by taking sides, made every effort to straddle the issue so as to appear neutral.[1]

Johnson soon learned of the plot and on January 7 asked his private secretary, Colonel William G. Moore, to write an order for Stanton's removal and prepare a brief message to the Senate advising them of the fact. He wanted the documents ready for signature "at any moment." If the Senate forced the issue of Stanton's reinstatement, Johnson also needed Grant's promise to not relinquish the office until the Tenure of Office Act could be tested by the Supreme Court. But would Grant cooperate? Not long after Stanton's suspension during the summer, Johnson had called upon Grant and asked what the general would do if the Senate attempted to reinstate the ex-secretary. Grant agreed to not become a party to the controversy, but agreed to return the office to the president "prior to a decision by the Senate," thereby providing Johnson with time to select another person for the office.[2]

On January 11 Johnson learned that the Senate did intend to reinstate Stanton, so once again he went to Grant to be doubly certain that the general would keep his word. Grant confirmed that he would either remain as head of the war department until the court ruled on the legality of Stanton's reinstatement, or he would vacate the office in sufficient time for Johnson to fill it before the Senate acted. Because the conversation took place on a Saturday, Grant promised to make a final decision no later than Monday.[3]

Edwin Stanton being congratulated by Radicals upon being reinstated as secretary of war. (Library of Congress, from Leslie's *Illustrated Weekly*.)

Monday came, but Johnson could not find Grant. While the president waited, the Senate sat for six hours in executive session discussing Stanton's reinstatement. During the debate Senator George F. Edmunds of Vermont introduced a resolution to inquire into the procedural rules for impeachment. Edmunds' motion did not need to be explained to be understood. Toward night-fall the Senate adopted a final resolution, declaring they did "not concur" with Stanton's suspension. A messenger delivered authenticated copies to Johnson, Grant, and Stanton. Finding himself in an awkward position, Grant sought advice from General Sherman. Together they decided that Grant should quickly extricate himself from the problem and, when doing so, suggest to Johnson the appointment of ex-governor Samuel Sunset Cox of Ohio as a replacement. Instead of disposing of the matter himself, Grant used Sherman to enlist the help of Reverdy Johnson. Both men went to the White House on Sunday to recommend Cox. Johnson still believed he had Grant's word and chose not to act. Sherman interposed himself on behalf of Grant and on Monday again met with the president. That evening the general and Mrs. Grant attended an affair at the White House. Though aware of the action of the Senate, Grant mentioned nothing of retracting his promise to the president. Therefore, Johnson expected Grant to retain his ad interim status and await the decision of the court.[4]

Very early Tuesday morning Grant called upon Assistant Adjutant General Edward D. Townsend and handed him the key to the war department, saying, "I am to be found over at my office at army headquarters. I was served with a copy of the Senate resolution last evening." Townsend went upstairs and delivered the key to Stanton, who by prearrangement was there and waiting for it. Stanton entered the office and drew $3,000 as back pay for the months of his suspension. He then issued a circular to Grant and bureau heads announcing his return to power.

Grant absented himself from the White House, though he sent his aide, General Cyrus B. Comstock, with a message to the president notifying him of the receipt of the resolution from the Senate. Grant concluded the message by saying that he complied with the conditions expressed in the Tenure of Office Act and that his ad interim status ended the moment he received notification from the Senate. Shocked by Grant's breach of faith, Johnson summoned the general to the White House and called a cabinet meeting.[5]

The general arrived to find the president, Seward, McCulloch, Welles, Browning, and Randall impatiently waiting. Grant said he came at the president's request though he considered himself relieved of his duties. Johnson asked if his surrender of the war department conformed to their previous understanding. Grant admitted having made such a promise. Johnson then asked was there not an understanding that the office be returned to the president should the general choose to vacate it. Grant again admitted having done so, but, he said, upon reviewing the second and fifth sections of the tenure act, he found himself unwilling to "suffer five years' imprisonment and pay ten thousand dollars fine." To the president's reminder that any fine would be paid by himself, Grant merely replied that he had attempted to alleviate the problem by sending Reverdy Johnson and General Sherman to the White House to propose Cox for the post. The president confirmed the meeting took place but expressed disappointment that Grant had chosen to not come himself. But why, he then asked, "did you give up the keys to Mr. Stanton and leave the department?" Grant fumbled for an answer, replying that he had given the keys to Townsend and sent word to the White House through General Comstock. "Yes," said Johnson, "but that, you know, was not our understanding." The general reddened with embarrassment, mumbling that he had been "busy with General Sherman" and not expecting the "Senate intended to act so soon." He then apologized and excused himself from the meeting. Though immensely irritated, Johnson remained calm and dignified during the interview. But as soon as Grant retired, Johnson turned to his secretary to say that if Stanton attempted to enter the president's office, to kick him out.[6]

Troubled by the rift with the president, Grant returned to the White House on Wednesday with Sherman. Both men offered to ask Stanton to resign. In the meantime the press picked up the story and condemned Grant's broken promises. The *New York World* denounced the act as unbecoming an officer and a gentlemen. Where the information came from cannot be traced to Johnson, but the content read like notes from the recent cabinet meeting. The general asked Johnson to repudiate the story, but the president said he had not read the article but would. All three men then fell into a friendly conversation. As Sherman and Grant departed, the latter turned to Johnson and said, "Mr. President, you should make some order that we of the army are not bound to obey the orders of Mr. Stanton as secretary of war." Johnson intimated that he might do so without being certain if he could.[7]

Returning to his office, Grant received a summons from Stanton to come to the war department. The secretary had an annoying way of issuing orders to generals as if they were foot soldiers. After the meeting Grant confided to Sherman his annoyance at Stanton's imperious conduct. Sherman disliked Stanton, and on January 18 he wrote Johnson that he and Grant would go to the war department to encourage the secretary to give up the office.[8]

The dates of the actual meeting became confused by different accounts. Grant appears to have gone to the war department alone, because on January 19 he wrote Johnson, "I had an interview alone with Mr. Stanton which led me to the conclusion that any advice to him of the kind would be useless, and I so informed General Sherman." Since Grant, on January 15, had asked Johnson for instructions to disregard all orders from Stanton, the president was now annoyed enough to issue such an order. Though there is some doubt of Grant's veracity in reporting to Johnson his conversation with Stanton, he did travel to Richmond two days later and confided to General Schofield that Stanton's conduct had been "intolerable." Grant appeared both sincere and emphatic when he declared his intention to demand Stanton's removal or the acceptance of his own resignation as general of the armies. Grant, however, had tied himself to the Radicals. Though squirming under a charge of treachery, and distressed by being drawn into embarrassing correspondence, Grant looked to the Radicals for salvation. They had no intention of letting him undermine their plot to oust Johnson or their plans to run him for president in 1868. With the Republican National Convention already scheduled, they were determined that if Grant was to have an altercation with anyone, it would be with Johnson — not Stanton.[9]

Donn Piatt, one of the men who knew Stanton well, wrote that the secretary disliked Grant and had no hesitation in expressing contempt for him. Piatt characterized Stanton as a person "without exception more subject to personal likes and dislikes, more vindictive in his gratification of the last, than any man ever called to public station." Whether Piatt deserved to be quoted may be questioned. One of Stanton's biographer's wrote that "it should be remembered that Piatt, according to a contemporary, was widely known in Washington as two of the three greatest liars in the town," but on his characterization of Stanton, Piatt may have been right.[10]

On January 24 Grant asked Johnson for confirmation that he need not take orders from Stanton. Four days later he asked again, this time requesting the orders be in writing, giving as a reason that his personal honor had been compromised by accounts in the press leaked by the White House. Then in a curious turnabout he publicly communicated his own views, denying any commitment to Johnson regarding his surrender of the war department. Grant's behavior suggested a man attempting to set a trap.[11]

Losing patience with Grant, Johnson grumbled that he had tried to be decent but would be "damned if some things have not gone about as far as they are to go." Referring to the general as "spoiled," Johnson felt inclined to ignore Grant's request, remarking to his private secretary that "the general had been very restive under Mr. Stanton, had been very glad to get rid of him, had now put him back in the war department," and should now be left to "fight it out."[12]

Concluding that Stanton and the general would not "fight it out," Johnson calmed down and sent Grant written instructions "to not obey any order from the war department ... unless such order is known by the general commanding the armies of the United States to have been authorized by the executive." Instead of following orders, Grant went to Stanton, who said that since the war department had received no instructions from the president "limiting or impairing his authority to issue orders to the army," he would therefore continue to issue whatever orders he saw fit. Grant returned to the White House to explain the turnabout to Johnson. Since the authority of Stanton had not been counter-manded by the president, the commanding general must therefore assume that any orders coming from the secretary were by direction of the president. In other words, Grant would follow the orders of Stanton regardless of whether they came from the president. Thus an impasse, for no president could function by circumventing the secretary of war and remain in accord with the general of the army.[13]

On February 3 Johnson received an indignant letter from Grant demanding the publication of all correspondence between himself and the president. The general sought exoneration from participating "in the resistance of law, for which you hesitated to assume responsibility in orders, and thus to destroy my character before the country." On the same day Chester Hubbard of West Virginia, a personal friend of Stanton's, introduced a resolution in the Senate calling for all the recent correspondence between Johnson, Grant, and Stanton. Hubbard knew Stanton already had the correspondence, but he went fishing for any other documents that might exonerate Grant and incriminate Johnson. Working in concert with Radicals, Stanton advised Speaker Colfax that he had received no "personal or written communication with the President since the 12th of August last."[14]

In a review of the documents, the cabinet judged them "highly discreditable to Grant's integrity, honor, ability, and truth," yet the general demanded they be published. Welles believed the general "played a false and treacherous part with the President throughout. From the first," he wrote, "[Grant] has studied to deceive the man who trusted him." Because the cabinet caught Grant in several lies, Welles concluded that "there is a conspiracy maturing for the overthrow of the administration and the subversion of the government and our federal system. The Radicals are using Grant as their tool; he is prepared to use them for his purpose." Johnson decided to spare Grant and gave nothing to the press. Grant, however, on February 6 published the documents that put himself before the public in the most favorable light.

Grant's behavior outraged the president. Though fully aware of the general's popularity, Johnson worked with the cabinet to prepare a rebuttal. On February 10 the press carried the president's reply, adding the documents Grant had omitted and reminding the general of his duty to obey the orders of the commander in chief of the army. The *New York World* observed that Johnson's "last letter is a document which General Grant's reputation can ill afford to have pass into history." In it, Johnson wrote:[15]

> You here admit that from the very beginning of what you term "the whole history" of your connection with Mr. Stanton's suspension, you intended to circumvent the President. It was to carry out that intent that you accepted the appointment.... You knew it was the President's purpose to prevent Mr. Stanton from resuming the office of Secretary of War, and you intended to defeat that purpose. You accepted the office not in the interest of the President but of Mr. Stanton.... You not only concealed your design from the President, but induced him to suppose that you would carry out his purpose to keep Mr. Stanton out of office, by retaining it yourself after an attempted restoration by the Senate, so as to require Mr. Stanton to establish his right by judicial decision.[16]

Having followed the break in relations between Johnson and Grant, a reporter from the *New York World* sought a comment from the head Radical. He found Stevens at home in an easy chair, looking exhausted. To the reporter's inquiry, Stevens replied, "What the devil do I care about the question of veracity between Johnson and Grant? Both may call each other liars if they want to; perhaps they both do lie a little, or, let us say, equivocate, though the president does seem to have the weight of evidence on his side.... If they want to settle the question between them, let them go out in any back yard and settle it." Stevens cared very much about Grant's reputation, and he deflected the nosy reporter with a harmless reply.[17]

For several months Johnson had attempted to keep Grant out of the hands of the Republicans, but the general succumbed to the influences of Radical power. Having joined them, Grant's break with Johnson became permanent. During the early aftermath of the crisis in the war department, Johnson missed an opportunity to square matters with Grant, who may have remained an ally had the president not stubbornly accused the general of duplicity. Instead, Johnson succeeded in pushing Grant into rapport with Stanton, who had considered giving up the office but not while under constant attack from the White House. By the slow process of self-destruction, Johnson's lack of political finesse began to isolate him from those who could help him win battles with Congress. Instead, to prove a point with the tenure act, he pitted himself against Congress and the army at a time when he and his administration were being discredited by the Radical press.[18]

Back on January 7 the president did not anticipate the defection of Grant when he asked Colonel Moore to prepare an order for the removal of Stanton. To test the tenure act, Stanton had to be removed and somebody put in his place. Grant's abdication of the office forced Johnson to look elsewhere, and no day passed without constant reminders of Stanton's unwanted presence. Neither spoke to the other, and the war department remained in a state of deliberate limbo.

Toward the latter part of January, Johnson contacted General Sherman and offered him the post ad interim. The president predicted that the tenure legislation "would not stand half an hour," but to bring it to court he needed to replace Stanton. Though Sherman respected the president and felt kindly toward him, he doubted whether Johnson had the power to suspend Stanton. He declined the offer, saying that he did "not want to live in Washington." To his wife he wrote, "I don't want to be involved in political combinations," but he also looked beyond the issue and said, "To remove Stanton by force, or a show of force, would be the very thing the enemies of the President want." In another letter to his wife he wrote, Washington is "full of spies and slanderers who stop at nothing to make game." Sherman understood his own fiery temperament and made a wise decision.[19]

Sherman escaped involvement with Johnson in bringing on the legal battle over the tenure act by judiciously extricating himself from a fight the president wanted. By detaching himself from what he called the "complications of politics," he forced Johnson to look for other alternatives, and none of them offered much promise.[20]

During the imbroglio with Johnson, Grant revealed flaws of character and judgment that would manifest themselves in the years to come. Easily influenced and easily led by persons who courted and befriended him, the general made an easy mark for unscrupulous predators who wanted something in return. Radicals promoted him for the presidency, but Grant did not know the personal price he would pay for the privilege. Welles captured the essence of Grant's weakness when on February 11 he wrote, "I presume he is surprised at his own folly and errors, and will, if he does not already, regret them. But he is now under the control of vicious and very bad men, who are using him for vicious purposes, and he assents with bad intent." Thad Stevens, one of the "bad men," validated Welles's opinion when he contemporaneously praised Grant's duplicity, saying "He is a bolder man than I thought him … now we will let him into the church."[21]

Stanton's occupation of the war department continued to perplex the administration. During a cabinet meeting on February 14, Welles asked, "Who is secretary of war?" Johnson replied, "That matter will be disposed of in one or two days." But Johnson could not find anybody foolish enough to act in an ad interim capacity just so the constitutionality of the act could be tested. The cabinet sought a person from the war department faithful to the president and suggested Edward D. Townsend, the assistant adjutant general, or John Potts, chief clerk of the war department, but Stanton had bullied the manhood out of both of them. That left sixty-three-year-old Adjutant General Lorenzo Thomas, an inept old army officer who Stanton kept busy far away from Washington. At Welles's suggestion, Johnson ordered Grant to restore Thomas to full control of the adjutant general's office and return him to the war department.

Ever since Lincoln took the oath of office in 1861, Lorenzo Thomas had held the same post. A typical army bureaucrat who had seen little action during the war, Thomas represented the older cadre of professional soldiers who understood military policy better than fighting. In Johnson's framework of thinking, Thomas' antipathy toward Stanton qualified him as a candidate for the office. The president did not expect Thomas to adapt well to a civilian role, but he intended the appointment to be an expedient and temporary. Brevet Major General Thomas returned to Washington, and on February 18 Johnson informed him of the possibility of becoming the interim secretary of war. Three days later the president summoned Thomas back to the White House and handed him two letters — one suspending Stanton for the second time and the other installing Thomas as secretary ad interim.[22]

Johnson's letter of suspension to Stanton read, "By virtue of the power and authority vested in me as President by the Constitution and the laws of the United States, you are hereby removed...." The words were vital because they expressed the precise premise on which Johnson wanted the tenure act adjudicated by the Supreme Court — the power of removal without the Senate's consent. The Constitution gave the president the "power to fill up all vacancies that may happen during the recess of the Senate," which he had done using Grant. In 1795 Congress enacted a law enabling the president to "authorize any person ... to perform the duties" of secretary of war "until a successor be appointed."[23]

Thomas accepted the appointment, marched to the war department, and handed Stanton the letter of suspension.

Stanton manifested a reluctance to open the letter but did. After digesting the contents he asked Thomas whether he should "vacate the office at once or will you give me time to remove my private property?" Thomas replied, "Act your pleasure." Stanton did not say how much time he needed, and Thomas did not ask. In the meantime Grant came into the room and Thomas showed him Stanton's letter. Grant asked for a copy, so Thomas departed and went to his office to copy and certify the order.[24]

During Thomas' absence, Stanton and Grant remained in conference. When Thomas returned, Stanton said, "I do not know whether I will obey your instructions or whether I will resist them." Thomas departed to report the interview to Johnson. When doing so he left the president with the impression that Stanton would vacate the department without a fuss. "Very well," said the president, "go and take charge of the office and perform the duties." Thinking that Thomas had assessed the situation accurately, Johnson notified his cabinet, saying, "perhaps he had delayed this step too long." Most members expressed relief that the ordeal had ended. Browning suggested that Stanton would probably resign now that he had been suspended. Welles said he doubted Stanton would do so unless the Radicals withdrew their support. He refused to believe that Stanton would "quietly surrender" and waited for confirmation that Thomas had actually taken physical possession of the office.[25]

Johnson promptly notified the Senate that Stanton had been suspended and Thomas appointed ad interim. Stanton immediately advised Thad Stevens' Reconstruction Committee that he had been ousted. In both chambers all regular business screeched to a halt. The House acted first. John Covode, an admitted illiterate, bounded to his feet with a resolution that Johnson "be impeached for high crimes and misdemeanors." Immediately afterwards the House sent a committee composed of Simon Cameron, Alexander G. Cattell, John Conness, and John M. Thayer to confer with Stanton on the use of different methods to resist the suspension.

A debate in the Senate raged late into the night. It finally ended with a party line vote resolving that "under the Constitution and laws of the United States, the President has no power to remove the Secretary of War and to designate any other officer to perform the duties of that office *ad interim.*" The Senate ruling, though expected, repudiated the agreement proposed by John Sherman that "the government will not be embarrassed by an attempt of a cabinet officer to hold on to his office despite the wish of the President."[26]

During the crisis in the war department, Lorenzo Thomas did nothing to assert himself. Instead, he returned to his hotel to prepare for a masked ball at Marini's Hall, where he openly gasconaded over becoming secretary of war. Walter Burleigh, a friend, asked Thomas, "When are you going to assume the duties of the office?" Thomas replied, "The next morning at ten o'clock." Burleigh seemed doubtful and asked, "Suppose Stanton objects to it, — resists?" "Well," Thomas replied, "I expect to meet force by force." "Suppose he bars the doors?" Burleigh asked. "I will break them down," Thomas said firmly, but Burleigh doubted whether the general possessed the fortitude to break anything down. Instead, Thomas remained away from the office throughout February 21, and Stanton remained in it.[27]

Thomas also failed to inform the president that the masked ball took precedence over his new responsibilities. When friends asked Johnson during the afternoon of the 21st whether Stanton opposed the order, Johnson replied, "There is no danger of that, as General Thomas [is] already in — This is but a temporary arrangement; I shall at once send in a good name for the office to the Senate."[28]

Thomas' glee over being named secretary lasted until 11:00 P.M., when J. W. Jones, an officer of the Senate, spotted the masked general and notified him in writing that the appointment was illegal. During the same evening a local socialite gave a large party that included officers from Major General William H. Emory's department of Washington. Edgar T. Welles, son of the secretary, attended the party and reported gaiety at its height when an orderly arrived with orders for the 5th Cavalry to report to headquarters. Later, a second orderly came with similar instructions to all officers of Emory's command. Puzzled by the flurry of activity, young Welles took leave and rushed home to report the matter to his father. The secretary directed his son to hurry to the White House and inform the president. Because of a diplomatic dinner, Edgar Welles could not get inside or find anyone to deliver the message, so he waited.[29]

Meanwhile, Stanton locked himself in the war department and met with Radical supporters. Together they composed an affidavit accusing Thomas of threatening Stanton with bodily harm if he refused to leave the office. They also accused Thomas of committing a "high misdemeanor" and demanded that a warrant be issued for his arrest. They addressed the document to David D.

Carrter, chief justice of the Supreme Court for the District of Columbia, one of Stanton's close friends. The committee got Carrter out of bed and obtained his signature on the warrant. Between two and three o'clock in the morning they roused the court clerk to get the judge's seal affixed to the warrant. Had events afterwards not moved so rapidly, Stanton and his cohorts may have blundered by opening the way for Johnson to challenge the tenure act.[30]

On the morning of February 22, before Lorenzo Thomas could rub the sleep from his eyes, U. S. Marshal David S. Gooding with two officers appeared at the general's home and arrested him. Thomas asked to speak with the president, and the party moved to the White House so the general could report his shocking surprise. Johnson listened then spoke, saying, "Very well, that is the place I want it in — the courts." He told Thomas to get help from Stanbery, so the party of four stopped at the attorney general's quarters before proceeding to the jail. Stanbery made a serious mistake by not advising Thomas to refuse bail and apply at once for a writ of habeas corpus, whereby the lawfulness of the arrest and the validity of the law under which the arrest had been made could be forced into court. Instead, Stanbery allowed Gooding to drag the badly shaken general into Judge Carrter's office without legal representation or anyone to advise him. Thomas finally sought legal counsel and obtained Richard T. Merrick, but not until after friends covered the $5,000 bail and secured Thomas' release. The general returned to the White House to report his troubles, but John-

son merely nodded with approval and said once more, "Very well, we want it in the courts."[31]

Bewildered, Thomas did not know what to do next, but believing he still occupied the office of secretary of war ad interim, he strolled over to the war department. Finding his own door locked, he climbed the stairs to Stanton's room. There he found the suspended secretary in conference with several members of Congress who had been with him through the night. Thomas offered to return later, but Stanton said, "Nothing private here, what do you want, sir?" Thomas demanded the office and ordered Stanton to leave. Stanton replied, "I deny your authority to act, and order you back to your own office." Thomas retorted, "I will stand here. I want no unpleasantness in the presence of these gentlemen." Stanton pompously replied, "You can stand there if you please, but you cannot act as Secretary of War. I am Secretary of War. I order you out of this office and to your own." The wrangle continued, and Thomas finally withdrew. He stepped across the hall and in an authoritative tone issued several orders to Townsend and Brevet Major General Edmund Schriver. Joined by two Congressmen, Stanton came into the room and rescinded the orders. Thomas hollered foul, and the bloodless conflict ignited all over again.[32]

The Congressmen withdrew, leaving Stanton and Thomas to settle their differences. Both men were exhausted, Stanton from a lack of sleep and Thomas from an excess of celebrating during the ball. "The next time you have me arrested," mumbled Thomas, "please do

Opposite: Cartoon of Stanton shutting door against General Thomas. (Leslie's *Illustrated Weekly*, March 7, 1868.)

not do it before I get something to eat." Sensing he had won, Stanton sidled over to Thomas and put his arm affectionately around the general's neck. Turning to Schriver, he said, "You have got a bottle here; bring it out." Schriver had only a vial, but a few minutes later a messenger arrived with a full bottle. "Now," said Stanton, as the two men heartily drank, "this at least is neutral ground."[33]

When Welles learned of the travesty at the war department, he declared Thomas unfit for any office of importance. "He is like a boy," wrote Welles, "ready to obey orders, but cannot himself act with decision or direct others, — is a mere child or worse in Stanton's presence. Instead of taking upon himself the duties of secretary of war and [countermanding] Stanton's orders, he is locked out of the department, laughed at, and treated with contempt." Johnson deserved a share of the blame because a prudent administrator would not have left the ousting of Stanton entirely in the hands of an incompetent general. Welles believed the consequences could have been averted had Johnson been more forthright with the cabinet and those in Congress who counted as his friends. One historian agreed, writing, "Johnson had overlearned the lesson of keeping his own counsel."[34]

Shortly after Thomas' arrest, Welles called upon the president to ask whether he had issued any orders mobilizing General Emory's command. When Johnson said he had not, Welles replied, "Some one has." The news disturbed Johnson because the orders would have come from either Stanton or Grant. Johnson summoned Emory and asked of any troop movements in the Washington area. Emory skirted the question, denying any outright activity but reminding Johnson

that "under a recent order ... founded upon a law of Congress, all orders had to be transmitted through General Grant to the army." He suggested that the president ask Grant. Johnson replied that under the Constitution the president is commander in chief and not Grant. Emory reminded Johnson that the latter had approved the Appropriation Act of 1867, which specifically provided that the general of the army would be headquartered in Washington and all military orders must come through him. Somewhat apologetically, Emory added, "We were bound by the order, constitutional or not constitutional." Now certain that Grant had issued the order, Johnson reflected a moment before dismissing Emory.[35]

As Emory departed, Thomas' attorney arrived at the White House with the court's papers. After Stanbery entered the conversation, the president asked Merrick whether the case could be brought before the Supreme Court immediately. Merrick did not know, so Stanbery asked him to find out.[36]

The president lacked confidence in Merrick, so he sent a carriage for attorney Walter S. Cox and summoned Thomas to the White House. When Cox arrived, he asked that necessary legal proceedings be initiated without delay to test Thomas' right to the war department. Cox agreed to taking the issue before the Supreme Court and withdrew to discuss the procedure with Stanbery.[37]

With this phase of the process underway, Johnson decided he had seen enough of Thomas and sent a message to the Senate nominating Thomas Ewing, Sr., of Ohio, as "Secretary of the Department of War." If Johnson could not get General Sherman to take the post, he would settle for the general's father-in-law. Colonel Moore carried the document to the Senate shortly after noon. The Senate had just adjourned, so Moore advised the House of the nomination. He returned to the White House and reported the lower chamber in the midst of a furious debate. Not until February 24 would the Senate officially see Johnson's message. By then, it would mean nothing.[38]

15

Johnson Is Impeached

It is difficult to understand how Johnson expected to overmatch Congress, even if the Supreme Court had been willing to stand against the legislature. Ever since the Milligan and test oath decisions a year earlier, the Radicals had bombasted the court with criticism. Proposals to limit the jurisdiction of the court, to require two-thirds of the judges to be in agreement on a verdict, to reduce its membership, even to abolish it altogether reflected the antagonistic attitude of the Radicals. The justices worried about this attack on their constitutional authority, but Johnson, at times, absorbed the threats impassively.

On crucial issues affecting the administration, he exacerbated the problems. He did not cleanse the cabinet of his enemies, fire the spies in the administration, or test the constitutionality of Congress' oppressive legislation in an expedient manner. He also bungled a most recent opportunity when on November 13, 1867, a Vicksburg editor and ex-Confederate colonel named William McCardle criticized General Ord, the district commander, and condemned the policy of Congress. Ord jailed McCardle, who petitioned the circuit court of Mississippi for a writ of habeas corpus. The circuit court denied the writ, but a law passed by Congress prior to the Reconstruction Acts enabled McCardle to appeal to the U. S. Supreme Court. The law had been passed to protect federal officers and other "loyal persons" against actions by state courts of the south. Though enacted to fetter southern courts, the McCardle case offered the Supreme Court an opportunity to strike away the chains and look into the constitutionality of Reconstruction. To start the ball rolling McCardle hired Jeremiah Black, a confidential adviser to the president but a former associate of Stanton.[1]

When 1867 elections went against the Radicals, the losses caused them to take special interest in this case. Grant asked Stanton and Senator Lyman Trumball to conduct Ord's defense, and Stanton added Matthew H. Carpenter of Wisconsin to the team. The three lawyers prepared a brief sustaining the legitimacy of the Reconstruction laws. Simultaneously, Congress began work on a measure of self-defense against the court.[2]

Johnson blundered by thrusting Black on McCardle. Critics accused the president of using his attorney to launch an attack on Congress and the army. Senator Doolittle warned the president to not get involved. On January 11 he warned again, this time advising Johnson that the Senate's military committee intended to reinstate Stanton as secretary of war. Johnson should have stood aside, but he believed Black would win the McCardle case. On January 17 the court agreed to hear arguments but not until the first Monday of March. The delay gave the Radicals time to block an adverse decision.[3]

Three days later the House attempted to pass a bill requiring a two-thirds vote for the passage of any decision by the Supreme Court, but the Senate rejected it. In the meantime Grant learned the Senate planned to sustain Stanton. He agreed to vacate the office the moment the Senate acted. Though Grant used the $10,000 fine imposed on interlopers as his reason for returning the keys to Stanton, he disapproved of the president's attack on Ord in the McCardle case. Johnson seemed unable to foresee how impulsive and indiscriminate acts alienated the people he needed.[4]

On February 22, soon after the Senate adjourned for the weekend, the House remained in session to debate impeachment, knowing the importance of having this done before the Supreme Court heard the McCardle case. House Radicals intended to thwart any exposure to having the Reconstruction Acts overturned. Word of the extended session leaked to the streets, and by noon spectators packed the galleries, crowded into the aisles, and flooded the hallways. Ben Wade, facing political extinction, ambled over from the Senate and took a seat beside Speaker Colfax. If the House impeached Johnson, the Senate Radicals would make Wade president. The House buzzed with feverish tension, stimulated by the rumor that men from Maryland were on the march to protect the president. Colfax could no longer bring the House to order or constrain the crowd, so he called for help from the capital police.[5]

Earlier, John Covode had proposed a vague resolution to impeach the president for unspecified high crimes and misdemeanors. Colfax turned the matter over to Stevens' Reconstruction Committee, and the members retired to a private room to compose a resolution. The galleries waited expectantly for the return of Stevens. At 2:20 P.M. he hobbled into the chamber, followed by his committee. No one needed to guess the outcome. Stevens declared that no debate was necessary — Johnson's crimes were too obvious for argument, his guilt too plain for discussion.[6]

Not all of Stevens' committee agreed. James Brooks of New York, one of two Democrats, argued against "this untoward, this unholy, this unconstitutional proceeding." He warned that if Congress stripped Johnson of power to make Ben Wade president, "you settle that hereafter a party having a sufficient majority in the House and the Senate can depose the President of the United States." This, of course, was exactly how the British Parliament worked — a system of government that men like Sumner preferred. The Democrats asked Stevens to give reasons for Johnson's impeachment. Edward R. Phelps of Maryland facetiously replied, "whether white men or negroes shall control ten states and through them the nation." Other members of the House demanded to know the specifics of the charges. Stevens had none, other than to condemn Johnson of atrocious attempts to "usurp the liberty and destroy the happiness of this nation as were ever perpetrated by the most detestable tyrant who ever oppressed his fellow man." He supported his views by reminding opponents that impeachment was a political rather than a criminal proceeding, confirming in his own words the warning of Brooks — that

Cartoon of "Old Thad" commanding impeachment. (*Harper's Weekly*, May 2, 1863.)

any president could be ousted if the House and Senate controlled the required majority. Holman of Indiana responded, arguing that Johnson committed a "crime" when he involved Grant in diminishing the intent of the tenure law by acting in defiance of the exclusive power of the Senate to do so. George Woodward, a Democrat from Pennsylvania, replied that Stanton had been appointed by Lincoln, therefore his office expired one month after Lincoln's death. Johnson could have removed him "within the strictest bounds of the Constitution" at any time without breaking any law.[7]

On into the night of February 22 the debate that Stevens wanted to avoid tempestuously raged until late afternoon on the 24th. At last came the vote, and by a margin of 126 to 47, the House decided — for the first time in American history — to impeach a president.[8]

Thaddeus Stevens being carried into the Senate in his chair. (Leslie's *Illustrated Weekly*, March 28, 1868.)

The vote fortified Stevens. Though quite feeble and slowly dying, he asked that two committees be established — a committee of two consisting of himself and John Bingham to notify the Senate, and a committee of seven to draft articles of impeachment. Stevens appeared to be hanging onto life for one reason, to destroy his archenemy, the president. On February 25 two black porters carried

Stevens announcing Johnson's impeachment to the Senate. (Leslie's *Illustrated Weekly*, March 14, 1868.)

him through the snow to the Senate. After they gently lowered his feet to the floor, Stevens took his cane in one hand and holding fast to Bingham with the other, walked down the aisle to the well. Wade looked down from the president's chair and waited anxiously to receive his friend's message. "Mr. President," said Stevens, "In obedience to the order of the House of Representatives we appear before you, and in the name of the House of Representatives and all the people of the United States, we do impeach Andrew Johnson ... of high crimes and misdemeanors in office." When asked for the articles of impeachment, Stevens replied that they were being drafted and would soon be available. He demanded that the Senate order the president to appear for trial. Wade, the expectant beneficiary of Johnson's removal, replied, "The

Senate will take order in the premises." Clutching Bingham's arm, Stevens retired from the chamber.[9]

Stevens and Bingham also served on the committee of seven, which included George S. Boutwell, George W. Julian, John A. Logan, James F. Wilson, and Hamilton Ward. After examining witnesses, the committee drafted nine articles charging Johnson with attempting to remove Stanton from office, appointing Thomas in his stead, and for informing General Emory that the law depriving the president of full command of the army was unconstitutional. The articles contained only weak accusations, but after hours of argument Stevens coerced the House into passing them. Each article pertained to the events of February 21–22, and each repeated some portion of another. Dissatisfied with the work of his own committee, Stevens asked Ben Butler to lend a hand and add at least two more articles with "real vigor in them." The deposed general needed a platform from which to promote his political ambitions and gladly accepted the invitation. He conceived Article 10, accusing Johnson of making inflammatory speeches designed to bring Congress into disrepute during the president's swing around the circle. Brainstorming gave rise to Article 11, drafted by Wilson, Butler, and Stevens. It contained a dazzling and somewhat incomprehensible array of all the previous charges, adding that the president violated the law when he disregarded Reconstruction Acts and declared the 40th Congress illegal because it excluded ten states of the south. The last article, wrote James F. Rhodes, was merely "a trick to catch wavering Senators." Taken together, all the charges represented "the most trifling crimes and misdemeanors which they could select from the official life of Andrew Johnson."[10]

On February 29 the House elected managers, naming Stevens, Bingham, Boutwell, Butler, Williams, John A. Logan, and James F. Wilson to present the case. Being too feeble to act as chairman, Stevens yielded to Boutwell, but Bingham demanded the chair and got it. On March 3, with finishing touches made to the articles, the managers strolled to the Senate. Stevens led the procession, carried once again in a chair by two muscular black porters.[11]

Bingham presented the articles to the Senate, which had already organized itself into a High Court of Impeachment with rules of procedure. One impediment to a fair trial involved Wade, who some members argued could not be partial because, as acting vice president, he

would become president upon Johnson's conviction. This did not dissuade the Radicals. Since Johnson's son-in-law, David T. Patterson, was entitled to a vote, they agreed to let Wade vote. The managers then asked that Johnson be summoned to testify and to respond no later than March 13. Having accomplished their purpose, the House managers withdrew.[12]

The Senate adopted its rules without conferring with Chief Justice Chase. They still thought of themselves as a legislative body and not a court. Chase made it clear that a trial must be conducted before the Senate, whose organization as a court must precede any action on the impeachment. Chase's charge went directly to the heart of the flimsy case concocted by the Radicals, who had attempted to unfetter themselves from any form of judicial restraint. But as a court, the Senate would be expected to prove the impeachment case within the principles of justice.[13]

Stevens did not like the rules. Word leaked that during the days before the trial began he had accosted each senator who might dare go against the party to coerce his vote. "It must shame and mortify some of the intelligent minds in the Senate," wrote Welles, "to be held in subjection and compelled to receive the excoriations and threatenings of this wicked and bad man, but it is questionable whether they have the moral courage and independence to do right, when the terrors of this party tyrant are before them."[14]

On Wednesday, February 26, while the House worked assiduously on drafting articles of impeachment, Lorenzo Thomas had his day in court. Cox and Merrick, Thomas's attorneys, decided that Stanbery had blundered by allowing

Johnson and disposed of the tenure law on constitutional grounds.[15]

In the meantime, Stanton surrounded himself with a company of infantry. With a box of cigars and a bottle of whiskey, he beleaguered himself in the war department. Grant provided the troops but privately condemned the secretary for behaving too much like a coward. Depictions by cartoonists of Stanton's "fortification and entrenchment" of the war department gave the president and his cabinet a rare moment of humor during the troubling days of the impeachment crisis.[16]

House members did not wait long to feel the impact of their impeachment vote. The New York police chief advised Colfax that nitroglycerine had disappeared from the city and warned it might be on the way to Washington. The news sent a shock wave through the Capitol. "Consternation of the gallant band of Radicals became excessive," and Congress adjourned while soldiers searched the building.[17]

Benjamin F. Butler, representative from Massachusetts, who became a leading and divisive prosecutor in the trial of Andrew Johnson. (Massachusetts Commandery Military Order of the Loyal Legion and the U.S. Army Military History Institute.)

the general to go free on bail. They planned to surrender Thomas to the jailer and then sue for a writ of habeas corpus. Judge Carrter had privately discussed this eventuality with Stanton and decided to foil the attempt. Because the House had impeached the president, Carrter dismissed the case, thereby depriving Johnson of his one chance to bring the tenure act before the Supreme Court. Welles lamented, "The President has from the first extended to Stanton a consideration and leniency that has surprised me, for he knew him to be false, remorseless, treacherous and base." Nearly sixty years passed before Chief Justice William Henry Taft vindicated

From north and south, veterans of the war flooded the White House with letters, offering to raise regiments to march on Washington and defend the president. In a few days thousands had volunteered to impede the actions of Congress — 2,000 from Pennsylvania, 5,000 from Indiana, 30,000 from Virginia, 100,000 from Tennessee. If Andrew Johnson wanted another civil war, he might have one. This time it was not the north against the south — it was the nation, or at least part of it, against the Radicals. Johnson appreciated the support, but he wanted no more bloody conflicts during his watch.[18]

Edwin Stanton beleaguered in the war department. (Library of Congress, from Leslie's *Illustrated Weekly*.)

From St. Louis, General Sherman warned his brother, "If the Democratic party intend[s] to fight on this impeachment ... you may count on 200,000 against you in the south. The negroes are no match for them." He also warned that Republicans would look bad if they all voted the same way. "They should act as judges," the general declared, "and not as partisans." Brother John replied, promising to give Johnson "a fair and impartial trial," but he blamed the impeachment impetus on the president, scornfully regarding him "as a foolish and stubborn man, doing even right things in a wrong way, and in a position where the evil that he does is immensely increased by his manner of doing it." Days before the trial began, John Sherman had decided how he would vote.[19]

On the morning of March 4 hundreds of the most fashionable women in Washington crowded into the Senate to hear the formal presentation of the articles of impeachment. By noon the galleries could hold no more. Shortly after 1:00 P.M. the main doors opened and the sergeant-at-arms announced the arrival of the House managers. Arm and arm, two by two, they made their entrance. First came Bingham and Boutwell, followed by Butler and Wilson, and finally Logan and Williams. Straggling in the rear hobbled Stevens, buttressed on both sides by friends and thumping his cane. Wade greeted the managers from the president's chair and asked them to take seats provided before the bar — Stevens, Bingham, Boutwell, and Logan on the left; Butler, Williams, and Wilson on the right.[20]

The House managers represented a cast of characters not uncommon in politics. George Boutwell, a narrow-minded and vindictive partisan, loved notoriety and hated Andrew Johnson. Thomas Williams, known as a remorseless manipulator, respected neither the Constitution nor the truth. He had been Stanton's partner in law. John Bingham, known as "a shrewd and tricky lawyer," once advocated sweeping away the Supreme Court's appellate jurisdiction in all cases. James Wilson had opposed impeachment, but fell into line with the Radicals as "a sinner come to repentance." John Logan had been among the hundred who recently guarded Stanton from the feeble efforts of Lorenzo Thomas to secure the war department. Ben Butler, potbellied, cross-eyed, and groveling to recapture lost political power, waited impatiently to employ his skills as the bullying barrister. And old Thad Stevens, with death at his doorstep, fought to live long enough to destroy Andrew Johnson.[21]

At Wade's bidding the sergeant-at-arms raised his voice and in clarion tones

pronounced: "Hear ye! Hear ye! Hear ye! All persons are commanded to keep silence in pain of imprisonment, while the House of Representatives is exhibiting to the Senate of the United States articles of impeachment against Andrew Johnson, President of the United States." Silence pervaded the chamber as the managers rose — all but Stevens — and Bingham unfolded two quires of foolscap paper stitched together in book form. Slowly, and in a measured tone that carried to all corners of the chamber, Bingham read the charges against Johnson. When done, he folded the booklets and sat down. The Senate moved for adjournment until the following day.[22]

On the morning of March 5 two important events seemed on a course for collision. The Supreme Court, with Chief Justice Chase presiding, opened its first day of hearings on the McCardle case. The arguments had just begun when a committee from the Senate entered the court to escort Chase to the impeachment trial. Entwined in both courts were the destinies of the south and of Andrew Johnson.[23]

Clad in his black judicial robes, the tall, elegant figure of Salmon P. Chase entered the Senate chamber and followed his escort to the bar. The crowded galleries barely uttered a breath as senators came to their feet and stood silently as Chase passed down the aisle. Wade rapped his gavel, and in obedience to the Constitution, surrendered his chair to the presiding chief justice. As Wade stepped down, Chase turned to Justice Samuel Nelson, who had accompanied him to the Senate, and said, "I am now ready to take the oath." With the galleries standing, Chase swore to "do impartial justice according to the Constitution and the laws; so help me God."[24]

Thaddeus Stevens and John A. Bingham before the Senate. (Library of Congress, from Leslie's *Illustrated Weekly*.)

After taking the oath, Chase ordered it administered to each senator. One by one the secretary called their names alphabetically, and each swore to "do impartial justice." They were now a High Court of impeachment and no longer merely politicians with party agendas.

Lord Macauley of Great Britain thought not, writing from experience, "They are all politicians. There is hardly one among them whose vote on impeachment may or may not be confidently predicted before a witness has been examined; and even if it were possible to rely on their

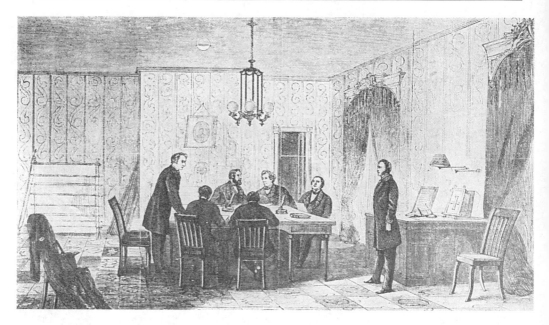

Andrew Johnson consulting with his counsel. (Library of Congress, from Leslie's *Illustrated Weekly*.)

justice, they would still be quite unfit to try such a cause."[25]

When the Senate secretary called for Wade to take the oath, Thomas A. Hendricks of Indiana objected, declaring Wade ineligible to take part in the trial. Because Wade would ascend to the presidency on Johnson's conviction, he would have a prejudicial interest "in the result of the proceedings." Hendricks cited the Constitution as providing that "in such a case the possible successor cannot even preside in ... the trial." The debate over the issue continued for the remainder of the day and eventually lapsed into the following day. Shouted down by Radicals from every corner of the chamber, Hendricks finally withdrew his objection with the understanding that he could present it again at a later time. Though Wade could have acted with honor and recused himself, his ebbing political prospects stimulated acts of flagrant desperation. He took the

oath of impartiality, and on March 6 the proceedings resumed.[26]

On March 7 the Senate served the president with a summons that did not require him to appear in person, and Johnson asked the advice of his cabinet. Some thought he should appear, but Welles dissented, arguing that doing so would give undeserved dignity to the proceedings and play directly into the hands of the conspirators. Welles prevailed, and the cabinet finally agreed that the president would be better represented by the appointment of competent attorneys. Perhaps they remembered Johnson's swing around the circle, because the president was still too much of a fighter to keep his mouth shut.[27]

The best minds in the cabinet worked with Johnson to develop a short list of potential lawyers to represent him at the trial. After much discussion they settled on Attorney General Stanbery, Jeremiah S. Black, Benjamin R. Curtis,

Benjamin R. Curtis, one of the president's distinguished lawyers during the impeachment trial. (Library of Congress.)

William M. Evarts, and Thomas A. R. Nelson of Tennessee. All were lawyers of the highest standing at the bar with the exception of Nelson, who, coming from the south, lacked the national exposure of the others. Stanbery, who had been ill, told the president that if he could keep well for the duration of the trial, he would be willing to be sick for the remainder of his life.[28]

Fifty-nine-year-old Benjamin Curtis came from Massachusetts, where he had established a reputation for being one of the finest representatives at the American bar. "He was," wrote one historian, "an ornament to the state that Benjamin F. Butler misrepresented." For six years Curtis sat on the bench of the United States Supreme Court before resigning the post to resume the practice of law. As a justice he wrote one of the great dissents in the Dred Scott case. Of these distinguished attainments, Andrew Johnson would need all.[29]

For the past two years Jeremiah Black had acted as Johnson's adviser and counsel, and the two men knew each other well. Black had been instrumental in coaxing from the Supreme Court a decision favorable to the president in the Milligan case. He also worked in preparing many of Johnson's veto messages and proclamations by applying constitutional law to the issues confronting the administration.[30]

Fifty-year-old William M. Evarts graduated from Yale and became the acknowledged leader of the New York bar. He stayed out of politics by choice, though he understood all the vicissitudes of political pandering. A man of great intellect, Evarts radiated confidence, moral persuasion, energy, and a capacity for hard work that few could match. Like

Jeremiah S. Black, counsel to president, fired by Johnson because of his involvement with Benjamin F. Butler. (Library of Congress.)

none other, he looked like what he was — a lawyer who could not be taken lightly in or out of any court of law.[31]

Thomas A. R. Nelson came from Johnson's hometown of Greeneville. They were old friends in a situation that neither of them understood. Nelson served briefly in Congress, but for the better part of thirty years he practiced law in the mountain towns of east Tennessee and worked every type of case that could be heard before a court of law. He brought to the team a rough, forensic force that men like Stanbery, Curtis, Black, and Evarts lacked.[32]

For the trial the Senate printed one thousand tickets, and no one, except those having the privileges of the floor, would be admitted without one. Four tickets went to each senator, forty to Washington diplomats, four to the chief justice, two to each member of the cabinet, twenty to the president, and sixty to the press. The remainder went to House members and other public officials.[33]

Not content with placing Johnson on trial, the Radicals committed one more equally contemptible act. Though they loathed Seward, they attempted to bribe him. If he would abandon Johnson, they would keep him in the state department after Wade became president. To their offer, Seward replied, "I will see you damned first, the impeachment of the president is the impeachment of the cabinet." When Seward informed Johnson of the bribe, the president replied, "I will have to insult some of these men yet."[34]

On March 9 Johnson anxiously

William M. Evarts, one of the country's most distinguished lawyers, who defended the president during the impeachment trial. (Library of Congress.)

watched as the Supreme Court reconvened to consider the McCardle case. Fearing an unfavorable opinion, Radicals took the matter into their own hands. On March 12 they rushed through an amendment on a pending measure in an effort to strip the Supreme Court of jurisdiction in the matter. Before the day ended, the bill passed in both houses. The *New York Herald* growled: "The country is in the hands of Congress. That Congress is the Radical majority, and that Radical majority is old Thad Stevens." But the Supreme Court still had time to act. The bill could not become law for at least ten days. An opinion in the McCardle case could be written in less time than that. The *Boston Post* agreed, writing that the great tribunal must act, if for no other reason than to protect its own dignity" and to show that the court cannot be trifled with by reckless partisans who flippantly speak of 'clipping the wings of the court.'" Six of the judges, including Chase, had examined the Reconstruction laws and believed them to be unconstitutional. But would they act? Did the great minds of the court possess the fortitude to resist Radical pressure and behave like an independent judiciary?[35]

On March 12 Stanbery resigned as attorney general to spend full time on Johnson's defense. Before departing from his final cabinet meeting, Stanbery turned to Johnson and said, "You are now, Mr. President, in the hands of your lawyers, who will speak and act for you, and I must begin by requesting that no further disclosures be made to newspaper correspondents.... They injure your case and embarrass your course." Stanbery had good reason for scolding Johnson. The president had leaked to the press an important precedent discovered by Seward that pertained to the removal of cabinet officers. It could be used by the defense to vindicate Johnson. Though Stanbery intended the caution to serve as friendly advice, the president felt rebuked. It was just what he needed.[36]

16

The Trial Begins

At eleven o'clock on the morning of Friday, March 13, 1868, the privileged ticket-holders for the trial of Andrew Johnson began filing into the Senate. Earlier, the ladies of Washington participated in a scramble for the last available tickets. Now bedecked in their frilly splendor, they fought for the best seats from which to witness the historical pageant. It did not matter if the trial would not start for another two hours, they would wait and defend their point of vantage. In a gallery designated for diplomats sat the wife and two daughters of Ben Wade. From their ringside seats the Wade family took a special interest in the proceedings. After the trial ended, they expected to occupy the White House.[1]

For Charles Sumner the affair marked the pinnacle of his fight to remove Johnson—a moment sought since 1865 when he and Johnson no longer agreed on policy. For more than two years Sumner denounced the president, often in frenzied demands for his impeachment. So agitated had he become at Johnson's condemnation of Congress that he threatened to reprimand the House if members failed to bring impeachment proceedings. After hoping that Johnson would suspend Stanton so a case could be made for the president's impeachment, Sumner flew into a rage when he learned that many House Re-

publicans believed the secretary's removal had been done properly and were more concerned about losses to Democrats during the 1867 election. "Those elections only show more imperatively the necessity of impeachment," declared Sumner. Though on numerous past occasions the House had defeated calls for Johnson's removal, the day of judgment had finally come, and Sumner believed, as did Wade and Stevens, that the president would be convicted.[2]

At one o'clock Chief Justice Chase entered the Senate. His daughter, Kate Chase Sprague, wife of Senator William Sprague of Rhode Island, sat among the diplomats and smiled approvingly as her father ambled solemnly toward his elevated but temporary throne. She still believed her father should be president.

Then came the House managers, who took seats arranged around a large table on the right side of the aisle. On the opposite side stood an empty table awaiting the attorneys for the defense. With standing room only in the rear of the chamber and the aisles and balconies filled to capacity, the chaplain opened the proceedings with a prayer. Invoking guidance from the Lord for those sitting in judgment, he prayed that their decisions in the trial "be sanctioned by the High Court of Heaven." The loud voice of the sergeant-at-arms interrupted a

The House managers being ushered into the Senate. (Library of Congress, from Leslie's *Illustrated Weekly*.)

moment of after-prayer silence. "Andrew Johnson, President of the United States ... appear and answer the articles of impeachment exhibited against you by the House of Representatives of the United States."[3]

But Andrew Johnson did not appear. Instead, Senator Reverdy Johnson announced that the president had retained counsel, who were waiting in a room outside the chamber. Presently Stanbery, Curtis, and Nelson entered and were ushered into chairs at the empty table across the aisle from the managers. Another shuffle ensued when members of the House filed into seats arranged in the aisles. When the commotion subsided, Chase called the chamber to order. "Gentlemen," he said, "the Senate is now sitting for the trial of articles of impeachment. The President of the United

States appears by counsel. The court will now hear you."[4]

Stanbery rose, qualifying himself and announcing Curtis, Black, Evarts, and Nelson as counsel for the president. He asked for "at least forty days" to prepare the defense. Stanbery not only needed the time, but he privately wanted to give the Supreme Court an opportunity to study the McCardle case and publish their opinion, which he hoped would be favorable to the president.[5]

Bingham objected. The House managers wanted no delay. He demanded that the president's answers to the charges be filed immediately and stressed that the trial must proceed on the assumption the president pleads "not guilty." Stanbery agreed with the plea, but he continued to argue for time, comparing the managers' demands to treating the president's trial "as if it were a matter before a police court." But Bingham wanted no time given for the president's defense. The debate heated to the point where the Senate asked for a recess to retire for consultation. Seventy-one minutes later the High Court returned, ruling that Johnson be given until March 23 to file his answer. Stanbery had asked for forty days; he received but nine.[6]

The date for the trial to resume became another subject of debate. Some senators suggested April 6, others wanted it to begin sooner. Ben Butler shifted into gear and demanded expedience. The president controlled too much power, he said, and to prevent its use, he must be removed. To observers it became clear that Butler wanted to conduct the prosecution — not with the decorum of good practice but as a horse thief case. No argument, no logic, no common sense put forth by the defense could quell Butler's demand for a fast trial. Even Chase failed to assert himself. After much discussion the Senate moved that the trial resume as Butler proposed, not on some day in April but on March 23. Welles, who had been ill, condemned the Senate as men "scarcely worthy to sit in judgment in such a case," adding that "a majority of the Senators have prejudged the case, and are ready to pronounce judgment without testimony."[7]

With the trial adjourned until March 23, the Radicals busied themselves counting noses in the Senate and canvassing the vote. There being fifty-four senators, thirty-six votes were required to convict the president. Of that total, twelve were Democrats. If seven Republicans defected, Johnson would be acquitted, and the Radicals resolved to not let that happen. They had a plan, purely political and purely corrupt. They

had their eye on Alabama, where operatives hurried to bring a state government into being with offices filled by Republicans. On March 11 Congress rushed through a law enabling Alabama to expedite the ratification of a state constitution. Could this be done in time to pack the court? And then there was the McCardle case, and in all aspects the Radicals must find a way to strike it down.[8]

While organizing the defense, Johnson developed problems with one of his attorneys. Jeremiah Black represented clients with interests in the guano island of Alta Vela off the coast of Haiti but occupied by the Dominican Republic. He asked Seward to have a gunboat sent to the island to protect American interests. Seward refused, relying on a precedent of noninterference established in 1857 by Black himself, when acting as attorney general in Buchanan's administration. Five days after the House filed impeachment articles, Black pressed Johnson to overrule Seward. He went ever further. Four days before the trial he obtained from Butler an opinion favorable to his claim. With Butler's statement in his pocket, he then obtained written concurrence from Stevens, Logan, and Bingham, and forwarded the documents to Johnson. For a little war with Santo Domingo, said Black, perhaps all charges would be dropped. He then went to Welles to ask if any naval vessels had been dispatched for the war. Welles answered no. Convinced his scheme would prevail, Black called on the president the following day. Johnson calmly replied that he had no constitutional authority to submit to the request, nor would he contravene Black's own ruling of noninterference.[9]

"I have pointed your way to acquit-

Ben Butler delivering the opening speech. (Library of Congress, from Leslie's *Illustrated Weekly*, April 18, 1868.)

tal," declared Black, "and advise you to pursue it. You decline to do so. You will be convicted and removed from office. I prefer not to have you convicted on my hands, therefore I resign as your counsel from the impeachment case."

Johnson looked Black squarely in the eyes and replied, "You try to force me to do a dishonorable act contrary to law ... and against my conscience, and rather than do your bidding I'll suffer my right arm torn from its socket. Yes, quit

as you have declared you will do. Just one word more: I regard you as a damned villain, and get out of my office or, damn you, I'll kick you out."

Black wrote the president the following day asking that "bygones be forgotten" and sheepishly offered to continue to act as the president's counsel. Johnson replied through Stanbery, "Tell General Black he is out of the case and will stay out." The Radicals propagandized Black's dismissal, declaring that the lawyer had quit the president's case "in disgust" because it offered no prospect for acquittal. For Johnson, Black presented a particularly troublesome problem because he still represented McCardle in the case before the Supreme Court.[10]

At 1:00 P.M. on Monday, March 23, the Senate came to order. Once again a thousand ticket holders squeezed into all corners of the chamber. Black no longer occupied a chair for the defense. In his place sat William S. Groesbeck of Ohio, a liberal Republican and able lawyer who supported Johnson's fidelity to the Constitution. Evarts also made his first appearance, giving the defense a touch of even greater distinction.[11]

The defense read the president's answer to the charges, thoroughly recounting the complete history of Stanton's suspension and removal. The statement denied any violation of the Constitution or the laws, any commission of high crimes and misdemeanors, and cited the act of 1795 as the authority for Grant's appointment. Upon the reinstatement of Stanton by the Senate, said Evarts, the president took such steps as legally required to "raise for a judicial decision the question affecting the lawful right" of Stanton to resume the office, and to that end had, on February 21, appointed General Thomas temporarily to the office. The president denied ever having advised General Emory to disobey any law and had merely expressed to the general the same opinion he had given to the House of Representatives. To the article accusing Johnson of disparaging Congress before the public, Evarts replied that the charge took the president's speeches out of context. He emphasized Johnson's right to speak to the people on any issue, including "legislation of Con-

gress, proposed or completed in respect to its wisdom, expediency, justice, worthiness, objects, purposes, and public and political motives." He had judiciously performed that duty and done nothing to besmirch the office of the presidency or cause it to come into "contempt, ridicule or disgrace."[12]

When the reading ended, Evarts asked for thirty days to prepare for trial. The managers bitterly opposed the request. After exhibiting outrage and condemning the president as "a criminal but not an ordinary one," they agreed to return the following day with their proposal. Evarts argued that the managers had no business dictating time requirements for the defense. Wilson angrily replied that the longer Johnson remained in office, the more time he would have to imperil the nation by his unlawful assumption of power. Stanbery made an appeal to saner minds, explaining that so much time had been spent responding to the articles that no thought had been given to providing witnesses for the defense. Bingham cared little about the problems of the defense, accusing the president of "trifling with the great power which the people, for wise purposes, have placed in the hands of ... Congress." The court finally adjourned, having resolved nothing on Evarts' request for time, but they returned on the 24th and granted the defense not thirty days but seven.[13]

By March 27 the cabinet, almost to a man, believed that the president would be convicted. Welles, however, would not acknowledge that the Senate, "feeble and timid as it is, will convict the President," but he also believed the entire body to be "subject to the dictation of Sumner, who is imperious." He said that Chandler was unprincipled — both are disliked and hated by a considerable portion of the Republicans, who nevertheless bow submissive to the violent extremists." Welles admitted that with Radicals losing power in the 1867 elections, they must have an ally as president to continue their policies — whether it be Wade now or Grant later. Welles believed that "Fraud or force would be resorted to if necessary to accomplish this end. Hence impeachment is necessary." Privately, he accused Radicals of shooting down the faithful sentinel because of his determination and loyalty to stand to his post.[14]

During the last days of March, Johnson's case received another blow. If the Supreme Court did not decide the McCardle case, the bill depriving it of jurisdiction would become law. Could Johnson afford to veto the bill while on trial? The Supreme Court had done nothing, not one thing to protect itself from an attempt by Congress to usurp judicial power. Assailed and harassed by Radicals every step along the way, Johnson threw caution to the wind and vetoed the bill, probably believing it would make no difference. If the Supreme Court would not protect itself, he would not be culpable for its diminishment. Shocked by Johnson's bold defiance, Congress repassed the bill two days later. The McCardle case could no longer be decided, and the Reconstruction Acts could not be upset until they had served their punitive purposes.[15]

On Monday, March 30, the trial resumed. Ben Butler's long-awaited moment came. He took command of the floor, bowing to the chief justice and then to the Senate. The spectators in the packed galleries leaned forward to hear the general's opening statement. Butler did not disappoint them, declaring that for the first time in the world a president had been brought before the "highest tribunal ... for trial and possible deposition from office." He wanted his audience to understand that nations in the past disposed of their despots by executing them, but in the civilized court of the Senate, bad presidents "shall be removed from office on impeachment for and conviction of treason, bribery or other high crimes and misdemeanors." Butler's opening address rang hollow because none of the articles of impeachment accused the president of any crime specified by the Constitution.[16]

Butler knew a majority of the Senate would convict Johnson without proof of guilt, but there were some who had taken the oath to do impartial justice that might be swayed by the absence of hard evidence. To that end Butler had to convince the doubters that high crimes and misdemeanors included other offenses. He composed his own list, including such offenses as subverting "some fundamental or essential principle of government, or [acts] highly prejudicial to the public interest.... This may," said Butler, "consist of a violation of the Constitution, of law, of an official oath, or of duty by an act committed or omitted, or, without violating a positive law, by the abuse of discretionary powers from improper motives for any improper purpose." Under Butler's law, any president could be impeached and convicted if enough senators did not like him.[17]

After Butler subverted the Constitution, he next wanted to do away with the proceedings as a "trial." He preferred to think of it as an "inquest of office," thereby obliterating not only the requirement for high crimes and misdemeanors but also the validity of a trial in context with the Constitution. Earlier, Bingham had declared that all senators were "a rule and a law to themselves." Butler expanded on Bingham's premise, proclaiming the Senate "bound by no law, either statute or common, which may limit your constitutional prerogative." Playing to men like Sumner, he compared the Senate to a body of parliamentarians, declaring, "You are a law unto yourselves, bound only by the natural principles of equity and justice." Having redefined the role of the Senate, Butler privately congratulated himself for having disposed of the president on the simple premise that two-thirds of the Senate no longer wanted Johnson in office.[18]

To further solidify his argument, Butler initiated a validation of the articles. Lumping the first eight articles together — those pertaining to the removal of Stanton and appointment of Thomas — Butler ridiculed Johnson's contention that the president still held the power of removal without the consent of the Senate. After launching an attack on Johnson's usurpation of the Tenure of Office Act, he spoke directly to any wavering senators, saying, "Whoever ... votes 'not guilty' on these articles votes to enchain our free institutions and to prostrate them at the feet of any man who being President may choose to control them."[19]

Butler worried a bit over John Sherman's declaration that "the government will not be embarrassed by an attempt by a cabinet officer to hold on to his office despite the wish of the President." Instead of responding to Sherman's words, Butler shifted his argument and praised Stanton as a "true patriot" who withstood the president's "unlooked-for treachery." Butler had built his reputation as a shrewd and unprincipled lawyer by using tricky tactics that evaded the issue but attacked the opponent. He aimed his arsenal of experience to bear on Johnson.[20]

To the statement by Johnson's attorneys that Stanton's removal had been necessary to test the constitutionality of the act, Butler minimized it as a subterfuge. He condemned Johnson for acting with defiance toward the Senate by attempting to remove Stanton. He suggested how a gentleman would have conducted himself when communicating with so august a body of legislators. This played well to the Senate, but not to Evarts, who later replied, "You as a court upon this manager's own argument are reduced to the necessity of removing the President of the United States, not for the act, but for the form and style in which it was done."[21]

Butler's lengthy discourse on the first eight articles put many in the Senate to sleep, and he still had three more articles to present. Having worked with Stevens and Wilson on preparing the tenth and eleventh articles, he switched to them and unleashed his well-known articulate dexterity for defamation. He granted the president freedom of speech but condemned him for improperly using it. Harkening back to the swing around the circle, Butler accused Johnson of addressing the public like a "ribald, scurrilous blasphemer, bandying epithets and taunts with a jeering mob." Butler stretched the Constitution by suggesting that such conduct rose to the level of "a high misdemeanor in office." He continued, setting new rules for presidential conduct in all matters public or otherwise. Though he did not challenge Johnson's words as being either true or false, he rested his case on "the scandal of the scene," which, he said, was purposely intended to "slander the Congress of the United States." All this occurred, Butler said, during the president's public appearances at Cleveland and St. Louis, where he mixed with "men and boys, washed and unwashed, drunk and sober, black and white," that had assembled on the street. He neglected to mention that the interruptions had been prearranged by fellow Radicals to disrupt the president's effectiveness.[22]

Butler continued the attack, shifting to the president's efforts to usurp the power of Congress. He knew Johnson's restoration of the south followed Lincoln's plan, and accused Lincoln of having "no intention of calling on Congress to assist in this matter."

In 1865 Butler had been relieved by Grant for military incompetence, and being uncertain of his standing with the Radicals, he sought an opportunity to market his skills. In April 1867, Butler had a conversation with Welles. On the subject of the Reconstruction Acts and the deployment of military tribunals, Butler said, "I do not indorse those acts nor approve them." He then asked, "Why does not the President test them? Why does he submit to such laws and attempt to carry them out? He declares them unconstitutional. If so they are no laws. Why does he obey them?" Welles replied that Johnson felt obliged to "see all laws faithfully executed." Butler suggested that Johnson should have no trouble getting a favorable decision from the Supreme Court and even outlined a method for the president to follow in doing so. Now, eleven months later, Butler operated on the other side and attacked the president for following advice similar to that which he had previously given.[23]

Though none of the articles charged Johnson with any crime or misdemeanor, Butler attempted to denounce all of the president's so-called reprehensible acts

as rising to a convictable level. In an effort to answer the question of where crimes or misdemeanors had been committed, he concocted a cunning but transparent summary by lumping all charges together in "the culmination of a series of wrongs, malfeasances and usurpations" that "need to be examined in the light of his precedent and concomitant acts to grasp their scope and design. The last three articles," Butler declared, "show the perversity and malignity with which he acted, so that the man as he is known to us may be clearly spread upon record to be seen and known of all men hereafter." Ending his opening statement, he challenged the Senate to safeguard the Constitution against usurpation. "The House of Representatives has done its duty," said Butler. "We have brought the criminal to your bar and demand judgment at your hands for his so great crimes. Never again if Andrew Johnson go quit and free this day, can the people of this or any other country by constitutional checks or guards stay the usurpations of executive power."[24]

Butler took his seat, and the trial moved to the presentation of the prosecution's evidence. James F. Wilson took the floor to present the proofs, which included such documents as Johnson's oath of office, Lincoln's nomination of Stanton, Johnson's message to the Senate advising of Stanton's removal, and other related material. Wilson asked that the documents not be read but entered into the record. Stanbery knew the documents contained exculpatory evidence and demanded a reading. Senator Sherman asked for adjournment midway through the reading, and the hearing of evidence moved to noon the following day.[25]

Butler's pyrotechnics received a mixed review — plaudits from his friends and scorn from his enemies. His opening statement provided no proof, only accusations, but Stanton rejoiced "at the mighty blow ... struck against the great enemy of the nation." A number of Republicans and all Democrats found nothing in Butler's allegations to justify conviction, so on Tuesday, March 31, they listened more intently as witnesses appeared to give testimony.[26]

Much of the evidence consisted of common knowledge — documentation chronologically tracking from the day of Stanton's suspension to the arrest of Lorenzo Thomas. Witnesses filled in the gaps with direct testimony during exchanges of correspondence between Johnson, the Senate, Grant, Thomas, and others.[27]

Throughout the questioning Chief Justice Chase attempted to maintain judicial decorum, ruling on what evidence could be admitted and what could not. Though many of Chase's rulings favored the prosecution, the Radicals did not want interference and plotted to muffle him. Once again Butler stepped into the spotlight, asking as a question of law whether the chief justice should be able "to stand between the Senate and the House and its prosecution?" He argued that if the chief justice could decide on the admissibility of evidence, then as a prosecutor he would be compelled "to withdraw and take instruction from the House before [laying] the rights of the House bound hand and foot at the feet of any man, however high or good or just he may be." Bingham put a motion on the floor to retire for consultation. The vote resulted in a tie. Having no precedent for tie-breaking during an impeachment trial, Chase broke the deadlock and voted "yea." The Senate retired to discuss the role of Chase. House members milled about the floor awaiting a decision.[28]

Several attempts by Sumner, Morrill, and others to confine the role of the chief justice to ruling strictly on points of order failed to pass. Hereafter Chase could issue a ruling on all questions of evidence and incidental questions, "which ruling shall stand as the judgment of the Senate" unless a formal vote upon the question was "submitted to the Senate for decision." If he chose, Chase could also submit questions to the Senate. However, on the following day Sumner objected to the chief justice voting and entered a resolution to deny it. The resolution failed to pass, and the outcome of Butler's effort to muffle the chief justice merely solidified Chase's authority to steer the trial, if he wished to do so, in an orderly fashion.[29]

On April 1 the trial continued. In their search for incriminating evidence, managers questioned more witnesses. Butler used any imaginable ruse to show that Johnson intended to use force to remove Stanton and that Thomas had been instructed to use force if necessary. He knew that no force had been involved or contemplated, but the witnesses had been coached. All the High Court learned, however, were of the silly declarations Thomas made at the masked ball. Stanton produced a witness who gave the prosecution some help because he cast so much ridicule on Thomas' clownish ballroom behavior that an abundance of derision rubbed off on the president who foolishly appointed him. Stanbery suspected that the witness had distorted the truth, and during cross-examination turned the absurdities back upon the testifier. Butler attempted to recover lost ground, but Curtis declared the witness incompetent. Butler argued but finally agreed to end the questioning. Having consumed the day without hearing any condemning evidence, the Senate adjourned.[30]

By April 2 people began to lose interest in a trial that seemed to be going nowhere. Two-thirds of the members of the House stayed away. They had seen enough documents and heard enough boring testimony. When the drama of the trial vanished, so did the people, but testimony continued.[31]

The managers called their tenth witness, General Emory, and prodded him to testify that Johnson had instructed army officers to not obey the laws of Congress. Emory admitted that Johnson had used words to that effect but in reference to a message sent to Congress and not as an order. Instead, Emory stated that Johnson had specifically told him to obey the order "whether it was constitutional or not." Finding Emory to be a poor witness for the prosecution, Wilson excused him from further questioning.[32]

Wilson believed the prosecution's case could best be validated by airing the relationship between the unpopular president and the popular General Grant. In his hand he held written documents from cabinet members disclosing Grant's bad faith, and he intended to use them to bolster his case. Stanbery protested to selective documents being read and asked for all of them to be put in evidence. His protest resulted in a debate, so Chase put the matter to a vote. The Senate decided that Wilson could proceed with whatever documents he wished to enter into the record and denied Stanbery's protest. As the testimony continued, however, the defense introduced most of the deleted documents, thereby frustrating Wilson's effort to distort events

without embarrassing the Radicals' favorite general.[33]

The prosecution held a full bag of tricks. After failing to make a case against Johnson over the Emory incident, Butler attempted to bring in William Chandler, a witness having no bearing on charges in the articles of impeachment. Stanbery accused the prosecution of attempting to "manufacture" new charges, arguing that such evidence fell outside the scope of the trial. If the managers wished to introduce new allegations, they must go first to the House and obtain approval for any "new article founded upon an illegal act." The prosecution haggled over Stanbery's protest until Chase put the matter before the Senate for a vote. Once again the Sumner coalition voted to allow unrelated testimony, but the majority of the Senate ruled it out.[34]

The managers then called Charles Tinker, another witness having nothing to do with the trial. Butler wanted Tinker's testimony to show that Johnson attempted on January 17, 1867, to obstruct the ratification of the Fourteenth Amendment in Alabama, but this happened three months prior to the passage of the Reconstruction Act. Another debate ensued during which applicable documents were introduced and read. Chase put the question of Tinker's testimony to a vote. Ten Senators abstained, leaving the final count deadlocked. Chase voted with the Sumner coalition. Since every document in question was entered into the record during the debate, Tinker's testimony lost its importance, so the Senate adjourned.[35]

Radicals throughout the country began to fear that the managers' case lacked substance. In an effort to salvage the party's reputation, coalitions met in different venues all over the north to pass resolutions imploring their senators to convict Johnson or suffer political consequences in the next election. Radical correspondents applied pressure with equally forcible persuasion. Senators squirmed, feeling hounded by internal and external influences. Sumnerites turned to the managers, urging them to strengthen the impeachment effort with better witnesses.[36]

Having successfully introduced documents dating back to 1867, the managers now tried to add evidence dating from June 22, 1866, a time when the president attempted to discourage Congress from passing amendments to the Constitution until all southern states had been admitted to legislature. After submitting the original copy of Johnson's message to Congress, Colonel Moore made some edits, but he dutifully forwarded to both chambers an edited copy when done. Butler tried to build a case of presidential deception, alleging that Johnson intended to submit different versions to different agencies. For two days reporters for the press testified why their accounts disagreed. Some correspondents admitted flavoring versions transcribed from notes with enhancements. The only reporters and stenographers called as witnesses by the managers were those who printed inflammatory accounts. Under cross-examination witnesses admitted using different methods of transcription. All depended upon stenographic techniques that left room for misinterpretation. They also admitted making editorial changes, changing phraseology to suit their style or fit their recollections. Nonetheless, Butler believed he had made a case for presidential duplicity — which he declared a high crime — and rested the prosecution's case.[37]

During the final days of listening to the prosecution's case, the defense made several motions to exclude testimony having no bearing on the articles of impeachment. The Senate consistently voted to uphold testimony from the managers' witnesses. To the president's counsel, it appeared that the Senate would let in any evidence if it helped build the prosecution's case.

Being Friday, the Senate moved to adjourn, allowing the defense five days to prepare its case. Simon Cameron objected, asking that the trial continue on Monday. The chief justice told Cameron he was out of order, rapped the gavel, and ordered the trial to resume at twelve o'clock on Thursday, April 9.[38]

Testimony from twenty-five prosecution witnesses produced no evidence of presidential crimes or misdemeanors. No new revelations surfaced. The court learned what they already knew — Johnson had removed Stanton, appointed Thomas temporarily in his place, had several conversations with army officers, and in 1866 made speeches criticizing Congress, none of which was denied. What worried the president's attorneys was the Senate's solidification behind the managers. Strong signs prevailed that the president — deservedly or not — would be convicted.

17

The President's Defense

On Thursday, April 9, ticket-holders who had become bored with the prosecution's case returned in huge numbers to see whether the battery of distinguished defense attorneys could save the president. The press observed the presence of General Sherman, who had wisely declined the contentious post of secretary of war. Next to him sat his father-in-law, Thomas Ewing, whose nomination for the same office lay unattended before the Senate. At twelve noon Chief Justice Chase entered the chamber, took his chair, and ordered the trial to resume.[1]

Benjamin R. Curtis opened for the defense. In stark contrast to Butler, Curtis manifested all the elegant and dignified qualities of a refined and honorable gentleman. His historic and well-known dissent in the Dred Scott case had elevated his public stature to the pinnacle of his profession. Dressed in a trim black suit fitted to his well-proportioned body, Curtis riveted his eyes on the Senate — not to intimidate and not to impress — but to grasp and hold their attention as he began to speak.

After extending the courtesies of recognition to the chief justice and the court, he reminded the Senate that "Here party spirit, political schemes, foregone conclusions, outrageous biases can have no fit operation. The Constitution re-quires that here should be a 'trial,' and as in that trial the oath which each one of you has taken is to administer 'impartial justice according to the Constitution and the laws,' the only appeal which I can make in behalf of the President is an appeal to the conscience and the reason of each judge who sits before me." He implored the Senate to pay close attention, drawing upon the "patience" of a judge to hear and deliver a verdict "upon the law and the facts, upon the judicial merits of the case" in view of the duties incumbent on a president in his "honest endeavor to discharge those duties."[2]

Curtis proceeded to rip to shreds the prosecution's case. He argued that the Tenure of Office Act provided no protection for Stanton because the secretary had been appointed during Lincoln's administration, and after thirty days, Johnson had a right by law to replace him at any time. He also reminded the court of Senator Sherman's post-script — that the law had not been intended to obstruct a president from removing a cabinet officer who refused, when asked, to resign. Curtis clarified how the president painstakingly examined the Constitution, the laws of the country, and obtained legal advice before coming to the conclusion that Stanton could be removed without the approval of the Senate. "How is it possible for this body to convict the President," Curtis asked, "for construing a law as those who made it construed it at the time when it was made?"[3]

Curtis continued, explaining why the president could not retain Stanton as one of his advisers or be responsible for his conduct in office. When graciously asked to resign, Stanton refused, forcing the president to suspend him until Congress reconvened. When the Senate reinstated Stanton, it forced Johnson to remove him to test the tenure act in court. "Let me ask any of you," said Curtis, "if you were the trustee for the rights of third persons, and those rights ... which they could not defend themselves by reason of sex or age, should be attacked by unconstitutional law, should you not deem it your sacred duty to resist it and have the question tried?" Curtis emphasized how the president acted as trustee of the public and honorably defended those powers confided in him by the Constitution. He could not "erect himself into a judicial court and decide [what] law is unconstitutional," but when the question arose "whether a particular law has cut off the power confided in him by the people, through the Constitution ... he alone can cause a judicial decision to come between the two branches of the government to say which of them is right ... and have it peacefully decided."[4]

As Curtis struck home his points, many of the extreme Radicals of the Senate, men such as Wade, Cameron, Harlan, and Williams, left the chamber. They did not want to be influenced by logic or legalities. Noticing their absence, Morrill of Vermont suggested the Senate adjourn for the day. By 35-2-17 the Senate voted to continue.[5]

The first eight articles addressed the tenure act. Curtis believed that by de-stroying the prosecution's case on the first article, the other seven would collapse in turn. He argued that the president attempted to avoid a conflict with Congress, and though he did not agree with the law, he felt bound to obey it. Only when the law prevented him from carrying on a proper and professional relationship with his cabinet was he forced to challenge the law. Stanton became a disruptive influence, Curtis said, and his reinstatement obstructed the administration from performing the duties of the executive branch. To test the law in court Stanton had to be removed. Curtis declared that the president acted with full justification in doing so. "The law may be a constitutional law," he said, but "if Mr. Stanton is not within the law ... the first article is entirely without foundation." Exhausted, Curtis asked for and received an adjournment until the following day.[6]

On April 10 he began his attack on article two, which charged that Johnson's letter of authority to Lorenzo Thomas violated both the Constitution and the tenure act. Curtis used precedents and laws still in force to validate the president's absolute authority to name any individual he chose to fill the office of secretary of war on a temporary basis. Therefore, naming General Thomas as ad interim secretary broke no law.[7]

Having dispatched article two, Curtis moved on to articles four and six, which charged Johnson with conspiring under the Act of July 31, 1861— a war measure defining conspiracies — to overthrow by force the government of the United States. According to the two articles, Johnson empowered Thomas to remove Stanton "by force." The opposite had already been established through cross-examination of the prosecution's witnesses. Curtis drove home the point that if the president could not allow Stanton to act as his adviser, then he had "full lawful power to remove him," and under such circumstances could rightfully give General Thomas an order to replace him. Curtis quickly disposed of articles four and six, which wiped out articles five and seven.[8]

He also dispensed with the ninth article that accused the president of ordering General Emory to disobey the tenure law so as to permit the physical ousting of Stanton from the war department. Earlier cross-examination of prosecution witnesses had already proved the president innocent of such action, so Curtis moved to the next article.[9]

The president's speeches formed the foundation for article ten, but to clarify the charge, Curtis wanted to first define what "high crimes and misdemeanors" did not mean. He argued that no law ever existed that declared any speech a crime of any kind. Nor could a law be enacted by Congress for the exclusive purpose of giving credibility to article ten. If in the opinion of the House the president had spoken improperly, or in disagreement with congressional policy, no crime could have been committed under the laws or the Constitution of the United States.[10]

After Curtis closed, he summed up the two-day session to a friend, writing: "There are from twenty-two to twenty-five Senators who began the trial with a fixed determination to convict. I have no reason to suppose any of them is shaken or will be. About twelve to fifteen of the dominant party had not abandoned all sense of right, and given themselves over to the party at any cost. What will become of them I know not, but the *result* is with them. The President himself preserves his calmness and to a great extent

his equanimity. My respect for the moral qualities of the man is greatly enhanced by the knowledge of him."

Later, one of the senators asked another whether Curtis' opening had made an impression. The other replied regretfully, "I was absent; but I have read it, and I wish I hadn't." And these were the men to judge the president.[11]

After a fifteen minute recess, Stanbery called Lorenzo Thomas, the first witness for the defense. The timorous general's comportment encouraged rough handling under cross-examination. Stanbery knew he had a scared rabbit for a witness and carefully guided him through the testimony. Butler interrupted, objected, and argued in an effort to destroy Thomas' testimony. Though he succeeded in dispensing ridicule, the general survived, making the point after two days of examination that at no time had the president authorized him to use force or threats to remove Stanton. That was all Stanbery wanted.[12]

The defense called General Sherman, who had been observing the trial from the gallery. Being a highly credible witness for the defense meant that the general could be a damaging witness for the prosecution, so Bingham and Butler conspired to block his testimony. If Sherman confirmed that the president never attempted "to get control of the military force of the government by the seizing of the Department of War" pursuant to Johnson's alleged design "to overthrow the Congress of the United States," then great damage would be done to the managers' case.

Five minutes into Sherman's testimony, Bingham attempted to stop it, arguing that conversations between Johnson and the general did not occur within the timeframe outlined in the articles.

Stanbery, however, continued, only to have Butler interrupt and demand that the question be presented in written form. Chief Justice Chase ruled that the question could be asked, but Senator John Conness of California moved that the matter of answering the question be put before the Senate. For more than an hour the attorneys battled over the admissibility of the question. Finally the Senate voted. The High Court knew their case would go up in smoke if Sherman testified and voted 28-23-3 to reject the question.[13]

Because of the importance of Sherman's testimony, Stanbery rephrased the question, hoping to pry from the general the information he wanted without further objections. Butler could not be fooled and challenged every question Stanbery asked, and the Senate voted each question inadmissible. Butler enjoyed riding high. He mirthfully ridiculed Stanbery's efforts to enter Sherman's testimony and drew laughter from the court. Stanbery replied, "Mr. Chief Justice, this is quite too serious a business that we are engaged in, and the responsibility is too great, the issues too important, to descend to the sort of controversy ... introduced here." Once more he attempted to draw out Sherman's testimony, only to be blocked again by the Senate. The general had been in the witness chair most of the afternoon, but he may as well have been in the washroom. The court adjourned until Monday, April 13, and Stanbery recalled Sherman. No matter how the defense phrased its questions to the general, the Senate sided with the prosecution and would not let him testify.[14]

Stanbery finally conceded to the Senate and called R. J. Meigs, clerk of the Supreme Court for the district of Co-

lumbia, to testify to the arrest and discharge of Lorenzo Thomas. Butler attempted to throw out Meigs' affidavit and all other documents related to Thomas' arrest arguing that the incident concerned Stanton and the general and not the president.[15]

While the debate over Meigs' testimony raged, Senator Reverdy Johnson gained the floor. Having observed General Sherman in the gallery, the senator asked the Chief Justice Chase for permission to direct a question to General Sherman. Chase recalled Sherman, and Johnson read the question: "When the President tendered to you the office of Secretary of War *ad interim* on the 27th of January, 1868, and on the 31st of the same month and year, did he, *at the very time of making such a tender, state to you what his purpose in doing so was?*" Bingham objected, so Chase referred the question to the Senate. This time the Senate by a narrow margin allowed the question. Sherman completed his testimony, confirming that the president only intended to test the constitutionality of the tenure act and at no time intimated the use of force. The prosecution successfully blocked from testimony Sherman's suggestion to the president that Stanton be removed, or that he and Grant intended to urge Stanton to resign.[16]

On Tuesday, April 14, Stanbery fell ill, so the Senate postponed the trial until Wednesday. To those watching, the tide seemed to be turning in favor of the president. Welles remained skeptical, writing, "Butler gives rules to the Senatorial judges and tells them how to vote, and they obey. They are less safe as triers than an ordinary intelligent jury." Though Welles admitted that "impeachment has lost ground in public estimation during the last few days; still I have no confidence in the partisan Senate." What is lacking, concluded Welles, is statesmanship.[17]

On Wednesday, Curtis and Evarts attempted to enter documents to prove the unconstitutionality of the Tenure of Office Act. They intended to show that the law did not apply to Stanton's case. The arguments of the defense supported the president's message to the Senate on February 22, 1868, which explained in detail the justification for Stanton's removal. Once again Butler and Bingham succeeded in blocking exculpatory evidence. Though most members of the Senate knew of Johnson's message, or could easily have found it in Senate documents, they nonetheless agreed to disallow it as trial evidence.[18]

On Thursday, April 16, Curtis called Walter S. Cox and Richard T. Merrick as witnesses for the defense. Both attorneys had represented Lorenzo Thomas. Curtis wanted to show that the president, by naming Thomas secretary ad interim, had merely intended to test the law. Despite Butler's constant objections and interruptions, Curtis made his point and put the testimony into the record. The defense had other witnesses to call, but because Stanbery remained ill, Curtis asked for another postponement.[19]

Butler sensed that despite support from the Senate, the prosecution's case had begun to unravel. Instead of respecting Curtis' request for adjournment, he launched a tirade against the president, demanding that he appear before the Senate and defend himself. "Now the whole legislation of this country is stopping," Butler declared, "the whole country waits upon us and our action, and it is not time now for the exhibitions of courtesy ... this is the closing up of a war

wherein three hundred thousand men laid down their lives to save the country ... and shall the country wait now in its march to safety because of the sickness of one man?" Having never experienced such shoddy courtroom behavior, Curtis and Evarts jumped to their feet and objected to Butler's harangue, but the manager refused to be interrupted. "Shall we delay this trial any longer," he shouted, "because of a question of courtesy?" Butler's tirade rang like a closing statement from a defense lawyer out of control — not an objection to a motion. He fabricated dozens of new charges never included in the articles. No senator stepped in to stop Butler on a point of order, nor did the chief justice. Evarts waited until Butler had winded himself and said, "I have never heard such a harangue before a court of justice, but I cannot say that I may not hear it again in this court." A few words of shame worked, and the Senate adjourned.[20]

On Friday, April 17, the defense addressed the article charging the president with committing slurs against Congress during his swing around the circle. Three editors appeared as witnesses, one from Cleveland and two from St. Louis. They admitted that their newspaper accounts did not properly represent Johnson's efforts to make an orderly address to the public. All three admitted the presence of agitators in the crowd and thought that Johnson handled the situation with acceptable skill and restraint.[21]

Evarts put Welles on the stand to testify to a conversation with Stanton. When the tenure bill became law, Johnson had discussed it with the cabinet. All members, Stanton included, declared the bill unconstitutional. Both Seward and Stanton agreed to prepare Johnson's veto message. Evarts' point was that even

Stanton opposed the bill. Butler saw his case evaporating and attempted to create a diversion by launching another diatribe. He succeeded in forestalling further testimony, thereby causing the Senate to call for adjournment. But Welles's testimony continued on the following day, as did the arguments. Chase admitted all of Welles' testimony, but before it could be given, the Senate interceded and rejected the testimony by a 20-29-5 vote. Evarts attempted to approach the issue by asking the question differently, but each time drew an objection from Butler. Evarts tried to show that the president had a "perfect right to suppose that Stanton would not oppose him." Once again, Chase wanted to hear evidence on the question, but the Senate overruled him again, voting 22-26-6. Had Welles been able to testify, Evarts would have called every member of the cabinet, including Stanton. Radicals feared this would happen and effectively stopped it.

Chase admitted being appalled by the Senate's unwillingness to do any justice, impartial or otherwise, and the same feeling began to pervade the public. Welles, after spending three hours on the witness stand, gave credit to Chase for acting with fairness, but he referred to twenty or so senators as a set of "stupid stolid creatures" who had been "ready from the first to vote to convict."[22]

By excluding reasonable and admissible evidence, the Radicals undermined their own case without realizing it. Ben Butler may have gleaned a little laughter for his wit — which always gave him special pleasure — but some members of the Senate developed a dislike for his bullying tactics. Butler's reputation as a shyster lawyer manifested itself too often to the detriment of the prosecution's case, but nobody muzzled him. Senator John

B. Henderson of Missouri spoke for many of his colleagues when he said that "competent evidence such as this, going to explain the character of his [the president's] intentions, should not have been rejected by the court. A verdict of guilty on these articles, after the exclusion of this testimony would fail to command the respect and approval of any enlightened public judgment."[23]

But the trial had not ended, nor the climax. Johnson waited patiently, but his anxiety increased as each day of the trial passed. He went about his work, as he had all the years of his life. If he had regrets, he mentioned them to no one, but the onus of being convicted of high crimes and misdemeanors and removed from office deeply troubled him. His attorneys gave him little encouragement, and for a man who stubbornly kept his own counsel, even his closest friends and associates found it difficult to know his mind.

Nobody understood Andrew Johnson better than his family, and they filled the White House with healing fun and laughter. During all the dark days of the impeachment crisis the president enjoyed the presence of his children. His five grandchildren romped with him on the grounds or tumbled on the floor and provided comic relief. With him were Colonel Robert Johnson, his oldest son, and Andrew, Jr., then thirteen. His daughter, Mrs. Daniel Stover, tried to watch after her three grandchildren, Sarah, Lillie, and Andrew, while his oldest daughter, Martha Patterson, the mistress of the White House, tended her two children, Mary Belle and Andrew Johnson Patterson. All enjoyed playing with their grandfather. While the president may not always have been generous with his comments to Congress, he seldom failed to listen to the problems of his grandchildren, and unlike his adversaries, they usually took his advice. His great sadness, however, concerned the failing health of his wife, to whom he owed so much. Though slowly dying of tuberculosis, she still comforted him. Watching as the disease sapped her life touched him harder than all the problems of office. Come what may, Congress may strip him of office, but Eliza McCardle would always be with him.[24]

Johnson often welcomed though not always adhered to the advice of others, but during the trial he wisely listened to his lawyers even when he disagreed with them. He had faced and weathered difficult problems all of his life, and he had enough confidence in himself to confront the Senate and the House prosecutors and speak in his own defense. To dissuade him from doing so required a coalition comprised of the cabinet, his attorneys, his family, and the guiding voice of his wife. Johnson felt an impulse to lash back at Butler and Bingham, and had he done so, the prosecutors would have chewed him to pieces before the Senate.[25]

While Johnson worried about conviction, Radicals worried about acquittal. Seven Republican defections could overturn the impeachment, and the Sumnerites went to work to ensure that nothing like that happened. Any Senator who dared to vote for acquittal would forever brand himself infamous. Even members of the House, who under the rules were not to tamper with the High Court, met privately with senators to inveigle their vote, declaring that the country's peace depended upon the president's conviction. So confident had the Radicals become that behind the scenes a cabinet had already been formed for Ben Wade with Butler as secretary of state. But the potential defectors remained obstinate, so much so that the Senate recruited Grant to sway the vote of General John B. Henderson of Missouri. The Senator no longer took orders from Grant and politely told him so.[26]

Some conservative Republicans felt more comfortable with Johnson in the White House than Wade. Speaking for this block, fellow Ohioan James A. Garfield described Wade as "a man of violent passions, extreme opinions and narrow views; a man who has never studied or thought carefully on any subject except slavery; a [man of] grossly profane, coarse nature who is surrounded by the worst and most violent elements in the Republican party." Another Ohioan, Chief Justice Chase, privately agreed with Garfield, which may explain why some of his rulings during the trial — though overturned by the Senate — favored the defense.[27]

Evarts knew he needed seven Republican senators to acquit the president. How to get them became the problem. Reverdy Johnson believed if the president could somehow assure the conservatives that he planned no rash acts during the balance of his administration, it would calm fears and perhaps secure votes. Evarts needed to develop a methodology for doing this without directly involving Johnson. He devised a scheme involving the replacement of Stanton with Major General John M. Schofield, a man supported by both Grant, a wartime friend, and the Senate. Schofield had a distinguished war record, and on April 21, one day before closing arguments were scheduled to begin, the general happened to be in town. Since the Senate had not acted on Ewing's nomination, why not send in Schofield's?

At 2:00 P.M. on the 21st, Evarts met with Schofield at Willard's Hotel and asked if the general would consent to serve as secretary of war if approved by the Senate. Before Schofield could respond, a courier brought a message to the room advising that Grant was waiting at the door. Schofield cut short the interview to discuss the matter with Grant. The latter unequivocally declared that the president would be convicted, but he would be delighted to see his friend as secretary of war for the remainder of "Mr. Wade's" term.[28]

Still undecided, Schofield returned to Willard's at 8:00 P.M. Evarts explained that a majority of Republicans, after finding "how slight is the evidence of guilty intent," regret the impeachment proceedings and now sought "to get out of the scrape." Evarts stated that prominent Republican senators had suggested Schofield for the post and hoped to see his name in nomination before the "vote upon the president's case." Schofield asked for time to discuss the matter once more with General Grant before making a decision. Grant told Schofield that Johnson would not be acquitted and to accept the nomination. But he also warned that if the Senate set Johnson free, the president would "trample the laws under foot and do whatever he pleased" and that Congress would have to remain in session all summer to watch him. Nevertheless, on the morning of April 22 Schofield informed Evarts that he would accept the nomination but to make no announcement until after the Senate confirmed his appointment.[29]

Schofield's consent to have his name put before the Senate gave Evarts a boost. Now perhaps he could save the president.

18

The Closing Arguments

On April 20 Evarts and Curtis called no more witnesses for the defense because the Senate refused by vote to deny further testimony that might vindicate the president. The Radical press heaped praise on Butler for outmaneuvering the defense and manipulating the Senate. As Evarts prepared to present his closing statements to the High Court, the *New York Tribune* promised, in bold letters, "Conviction Almost a Certainty." And now came the time to hear from the other managers. John A. Logan of Illinois prepared more than a hundred pages of argument, but on the advice of his colleagues to not read it, he filed it with the court.[1]

Boutwell, however, wanted to be heard. He at least voiced a partial truth when he declared: "The crime of the President" had nothing to do with violating "a constitutional law." He explained that Johnson's crime "is that he has violated a law, and in his defense no inquiry can be made whether the [tenure] law is constitutional." Curtis had exposed the true nature of the prosecution's case, giving Boutwell much trouble with the logic of his argument. The Tenure of Office Act did not protect Stanton, but if it did, it violated the Constitution as construed since 1789. The president merely attempted to seek a judicial decision on the validity of the act.

Instead of making his closing statement apply to the articles of impeachment, Boutwell diverted his argument to the real substance of the case — Johnson's interference with Republican patronage and his disagreement with the Reconstruction Acts. On the patronage issue, Boutwell warned the Senate that by acquitting the president, "you surrender the government into the hands of a usurping and unscrupulous man, who will use all the vast power he now claims for the corruption of every branch of the public service, and the final overthrow of public liberties." Those who followed the trial might ask — Had there been any trace of corruption on Johnson's part, would this not have appeared in one of the articles of impeachment?[2]

After accusing the president of all the blackguard measures that a human being could possibly commit short of murder, rape, or treason, Boutwell failed to make a case for Johnson's conviction on the articles of impeachment. Though hindered by the absence of compelling evidence, he resorted to the charade of pious hypocrisy when he said, "The House of Representatives does not demand the conviction of Andrew Johnson unless he is guilty in the manner charged by the articles of impeachment; nor does the House expect the managers to seek conviction except upon the law and facts considered within judicial impartiality." Boutwell's rantings carried over to a second day, and his outbursts of pure political bombast were noted by some observers as desperate worry on the part of the most extreme Radicals.[3]

For the defense came Thomas A. R. Nelson, the country lawyer from Tennessee whom one might expect to be outmatched by the high-powered attorneys arguing the impeachment case. When rising to his feet he metamorphosed into a tall, striking, and clean shaven figure with piercing eyes, a firm mouth, and an aura of dignified honesty. To the Senate's surprise, Nelson emanated emotional power. He could speak from the heart and did so, scolding the managers for characterizing Johnson as a "usurper," a "traitor," and a "criminal but not an ordinary one." But, Nelson asked, "Who is Andrew Johnson?" — and then proceeded to sketch the astonishing career of his fellow townsman. Many in the chamber knew Johnson as a courageous senator who had forsaken the south to stand with the Union. Had they forgotten the Tennessean's fight, his personal ordeal to bring his state and the entire south back into the Union? Had he usurped the Constitution by upholding its laws and its virtues? Was he a traitor to challenge laws he lived by when constitutionality came into question?[4]

Nelson questioned the High Court indirectly — What would the Senate have done if Lincoln had lived? Nelson argued that in good faith Johnson undertook Lincoln's plan of restoration. "He retained the cabinet Mr. Lincoln left. He manifested no desire to segregate himself from the party by whom he had been elected." In regard to Louisiana and Arkansas, he followed in the spirit of Lincoln's proclamations and efforts "to restore the southern states to the relations which they had maintained to our common Union before the civil war commenced. I ask who can say there was guilt in all this? He was anxious to … heal the wounds of his distracted country. If he erred in this, it was almost a divine error. If he erred in this, it was a noble error. It was an error … intended to restore peace and harmony to our bleeding country."[5]

Nelson's argument continued the following morning. Though long, it offended no one, nor did he put anyone to sleep. He manifested a marvelous manner for holding the attention of even those who did not want to listen. There are those among you, said Nelson, who "know little of the President of the United States, far less than your humble servant knows, who imagine that they can force or drive or compel him, under any imaginable state of circumstances, to do what he believes to be wrong. He is a man of peculiar temperament and disposition. By careful management and proper manipulation he may, perhaps, be gently led; [but] no power under the heavens can compel him to go one inch beyond what he believes to be right." Perhaps for the first time some members of the High Court began to understand Andrew Johnson. Through much of his closing argument Nelson extemporized, giving his words an empathetic affect of sincerity that struck gently at some of the hardened hearts of the jurists. Because the High Court now better understood the man they had come to convict did not mean that minds had been changed, but Nelson made an impression.[6]

As Nelson closed, Seward watched the faces of the gallery and of the Senate. Later, when with Welles, he predicted acquittal. Horace Greeley's *Tribune* printed an unusually scathing editorial in response to Nelson's closing argument, giving Seward the impression that Greeley, too, feared that Johnson might be acquitted. If so, said Seward, then the Radicals must be worried as a whole.[7]

On the morning of Saturday, April 25, as William Groesbeck rose to make the second closing argument for the defense, jurists of the High Court circulated Greeley's editorial among its members. Groesbeck, though a sick man, ignored the intrusion. Mincing none of the words he had come to speak, he said, "You are to try the charges contained in these articles of impeachment and nothing else ... not upon newspaper rumor; not upon any views of party policy; you are to try them upon the evidence offered here and nothing else, by the obligation of your oaths." He reminded the High Court that seventy-eight years earlier Congress had upheld the right of the president to make removals without the consent of the Senate. So, he asked, "Is this Senate prepared to drag a President in here and convict him of crime because he believed as every other President believed, as the Supreme Court believed, as thirty-eight of thirty-nine Congresses believed? ... He shall execute your laws; he shall execute even doubtful laws; but when you bring to him a question like this, when he has all this precedent behind him and around him ... as to what is the right interpretation of the Constitution, and only one the other way, I say you are going too far to undertake to brand him with criminality, because he proposed to go to the Supreme Court.... To go there is peaceable, is constitutional, is lawful. What is the tribunal there for? For this very purpose."[8]

Groesbeck reviewed all the charges, giving special attention to those brandished and embellished by Butler — articles ten and eleven. His ridicule of the silly charges in article ten drew laughter from the High Court. He then attacked the House's interpretation of the Tenure of Office Act, showing that the managers had not presented one item of incriminating evidence. "It almost shocks me to think that the President of the United States is to be dragged out of his office on these miserable little questions, whether he could make an ad interim appointment for a single day, or whether in anything he did there was so great a crime that you should break the even flow of the administration of the country, disturb the quiet of the people, and impair their confidence ... in the stability of their government; that you should, in a word, take possession of the Executive ... empty the office, *and fill it with your own people.*" Having voiced the essence of the conspiracy, Groesbeck added, "I cannot understand how such a thing can possibly be done. How miserable is this case!"[9]

Groesbeck's closing so captivated the attention of the Senate and the galleries that barely a sound other than the speaker's voice penetrated the crowded chamber. He reminded the High Court that pacification and restoration, in keeping with Lincoln's "charity for all, malice toward none," had become the administration's great benevolent objective. The president "thought the war was ended," said Groesbeck. "The drums were all silent; the arsenals were all shut, the roar of cannon had died away ... the army was disbanded, not a single enemy confronted us on the field." Referring to the charges against the president, Groesbeck declared — "Ah, he was too eager, too forgiving, too kind. The hand of conciliation was stretched out to him [by the South] and he took it. It may be he should have put it away, but was it a crime to take it? Kindness, forgiveness, a crime? Kindness a crime? Kindness is omnipotent for good, more powerful than gunpowder or cannon. Kindness is statesmanship.... What shall I say of this man?" Groesbeck asked. "He is no theorist; he is no reformer, I have looked over his life. He has ever walked in beaten paths, and by the light of the Constitution.... He loves the Constitution. It has been the study of his life.... He is a patriot, second to no one of you in the measure of his patriotism. He loves his country."[10]

In closing Groesbeck referred again to the impeachment of a president. "No good can come of it, senators, and how much will the heart of the nation be refreshed if at last the Senate of the United States can, in its judgment upon this case, maintain its ancient dignity and high character in the midst of storm and passion and strife."[11]

Weak from illness and hoarse from his exertions, Groesbeck slumped into his chair. Men crowded forward to congratulate him. It had been a stunning closing argument, delivered from the heart by a man nobody knew. Now the country would become acquainted with William Groesbeck. The Radicals were still reeling from his assaults when they learned that Andrew Johnson, the previous day, had withdrawn the name of Thomas Ewing, Sr., for secretary of war and replaced it by nominating General Schofield.[12]

With senators beginning to waver on conviction, the Radicals accosted Grant, asking if he knew of Schofield's nomination. Grant sheepishly replied he did not, but agreed to correct the problem. He asked Schofield to decline. "I

have already promised not to decline the nomination," Schofield replied, "in advance of any action of the Senate."[13]

Consternation gripped the managers, but Ben Butler conceived a plan. During the trial he had spoken of supposed frauds in the treasury, inferring that the president was somehow implicated in the conspiracy. By vote, the Senate struck the inappropriate allegation from the record. To put pressure on the High Court, however, Butler printed twenty thousand copies of his expunged lie and circulated at least one copy to every newspaper in the United States. Horace Greeley consumed the allegation and introduced it to the public through the *Tribune*.[14]

On Monday, April 27, the High Court reconvened to hear closing arguments by Thad Stevens — the man who had masterminded the impeachment scandal. Through most of the long days of the trial, Charles Sumner had sat beside him at the managers' table. The eleventh article — Stevens' personal pet — contained a consolidation of the first ten articles. Conviction on article eleven would establish the basis needed for conviction on the other articles. Stevens would not risk an extemporaneous closing. Three times had he reviewed and corrected his speech. He would read it, every word of it, for he believed the president's conviction depended upon his remarks.[15]

When Stevens took the floor he already knew the level to which the managers' case had fallen. Sumner urged him on, reminding him that impeachment was not a trial but "a political proceeding before a political body with a political purpose." Stevens, the "malicious master of discord," concentrated on an old theme — the mere removal of Stanton and the appointment of Thomas, irrespective of the motives that prompted them, as being sufficient for conviction. Taking up the Grant-Johnson correspondence, he declared it "wholly immaterial" who had told the truth, but asked, "Who can hesitate to choose between the words of a gallant soldier and the pettifogging of a political trickster?" Though at the beginning of his statement Stevens promised no "mean spirit of malignity or vituperation," his closing argument consisted of nothing else. Halfway through the discourse, Stevens handed the speech to Butler and collapsed in his chair. Some forty pages remained, and each page contained more maledictions upon the president but no incriminating evidence. Butler read the words with marvelous flourish and closed by suggesting that the founding fathers, when they created the laws of the United States, never anticipated an individual of such low character ever occupying the office of the president.[16]

Another day passed, and on April 28 Manager Thomas Williams, Stanton's one-time law partner, took the floor to arraign the man whom his colleague had betrayed. Though Williams' closing consumed more than two hours, he neither added nor supported any evidence given in the case. He concentrated on berating Johnson's character, declaring that the president's differences with Congress as sufficient cause to throw him out of office. Williams' declarations contained little substance, but he delivered them with force and emotion — which seemed to be the only attribute of the managers' case.[17]

When Williams finished, Butler sought an opportunity to recapture the floor to argue a point made by the defense earlier in the trial. The timing suited him because the galleries were filled. He also had a second motive for interrupting. With Evarts scheduled to take the floor, Butler wanted the opportunity to sidetrack and diminish the closing arguments of the defense's most gifted orator. The issue in question pertained to Alta Vela, the removal of Jeremiah Black from the defense, and the involvement of Butler with the scheme. Four days earlier Nelson had exposed Butler's nefarious involvement in the Alta Vela affair. To cleanse himself before the public, Butler now tried to implicate Johnson. Nelson angrily roared back, and if duels had been legal, there would have been a settlement at sunrise on the lawn of the Capitol. The Senate interceded and stopped the debate. Butler had managed to send up a smoke screen, but as an effort to rattle Evarts, the maneuver failed.[18]

Evarts outclassed them all. His forensic power, masterful eloquence, charming wit, unerring logic, dignified force, and precise comprehension of the real issues before the High Court could not be matched by the disgruntled managers who sat by and listened. One historian noted that "The contrast between the effect of his presence and that of Butler's is a striking illustration of the importance of character when a great case is tried at the bar."[19]

Logically and deliberately, Evarts explained the purpose of impeachment, defining treason, bribery, high crimes and misdemeanors. He said the people of America wanted to know which of those heinous crimes the president committed. "And when informed that none of these things are charged, imputed, or even declaimed about," Evarts declared, "they yet seek further information and are told that he has removed a member of his cabinet." Continuing, Evarts showed that the public did not understand why Stanton's removal could not be done or why doing so rose to the level of a high crime or misdemeanor when every president before him did the same. "He undertook to make an ad interim secretary of war," Evarts declared, so you [the Senate] can now make for yourselves "an ad interim President." Before the High Court adjourned for the day, Evarts gave them much to think about, including whether they were a court of justice or a court to accommodate party interests as Sumner claimed.[20]

When the trial opened on April 29, Butler once again attempted to derail the defense and exonerate himself by arguing that his opinion in the Alta Vela matter preceded the impeachment investigation. Nelson reached into his folder and produced a copy of the original manuscript of Butler's opinion, dated March 9, 1868, and presented it to the court. Caught in a lie, Butler fell silent, but Sumner rushed to the manager's defense in an effort to suppress the documents. Butler finally agreed to let the documents stand in the record as long as they were not read to the court.[21]

Evarts went back to work characterizing the articles for what they were — a litany of charges having no substance. He not only accused the House of concocting a humbug of hypocrisy, he also leveled criticism on the Radical press. "But the idea that a President is to be brought into the procedure of this court by a limited accusation, found 'not guilty' under that, and convicted on an indictment that the House refused to sustain, or upon the wider indictment of the newspaper press, and without any opportunity to bring proof or make arguments on the subject, seems to us too monstrous for any intelligence within or without this political circle ... to main-

tain for a moment." In a subtle and gentlemanly manner, Evarts suggested to the Senate that they had been duped by the House into trying a silly and unsubstantiated impeachment case.[22]

On April 30, before Evarts could take the floor to conclude his closing statement, Sumner called for action on a resolution to discipline Nelson for his willingness to fight a duel with Butler. The extreme Radicals felt obliged to resort to any musterable ruse to embarrass the prosecution. Nelson suggested that a review of the testimony would show Butler as the instigator and not he, but if Butler wanted a duel, he would oblige. Reverdy Johnson moved that the resolution be laid on the table, and by a vote of 35-10-9, the Senate quashed Sumner's motion.[23]

Evarts returned to the floor and occupied it for two more days. Like a surgeon operating with a razor-sharp scalpel, he sliced through the arguments of all the managers and each of their witnesses. Using doses of humor, he dismantled the tainted testimony. He also criticized the charges. To the allegation accusing the president of being "unmindful of the harmony and courtesies which ought to exist and be maintained between the executive and legislative branches of the government," he replied, "If it prevails from the executive toward the legislative, it should prevail from the legislative to the executive, unless I am to be met with what I must regard as a most novel view presented by Mr. Manager Williams ... that ... it is a rule that does not work both ways." The Senate erupted with laughter, but Evarts also had words for them. He reminded the High Court of Sumner's references to the president as "the enemy of the country." He recalled how, when called to order by his peers,

Senator Sherman supported Sumner, saying, "I think the words objected to are clearly in order. I have heard similar remarks fifty times without any question of order being raised." So when the issue came to a vote in the Senate, Evarts said, it was "laid on the table by 29 yeas and 10 nays ... which remind me of some of the votes on evidence that we have had in this trial." Again the Senate laughed, this time at themselves.[24]

Evarts closing argument lasted fourteen hours. Because of interruptions by Butler and others, the speech spanned four days. After exposing the impeachment case as an unwarranted conspiracy hatched by Radicals in the House, Evarts exhorted the High Court to ignore politics and render a verdict on the same proofs they would apply to men like Lincoln or Washington. Evarts had examined and destroyed the prosecution's case, and the managers knew it. The conspiracy had been shaken but not shattered. There was still time to repair the damage — Bingham would have the last word.[25]

On Monday, May 4, John Bingham began the final argument for the prosecution. Welles characterized Bingham as a "shrewd, sinuous, tricky lawyer," and the public, knowing of his reputation, demonstrated their interest in his closing remarks by jamming the Senate to the point of suffocation. Bingham intended to use every deception concoctable by the human mind to win back wavering senators. For the past few days those same senators had been inundated with letters from the Radical party machine demanding conviction. The notes came in all forms, some signed, some forged, and some unsigned. Many letters threatened to expose an incumbent's private life or promised some form of personal harm. Senators brought the letters into the chamber and passed them among their colleagues. Bingham knew all about the letters and the threats, and it was with this knowledge that he directed his closing statement to the undecided senators.[26]

Bingham's address contained the fervor of a zealot and the intellectual dishonesty of a political partisan. As one historian noted, Bingham had a loud voice and a confidant bearing, "but his law was partisanship, his logic unbridled political passion, and his history came from the grammar school." Rather than concentrate on supporting the articles, Bingham attacked the president for "the disgraceful part [he] played upon the tribune of the Senate on the 4th day of March 1865, and accepted the oath thus taken by him as the successor of Abraham Lincoln as confirmation and assurance that he would take care that the laws be faithfully executed." Instead, Bingham said, the president played "king of the people" and decided which laws were to be obeyed and which were not. Butler rejoiced at the oratory, writing to the Republican Convention of New Hampshire, "The removal of the great obstruction is certain. Wade and prosperity are sure to come with the apple blossoms."[27]

When Bingham closed on Wednesday, May 6, the chamber exploded with thunderous applause, roaring cheers, and wild, uncontrollable tumult. Chief Justice Chase pounded the gavel, shouting for order and threatening to clear the galleries. The crowd hissed, shouted him down, and continued rollicking about and making noise. Chase ordered the galleries emptied and the offenders arrested, but Cameron shouted back, "I hope the galleries will not be cleared." The demonstration had been organized by Radicals, and many senators demanded that order be restored, but pandemonium continued. Beset by demands from dozens of senators simultaneously, Chase finally restored order, and the trial ended.[28]

The Senate set Monday, May 11, as the date to debate the articles of impeachment. The session now stood closed to the public. No record of the debate exists, but thirty senators eventually filed written opinions. Sumner declared the trial "one of the last great battles with slavery" and demanded "action at once" to preserve the "safety of the Republic." John Sherman's opinion smacked of hypocrisy. Having once declared that the Tenure of Office Act did not prevent Stanton's removal, he now found guilt in the ad interim appointment of Lorenzo Thomas. Welles summed up the senator's duplicity, writing: "Sherman declared himself opposed to the first article, but would vote for the second. In other words, the President had the right to remove Stanton, but no right to order another to discharge the duties. Poor Sherman! He thinks the people fools; they know him better than he does them."[29]

The closed door debate produced opinions from three Republican party defectors, Fessenden, Trumbull, and Grimes, all of whom denounced the articles as absurd and not within the constitutional meaning of high crimes and misdemeanors. Were other defections imminent? All the president needed for acquittal were four more Republicans. The Radicals denounced the opinions of the three defectors and promised political reprisals if minds did not change. Justin S. Morrill of Vermont, one of Fessenden's closest friends, warned against voting for acquittal, writing, "As an idol of a very large portion of our people, you would be knocked off your pedestal. Then, the sharp pens of all the press would be stuck into you for years, tip'd with fire, and it would sour the rest of your life." Morrill expressed the fears of many Radicals when he added that his vote for conviction "may be selfish, but I know there is no other aspect of this case where any particle of self crops in." Fessenden, Trumbull, and Grimes were not of a character to change their minds. But if there were others, could they stand the blood-boiling pressure imposed upon them by the conspirators?[30]

19

The Verdict

The Radical press went to work and applied coercive pressure on undecided senators to convict. Men like Horace Greeley had a telling effect because no newspaper could arouse public sentiment more ardently than the *New York Tribune*. Greeley abhorred Johnson, but his bitterness had so contaminated the pages of his press that people had become apathetic toward his editorial diatribes. On May 6 Greeley compared the president's treason to that of Benedict Arnold and declared any senator so base as to vote for acquittal would stand "in history as the partner of his crimes." In another editorial he wrote, "We are certain that neither money nor revenge will seduce any Senator into an infamous association with America's most degraded son." Under the Constitution, impeachable offenses included bribery, giving rise to speculation that Greeley had been obtaining editorial advice from Butler?[1]

Five Republican senators remained on the Radicals' list of potential defectors: Waitman T. Willey and Peter G. Van Winkle of West Virginia; Joseph S. Fowler and John B. Henderson of Missouri; and Edmund G. Ross of Kansas. If four stood for the president, Johnson would be acquitted. Every manager knew this, and Stevens, after squandering so many months of failing health to impeach the president, now marshaled his remaining strength to destroy him.

Stevens' earlier effort to pack the court by seating representatives from Arkansas had failed. The state had now fallen under carpetbag rule, and its senators made reliable allies. Stevens studied the matter closely and on May 8 reported a bill to admit Arkansas as a state. No matter that her senators had not participated in the trial, heard testimony, or sworn impartial justice. Of utmost importance was to get them sworn in so their two votes could be counted, thereby neutralizing a fourth defector should there be one. "There are reasons which I do not think it proper or necessary to mention now," said Stevens, "why this bill should be considered, passed and sent to the Senate before next Monday!" Why should anyone need to discuss the obvious?[2]

On May 11, without waiting for the Senate to act on the Arkansas bill, Stevens took a bigger step, announcing a bill for the admission of Louisiana, Georgia, Alabama, and the Carolinas. Ten more senators from the carpetbag legislatures would ensure conviction in the High Court. What a marvelous statesmanlike idea. But did the Senate have the fortitude to join in the conspiracy? If not, other tactics must be employed.[3]

Armed for battle, House Radicals

descended on the five undecided Senators. Missouri's representatives fell upon Henderson with fangs bared and threatened to rip away his career in the Senate. They badgered him outside the Senate, in his office, on the street, and on the day of the vote, at his home. Disgusted, Henderson decided to resign, but no, said the Radicals, they did not want his resignation — they wanted his vote. So Henderson pondered his manhood, undecided what to do.[4]

Wielding all his remaining physical strength and political power, Stevens used operatives to warn Senators Willey and Van Winkle that if they voted for acquittal, West Virginia would cease to exist as a state.[5]

As time ran out on the Radicals, Jacob Howard of Michigan reported sick. Zachariah Chandler rose on behalf of his colleague and asked for a postponement. The Radicals needed Howard's ballot and moved to delay the decision until Saturday the 16th, thereby providing themselves with four more days to work on doubtful senators, all of whom wanted to vote and be done with the trial.[6]

Radicals recruited the Union Congressional Committee, chaired by Robert Schenck of Ohio, beseeching it to send out hundreds of telegrams to the Loyal Leagues. To the state of every wavering senator went the message: "Great danger to the peace of the country and the Republican cause if impeachment fails. Send to your Senators public opinion by resolutions, letters, and delegations." Respondents jammed the telegraph office and messages with warnings and demands flooded the offices of the four announced defectors and the five undecided senators.[7]

During the interregnum Grant exerted his influence in support of the managers. Stanton worked night and day, stirring activity in the war department. Both induced officers at all levels of the military to speak and act in the interest of the Radicals. No political defectors had ever been so unceasingly subjected to such intense fire from their party than the nine Republican senators under attack.[8]

Horace Greeley, having developed a fondness for comparing political enemies to Benedict Arnold, now applied his pet cognomen to James Grimes of Iowa. As the *Tribune* hit the street, Grimes suffered a paralyzing stroke — another victory for the house managers, or so they thought.[9]

As the day of decision drew near, Radicals focused their efforts on Edmund Ross of Kansas. Sumner did not believe that a Kansas man would defect, but the managers worried he might. They recruited spies to watch and track his moves. Detectives probed into his background, smelling around for blackmail material. They discovered that Ross made frequent calls at a studio where a young girl worked. Thinking the evidence strong enough to create a scandal, they approached Ross with an "or else" option. To cover their plot, they sent George Julian to induce the girl to cooperate. That he threatened her to do so was later charged on the floor of the House, but he denied it.[10]

The House continued to pester and intimidate Ross. They recruited Samuel C. Pomeroy, senior senator from Kansas, who blatantly demanded of Ross an answer on how he would vote. Ross replied that he had not decided. Pomeroy relentlessly badgered Ross for an answer and the following day found him in the company of Willey, Henderson, Trumbull, and Van Winkle. Pomeroy stepped into the room and informed the gathering that the president would be convicted on article eleven by one vote—Ross's vote. Ross replied, "Do not count on my vote for conviction under any circumstances." The following morning a telegram arrived from Leavenworth for Ross: "Kansas has heard the evidence and demands the conviction of the President." Though signed by "D. R. Anthony and 1000 Others," Ross suspected Pomeroy of instigating the telegram. At midnight, May 14, Pomeroy made one more attempt. He went to Ross's room but did not find him there. He waited until 4:00 A.M., but Ross never returned. Disgusted, Pomeroy retired, suspicious but no wiser for his efforts.[11]

On May 15 Horace Greeley published all the reasons why the president should be convicted and effusively predicted his removal. Behaving much like the managers, he ignored the evidence and merely proclaimed that impeachment was not so much intended to punish guilt but to "exchange a bad officer for a good one." Many senators believed that exchanging Wade for Johnson improved nothing. Greeley, however, always looked for an authority to quote when expressing his views, and what better spokesman could he find than the ever-popular Grant, who, quoted the editor, "declares that the acquittal of Johnson would threaten the country and especially the south with revolution and bloodshed." If Grant made the statement, those who knew him well would doubt he really believed it.[12]

The president's judgment day, May 16, came at last. A few days earlier Johnson spoke to a correspondent from the *New York World* and said, "I have never allowed myself to believe or feel that the American Senate would prostitute its great power of impeachment to base party purposes, and I shall not believe it until I know the vote for conviction has been recorded." Was Johnson wishfully predicting his acquittal or expressing a conviction in the integrity of the Senate? Now he would have his answer.[13]

The Senate had studied all eleven articles, searching for one that would attract the greatest number of votes for conviction. Separate caucuses reviewed the question and eventually agreed to vote first on article eleven, the most comprehensive and least understood of all the articles. Stevens and Butler had designed it that way, hoping to snare wavering senators. Surely, thought the managers, the article contained at least one accusation no senator could deny. And while they caucused, they finally put their stamp of approval on Ben Wade's cabinet. Feeling confident they would prevail, all that remained was to vote.[14]

Ten minutes before noon, the time set for reconvening, Pomeroy observed Ross in the lobby of the Senate. Nearby sat Stevens, who listened with grim approval as Pomeroy admonished Ross that a vote for acquittal spelled political death and insinuated that the latter might find himself embroiled in a charge of bribery. Though baffled by Pomeroy's reference to bribery, Ross had become ambivalent about his political career after witnessing how his so-called distinguished colleagues operated.[15]

At twelve noon Chief Justice Chase entered the Senate in flowing black robes, and the sergeant-at-arms called the High Court to order. After the opening formalities ended, Senator Williams, by prearrangement, took the floor and entered a motion for the first vote to be taken on the eleventh article—Stevens' catch-all blunderbuss. Chase ordered the yeas and nays, and the motion passed, 34-19-1. All the doubtful senators voted against the motion, all but Grimes, who was not in the Senate. A new voice spoke in the majority, Ben Wade — his first vote. No longer would he keep silent, impartial justice or not, for today he would become president.[16]

Fessenden requested a half hour recess before proceeding to a final vote. Grimes, who three days before had suffered a stroke, promised to be in the Senate, but when he failed to show, Fessenden wanted time to get him. Reverdy Johnson interrupted and said, "He is downstairs. He will be in the chamber in a moment." As he spoke Grimes came through the door, carried by two porters who deposited the senator in his seat. Though physically shattered by paralysis, Grimes faced death by coming to the Senate. He knew the odds against Johnson, against his own health, and the importance of a single ballot.[17]

The galleries stirred restlessly, waiting for the grand finale to one of the greatest moments in American history. The chief justice called for absolute quiet, and the chamber hushed to the silence of a mortuary. Barely a breath stirred. Friends and foes alike fixed pallid stares upon the chief justice, waiting for the call of the roll. "Some of the members of the House near me," Julian recalled, "grew pale and sick under the burden of suspense." In another building not far away another assembly suffered the burden of uncertainty. The president, with his wife and family by his side, waited for the verdict.[18]

Taking his cue from Chase, the Senate clerk read article eleven to the High Court. A masterpiece of mumbo jumbo, only bits and pieces of the verbiage could be intelligibly connected to the case of the managers. Would it be enough? Stevens thought so, and so did Wade.[19]

Chief Justice Chase ordered the roll called. One by one, senators responded. As the clerk took the tally, hundreds in the galleries, every member of the House and Senate, guests of the diplomatic corps, all scratched the count on clip boards, tablets, backs of envelopes, or scraps of paper. When the chief justice called, "Mr. Grimes," he excused the disabled senator from rising, but Grimes had come this far and with help struggled to his feet, answering weakly, "Not guilty." Henderson followed Harlan, adding another "not guilty" to the slowly growing number. Four of the doubtful senators had voted, all of them for acquittal. Fifteen more votes follow, ten for conviction, five for acquittal, and then the chief justice called, "Mr. Ross." In a thin voice, the senator from Kansas replied "Not guilty." Only four more votes were needed for acquittal. Saulsbury, voting next, voiced one of them, but Sherman, Sprague, Stewart, and Sumner followed with two others for conviction. Trumbull, Van Winkle, and Vickers came next, and all three voted for acquittal, thereby settling the impeachment issue on article eleven by a single vote. The roll continued with Wade, Willey, Williams, Wilson, and Yates all voting for conviction, but to no avail.[20]

"Upon this article," the chief justice announced, "35 Senators vote 'guilty' and 19 Senators vote 'not guilty.' Two-thirds not having pronounced guilty, the President is therefore acquitted on this article." It was not necessary to say "by one vote." Every person in the chamber held their own scorecards.[21]

In the absence of modern technology, fleet-footed Colonel Crook, the president's bodyguard, bolted out of the

Tallying and impeachment vote. (Library of Congress, from Leslie's *Illustrated Weekly*.)

Senate and ran the length of Pennsylvania Avenue to the White House. The president waited in the library, surrounded by friends and family. Though ostensibly a hard man, he could no longer suppress his emotions. To Crook's congratulations tears rolled down the president's weathered face, and he motioned the colonel to go upstairs and inform the first lady. There she sat, calmly sewing in her rocking chair. "He's acquitted," said colonel jubilantly, encasing her tiny hands in his. "Crook," she replied, "I knew he would be acquitted; I knew it."[22]

But the ordeal did not end. Ten more articles awaited a decision, and conviction on any one of them could oust the president. Outraged that they had lost the battle on article eleven, the Radicals moved for adjournment until Tuesday, May 26. Chase called the motion out of order, but deferred to the Senate. With the Republican National Convention scheduled to meet on May 20 in Chicago, the Radicals hoped to use the occasion to apply more pressure on the defectors and perhaps scrape together one more vote. By 36-21-1, the Senate voted to adjourn, the absent vote being Grimes', who had departed from the chamber exhausted. So the fate of the president lay in limbo for another ten days, as did the political future of Wade, who no longer withheld his vote out of deference to honorable conduct.[23]

From New York Horace Greeley condemned the Radicals for injudiciously voting the eleventh article first. "This failing," he said, "all fails." Whether Greeley's prediction would prevail could not be determined for another eight days. Meanwhile, the Radicals had time to coerce and, if possible, bribe the defectors.[24]

Matters at the Chicago convention soon cheered the gloomy Radicals. With great enthusiasm six hundred fifty delegates nominated by acclamation Grant for president. Sumner and a few of the ultra Radicals would have preferred Chase, but Sumner's attacks on anyone who disagreed with him had finally diluted his influence. Aside from contumations and occasional outbursts of meanness and hatred, nobody gave Johnson a word of praise. When developing their platform, they extolled Lincoln as the grand champion of the party, but said nothing about Johnson's efforts to implement the great liberator's policies. At their own convention the Radicals could say whatever they wished, and what they said need not be true. Many of them arrived from the impeachment trial, and though article eleven had gone down in infamy, the Radicals brazenly declared that the president had been "justly impeached for high crimes and misdemeanors, and properly pronounced guilty thereof by the vote of thirty-five Senators." Statements like this were meant to salve wounds, and with ten articles to go, the Radicals were doing a marvelous job of making themselves feel better.[25]

The second plank of the Radical platform disgusted even many of the Republicans. It called for "equal suffrage to all loyal men of the south" while leaving equal suffrage in the north up to the individual states. Since some northern states would not grant suffrage to blacks, the only states feeling the imposition of suffrage would be those of the south. Men like James Blaine denounced the platform, condemning it "unworthy of the Republican party" and "a mere stroke of expediency to escape the prejudices which negro suffrage would encounter in a majority of the loyal states." The actual wording of the document contained the same intellectual chicanery and confusion of understanding that marked the eleventh article of impeachment and would eventually embarrass the Radicals.[26]

The choice of vice president came as a great disappointment to Wade. Had Johnson been convicted, Wade would have become Grant's vice president, a post the senator desperately needed and dearly wanted. Everything that had been decided in advance assumed Johnson's conviction. With five candidates in the running for vice president, Wade easily won a plurality on the first vote, but it took only five ballots to dispose of him and give the nomination to Schuyler Colfax. Perhaps it was fateful. Colfax fit nicely into the corruption and graft that would eventually shame the Grant administration.[27]

With the convention behind them, members of Congress returned to Washington to congratulate Grant and to finish the work of impeachment. During the recess the managers had busied themselves by probing into the backgrounds of dissident senators. Butler took charge of the inquisition—a talent honed in 1862 as military governor of Louisiana. For headquarters, he chose a section of the basement in the Capitol. Edmund Ross, the most vulnerable of young senators, became the focus of Butler's attack. He poured over the bank accounts of Ross, Trumbull, Van Winkle, and others looking for clues that could be used for blackmail. Butler hired detectives and sent them to the Baltimore and Washington telegraph offices with orders to confiscate all messages sent or received during the four days preceding May 16.[28]

Desperate acts also pervaded the Senate. Having been defeated on the eleventh article, Radicals reconvened immediately after the vote in an effort to push through the House bill admitting Alabama, Georgia, Louisiana, and the Carolinas "before the sun goes down." Saner minds asked whether senators from those states could judge an impeachment case having not heard the evidence. "Of course they can," replied Sumner. Others disagreed, and Sumner lost the argument.[29]

Butler's inquisitors came up empty at the banks and telegraph offices, but detectives discovered widespread betting on the president's conviction. Small fortunes had been wagered by lobbyists, claim agents, gold speculators, and whiskey brokers. Without the time or interest for verifying stories concocted by big money gamblers, Horace Greeley took Butler's report and printed it for public consumption under the headline "The Impeachment Manager's Report — Conclusive Evidence of Corruption." Though cleverly crafted to make innocent senators appear guilty, Butler's reported findings were a disgraceful distortion of fact. But what care the Radicals if lies could coerce one more vote for conviction.[30]

On May 26 the Senate reconvened to vote on the first ten articles and settle the presidential issue until the fall elections. The Radicals did not have the votes to convict, and they knew it. During the recess some senators who had voted for conviction now harbored misgivings, but would they change their vote? A motion went to the floor to adjourn until June 23. Ross objected and asked that the date be amended to Sep-

tember first. Ross' motion raised concern among the defense. Was Ross defecting? A messenger jogged to the White House to warn Johnson of possible catastrophe. But the Senate voted down both measures.[31]

After a quick caucus the Senate decided to vote first on articles two and three. The suspense that pervaded the chamber on May 16 once more revisited the floor and galleries of the Senate. Throughout the call of the roll, not a senator changed his vote, and then came Ross's turn. All eyes turned to the junior senator from Kansas, who rose deliberately and said, "Not guilty." Butler's tricks had failed. By a measure of 35-19, the Senate acquitted Johnson on the second article. Without further delay, Chase put the third article before the High Court and called the roll. Gone was the suspense, along with the hopes of the Radicals. Ross held firm, and the chief justice reported that, "the President of the United States stands acquitted upon this article."[32]

Early on the afternoon of May 26 the conspiracy to oust the president ended, and with it the career of Ben Wade. Senator Williams moved that the "Senate sitting as a Court of Impeachment do now adjourn *sine die*." The motion passed 34-16-4 without ever voting on the remaining articles, nor would they ever come before the court again.[33]

With courage, honor, and distinction, seven Republican defectors destroyed the Radical conspiracy. Their names deserve to be remembered: Fessenden of Maine, Fowler of Tennessee, Grimes of Indiana, Henderson of Missouri, Ross of Kansas, Trumbull of Illinois, and Van Winkle of West Virginia. But proscription rather than praise greeted them, and the Radicals used the press and their vast connections to destroy and defame the seven members who broke ranks to do impartial justice. Chicago warned Trumbull to never show his face on the streets of the Windy City unless he wished to be hung. Radicals treated Ross as a leper, destroyed his political career, and left him desperately poor. Sixteen years later, the party forgave Henderson and made him chairman of the committee that nominated Blaine for president. Grimes never completely recovered from his stroke, but along the way Chief Justice chase paid him a visit and said, "I would rather be in your place, Mr. Grimes, than to receive any honor in the gift of our people." Chase no longer wanted to be associated with Radicals, but the presidency he cherished remained forever unattainable. The trial turned Chase away from the Republicans, and in frustration he drifted toward the new party being built by Democrats.[34]

Years later George Julian admitted that "The idea of making the question of impeachment a matter of party discipline was utterly indefensible and preposterous." Writing in 1884, James Blaine observed that "many who favored impeachment" had come to admit that "it was not justifiable on the charges made, and that its success would have resulted in greater injury to free institutions than Andrew Johnson in his utmost endeavor was able to inflict." A most peculiar comment came from John Sherman, who wrote, "I felt bound, with much regret, to vote 'guilty' in response to my name, but I was entirely satisfied with the result of the vote, brought about by several Republican Senators." Of those seven defectors, Senator Justin Morrill's biographer wrote, they voted "for acquittal against their party, but to their everlasting honor; one could wish to [have seen]

Morrill's name included in that list." Perhaps the strangest admission of all came from Charles Sumner, who late one night took Henderson aside and said, "I don't want to die without making this confession, that in the matter of impeachment you were right and I was wrong." All the exculpatory afterthoughts surfaced many years after the trial of Andrew Johnson — the time when the blood ran hot during the days of Thad Stevens, Ben Butler, John Bingham, Ben Wade, Charles Sumner, and their band of zealots.[35]

Three friends of the president who voted against him deserved a small white feather. Morgan of New York, Sprague of Rhode Island, and Willey of West Virginia all told Johnson that should their votes be needed, they would vote for acquittal. So great were the powers of the Radicals that such men as Morgan, Sprague, and Willey would cravenly slink behind the courage of Edmund Ross of Kansas.[36]

On May 26, when word of the president's acquittal reached the war department, Stanton surrendered the office. In a matter of days the Senate confirmed Schofield. To enable Stanton to exit graciously, they emphasized that he had not been "legally removed" but had merely "relinquished his place as Secretary of War for causes stated in his note to the President." The Senate thanked Stanton for his services under hostile conditions that threatened the work of Congress "in the restoration of a real and permanent peace."[37]

Political spitefulness dominated the Senate when they rejected Johnson's effort to reinstate Stanbery as attorney general. Curtis refused the post, and Johnson finally settled upon Evarts. Even the most disaffected Senators could not reject a man of Evarts distinguished record, so Johnson added to his cabinet for the remainder of his term one of the most brilliant men in the country.[38]

As May 1868 came to an end, Johnson had little more than nine months to finish what started as Lincoln's second term. For most of those three years in office, he had been at war with Congress. He could not predict whether the trouble would continue, but his career as a Republican had come to an end. Before the war he had been a southern Jacksonian Democrat, and by his actions as president, he became one again.

Now he needed political allies, but who would have him — an impeached and tainted president without a constituency?

20

Last Days of
the Presidency

During the trial, Chief Justice Chase conducted himself with dignity, impartiality, and skill, but at night he penned letters which one historian described as "unworthy of a college sophomore." His motive — to angle for the Democratic presidential nomination — an "act of folly as to render him ludicrous and his judicial robes less than immaculate." Four days after the president's acquittal, Chase wrote August Belmont that he did not know whether he was a "suitable candidate for any party," but if his fellow countrymen should seek his services "they are without doubt entitled to them." With that letter more than any other, Chase announced his wish to become the Democratic nominee for president.[1]

Andrew Johnson, having openly repudiated the Republican cause, also felt entitled to consideration from the Democrats. He had a claim to the presidency and wanted another term. But Johnson's public image had been so debased by the Radical press that it presented a problem for the Democrats.[2]

Other candidates seemed more promising than either Johnson or Chase, and there were many. George H. Pendleton advocated a plan to liquidate the federal debt using greenbacks rather than gold. His proposal had little popular appeal except in the west. Major General Winfield S. Hancock's distinguished service in the Army of the Potomac made him a good candidate to run against Grant. And there were others, James R. Doolittle of Wisconsin, who had supported Johnson's administration; Thomas A. Hendricks of Indiana, who had tried to prevent Wade from sitting on the High Court; Joel Parker of New Jersey; Asa Packer of Pennsylvania; Sanford E. Church of New York; and Horatio Seymour, also of New York and chairman of the convention. Some New Yorkers favored Chase, and they planned to design a platform omitting those issues he opposed.[3]

On July 4, 1868, a new "Wigwam" on New York's Fourteenth Street housed the Democratic Convention. When the delegates shuffled inside to take their seats, observers noted many former rebel leaders dressed in gray. Johnson had issued full pardons to all Confederate officers and politicians except those under indictment for treason, such as Jefferson Davis. The delegates worked assiduously on designing their platform, and as the document neared completion, it took on the character of Johnson's veto messages on the Tenure of Office Act, the Freed-men's Bureau Act, and the Reconstruc-tion Acts. Had the Democrats stopped there, they might have beaten Grant, but they included Pendleton's heretical green-back plan for liquidating the federal debt and irritated every section of the coun-try but the west.[4]

Johnson and Chase remained in Washington during the convention, but each had sponsors and advocates work-ing delegates for votes. Word came back from New York encouraging Johnson to remove McCulloch and Seward, the two most traditional Republicans in the cab-inet, and replace them with Democrats. The president refused the request. He could not have gotten through the im-peachment troubles without their sup-port and loyalty.[5]

Thomas A. R. Nelson, fresh from the trial and flush with victory, nomi-nated Johnson for president, heralding him as the man who stood against the Radicals and protected the Constitution. Nelson won enormous applause, and Johnson's name went before the conven-tion along with those of Pendleton, Han-cock, Church, and others. On the first ballot Pendleton won the plurality with Johnson second, but Chase did not re-ceive a single vote. Johnson expressed gratification with the vote, but the cab-inet doubted whether he would take the lead.[6]

The balloting continued for three days. When none of the front-runners made gains, the ballots for Hancock and Hendricks picked up votes but no com-manding plurality. On the fourth ballot North Carolina slipped in the name of Seymour, who halfheartedly attempted to decline on the premise that he chaired the convention. No candidate could mus-ter the required two-thirds majority, and

by the eighteenth ballot, Johnson carried only ten votes. The scoundrels in New York's Tammany Hall had been maneu-vering since the convention began and asked, Why not Horatio Seymour? Be-cause the Radicals had committed so many blunders, the Democrats foolishly believed that anyone they nominated could beat Grant.[7]

From 1862 to 1864 Seymour had been governor of New York. The New York draft riots occurred midway through his term, and Seymour associated him-self with the rioters. He pestered Lincoln through the latter years of the war, com-plaining of the unfairness of quotas and demanded that draft laws be suspended until tested in the courts. Lincoln could not stop the war to grant Seymour's silly request. While New York liked their man, his popularity did not extend much be-yond the borders of the Empire State. Though Hendricks and Hancock con-tinued to make small gains, Tammany Hall wanted neither man. During the twenty-second roll call, Brevet Major General Alexander M. McCook of Ohio sprang to his feet and in a stirring speech nominated Seymour. The ex-governor replied, "Gentlemen, I thank you and may God bless you for your kindness to me, but your candidate I cannot be." The "Wigwam" erupted in cheers for the New Yorker. One state after another ral-lied to his support, and in a blink of an eye, Seymour won the nomination by unanimous acclaim, coyly admitting he had been "unable to resist."[8]

For vice president the convention elected Brevet Major General Francis P. Blair, Jr., who had staunchly supported Lincoln throughout the war and Johnson after the war. He believed that the presi-dent should restore the government and the Constitution by declaring all reconstruction acts "null and void, compel the army to undo its usurpations in the south, dispossess the carpetbag state governments, allow the white people to reorganize their own governments and elect Senators and Representatives." Blair would have made a much better vice president for Johnson than for Seymour.[9]

Had Johnson won the nomination, the Democrats might have altered the course of history, but in Seymour they chose a politician who, during the war, so embarrassed the Lincoln administration as to raise questions of his personal loyalty. Seymour's candidacy came as a boon to the Radicals and all but assured Grant's election. Nonetheless, Stevens took no chances. On June 20, after Arkansas adopted the Fourteenth Amendment, he rushed through both Houses a bill for the state's readmission. Five days later he pushed through the so-called Omnibus Bill to admit Alabama, Florida, Georgia, Louisiana, and the two Carolinas. Stevens made his motives clear when he said, "I trust the Almighty ruler of nations will never again permit this land to be made slave; or in other words that he will never permit the Democratic party to gain the ascendancy." By July 20, all seven states had ratified the Fourteenth Amendment.[10]

Johnson vetoed both bills, writing, "I could not consent to ... the assumption ... that Congress may at its pleasure expel or exclude a state from the Union." Not even impeachment had moderated Johnson's response to efforts by the Radicals to defy the Constitution. Nor had the Radicals attempted to moderate their relationship with the president and repassed both bills over his vetoes.[11]

Seward challenged the legality of the Fourteenth Amendment, arguing that the newly formed state governments of the south may not, in themselves, have been legally organized under the Constitution. Grant never questioned the amendment, and he probably never reflected on the many thousands of paroles written during the war which enabled every man "to return to their homes, not to be disturbed by United States authority so long as they observe their paroles and the laws in force where they may reside." Seward's argument fell on deaf ears in Congress, and on July 28, he had no alternative but to comply with the amendment. Writing on the Fourteenth Amendment in 1885, Samuel S. Cox corroborated Seward's dissenting argument. He called the action of Congress in promulgating the act and coercing its acceptance by bribing southerners with statehood "a monument to the satanic malice of the Radical party. It is a warning to succeeding generations of the excesses of partisan lust."[12]

Because Mississippi, Texas, and Virginia did not comply with Radical demands, Congress passed a joint resolution excluding from the electoral college "the votes of states lately in rebellion which shall not have been reorganized." Johnson observed a contradiction in the resolution to which he replied, "If this position is correct, it follows that [the states] were taken out of the Union by virtue of the acts of secession and hence that the war waged against them was illegal and unconstitutional." Congress had no power under the Constitution to reject the electoral vote of any state. The Radicals paid as little heed to the Constitution as they did presidential vetoes. Johnson's argument made no impression on them. They considered logic and the Constitution an inconvenient encumbrance that could be nullified by votes, so they repassed the joint resolution and excluded three southern states from the count.[13]

The president watched as the carpetbag regime filed into Congress. Ten of the fourteen senators came from the north, as did sixteen representatives. Some were foreigners by birth and one had served in the Union army. They had no social standing or any political influence with their constituency. They were mere creations of the Radicals and protected by federal troops stationed in their districts. The Radicals wanted no surprises with elections fast approaching.[14]

Congress adjourned on July 27 after Thomas Williams of Pennsylvania failed to reimpeach the president by authoring and presenting fourteen new articles. Though the juice of life ebbed slowly from his body, Stevens offered three more articles. His determination to destroy Johnson seemed to keep him alive. Thriving mainly on brandy, Stevens lashed out, suggesting that Johnson be brought to the block and decapitated. Though support came from the carpetbaggers, the Radicals wanted no more impeachment embarrassments. Johnson would soon be gone from the presidency, and Grant would follow their lead. After Congress adjourned, Stevens remained behind, too ill to return to Lancaster.

When John W. Forney, publisher of the *Philadelphia Press,* visited the emaciated impeacher in Washington, Stevens said "it is not my appearance but my disappearance that troubles me." As one historian wrote, Stevens performed a lasting service to the country when on August 11, he died. Sumner bewailed the loss, delivering a maudlin eulogy to the "hero statesman [who] passes to his reward." But Stevens seldom applied his mind to constructive or statesmanlike work. Though he fathered the reconstruction measures, time exposed them as more destructive than constructive.[15]

With Congress adjourned, the presidential campaign of 1868 took center stage across the nation. The Democrats had chosen Johnson's program as their platform, but in Seymour they had chosen a man "who had not lifted a finger" to sustain the president during his three-year administration. Seymour's affiliation with Tammany Hall, combined with an undistinguished war record, gave him a low standing when publicly compared with Grant. The ticket may have had a better chance had Blair been the candidate instead of Seymour, but the Democrats would have had their best chance with Johnson. The country knew where Johnson stood on national issues; no one knew where Seymour stood.[16]

For Seymour, the campaign would be an uphill battle with an unattainable goal. Agents of the Freedmen's Bureau sniffed the air for political opportunities. They stimulated the blacks and in a backhanded way created enough race dissension to enable Radicals to claim "outrages" again. To combat this power the Ku Klux Klan, organized in 1868, now numbered more than half a million members. The manhood of the south, said historian James F. Rhodes, "rallied to the defense of wives and daughters." Doing so strained the Democratic platform and reinforced the policies of the Radicals.[17]

Grant conducted his well-planned campaign by doing nothing. Seymour made no speeches until October. Thomas Nast caricatured the differences between the two men in a telling cartoon, depicting on one side Grant demanding the surrender of Vicksburg on July 1863, and on the other Seymour, addressing the New York draft rioters as "my friends."

To win, Grant needed no more than his war record and Seymour's lack of one.[18]

Andrew Johnson played no role in the campaign. With dignity and without bitterness he reconciled himself to the remaining months of the presidency. He felt powerless to aid Seymour, whose awkward fumbling of the issues before the country helped Grant's race to victory. When reflecting on Grant, Johnson remembered the general's help during the first two years of the administration, but lamented that "Grant saw the Radical handwriting on the wall, and heeded it. I did not see it or if seeing it did not heed it. Grant did the proper thing to save Grant, but it pretty nearly ruined me." On the subject of secession, however, Johnson said, "I shall go down to my grave with the firm belief that Davis [Howell] Cobb, [Robert A.] Toombs, and a few other of the arch conspirators should have been tried, convicted, and hanged for treason. There was too much precious blood spilled on both sides not to have held the leading traitors responsible." Johnson remained a man of convictions, and nothing about his life suggested any change.[19]

Johnson predicted that Grant would win the presidency, and knowing that he could do nothing to influence the outcome, avoided aligning himself with any party. Welles followed the campaign with interest, writing in September, "There is no love for Grant, there is a positive dislike of Seymour." Neither party talked about the great problems facing the nation — "the rights of man, the rights of states, the grants and limitations of the Constitution." It was, as George F. Milton entitled his book, *The Age of Hate*, and both parties regurgitated their share upon the American public.[20]

On October 13 a poll covering Pennsylvania, Indiana, Ohio, and Nebraska showed Grant well ahead of Seymour. Shocked by the data, the *New York World* demanded that Seymour and Blair be dropped from the Democratic ticket and replaced by better candidates. Many agreed, some suggesting Johnson, some Chase. The Democrats refused to budge, preferring defeat to a change in the ticket. Many callers descended on the White House, beseeching Johnson to express a willingness to step into the competition, but the president distanced himself from such schemes.[21]

When November 3 finally arrived, the Radicals had so positioned themselves that every state in the south but Georgia voted for Grant. As expected, New York and New Jersey gave their majorities to Seymour. Across the country, however, Grant's popular majority barely exceeded 300,000, a miserably small margin. Without enforced aid from military tribunals, carpetbag administrations in the south, and the exclusion of Virginia, Texas, and Mississippi from the election, Grant may have been defeated. The Radicals had their way, but would it last?[22]

Congress reconvened on December 5, 1869. Four days later Johnson issued his last annual message. He wrote in the spirit of conciliation, though not budging an inch from his previous stand on the Constitution or departing from the great work once envisioned by his predecessor. If anything, he lectured too much to a legislature preferring to hear nothing from him at all. Few in Congress wanted his message, and Johnson's counsel and advice went unheeded, and for the most part unheard until 1907, when James D. Richardson compiled the *Messages and Papers of the Presidents*. After putting eleven volumes together, Richardson remarked one day to a friend that he was probably the only person who had ever read all the messages of the presidents. Next to Jefferson and Lincoln, said Richardson, those of Johnson were the greatest.[23]

Congress did not like to be scolded by the president. The message, having been read in both Houses, drew harsh denouncements from Radicals. The *New York Tribune* labeled the message as Johnson's "worst and fortunately last insult to the American people." Horace Greeley deserved some measure of thanks. Without criticism from his press, few people would have read Johnson's meritorious message.[24]

On Christmas Day, with little more than two months remaining on his term in office, Johnson issued his last proclamation — a befitting gift to those in need. To all who had participated in the late rebellion he granted a "full pardon and amnesty for the offense of treason against the United States." It brought an end to the Jefferson Davis case. The Senate asked on what "authority of law" could such a proclamation be made? Johnson replied, "The second section of article second" of the Constitution. The Senate withdrew its challenge.[25]

On December 30 the president celebrated his sixtieth birthday. He gave a party for his grandchildren and invited three hundred children to the White House. At the appointed hour they converged on the East Room and danced away the evening. Nothing could have given more enjoyment to the president and his family. The first lady made a brief public appearance, her second since moving into the White House. His hard life, his unrelenting struggle with poverty, the war, and his fight with Congress had suppressed his lighter moods. To him, life had been no laughing matter. But on

this day he no longer appeared as the "grimly stern great man" who paced the White House, cracked no jokes, told no stories, and bore the burden of restoration. One of his secretaries observed, "I have seen him greet friends with pleasure portrayed in his countenance, and have seen him with a grim cast-iron wrinkle on the nether half of his face at public receptions, but his eye lacked the luster of a light heart"—but everything changed on the president's birthday when the children came.[26]

On New Year's Day the president held his annual reception at the White House. Grant shunned the invitation, unable to forget or forgive the embarrassing correspondence between himself and the president during the days of Stanton's suspension. Unexpectedly, Ben Butler made an appearance. He pushed his way through the crowd, grasped the president's hand, and explained that though he discriminated "between the President and the man," he had "no controversy or differences with Andrew Johnson." The president, though courteous, "expressed no opinion" as to the propriety of the visit. Welles condemned Butler's explanation as "worthy of the cad of New Orleans," but Johnson sidestepped neither man nor devil. He nursed no resentments and could grasp the proffered hand of Butler, offer his own to Oliver P. Morton, who had deserted to become one of the president's most ferocious foes, or speak kindly of Parson Brownlow, who had called him "the dead dog in the White House."[27]

Yet on January 11 Butler attempted to repeal the Tenure of Office Act. He carried it through the House, but the Senate failed to act. Welles suspected that Butler merely intended to show that the act had been passed for the sole purpose of blocking Johnson's effort to oust Stanton and was now no longer necessary — especially with Grant about to take office. Under Grant's administration, Congress eventually changed the law to allow a president to suspend civil officers until the next session, but the Senate still retained its right to restore the suspended officer. "Casting off all political disguises," the speaker of the House later admitted, "the simple truth remains that the Tenure-of-Office Law was enacted lest President Johnson should remove Republican officeholders too rapidly, and it was practically repealed lest General Grant should not remove Democratic officeholders rapidly enough."[28]

After the Christmas recess, the Radicals returned to their work — debating the Fifteenth Amendment to the Constitution. When finished, it read, "The rights of citizens of the United States to vote shall not be denied or abridged by the United States or by any state on account of race, color or previous condition of servitude." This was necessary, said the Radicals, in order to make "permanent the results of the Union victory in the Civil War." But any law to be accepted and respected by the people must express the will of the great mass it affects. By the end of February the new amendment was ready for submission to the states — those free and those in the custody of carpetbaggers, blacks, and military tribunals.[29]

With Grant's inauguration day fast approaching, one of the questions troubling Johnson's cabinet was deciding what part the president should play in the ceremony. Grant refused to ride in the same carriage with Johnson or to speak with him. The committee solved the problem by settling upon two carriages, each to proceed up Pennsylvania Avenue side-by-side with Johnson on the right and Grant on the left. The cabinet discouraged the president from attending the inaugural, but Johnson demurred. He would decide later.[30]

By March 3 the streets of Washington overflowed with office-seekers, sightseers, well-wishers, friends and officials paying their respects. With them came hundreds of black vagabonds. The Radicals saw an opportunity to express their affection for the blacks and passed a resolution to provide them with muskets. Johnson thought the idea insane, and in his last official act, he vetoed the resolution.[31]

Early on the morning of March 4 the cabinet assembled at the White House for the trip to the other end of Pennsylvania Avenue. They found the president behind his desk and urged him to hurry. Johnson replied, "I think we will finish our work here without going to the Capitol." Half of the cabinet reacted with disappointment, the others with satisfaction. "After the offensive, silly, arrogant, and insolent declarations of Grant that he would not speak to his official superior and predecessor, nor ride, nor associate with him," said Welles, we "could not compose a part in the pageant to glorify Grant without a feeling of abasement." McCulloch, among others, expressed his disappointment to Welles, grumbling, "Well, you have carried your point."[32]

The inaugural procession passed down Pennsylvania Avenue without the outgoing president. Blacks composed about two-thirds of the marchers, and thanks to Johnson, none of them carried arms. Grant drove to the Capitol in a dog cart with an old friend from army days. His short, flat, and trite address carried subtle undertones of the Radicals, causing some observers to conclude that the general could be easily led by others. Grant's inaugural address revealed no statements of policy but disclosed how little the general understood the task before him or of his own limitations to perform it.[33]

While Grant delivered his inaugural, Andrew Johnson sent his farewell message across the wires. In the tradition of Abe Lincoln, he said, "My thoughts have been those of peace, and my effort has ever been to allay contention among my countrymen. Forgetting the past let us return to the first principles of the government, and, unfurling the banner of our country, inscribe upon it in ineffaceable characters 'the Constitution and the Union, one and inseparable.'"[34]

A few minutes after noon Johnson rose to his feet, shook hands with his cabinet, expressed his deepest gratitude for their friendship and support, and said that the time of parting had come. He passed out the door and onto the portico, where carriages waited. Slowly, they all drove away. A few minutes later the president and Mrs. Grant headed down Pennsylvania Avenue to their new home, where hundreds of gleeful supporters had gathered to greet them.[35]

So on March 4, 1869, Andrew Johnson departed from the White House forever. His impeachment would never be forgotten, but his work had not yet finished.

21

Vindication

For the first time in thirty years, Andrew Johnson enjoyed life as a private citizen. For twelve days he and his family stayed with friends in Washington, but all were anxious to get back to Tennessee. Before departing he made purchases for his old home in Greeneville, which he had not seen since 1861. At banquets held in his honor, speakers talked of his retirement, but Johnson thought of himself as temporarily unemployed, not retired. To get back to work he needed to first resettle his family and see to their comfort, and he could not do that in Washington.[1]

Johnson was still in Washington when Grant announced his cabinet appointments. They were not men of experience or credibility, but rather personal friends or benefactors. Wealthy storekeeper A. T Stewart, nominee for the treasury, recently handed Grant a check for $65,000 for a property worth half the amount. The Senate disqualified Stewart because his business involved "trade or commerce." The Senate also rejected the president's request for an exception, so in Stewart's place Grant nominated George S. Boutwell, who critics disclaimed as a "lugubrious joke," but the Senate approved. Grant then named fellow townsman Elihu B. Washburne secretary of state. Of foreign affairs Washburne knew nothing. Horace White

called him impulsive, headstrong, combative, and unbalanced. Grant later changed his mind and appointed Hamilton Fish, who, wrote Hugh McCulloch, "seemed to belong to a past generation, to be politically superannuated." Grant had once spent time in Fish's mansion on the Hudson, and by dumb luck rather than good insight, Fish became one of the general's better appointments.[2]

For secretary of war, Grant selected John A. Rawlins, another friend and fellow townsman from Galena, Ohio. During the war Rawlins served as Grant's adjutant general, whose duties included keeping his boss sober. Whenever Grant broke the pledge, Rawlins used anger and profanity to bring the general back into line.[3]

Grant's final three appointments were remarkable for their inconsistency. Attorney General E. Rockwood Hoar became the most distinguished and useful member of Grant's cabinet, but the president fed gross incompetents into the remaining two posts — John A. J. Creswell of Maryland as postmaster general and Adolph E. Borie of Philadelphia as secretary of the navy. Creswell, having been a secessionist, did not fit well with the Radicals, and nobody had ever heard of Borie, who had once offered Grant a home in Philadelphia. Borie lasted three months. Such were the first cabinet appointments of the eighteenth president.[4]

Enthusiastic celebrations greeted Johnson on his arrival home, where a large crowd turned out to welcome him back. Before he could catch his breath, cities from one end of Tennessee to the other competed for his presence. The old spokesman for constitutional freedom found himself in politics once more. Before settling into the comforts of his Greeneville home, invitations drew him to Knoxville, Chattanooga, Memphis, and finally to Nashville, the state capital. He had come to Tennessee, he said, to "lay my weary bones down in peace," but if the people had their way, peace would not come to Andy Johnson. Those who saw him remarked how little he had changed. Aside from a few gray hairs he seemed as vigorous and self-reliant as when thirty-some years ago they first heard him speak.[5]

Unlike most presidents who happily retire into private life, Johnson considered returning to Washington as a senator. He still had more denouncing to do, and the Senate provided the best platform for expressing one's mind. One person stood in the way — an old enemy, Parson Brownlow, who in 1867 had been reelected governor of Tennessee. The state convention nominating Brownlow had declared itself "ashamed of the unprincipled adopted son of Tennessee, now President of the United States, for his deception and degeneracy." It promised to "endorse any action of Congress that will legitimately deprive him of continued power." In the next session the state legislature elected Brownlow to the United States Senate, thereby ousting David Patterson, Johnson's son-in-law. Brownlow's term began the day Grant took office.[6]

For Johnson, any quest for a Senate seat promised to be an uphill climb. For more than two years the Radicals had controlled the state. At the time Johnson returned to Tennessee, Brownlow was in Washington, but the parson's twelve companies of "county guards" remained active on behalf of the local political machine. They appeared at public meetings to "protect" Republicans in the rights of free speech and to repress opposing views by sending the spokesperson for a ride on the rails.[7]

By the time Johnson reached Nashville he knew what to expect. Carpetbaggers ran the city, and by frauds upon the public treasury, they lived luxurious lives — all aided and abetted by Brownlow's guards. Many of the whites in central and west Tennessee had been disenfranchised and their places at the ballot boxes taken by blacks. The Ku Klux Klan's activities escalated and caused more outrages on freedmen. The political condition of whites grew worse, and their taxes increased. Johnson found similar problems in Mississippi, Georgia, and Alabama. All his fears of reconstruction lay before him, but what could he do to correct the problem?[8]

Johnson realized the importance of remaining politically active and immediately took steps to do so. After Brownlow's departure, DeWitt C. Senter became the acting governor and a candidate to succeed himself. Because of Senter's moderate views, the Republicans recruited Colonel William Stokes to defeat him. Senter campaigned for restoring the franchise to whites. Stokes took the Radical position. The Republican camp split with two candidates for governor, the Democrats had none. Johnson threw himself into the contest and stumped the state for Senter. On August

5 Senter won by a landslide, pulling with him a Democratic legislature. In six months Johnson had repositioned himself as a political force in Tennessee. Men began predicting that he would be returned to the United States Senate when Joseph S. Fowler's term expired.[9]

Johnson's time came in October 1869, when the state legislature convened to elect the next United States Senator. Most of Senter's coalition pledged their votes to Johnson, but the ex-president's enemies had been diligently applying coercive persuasion to prevent it. Grant voiced a warning, saying that if Johnson returned to the Senate, he would consider it a personal insult. The Radicals put up a good candidate, conservative Unionist Emerson Etherbridge. On October 21 Johnson led, 48-41, with seventeen votes scattered among others. Johnson continued to pick up votes, coming within the two he needed to win. Edmund Cooper, who had been one of the president's secretaries in Washington, approached Johnson with the news that he had secured a majority by buying "the necessary two votes" for $1,000 each. Johnson replied, "You will do no such thing, go tell the rascals the deal is off." Cooper objected, declaring, "I can't do that. I am honor bound." But Johnson refused and it cost him the election. The Radicals and secessionists met in caucus and decided to go with Judge Henry Cooper, Edmund Cooper's relative. Johnson lost on the final ballot, 55-51.[10]

Though disappointed, Johnson returned home to rethink his future and care for his invalid wife. He observed reconstruction at work and looked for one more chance to strike it down. He watched as Congress coerced Mississippi, Texas, and Virginia to adopt state constitutions consistent with the Reconstruction Acts while imposing an additional requirement for admission — the ratification of the Fifteenth Amendment. The three states complied and rejoined the Union in March 1870. All eleven states of the south were now back in the Union, but their representation in Congress originated mainly from the north. One senator came from the south, Hiram R. Revels of Mississippi. He especially pleased the Radicals because he was black and took Jefferson Davis' seat in the Senate. Charles Sumner could not contain his glee.[11]

Johnson watched as carpetbaggers sowed the seeds of hatred throughout the south. It made no difference to the Radicals that the proud, high-spirited, and self-governing people of the south were trampled under foot by freedmen armed and protected by the laws of Congress. To maintain themselves in power, the carpetbaggers parceled out the lesser spoils to ex-slaves while reaping the real harvest for themselves. They organized and drilled black constabularies and militias. South Carolina, the first state to secede, bore the worst punishments reconstruction could impose. Bribery, corruption, embezzlement, fraud, infamy, and demoralization flourished like a raging pestilence. To support grand larceny, the governor enrolled 96,000 blacks and armed 20,000 of them. In two years South Carolina's public debt leaped from seven million to twenty-nine million dollars. During the same period Louisiana's governor recruited a black standing army — the Metropolitan Guard. Whites everywhere were disarmed, their companies disbanded. Despite occasional disturbances by the Ku Klux Klan, Samuel Cox wrote, "No brave people, accustomed to be free, ever endured oppression so peacefully or so wisely."[12]

Johnson also looked to Washington, where he observed Grant whipped into the Radical conspiracy, confused and dazed, pliant and yielding, no longer the man of Appomattox. The general had forsaken the conciliation he once expressed on the battlefield. Being so completely out of his element, he seemed bewildered by the swirl of greed enveloping his office. Johnson watched as public sentiment in the north began to change. Corruption pervaded Grant's administration. A resurgence of fair-mindedness might yet be aroused, but it needed a voice. He felt the call and resolved, one way or another, to go back to Washington.[13]

The sign of the times manifested itself in 1872 when the Democrats nominated Horace Greeley for president and B. Gratz Brown for vice president. The move started in 1870 when a group from Missouri calling themselves Liberal Republicans began to break with the central party. In 1872 the Radical Republicans wanted Grant returned to office, so the Democrats pursued Greeley and Brown. Most of country knew Greeley only as a Radical and not as a disaffected Republican. Under those circumstances Greeley could not win against Grant, but the Democratic tide — right along with Greeley's principles — began to change. Never did politics present a stranger spectacle than acceptance by Democrats of Greeley, who had been one of their bitterist enemies. Equally strange, Johnson supported Greeley's candidacy "on the principle of universal pressure of circumstances beyond human control." Even Sumner came out for Greeley, which marked one of the few moments in history when Johnson found himself in the same camp with two of his former antagonists.[14]

The time for liberalism had not yet arrived, and Greeley suffered a disastrous defeat in the fall elections. He carried no northern states but won six in the south, among them Tennessee. One month later Greeley died, but the campaign rejuvenated opportunities for Johnson.[15]

The Democratic State Convention met at Nashville to nominate a candidate for Congress, and Johnson suspected they might select him. He wanted to be in the Senate, so he took Colonel E. C. Reeves aside and told him to go to the convention, "and if my name is put in nomination, promptly withdraw it on my authority." Reeves did so, and the convention nominated Benjamin F. Cheatham, an ex-Confederate major general who was part of the military clique that defeated Johnson's chance for election to the Senate in 1869. On the way home Reeves learned that at Nashville Johnson had announced himself as an independent candidate for the open seat in the House. Johnson decided to run as an independent only after he learned that Cheatham had won the nomination. Johnson still had his eye on the Senate, but he believed that by entering the race, Horace Maynard, the Republican candidate would win. By swinging the election to Maynard, Johnson hoped to accumulate enough political capital from liberal Republicans to capture the next Senate seat.

Johnson vigorously worked the campaign trail, stumping the state, and as an independent candidate, he probably exerted more effort putting himself before the public than ever before. He used the opportunity to vindicate his policies as president. Until the public heard his side of the battle with Radicals, they believed only what they had read in the papers. The debates did much to wound the prospects of Cheatham and reestablish Johnson as a man of the people. As expected, he lost his fight for Congress and swung the election for Maynard. Johnson tallied 37,903 votes but came in last. At least one part of his strategy worked. As one newspaper reported:

> A more striking illustration of one man's power was never before given in this country than in Mr. Johnson's canvass of the state; and though not elected, he is more firmly entrenched in the hearts of the people, and more conscious of his hold upon their confidence than at any time since 1860.

Johnson returned once more to Greeneville, speaking neither of his defeat nor of his future plans.[16]

The year of 1872 ended with Grant's reelection and new allegations of corruption at the highest level of government. Scandals spread, and so did financial mismanagement. Tentacles from the Credit Mobilier bribery reached into Congress and implicated Oakes Ames, who had sold stock to members of the House at bargain-basement prices to win their vote for a $27,000,000 interest-free thirty-year government loan. Ames survived with a censure, and the others, all Republicans, absolved themselves "from any corrupt motive or purpose" by their Radical peers. It would not look good for Republicans to appear dishonest, though as Ames's checkbook showed, several House members benefited from the scam.[17]

The year of 1873 came and went, bringing with it a different form of trouble for Andrew Johnson. During the summer, cholera struck Tennessee, creating a mass exodus to healthier districts. Johnson stayed in Greeneville to aid the sick, only to be smitten himself. He expected to die and left for posterity a farewell message. Adversity never stopped him before, and cholera did no better. He survived the attack and soon regained his health.[18]

A different kind of disaster struck during the fall. The banking firm of Jay Cooke failed, ushering in a depression that threatened to impoverish Johnson. When leaving the presidency, Johnson converted $60,000 in bonds to cash and deposited it at 6 percent per annum in the First National Bank of Washington — presumably among the safest depositories in the country. When the First National went under, Johnson's deposits of $73,000 seemed lost. Despite predictions of his ruin, Johnson maintained other holdings. Though more than half of his assets were at risk, he eventually recovered most of his money from the bank.[19]

In the 1874 elections a disaffected country marked its disapproval of Grant's administration and chose a Democratic House of Representative — the first in fourteen years. In Massachusetts Ben Butler lost his seat in Congress. Nearly ten years had passed since the rebellion, and the charges of graft and corruption permeating all levels of government gave hope to the struggling south. The Republican strategy to remain in power using black suffrage lasted eight years. Its collapse resulted from mishandling their own legislative authority.[20]

With Democrats regaining power, Andrew Johnson once again saw an opportunity for vindication. In early 1875 the Tennessee legislature began looking for a successor to Senator Brownlow. Johnson jumped into the campaign and once more canvassed the state for support. His opponents and old enemies took pains to obstruct his appearances, but Johnson always found ways to frustrate their efforts and get his message to the public. The contest intensified as it gathered steam. Johnson faced six competitors, among them Governor John C. Brown of Tennessee; three high-ranking ex-Confederate officers, William B. Bate, William A. Quarles, and Colonel John H. Stephens; a former Democratic congressman, John H. Savage; and Gustavus A. Henry, whom Johnson had defeated for governor in 1853.[21]

For all candidates, and especially for Johnson, the contest became desperate. No one believed the ex-president could win, but Johnson pressed forward with confidence. While the legislature debated, he directed his small band of supporters like a master tactician. Thirty legislators never wavered in their support, but whether they could persuade others to support Johnson remained an unanswered question.

On January 20, 1875, packed galleries watched as the balloting began. The first vote gave Johnson 30, Stephens 16, Brown 15, Bate 13, Savage 10, and spread 15 to others. After two days of fighting and bitterness, no clear winner emerged. Judge Oliver P. Temple observed, "Never did the invincible will of Mr. Johnson to control men appear to more conspicuous advantage than during this memorable contest. All the opposition to him in the state, which had been gathering for forty years, was concentrated in an unrelenting, determined effort to overthrow him." On January 23, after the thirty-fifth ballot, Brown withdrew and swung his votes to Bate. On the forty-fourth ballot, Bate came within two votes of winning election, but Johnson remained close with five fewer. Of ninety-two Democrats, Bate controlled a slim majority, but for Johnson to win, he needed to capture the votes of all eight Republicans.[22]

Republicans, having lost power in Tennessee, welcomed overtures from the former president. Johnson sought out Henry R. Gibson, an east Tennessee Republican, and promised, if elected, to not advocate any radical measures or oppose Grant's policies except in extreme instances. "I will never forget," he said, "what I owe [the Republican] party." Johnson also agreed that if he went to Washington, he would go as an independent and not as a Democrat, emphasizing that all Unionists must stick together.[23]

Learning of Johnson's maneuver, the opposition met in caucus on January 25 to find a candidate on whom all could agree. Failing to do so, they streamed into the legislature on the following morning with no specific counter-plan. On the fifty-fourth ballot, Johnson took the lead with forty-seven votes. One member after another began taking the floor to explain why they had decided to switch their vote to Johnson. Before long, Johnson captured 52 votes. The House exploded in cheers, the galleries rose to their feet, and Alfred E. Taylor, one of Johnson's supporters, ran as fast as his legs could carry him to the Maxwell House. He burst into the room and said, "Mr. Johnson, you are elected." Taylor collapsed from exhaustion, and when Colonel Reeves arrived to deliver the same message, he found Johnson kneeling by Taylor and splashing water in his face. In response to the good news, Johnson remained thoughtful for a few moments before remarking: "Well, well, well, I'd rather have this information than to learn that I had been elected President of the United States. Thank God for the vindication."[24]

The throng filling the galleries at the state house pushed through the doors to the street, cheering and gathering momentum as they made their way to the Maxwell House. They piled into the rotunda to congratulate the senator-elect. That evening ten thousand men, women, and children gathered in the public square to hear the old fighter speak. Unlike his swing around the circle, Johnson delivered a marvelous speech, assuring the public that he would return to Washington with no personal hostility toward anyone. He would work for a union of all men who loved their country and would resist any further aggression on the Constitution. He also promised to devote his remaining years to the country which from childhood he had loved more than life itself. Some in the crowd urged Johnson to run for president in 1876.

Even the Radical press, which had once tried to deride and bully him, agreed that Johnson would be an attribute in the Senate, one writing, "Who, ten years ago, would have thought such a thing possible?" The *New York Times* declared, "We shall not be sorry to see him again in public life. Whatever his faults as President may have been, at any rate he went out of the White House as poor as he entered it and that is something to say in these times. The public generally take a more favorable view of Mr. Johnson's character now." But it took ten years for the press and the public to witness and digest the political avarice that Johnson fought so stubbornly to defeat during his tenure as president.[25]

No election in the country captivated the public's attention more than the senatorial race in Tennessee, and for a few days no politician absorbed the public's imagination more than Johnson. He had been scorned, branded a traitor, impeached, and his administration condemned—but all that happened before

Grant infused the presidency with a more reprehensible brand of infamy. The *New York Herald* praised Johnson's return to politics, cheerfully reporting that he had "lived to see his vindication.... He is the best man Tennessee could have chosen, not merely for herself but for democracy of North and South.... The Senate needs men who have the courage to speak the truth.... It is now generally conceded that the imaginary misdemeanors of 1868 ... were in fact official merits." The public demonstrated their agreement, and an outpouring of congratulations flooded the post office and telegraph in Greeneville. Gideon Welles, who had watched the election in Nashville with keen interest, wrote from Hartford, "The indications are that the 'gospel of hate' is drawing to a close, and that we may now hope for peace and reconciliation and a return to the true principles of the Constitution,—a restoration of the states to their rights." Johnson hoped so, too.[26]

Under normal circumstances Johnson would not have entered upon his duties until December, but Grant convened the Senate on March 4 to act upon a reciprocity treaty with King Kalakaua of Hawaii. Johnson's initial meeting with senators who had tried to impeach him was watched with great interest by the public. By coming to the Senate as an independent, some believed that Johnson would do as much damage to the Republicans as to the Democrats, making it very uncomfortable for those who attempted to stray from the Constitution. Even the *New York Tribune*, which during Greeley's lifetime had scorned Johnson's presidency, now admitted that honesty must be restored to government. It wrote, "In these days of moral and official delinquency, it is no ordinary gratification for the people at large to have their national councils honored by the presence of such a man."[27]

On March 5 Vice President Henry Wilson, one of the Radicals who had voted for Johnson's impeachment, called the Senate into session. Once again Johnson came face to face with Lincoln's first vice president, Hannibal Hamlin of Maine, whose resentment of Johnson led to the flask of brandy responsible for the latter's intoxication during Lincoln's second inaugural. Never a forgiving man, Hamlin had taken to the stump in 1866 to demand the impeachment of Johnson, accusing him of responsibility for the New Orleans massacre. Both Wilson and Hamlin were tall men, but as one observer noted, Andrew Johnson may have been short, "but to everyone present there was no taller man in the Senate that day." Without hesitation, Johnson shook hands with all of his former adversaries.[28]

Crowds gathered at the Capitol to see the ex-president, and he entered the Senate chamber to a standing ovation. After the formalities, Lewis V. Bogy, a conservative friend and Democrat from Missouri, took him aside. Johnson knew the purpose of the meeting. True to the Republicans in Tennessee, whose votes brought him back to the Senate, Johnson retained his independence and refused to join the Democratic caucus.[29]

Faces in the Senate were all too familiar to Andrew Johnson. John A. Logan and George S. Boutwell, now both senators, had been managers during the impeachment trial. In a curious statement, Boutwell once remarked that Johnson's courage "passed far beyond the line of obstinacy." Some of the old guard voting for conviction still held seats; Frederick T. Frelinghuysen of New Jersey, Anthony of Rhode Island, Sherman of Ohio,

Cameron of Pennsylvania, Howe of Wisconsin, Morrill of Maine, and Conkling of New York. Absent among the Radicals were Sumner, who had died. Wade abandoned politics to act as counsel for the Northern Pacific Railway. Of the seven stalwart Republicans who voted for Johnson's acquittal, Grimes lay physically dead while five of the other six senators were numbered among the politically dead.[30]

When the ceremony ended Johnson exchanged greetings with his old enemies and retired to his office. He found his desk heaped with flowers from admirers. The New York Tribune reported the occasion, writing, "Mr. Johnson has always been popular in Washington, where he is regarded as a dignified, considerate and large-hearted gentleman. He bore himself with great self composure." This was not the kind of statement made by Greeley's organ in 1868. The same reporter asked the senator if he intended "to pay off some old scores"? Johnson replied in the negative, saying, "I have no enemies to punish or friends to reward." It was a good reply, now all Johnson needed to do was to live by his statement. The reporter noted that the two rooms occupied by the senator on the second floor of Willard's Hotel were not hardly as commodious as those which he once occupied a short distance up Pennsylvania Avenue. Johnson agreed, but with a merry twinkle in his eye, said they were a darned sight more comfortable.[31]

Johnson had promised his Republican supporters in Tennessee to not interfere with Grant so long as the president attempted no radical measures. Not long after the special March session convened, Frelinghuysen introduced a resolution approving Grant's policies in

Louisiana, where the army had interfered in disputed elections and ejected five assemblymen from their seats in the legislature. Johnson understood the background of the problem. The notorious Henry C. Warmouth had come to Louisiana with the army and made himself governor and the terror of the state. "Corruption is the fashion," he declared. "I do not pretend to be honest, but only as honest as anybody in politics." Having no assets at the beginning of his reign, he left office in 1872 with a tidy fortune. So little did the lawmakers think of bribery that it had become a public virtue and not a crime. When a congressional investigating committee looked into the matter, one member facetiously asked, "What is the price of a senator?" The deponent replied, "I think six hundred dollars."[32]

In 1872 the Republicans running Louisiana split, one faction backing Warmouth and the other the "custom house ring" led by Mrs. Grant's brother-in-law, James F. Casey, who held the post of Collector of the Port of New Orleans. He and his adherents had involved themselves in a squabble with Warmouth over the division of spoils. Each accused the other of numerous crimes. The rift caused the black lieutenant governor, P. B. S. Pinchback, who usually abetted Warmouth, to defect and create a third faction. Pinchback eventually sided with Mrs. Grant's brother-in-law to further the candidacy of William Kellogg, a carpetbagger from Vermont who wanted to oust Warmouth's candidate, John McEnery, and become governor. After tallying the election returns, Warmouth declared McEnery victor, but Casey declared Kellogg the winner. Casey appealed to Edmund H. Durrell of the United States district court, and the judge

obligingly issued an order directing the marshal and the local commander of federal troops to take possession of the state house and hold it for Kellogg. Soon thereafter, Kellogg entered the building with the new legislature and all were installed, but he knew he would lose possession of the state house the moment troops withdrew.[33]

The inevitable result of federal meddling led to a clash of arms and a spilling of blood. White men of Louisiana had read Grant's message of February 1873, in which he said that if Congress did not interfere to support the Kellogg government, he would. Soon thereafter Grant delivered his second inaugural and said, "The states lately at war with the General Government are now happily rehabilitated." A few days later in Grant Parish, a clash occurred between Kellogg's appointees and those who did not recognize his authority. Fifty-nine blacks and two whites were killed. Because of the relationship between Grant and Casey, Kellogg received the support of the federal government. McEnery, who had a legitimate claim to the governorship, received orders from Grant to retire peacefully and submit to the "constituted authorities" of the state.[34]

During late summer in 1874 another civil disturbance occurred during Kellogg's administration — this one on Canal Street in New Orleans. In a bloody struggle, native whites overwhelmed the black metropolitan police and marched to the state house. Kellogg fled and took shelter in Casey's customhouse. Temporarily, the city's carpetbag rule had been ousted. Grant, however, had no intention of leaving matters in the hands of Casey's enemies. On the day following the Canal Street disturbance, he issued a proclamation ordering "turbulent and disorderly persons to disperse." Three days later soldiers forced the surrender of the native whites and reinstated carpetbag rule. When the state legislature met in January 1875, the question arose whether carpetbaggers or native whites were entitled to legal control of the state. Federal soldiers arrived with bayonets. Five soldiers advanced on five members of the legislature and drove them from the state house.[35]

Grant decided to put an end to Casey's worries. Without consulting General Sherman, the general of the army, Grant sent General Sheridan to New Orleans to maintain order. Eight years earlier, Johnson had dismissed Sheridan from command of the district because he had, at least in Johnson's opinion, abused his power. After expelling five assemblymen, Sheridan asked Congress to issue a proclamation declaring all whites in opposition to the carpetbag administration "banditti" and to provide a military tribunal to try them. A wave of indignation swept the country when Sheridan's message became public. Two of Grant's cabinet denounced Sheridan and threatened to resign.[36]

Criticism of the civil strife in Louisiana prompted Senator Frelinghuysen to present the resolution approving Grant's policies for suppressing the disturbances. Knowing the background of the problem, Johnson took the Senate floor on March 20, 1875, and began by questioning the right of the Senate to debate a matter during a special session called to discuss other issues. Besides, he argued, "The President of the United States assumes to take command of the state and assign these people a governor. What does he say himself on this point?" Johnson then read from Grant's message: "It has been bitterly alleged that Kellogg

was not elected. Whether he was or not is not altogether certain, nor is it any more certain that his competitor McEnery was chosen. The election was a gigantic fraud and there are no reliable returns of its result." If, Johnson continued, there had been fraud, then both contestants should be disqualified, "but the President finds a usurper in power, and he takes it upon himself to make the government of the United States a party to this usurpation.... Is not this monstrous in a free government?"

Knowing that Grant wanted a third term, Johnson added, "The people of Louisiana were anxious for full restoration to the Union, but what is that to those acting behind the curtain and who are aspiring to retain power, and if it cannot be by popular contest ... would inaugurate a system of terrorism, and ... in the midst of the war-cry triumphantly ride into the Presidency for a third term. And when this is done, farewell to the liberties of the country." The chamber and galleries erupted in applause. The sixty-seven-year-old warrior from Tennessee had not budged an inch from his protection of the Constitution.[37]

The time had come for someone to speak out against Grant's policies. His craving for a third term had become as scandalous as his graft-ridden administration. Johnson's speech shook the rafters of the Senate. He voiced what had not been said but needed to be said. It put all the evils of Grant's administration toward the south in perspective and shook awake the sleeping conscience of the north.

Two days after his denunciation of Grant's policies, the special session ended, and Johnson returned to Greeneville. President Grant never received Frelinghuysen's face-saving resolution. It died in the Senate, killed by Andrew Johnson.

22

Epilogue

At home once more, Johnson relaxed and enjoyed the fresh fragrances of spring. He felt vigorous and looked forward to the next session. The country needed him. Being the first ex-president ever to be returned to the Senate, he contemplated a future run for the presidency, perhaps as soon as 1876. He did not know his work was done.

During the last torrid days of July he traveled into Carter County, some forty miles away, to visit his daughter, Mary Stover. There he sat with granddaughter Lillie, and as they discussed her forthcoming marriage, he collapsed. Physicians came but could do nothing. Thirty-six hours later, July 31, Andrew Johnson died of a paralyzing stroke.[1]

In one of his greatest speeches Johnson once said, "When I die, I desire no better winding sheet than the Stars and Stripes, and no softer pillow than the Constitution of my country." Loving hands now granted him his wish. Wrapped in a flag and pillowed on the Constitution, family and friends brought the old campaigner back to Greeneville. Washington draped itself in black. Even Grant paid homage to his old nemesis by ordering a tribute fired at each naval station and by the battleships of war. But in Greeneville the masses came from the country, some on horseback, some in carriages, and some on foot. They came for the last time to honor their distinguished neighbor. Together they followed the funeral procession to a windswept conical knoll not far from town, and there, in a place chosen by Johnson, they watched as the great patriot sank softly to his place of rest. With the pious efforts of his most devoted daughter, there now stands a tall, graceful pillar of granite marking his grave. On its top is an eagle with wings outstretched, and on its base an inscription: "Andrew Johnson, Seventeenth President of the United States. His faith in the people never wavered"— true words, but touched by an element of sadness. As one biographer observed, "There, surrounded by his kindred dead, after his lifelong battle, rests, at last, the stubbornist fighter in civil affairs among the self-made champions of modern democracy."[2]

Johnson's estate exceeded $100,000, but he left no will. He had already deeded a farm near Greeneville to Martha. Andrew, Jr., retained possession of the homestead, and Eliza, though quite feeble, became administratrix but died six months later. Andrew, Jr., took over the settlement of the estate until March 1879, when he, too, died. Because his sisters had surrendered their interests to him, Andrew's widow made inappropriate claims of ownership. The sisters sued for their portion of the property. The heirs eventually reached a compromise, and the case settled. Why Johnson never executed a will can only be explained by his intention to go on with life forever, though in 1873 he nearly died from a bout with cholera.[3]

Johnson's departure from a life of politics left him with a legacy unlike any other president. Because he held office during the period of Reconstruction when Radicals ruled, his reputation alternately rose and fell depending upon the opinions of both advocates and detractors. No impeached president can escape criticism, regardless of the validity of the underlying reasons. Johnson's courageous protection of the Constitution cannot be challenged on its merits, but his obstinate methods can be questioned because compromise never came easy for Andrew Johnson.

Like his predecessor, Johnson was unfashionable among public men of the period because of his meticulous honesty. When a group from New York City offered him a fine carriage and a span of horses, he rejected the offer on the ground that he had always made it a practice to refuse gifts while in public station. When handling millions of dollars as military governor of Tennessee, he left office poorer than when he entered it — which many patriots of the time condemned as outright stupidity. The House Impeachment Committee spent two years investigating every transaction Johnson made and never found so much as a scrap on which to hang an allegation. Scarcely one among his traducers could have stood the same microscopic test without suffering political pain.[4]

Among a number of capable historical scholars, one discovered that Johnson, when preparing speeches or veto messages, formed his "opinions on great questions of public policy as diligent as any man in seeking and weighing the views of all who were competent to aid him." The White House staff were amazed at his tireless energy. He kept six secretaries busy and "except for an hour or so in the afternoon and at meal times rarely left his desk until midnight." Henry Adams, an intellectual both admired and criticized for his snobbery, admitted when recalling his youthful prejudices of being "surprised to realize how strong the Executive was in 1868 — perhaps the strongest he was ever to see."[5]

When the Supreme Court overturned the Tenure of Office Act in the 1920s, historians took another look at Andrew Johnson and revived his attributes. When civil rights issues erupted in the 1960s, scholars looked once more at Johnson's policies and blamed him for repressing racial solutions for one hundred years. The Radicals, however, overturned presidential vetoes on every important civil rights issue. Although many in the south heard Johnson's voice, he cannot be blamed for the corrupt carpetbaggers who, supported by Radical legislation, created the polarization between blacks and whites that continued through the twentieth century.

Johnson understood life in the south better than he understood life in the north. Radicals only understood life in the north. The day of the Jacksonian Democrat passed before the Civil War began, and Johnson held himself back by not making the adjustment. He also lacked the guiding hand a president needed when dealing with such contentious issues as the restoration of eleven rebellious states. As a Republican president, he lost an opportunity to work with a Republican Congress because he could not shed his Jacksonian ways.

Another factor leading to Johnson's war with the Radicals involved Lincoln and the exercise of war powers. Prior to the Civil War Congress represented the people, enacted the laws, and the president seldom vetoed or interfered with the passage of laws. Because of the Civil War, Lincoln stretched executive authority and used power once enjoyed exclusively by Congress. When the war ended, Lincoln died and Congress reasserted its prewar prerogatives and reclaimed its lost power. The effort resulted in open conflict between the executive and legislative branches of government.

Because the Radicals could muster a two-thirds vote any day of any week, they could write laws and pass them over the veto of the president. Johnson recognized this, but unlike Lincoln, he made little effort to work with Congress to find common ground and strike a compromise. Lincoln understood the importance of working with those in Congress who opposed him, but Johnson never had the opportunity of witnessing Lincoln's methods or of understanding how his predecessor got his way. Instead, Johnson chose to promulgate vetoes that lectured on the Constitution. He failed in his efforts to restore the south because early in his administration he lost the trust of those in Congress who attempted to communicate with him on national issues. The Radicals failed to restore the south because their strategy focused too much on political power and punishment, and not enough on reunifying the southern states in a forgiving and respectful manner.

Samuel "Sunset" Cox, New York City's representative to Congress, spoke of the times as well as anyone when he blamed the Radical Republicans for tearing the Union apart, writing, "What neither secession nor war ... could do was now done by act of Congress and radical hate.... Here began the second contest to save the Union; a contest no less pregnant with the fate of American Institutions, and no less bitterly fought.... It took almost a quarter of a century to silence the guns of Moultrie and Sumter."[6]

Impeachment of a president should never occur in a political atmosphere of good statesmanship. In 1868 statesmanship failed in all three branches of the government. Statesmanship is especially vulnerable to failure when one branch of the government can induce its will on the other two branches. The consequences for a country are never good. Neither Congress, the Supreme Court, nor Johnson as president grew with the times, and when distributing blame, it must fall upon all. Like every political error, it is not the politicians who suffer, it is the people they represent, and neither Johnson, the Radicals, nor the Supreme Court left for the future a good legacy on Reconstruction.

However, Johnson's formula for peaceful reconciliation had merits. Unlike the Radicals, he did not seek political domination of the nation through the smoke screen of civil rights legislation. He foresaw the evils of Reconstruction legislated by Congress and predicted the disastrous outcome. He advocated reconciliation and gradual civil rights legislation, leaving the latter issue to the individual states, as done in the north. He failed as chief executive to alter the policies imposed upon the country by Radical Republicans. Whether Abraham Lincoln could have changed the course of history remains an unanswerable question. The same could be asked of Andrew Johnson. Radical power reigned supreme. It must never be allowed to happen again — in any branch of the government.

Chapter Notes

Abbreviations

AJP: Andrew Johnson Papers in LeRoy P. Graf and Ralph W. Haskins, Ralph W. et al., eds. *The Papers of Andrew Johnson.* 14 vols. Knoxville: The University of Tennessee Press, 1967–97.

CWD: Mark M. Boatner, III, *The Civil War Dictionary.* New York, David McKay Company, Inc., 1959.

HL: Huntington Library, Harvard University

HSP: Historical Society of Pennsylvania

HTI: Patricia L. Faust, ed., *Historical Times Illustrated Encyclopedia of the Civil War.* New York, Harper and Row, 1986.

IHS: Indiana Historical Society

LC: Library of Congress

NA: National Archives

IIYHS: New York Historical Society

NYPL: New York Public Library

OR: *War of the Rebellion: A Compilation of the Official Records of the Union and Confederate Armies.* 128 vols. Harrisburg: National Historical Society, 1971.

TSLA: Tennessee State Library and Archives

Introduction

1. John Savage, *Life and Public Services of Andrew Johnson* (New York: Derby & Miller Publishers, 1866), 13; Ida Tarbell, *The Life of Abraham Lincoln,* 4 vols. (New York: Lincoln History Society, 1904), I, 59–62; Patricia L. Faust, ed., *HTI* (Harper and Row, 1986), 395–96.

2. Savage, *Life of Johnson,* 123.

3. Roy P. Basler, ed. *The Collected Works of Abraham Lincoln,* 9 vols. (New Brunswick: Rutgers University Press, 1953–55), V, 388.

4. James D. Richardson, *A Compilation of the Messages and Papers of the Presidents, 1789–1897.* 11 vols. (Washington: Bureau of National Literature and Art, 1897–1907), VI, 67; Basler, *Works of Lincoln,* I, 318–20, 327–45; Savage, *Life of Johnson,* 41.

5. Gideon Welles, *Diary of Gideon Welles, Secretary of the Navy under Lincoln and Johnson,* 3 vols. (Boston and New York: Houghton Mifflin Company, 1911), I, 502; Hugh McCulloch, *Men and Measures of Half a Century* (New York, DaCapo Press, 1970), 233–34; Gamaliel Bradford, *Union Portraits* (Boston: Houghton Mifflin & Company, 1916), 245–56.

6. Pierce, Edward L., *Memoir and Letters of Charles Sumner,* 4 vols. (Boston: Roberts Brothers, 1893), I, 196; William M. Stewart, *Reminiscences;* George Rothwell Brown, ed. (Washington, D.C.: Neale, 1908), 239; Henry Adams, *The Education of Henry Adams, An Autobiography* (Boston: Houghton Mifflin Company, 1918), 251–52; George F. Hoar, *Autobiography of Seventy Years.* 2 vols. (New York: Scribner's Sons, 1903), I, 214.

7. Faust, *HTI,* 794; Hans L. Trefousse, *Benjamin Franklin Wade: Radical Republican from Ohio* (New York: Twain Publishers, Inc., 1963), 18.

8. Claude Bowers, *The Tragic Era: The Revolution After Lincoln* (Cambridge: Houghton Mifflin Company, 1929), 88, 158, 159; George Fort Milton, *The Age of Hate: Andrew Johnson and the Radicals* (New York: Coward McCann, 1930), 34.

9. James Albert Woodburn, *The Life of Thaddeus Stevens* (Indianapolis: Bobbs, Merrill Company, 1913), 14.

10. Samuel W. McCall, *Thaddeus Stevens* (Boston: Houghton Mifflin & Co., 1899), 31, 32, 61; James Ford Rhodes, *History*

of the United States from the Compromise of 1850 to the Final Restoration of Home Rule in the South in 1877, 7 vols. (New York: Macmillan Company, 1910), V, 542.

11. James G. Blaine, *Twenty Years in Congress, 1861–1881,* 2 vols. (Norwich, CT: Henry Bill Publishing Company, 1884), I, 325; Woodburn, *Life of Stevens,* 112, 601–602; Bowers, *The Tragic Era,* 79.

12. Carl Schurz, *The Reminiscences of Carl Schurz,* 3 vols. (New York: Doubleday, Page & Company, 1908), III, 212–17; *The Nation,* August 20, 1868; Bowers, *The Tragic Era,* 67; George S. Boutwell, *Reminiscences of Sixty Years in Public Affairs,* 2 vols. (New York: McClure Phillips & Company, 1902), II, 9.

13. Faust, *HTI,* 712–13; David Miller DeWitt, *The Impeachment and Trial of Andrew Johnson* (New York: Macmillan Company, 1902), 246–47.

14. Welles, *Diary,* I, xxxi; Herndon to Weik, January 6, 1887, Herndon-Weik Papers, LC.

15. William B. Parker, *The Life and Public Services of Justin Smith Morrill* (Boston: Houghton Mifflin Company, 1924), 209–10.

16. John J. Craven, *Prison Life of Jefferson Davis* (New York: Carleton Publisher, 1866), 261.

Chapter 1

1. Savage, *Life of Johnson,* 13–16; Hans L. Trefousse, *Andrew Johnson* (New York: W.W. Norton & Co., 1989), 17–20; Milton, *Age of Hate,* 60–61.

2. Savage, *Life of Johnson,* 13–15, 23; William J. Anderson to Johnson, April 8, 1869, Johnson Papers, LC; Trefousse, *Andrew Johnson,* 20; Oliver P. Temple, *Notable Men of Tennessee, from 1833–1875* (New York: Cosmopolitan Press, 1912), 360–61; Harriet S. Turner, "Recollections of Andrew Johnson," *Harper's Monthly,* no. 120 (January 1910), 170.

3. Savage, *Life of Johnson,* 16–17; Fay W. Brabson, *Andrew Johnson: A Life in Pursuit of the Right Course, 1808–1875* (Durham: Duke University Press, 1972), 6; W. H. Griffin to Johnson, August 20, 1865, Johnson Papers, LC; Robert W. Winston, *Andrew Johnson: Plebeian and Patriot* (New York: Henry Holt, 1928), 11.

4. Milton, *Age of Hate,* 65–66; A. D. February to Johnson, October 6, 1868, Johnson Papers, LC; Brabson, *Andrew Johnson,* 8–9; Trefousse, *Andrew Johnson,* 25–28; Johnson's Marriage License and Certificate, LeRoy P. Graf and Ralph W. Haskins, et al., eds. *AJP,* 14 vols. (Knoxville: The University of Tennessee Press, 1967–97), I, 4.

5. James S. Jones, *Life of Andrew Johnson* (Greeneville, TN: Greeneville Publishing Company, 1901), 17–18; Temple, *Notable Men,* 361–62; Richardson, *Messages and Papers,* VI, 301.

6. Jones, *Life of Johnson,* 28–29; Deed to Johnson home, September 10, 1865, *AJP,* I, 624–25; Trefousse, *Andrew Johnson,* 30.

7. Jones, *Life of Johnson,* 19; Savage, *Life of Johnson,* 20.

8. Savage, *Life of Johnson,* 22; Milton, *Age of Hate,* 74–75.

9. Trefousse, *Andrew Johnson,* 33, 34.

10. Savage, *Life of Johnson,* 26; Hans L Trefousse, *Impeachment of a President* (Knoxville: University of Tennessee Press, 1975), 4–5.

11. Temple, *Notable Men,* 363–64; Jones, *Life of Johnson,* 21–22; *Journal of the House of Representatives of the State of Tennessee at the 21st General Assembly* (Knoxville, 1836), 3.

12. Easton Morris, *The Tennessee Gazetteer or Topographical Dictionary* (Nashville, 1834), xviii: Hall, *Andrew Johnson,* 4; Jones, *Life of Johnson,* 11, 29–30.

13. Savage, *Life of Johnson,* 27; Jones, *Life of Johnson,* 22; Lloyd Paul Stryker, *Andrew Johnson, A Study in Courage* (New York, The Macmillan Company, 1929), 9.

14. Savage, *Life of Johnson,* 28; Temple, *Notable Men,* 364–65; Brabson, *Andrew Johnson,* 15–16.

15. Johnson to George W. Jones, December 25, 1836, and Johnson to John Young, March 10, 1840, *AJP,* I: 18–20, 26–27; Nashville *Union,* February 11, 1840, August 16, 1841; Brabson, *Andrew Johnson,* 16–17: Savage, *Life of Johnson,* 28.

16. Richardson, *Messages and Papers,* VI, 302; Temple, *Notable Men,* 216–17; Nashville *Union,* August 8, 11, 1843; Jones, *Life of Johnson,* 40.

17. Kenneth M. Stampp, *The Era of Reconstruction, 1865–1877* (New York: Alfred A. Knopf, 1965), 55–56; Eric L. McKitrick, *An-*

drew Johnson and Reconstruction (New York: Oxford University Press, 1988), 85–92, especially p. 86; *Cong. Globe,* 29 Cong., 2 Sess., App. 160–63.

18. Winston, *Andrew Johnson,* 40; Savage, *Life of Johnson,* 35.

19. *Cong. Globe,* 28 Cong., 2 Sess., 170, App. 219–23, and 30 Cong., 2 Sess., 22–28, 334–36; Savage, *Life of Johnson,* 31–32; St. George L. Sioussat, "Andrew Johnson and the Early Phases of the Homestead Bill," *Tennessee Historical Magazine,* VI (1920), 14–75.

20. Jones, *Life of Johnson,* 39–40; *Cong. Globe,* 31 Cong., 1 Sess., 515, 1127, App. 669–73; Frank Moore, Comp., *Speeches of Andrew Johnson* (Boston: Little Brown & Company, 1866), 253.

21. Rhodes, *History of the United States,* I, 439, 475; Moore, *Speeches,* 63.

22. Moore, *Speeches,* 48, 63, 289; Nashville *Union and American,* January 16, 1855; Jones, *Life of Johnson,* 56.

23. Jones, *Life of Johnson,* 59, 70; Trefousse, *Andrew Johnson,* 92.

24. Moore, *Speeches,* 66.

25. Hans L. Trefousse, *The Radical Republicans: Lincoln's Vanguard for Racial Justice* (New York: Alfred P. Knopf, 1969), 91ff.; Savage, *Life of Johnson,* 51, 150.

26. Moore, *Speeches,* 16, 28, 34, 44, 52, 54–57, 65–68, 76.

27. Trefousse, *Andrew Johnson,* 71, 117.

28. David H. Donald, *Charles Sumner and the Coming of the Civil War* (New York: Alfred A. Knopf, 1967), 289–304.

29. Frederic Bancroft, *Life of William H. Seward,* 2 vols. (New York: Harper & Brothers, 1900), I, 458–61.

30. Moore, *Speeches,* 259–63.

31. Woodrow Wilson, *Division and Reunion* (Longmans Green & Company, 1925, 205; Jones, *Life of Johnson,* 64–65, 68; Savage, *Life of Johnson,* 148.

32. Results of the popular vote: Lincoln, 1,866,452, Douglas, 1,376,957; Breckinridge, 849,781; Bell 588,879. Electoral vote: Lincoln, 180; Breckinridge, 72; Bell, 39; Douglas, 12, Faust, *HTI,* 238.

33. Moore, *Speeches,* 79–80, 150.

34. Richardson, *Messages and Papers,* V, 626ff. For Buchanan's position on secession, see John Bassett Moore, ed., *The Works of James Buchanan, Comprising His Speeches,* *State Papers, and Private Correspondence* (New York: Antiquarian Press, 1960), 159–210.

35. DeWitt, *Impeachment and Trial,* 247, 252–53.

36. Ibid., 248, 254.

37. Moore, *Speeches,* 153, 311–13, 325–27; Temple, *Notable Men,* 400.

38. Richardson, *Messages and Papers,* VI, 5, 7; Roy P. Basler, ed., *Collected Works,* IV, 262–71.

39. Stryker, *Andrew Johnson,* 78. For a slightly different eye-witness account, see James Morris Morgan, *Recollections of a Rebel Reefer* (Boston: Houghton Mifflin Company, 1917), 36–37.

40. Moore, *Speeches,* 395; Clifton R. Hall, *Andrew Johnson, Military Governor of Tennessee* (Princeton, Princeton University Press, 1916), 10.

41. Wilson, *Division and Reunion,* 219.

Chapter 2

1. Faust, *HTI,* 90–92; Samuel S. Cox, *Three Decades of Federal Legislation* (Providence: J.A. and R.H. Reid, 1885), 158.

2. George Ticknor Curtis, *Life of James Buchanan,* 2 vols. (New York: Harper & Brothers, 1883), II, 559.

3. Moore, *Speeches,* 330–404 passim; Gamaliel Bradford, *Confederate Portraits* (Boston: Houghton Mifflin Company, 1912), 153–81; Hall, *Andrew Johnson,* 29–31.

4. Curtis, *Life of Buchanan,* II, 518–21, 524–25, 538–39, 545, 559.

5. Erwin Stanley Bradbury, *Simon Cameron, Lincoln's Secretary of War* (Philadelphia: University of Pennsylvania Press, 1966), 149–51, 173–74, 214–15, 217–19. See also Frank Abial Flower, *Edwin McMaster's Stanton, The Autocrat of Rebellion, Emancipation, and Reconstruction* (Akron:Saalfield Publishing Company, 1905), 105–13.

6. Benjamin Thomas and Harold M. Hyman, *Stanton: The Life and Times of Lincoln's Secretary of War* (New York: Alfred A. Knopf, 1962), 126–27, 135, 136–37; Flower, *Stanton,* 117; Chase to Jeremiah H. Black, July 4, 1870, Black Papers, LC; Maunsell B. Field, *Memories of Many Men and Some Women* (New York: Harpers Brothers, 1874), 266–69; David H. Donald, *Inside Lincoln's Cabinet: The Civil War Diaries of Salmon P. Chase*

(New York: Longmans Green & Company, 1954), 62.

7. Welles, *Diary*, I, xxxi, 128–29; John T. Morse, Jr., *Abraham Lincoln*, 2 vols. (Boston: Houghton Mifflin, 1893), 328.

8. Hall, *Andrew Johnson*, 14–16.

9. Graf and Haskins, *AJP*, V, 43–44; Moore, *Speeches*, 428–30, 444–47.

10. Hall, *Andrew Johnson*, 17–19; Jones, *Life of Johnson*, 76; *War of the Rebellion: A Compilation of the Official Records of the Union and Confederate Armies*, 128 vols. (Harrisburg: National Historical Society, 1971), IV, 324–25, 303, 342–43, 347; VII, 443–44, 480. Hereinafter cited as *OR*. All references are to Series I unless specified otherwise.

11. Stanton to Johnson, March 4, 1862, Stanton Papers, LC; Hall, *Andrew Johnson*, 32–33, 40; Stanton to Johnson, March 4, 1862, *AJP*, V, 177–78, 182.

12. Hall, *Andrew Johnson*, 34.

13. Edward Belcher Callender, *Thaddeus Stevens, Commoner* (Boston: Houghton Mifflin, 1882), 111.

14. Ibid. 38; William Nelson to Chase, February 28, 1862, Chase Papers, HSP; Johnson to Senate, January 31, 1862, V, 114ff., *AJP*; Jones, *Life of Johnson*, 77.

15. Nashville Speech, March 13, 18, 1862, *AJP* V: 202–4, 222–41; Jones, *Life of Johnson*, 77–78.

16. Henry Villard, *Memoirs of Henry Villard, Journalist and Financier, 1835–1900*, 2 vols. (Boston: Houghton Mifflin Company, 1904), I, 233; Johnson to Stanley Matthews, March 17, 29, Johnson to Nashville City Council, March 25, and City Council to Johnson, March 27, 1862, Interview with Clergy, n.d., *AJP*, V, 208–12, 244–45, 247–48, 253–54, 587–90; Hall, *Andrew Johnson*, 42–43; Moore, *Speeches*, 455; *New York Tribune*, July 4, 1862.

17. Hall, *Andrew Johnson*, 51–53, 55, 64; Johnson to Lincoln, July 10, Lincoln to Johnson, July 11, 1862, *AJP*, V, 549–50, 551–52; Mark M. Boatner, III, *The Civil War Dictionary* (New York: David McKay Company, Inc., 1959), 289, hereinafter Boatner, *CWD*.

18. *OR*, XVI, Pt. 1, 59–60, 697–98, Pt. 2, 242, 490; Lincoln to Johnson, July 11, Johnson to Halleck, July 13, 1862, *AJP*, V, 551–52, 556–57.

19. Savage, *Life of Johnson*, 273–74; *New York Tribune*, November 18, 1862; *OR* XVI, Pt. 2, 490; Boatner, *CWD*, 708.

20. Johnson to Lincoln, September 1, October 29, Lincoln to Johnson, October 31, 1862, *AJP*, VI, 4–6, 44–45; Jones, *Life of Johnson*, 80; Hall, *Andrew Johnson*, 78, 80–81.

21. Basler, *Collected Works*, V, 433–36; Blaine, *Twenty Years*, I, 446; Petition to Lincoln, December 4, 1862, Johnson to Lincoln, January 11, 1863, *AJP*, VI, 685–86, 114.

22. *New York Times*, January 25, 1862.

23. Johnson's Speech, July 4, 1862, Johnson Papers, LC.

24. John M. Palmer, *Personal Recollections of John M. Palmer; The Story of an Earnest Life* (Cincinnati: R. Clarke Company, 1901), 127.

25. Faust, *HTI*, 722–23; Johnson to Lincoln, January 11, 1863, *AJP*, VI, 6:114; Hall, *Andrew Johnson*, 89–90.

26. For correspondence concerning Johnson's military build up, see *AJP*, V, 181, 326–27, 461–62, 495–96, 587, VI, 194–95, 198–99, 205, 211–13, 376–77, 378–79, 384, 488–92; for Johnson's disputes with army officers, see *AJP*, V, 485–86, 487, VI, 32–33, 48–48, and *OR*, XXVI, pt. 2, 72; Hall, *Andrew Johnson*, 178–82; Brabson, *Andrew Johnson*, 87.

27. Hall, *Andrew Johnson*, 95–99.

28. Faust, *HTI*, 643; Boatner, *CWD*, 466–68; Hall, *Andrew Johnson*, 101.

29. Basler, *Works of Lincoln*, VI, 440.

30. Faust, *HTI*, 136–38, 420–21.

31. Hall, *Andrew Johnson*, 198.

32. Hall, *Andrew Johnson*, 212, 205–6; Basler, *Works of Lincoln*, VII, 53–56; Lincoln to Johnson, December 10, 1863, Johnson's Speech on Slavery, January 8, Johnson's Speech on Restoration, January 21, Proclamation Ordering Elections, January 26, 1864, *AJP*, VI, 514, 548–51, 574–90, 594–96; John G. Nicolay and John Hay, *Abraham Lincoln, A History*, 10 vols. (New York: The Century Company, 1894–1905), VIII, 443.

33. Proclamation Ordering Election, January 26, Ewing to Johnson, February 1, 1868, *AJP*, VI, 594–96, 601–2; Richardson, *Messages and Papers*, VI, 7, 27; Basler, *Works of Lincoln*, VII, 183–84, 196.

34. Temple, *Notable Men*, 407–9; Johnson to Brownlow, April 6, Johnson to Lincoln, April 11, Speech at Athens, April 11, Speech at Knoxville, April 12, 16, 1864, *AJP*, VI, 663, 669–79.

35. Basler, *Works of Lincoln*, VII, 53–56; Richardson, *Messages and Papers*, VI, 213–14.

36. Basler, *Works of Lincoln*, VII, 56.

37. Ibid. V, 145–46. See note 1 for the resolution of Congress; Richardson, *Messages and Papers*, 126–42.

38. Charles H. McCarthy, *Lincoln's Plan of Reconstruction* (New York: AMS Press, 1966), 196–97, 216; *Congressional Globe*, 37 Cong., 1 Sess., 239–43.

39. McCarthy, *Lincoln's Plan*, 217.

40. Faust, *HTI*, 207; McCarthy, *Lincoln's Plan*, 224, 226.

41. McCarthy, *Lincoln's Plan*, 226–36, 248; *Cong. Globe*, 38 Cong., 1 Sess., 2039–41.

42. *Cong. Globe*, 38 Cong., 1 Sess., 2108; Blaine, *Twenty Years*, II, 42; T. Harry Williams, *Lincoln and the Radicals* (Madison: University of Wisconsin Press, 1941), 318–21; Moorfield Storey, *Charles Sumner* (Boston: Houghton Mifflin Company, 1900.

43. Nicolay and Hay, *Abraham Lincoln*, IX, 120–22; Richardson, *Messages and Papers*, VI, McCarthy, *Lincoln's Plan*, 273–74; Stevens to Edward McPherson, July 10, 1864, McPherson Papers, LC; Blaine, *Twenty Years*, II, 44.

Chapter 3

1. *Nashville Union*, June 4, 1864; Rhodes, *History of the United States*, IV, 456.

2. Rhodes, History of the United States, IV, 457–60; Nicolay and Hay, *Abraham Lincoln*, VIII, 316; Lord Charnwood, *Abraham Lincoln* (New York: Henry Holt and Company, 1917), 329.

3. Rhodes, *History of the United States*, IV, 462–63, 468; Faust, *HTI*, 608.

4. Blaine, *Twenty Years*, I, 517, 520.

5. Rhodes, *History of the United States*, IV, 470; Blaine, *Twenty Years*, I, 522.

6. Edward Stanwood, *A History of the Presidency from 1788 to 1897*, 2 vols. (Boston: Houghton Mifflin & Company, 1916), I, 303–304; Morse, *Abraham Lincoln*, II, 264; Alexander K. McClure, *Abraham Lincoln and Men of War-Times* (Philadelphia: Times Publishing Company, 1892), 115.

7. Welles, *Diary*, II, 47; Chauncey M. Depew, *My Memories of Eighty Years* (New York: Macmillan Company, 1922), 60.

8. Gustave Koerner to Lyman Trumbull, March 10, 1866, Trumbull Papers, LC; Charles Eugene Hamlin, *Life and Times of Hannibal Hamlin* (Cambridge, Riverside

Press, 1899), 472; Rhodes, *History of the United States*, V, 543.

9. Horace Greeley, *Proceedings of the First Three Republican National Conventions, 1856, 1860, and 1864* (Minneapolis: 1893), 188–239 passim; Blaine, *Twenty Years*, I, 522; *New York World*, June 9, 1864; *New York Herald*, June 9, 1864.

10. Stanwood, *History of the Presidency*, I, 304.

11. Stanwood, *History of the Presidency*, I, 301.

12. Speech on Vice Presidential Nomination, June 9, 1864, *AJP*, VI, 723–28; Savage, *Life of Johnson*, 291, 293–97; Stanwood, *History of the Presidency*, I, 302.

13. Faust, *HTI*, 794; Johnson to Lincoln, July 13, 1864, January 13, 1865, *AJP*, VII, 30, 404; McKitrick, *Andrew Johnson*, 128–33.

14. *New York Tribune*, August 18, 1864; Rhodes, *History of the United States*, IV, 518; Henry Greenleaf Pearson, *The Life of John A. Andrew, Governor of Massachusetts 1861–1865*, 2 vols. (Boston: Houghton Mifflin Company, 1904), II, 159.

15. *New York Tribune*, August 5, 1864; William F. Zornow, *Lincoln and the Party Divided* (Norman: University of Oklahoma Press, 1954), 114–17; *New York Herald*, August 5, 1864.

16. Rhodes, *History of the United States*, IV, 523, 526, 536; N. P. Sawyer to Frémont, September 13, 1864, Johnson Papers, LC; *New York World*, September 22, October 1, 1864.

17. Stanwood, *History of the Presidency*, I, 308.

18. Faust, *HTI*, 741–42; Rhodes, *History of the United States*, V, 46; Chase to Lincoln, December 6, 1864, Chase Papers, LC.

19. Welles, *Diary*, II, 192–93.

20. Basler, *Works of Lincoln*, VIII, 136–53; Faust, *HTI*, 752–53.

21. *Cong. Globe*, 38 Cong., 2 Sess., 969–70; McCarthy, *Lincoln's Plan*, 289, 313.

22. Jacob D. Cox, *Military Reminiscences of the Civil War*, 2 vols. (New York: Scribner's, 1900), II, 396.

23. Alexander H. Stephens, *A Constitutional View of the Late War Between the States*, 2 vols. (Philadelphia: National Publishing Company, 1868–1870), II, 594–617 passim.

24. James D. Richardson, *A Compilation of the Messages and Papers of the Confederacy,*

2 vols. (Washington, Bureau of National Literature and Art, 1896–99), I, 551.

25. Ibid. 617; Blaine, *Twenty Years*, II, 25; *Cong. Globe*, 38 Cong. 2 Sess., 969–70.

26. Johnson to Brownlow, December 22, 1864, Speech to the Union Convention, January 12, 1865, *AJP*, VII, 350, 398; Hall, *Andrew Johnson*, 159–70.

27. Johnson to Lincoln, January 13, 1865, *AJP*, vii, 404; Hall, *Andrew Johnson*, 173.

28. Basler, *Works of Lincoln*, VIII, 235; Jones, *Life of Johnson*, 89; Johnson to Lincoln, January 12, John W. Forney to Johnson, January 27, 1865, *AJP*, VII, 420–21, 439.

29. McCarthy, *Lincoln's Plan*, 46, 70; Rhodes, *History of the United States*, V, 52.

30. *Cong. Globe*, 38 Cong., 2 Sess., 1129.

31. Ibid. 1128; Rhodes, *History of the United States*, V, 55.

32. McCarthy, *Lincoln's Plan*, 129, 338; Rhodes, *History of the United States*, V, 51; *Cong. Globe*, 38 Cong., 2 Sess., 556.

33. Johnson to Stanton, March 3, Stanton, March 3, 1865, *AJP*, VII, 491–92, 494; Forney to Johnson, March 2, 1865, Johnson Papers, LC.

34. Basler, *Works of Lincoln*, VIII, 333.

35. *New York Tribune*, March 6, 1865; John Niven, *Gideon Welles, Secretary of the Navy* (New York, Oxford University Press, 1973), 489.

36. McCulloch, *Men and Measures*, 373; Hamlin, *Life and Times*, 497–98; Welles, *Diary*, II, 251–52; *New York Herald*, March 5, 1865.

37. Hamlin, *Life and Times*, 498, 504; *New York World*, March 7, 1865; John Niven, *Salmon P. Chase, A Biography* (New York, Oxford University Press), 1995), 379.

38. McCulloch, *Men and Measures*, 373; John W. Forney, *Anecdotes of Public Men*, 2 vols. (New York: Harper's Bros., 1873–1881), I, 177; William H. Crook, *Through Five Administrations: Reminiscences of Colonel William H. Crook, Body-guard to President Lincoln*. Margarita Spalding Gerry, ed. (New York: Harper's Brothers, 1910), 83.

39. David Donald, *Charles Sumner and the Rights of Man*. (New York: Alfred A. Knopf, 1970) 218–19.

Chapter 4

1. John S. Barnes, "With Lincoln from Washington to Richmond in 1862," *Appleton's Magazine*, vol. 11 (June 1907), 746–50; William H. Crook, "Lincoln's Last Day; new facts now told for the first time. Compiled and written down by Margarita S. Gerry." *Harper's Monthly Magazine*, vol. 115, (September 1907), 519–30; Basler, *Collected Works*, VIII, 389.

2. Walter Lynwood Fleming, *The Sequel to Appomattox* (New Haven, Yale University Press, 1919), 67; Welles, *Diary*, II, 279–80; Basler, *Collected Works*, VIII, 405, 406–7.

3. Ulysses S. Grant, *Personal Memoirs of Ulysses S. Grant*, 2 vols. (New York: Charles L. Webster & Company, 1885), II, 493.

4. Welles, *Diary*, II, 278; Basler, *Collected Works*, VIII, 393; Washington *Daily National Intelligencer*, April 11, 1865.

5. Basler, *Collected Works*, VIII, 399–405; Chase to Lincoln, April 11, 1865, Robert T. Lincoln Collection, LC.

6. Basler, *Collected Works*, VIII, 399–405; Pierce, *Memoir and Letters*, IV, 236; Rhodes, *History of the United States*, V, 138.

7. Nicolay and Hay, *Abraham Lincoln*, X, 291–302; Otto Eisenschmil, *In the Shadow of Lincoln's Death* (New York, Funk and Wagnels, 1940), 348–52.

8. Boatner, *CWD*, 484; William Hanchett, *The Lincoln Murder Conspiracies* (Urbana: 1983), 83–85; Rhodes, *History of the United States*, V, 145–50.

9. Chase "Diary," April 15, 1865, NYHS, also in HSP; Welles *Diary*, II, 287, 288, 290–93; Blaine, *Twenty Years*, II, 1–2; J. W. Schuckers, *The Life and Public Services of Salmon Portland Chase*. (New York: D. Appleton and Company, 1874), 519; Remarks on Assuming the Presidency, April 15, 1865, *AJP*, VII, 553–54; *New York Herald*, April 16, 1865.

10. McCulloch, *Men and Measures*, 376; Richardson, *Messages and Papers*, VI, 305; Welles, *Diary*, II, 289; Cabinet to Johnson, April 15, Remarks on Assuming the Presidency, April 15, 1865, *AJP*, VII, 553–54.

11. Frederick W. Seward, *Reminiscences of a War-Time Statesman and Diplomat, 1830–1915* (New York and London: G. P. Putnam's Sons, 1916), 251, 258–61.

12. Faust, *HTI*, 668–69; Harriet A.

Weed, ed., *The Life of Thurlow Weed*. 2 vols. (Boston: Houghton Mifflin Company, 1884), I, 423.

13. Thornton K. Lothrop, *William Henry Seward* (Boston: Houghton Mifflin & Co., 1896), 203; Savage, *Life of Andrew Johnson*, 222.

14. Frederic Bancroft, *The Life of William H. Seward*. 2 vols. (New York: Harper & Brothers, 1900, 243–63; G. E. Baker, ed., *The Works of William H. Seward*. 5 vols. (Boston: Houghton Mifflin & Company, 1884), IV, 600; Basler, *Collected Works*, IV, 50.

15. Lothrop, *William Seward*, 150, 155, 215, 219; Weed, *Life of Thurlow Weed*, II, 277; Rhodes, *History of the United States*, II, 471.

16. J. G. Randall, *Lincoln the President*. 4 vols. (New York: Dodd, Mead & Co., 1945–55) I, 258–60, 291–92.

17. Rhodes, *History of the United States*, III, 320, n.3; Nicolay and Hay, *Abraham Lincoln*, III, 445–49; Lothrop, *William Seward*, 361.

18. Glyndon Van Deusen, *William Henry Seward: Lincoln's Secretary of State* (New York: Oxford University Press, 1967), 338–48; Welles, *Diary*, I, 203; Nicolay and Hay, *Abraham Lincoln*, VI, 268.

19. Bradford, *Union Portraits*, 199–203.

20. Faust, *HTI*, 712–13; Welles, *Diary*, I, 203. II, 17.

21. Faust, *HTI*, 813; Welles, *Diary*, I, xxxviii, xxxix.

22. Welles, *Diary*, I, xlii.

23. Faust, *HTI*, 257–58, 459; Welles, *Diary*, II, 576–77.

24. Faust, *HTI*, 215, 340, 708; Blaine, *Twenty Years*, II, 61–62; Rhodes, *History of the United States*, IV, 529; William H. Herndon and Jesse W. Weik, *Abraham Lincoln*, 2 vols. (New York: D. Appleton and Company, 1896), I, 175, 195.

25. Remarks on Assuming the Presidency, April 15, 1865, *AJP*, VII, 553–54.

26. Moore, *Speeches*, 294.

27. Ibid. 456.

28. George W. Julian, *Political Recollections, 1840–1872* (Chicago: Jansen McClurg & Company, 1884), 255–56.

29. Rhodes, *History of the United States*, V, 153–55, 159; *New York Tribune*, April 17, 1865.

30. Richardson, *Messages and Papers*, VI, 305.

31. Julian, *Political Recollections*, 258–59.

32. Welles, *Diary*, II, 291; Quotes from Donald, *Charles Sumner*, 219–22; Charles Sumner, *The Works of Charles Sumner*, 15 vols. (Boston: Lee and Shephard, 1870–1883), XI, 20; Pierce, *Memoir and Letters*, IV, 242, 243.

33. Chase Diary, April 29, 1865, Chase Papers, HSP. See also "Address to the People of the United States," written in Chase's hand, in Johnson Papers, LC.

34. Justin G. Turner and Linda Levitt Turner, *Mary Todd Lincoln, Her Life and Letters* (New York: Alfred P. Knopf, 1972), 225–26; McCulloch, *Men and Measures*, 374.

35. McCulloch, *Men and Measures*, 374.

36. Moore, *Speeches*, 483–84.

37. Basler, *Collected Works*, VIII, 399–408.

38. Schurz, *Reminiscences*, III, 221–23; Michael Les Benedict, *A Compromise of Principle: Congressional Republicans and Reconstruction* (New York: W. W. Norton, 1974), 73; Weed, *Life of Thurlow Weed*, II, 450.

Chapter 5

1. Faust, *HTI*, 154–55; Julian, *Political Recollections*, 257; George W. Julian to Mrs. Julian, April 17, 1865, Julian Papers, Indiana Historical Society.

2. Julian, *Political Recollections*, 257.

3. Faust, *HTI*, 98–99; Blaine, *Twenty Years*, II, 14.

4. George W. Julian to Mrs. Julian, April 17, 1865, Julian Papers, Indiana Historical Society; Moore, *Speeches*, 470.

5. Moore, *Speeches*, 471.

6. Welles, *Diary*, II, 291.

7. Moore, *Speeches*, 478.

8. Ibid. 479–80.

9. Ibid. 480–81.

10. William T. Sherman, *Home Letters of General Sherman*, M. A. DeWolfe Howe, ed. (New York, Charles Scribner's Sons, 1909), 349–50; Rhodes, *History of the United States*, V, 168–69; Faust, *HTI*, 114.

11. *OR*, XLVII, Pt. 3, 263, 285, 292–93; Sherman to Grant, May 28, 1865, Sherman Papers, HL; William T. Sherman, *Memoirs of General William T. Sherman*, 2 vols. (New York: D. Appleton & Company, 1875), II,

325–72 passim; Sherman to Schofield, May 28, 1865, Sherman Papers, LC.

12. Rhodes, *History of the United States*, V, 525, 527–28, VI, 34.

13. Welles, *Diary*, 302–3.

14. Sherman, *Memoirs*, 376.

15. Whitelaw Reid, *After the War: A Southern Tour, May 1, 1865 to May 1, 1866* (London: Sampson Low, Son, & Marston, 1866), 304–5; *New York Herald*, June 27, July 6, 1865; Welles, *Diary*, II, 327.

16. Richardson, *Messages and Papers*, VI, 310.

17. Ibid. IV, 213–15, 311–12.

18. Blaine, *Twenty Years*, II, 67–68; Rhodes, *History of the United States*, V, 535; Bancroft, *Life of Seward*, II, 447.

19. Richardson, *Messages and Papers*, VI, 312–13.

20. Ibid. 313; Sumner to Carl Schurz, June 19, 1865, Sumner Papers, LC; Sumner, *Works*, XI, 22.

21. Turner and Turner, *Mary Todd Lincoln*, 235; *New York Tribune*, June 10, 1865; Rhodes, *History of the United States*, V, 137.

22. Chase to Johnson, May 17, 1865, Johnson Papers, LC.

23. Richardson, *Messages and Papers*, VI, 315–31.

24. Sumner to Chase, June 25, 1865, Chase Papers, LC; Sumner to Wade, June 12, 1865, Wade Papers, LC; Sumner, *Works*, IX, 441–77.

25. Edward McPherson, *The Political History of the United States of America During the Period of Reconstruction* (Chicago: James J. Chapman, 1880), 18–28.

26. Ibid. 49; Blaine, *Twenty Years*, II, 76.

27. *New York Herald*, May 10, 31, 1865.

28. Welles, *Diary*, II, 355–56.

29. McCulloch, *Men and Measures*, 378; Rhodes, *History of the United States*, V, 533–34; Welles, *Diary*, II, 364.

30. Welles, *Diary*, II, 363, 369.

31. *New York Herald*, June 2, 1865; *New York World*, October 19, 1865.

32. Rhodes, *History of the United States*, V, 533–34; Wade to Sumner, July 29, 1865, Wade Papers, LC.

33. Pierce, *Memoir and Letters*, IV, 242; Reid, *After the War*, 26–33.

34. Reid, *After the War*, 51–52, 80–86.

35. Hamilton, *Papers of Thomas Ruffin*,

35; From a Lancaster pamphlet quoted in Bowers, *The Tragic Era*, 21.

36. Chase to Sumner, June 25, 1865, Chase Papers, LC; Beverly Palmer, ed., *The Selected Letters of Charles Sumner*, 2 vols. (Boston: 1990) II, 313–19.

37. McPherson, *Political History*, 49–51.

38. DeWitt, *Impeachment and Trial*, 22.

Chapter 6

1. McPherson, *Political History*, 107, 109.

2. C. J. Hollister, *Life of Schuyler Colfax* (New York: 1886), 372; Welles, *Diary*, II, 385; Sumner to Wade, August 3, 1865, Wade Papers, LC; Sumner to Schurz, August 28, 1865, Schurz Papers, LC.

3. Welles, *Diary*, II 387; Thomas Frederick Woodley, *Thaddeus Stevens* (Harrisburg: Telegraph Press, 1934), 416–17; Cox, *Three Decades*, 365; Schurz, *Reminiscences*, II, 214.

4. Ibid. II, 388; McPherson, *Political History*, 108; Blaine, *Twenty Years*, II, 112–13; Edward McPherson Papers, no. 53297, LC.

5. McCall, *Thaddeus Stevens*, 257.

6. Ibid. 253, 257–59; Blaine, *Twenty Years*, II, 113; Stryker, *Andrew Johnson*, 233; Edward McPherson Papers, no. 53297, and Theodore Tilton to Stevens, December 6, 1865, Stevens Papers, LC.

7. Blaine, *Twenty Years*, II, 113–14; Storey, *Charles Sumner*, 299–300; Donald, *Charles Sumner*, 243–44.

8. Pierce, *Works of Sumner*, IV, 286, 289; Donald, *Charles Sumner*, 237–38, 241.

9. Richardson, *Messages and Papers*, VI, 353.

10. Ibid. 355–57.

11. Ibid. 357–58; McPherson, *Political History*, 18–28.

12. Richardson, *Messages and Papers*, VI, 359–60.

13. Ibid. 360.

14. Rhodes, *History of the United States*, V, 546, 548; *New York Tribune*, December 6, 1865; *New York Times*, December 6, 1865.

15. Rhodes, *History of the United States*, V, 546, 548; Welles, *Diary*, II, 392; Milton, *Age of Hate*, 386–87.

16. Richardson, *Messages and Papers*,

VI, 214; Blaine, *Twenty Years*, II, 163; Rhodes, *History of the United States*, V, 557–58.

17. McPherson, *Political History*, 28–44; John W. Burgess, *Reconstruction and the Constitution, 1866–1876* (New York: DaCapo Press, 1970), 46–53.

18. Blaine, *Twenty Years*, II, 112–21.

19. Storey, *Charles Sumner*, 302–303.

20. Welles, *Diary*, II, 393–94.

21. Ibid. 395.

22. Francis Fessenden, *Life and Public Services of William Pitt Fessenden*. 2 vols. (Boston: Houghton, Mifflin and Co., 1907), II, 19–20.

23. Ibid. 19–20.

24. Blaine, *Twenty Years*, II, 127; Woodley, *Thaddeus Stevens*, 419.

25. Welles, *Diary*, II, 397–98.

26. Ibid. 396–97; Schurz, *Reminiscences*, III, 195–209; Blaine, *Twenty Years*, II, 147; Richardson, *Messages and Papers*, VI, 372–73. For Schurz Report, see "Report of Carl Schurz on the States of South Carolina, Georgia, Alabama, Mississippi, and Louisiana," *Sen. Ex. Doc. no. 2, 39 Cong., 1 Sess.,* 2–105.

27. Blaine, *Twenty Years*, II, 153; Schurz, *Reminiscences*, III, 200–201; Brooks D. Simpson, et al., *Advice After Appomattox: Letters to Andrew Johnson, 1865–1866* (Knoxville: University of Tennessee Press, 1987), 76–77.

28. Storey, *Charles Sumner*, 305–7; Schurz, *Reminiscences*, III, 209; Sumner, *Works of Sumner*, XI, 25.

29. *Cong. Globe*, 39 Cong., 1 Sess., 72–73; Blaine, *Twenty Years*, II, 130. Mississippi, Florida, and Texas had not yet ratified the Thirteenth Amendment.

30. McPherson, *Political History*, 6; Bancroft, *Life of Seward*, II, 452.

31. Blaine, *Twenty Years*, II, 136–37; Welles, *Diary*, II, 412.

32. Bowers, *The Tragic Era*, 84; Welles, *Diary*, II, 435.

Chapter 7

1. House Exec. Doc. 39 Cong., 1 Sess., no. 70, 394; Burgess, *Reconstruction*, 44–45; *Cong. Globe*, 38 Cong., 1 Sess., 2972, 3331; See Benjamin C. Truman's Report, Senate Ex. Doc., 39 Cong., 1 Sess., No. 43, and *Report of the Joint Committee on Reconstruction at the First Session Thirty-ninth Congress*

(Washington: Government Printing Office, 1866), pt. II, 123, 156, pt. IV, 148.

2. Ulysses S. Grant Report, Senate Ex. Doc., 39 Cong., 1st Sess., no. 2, 117; *Cong. Globe*, 39 Cong., 1 Sess., 129.

3. Fessenden, *Life and Public Services*, II, 21–22.

4. Ibid. 73–74; Burgess, *Reconstruction*, 7.

5. Welles, *Diary*, II, 414.

6. Ibid. II, 415–16.

7. Ibid. II, 417

8. McPherson, *Political History*, 74; Welles, *Diary*, II, 419, 421; Stryker, *Andrew Johnson*, 265.

9. Welles, *Diary*, II, 430–31.

10. Rachel Sherman Thorndike, ed. *The Sherman Letters: Correspondence Between General and Senator Sherman from 1837 to 1891* (New York: Charles Scribner's Sons, 1894), 262.

11. Welles, *Diary*, II, 432.

12. Ibid. II, 434; Fessenden, *Life and Public Services*, II, 26.

13. Welles, *Diary*, II, 434–35.

14. Richardson, *Messages and Papers*, VI, 398–99, 403.

15. Ibid. VI, 402–403.

16. Welles, *Diary*, II, 438.

17. McCulloch, *Men and Measures*, 393; Blaine, *Twenty Years*, II, 181; McPherson, *Political History*, 58–60; McKitrick, *Andrew Johnson and Reconstruction*, 293. The references are to Jefferson Davis, Confederate president, Robert A. Toombs, Confederate secretary of state, and John Slidell, Confederate commissioner to France, all former United States senators.

18. *New York Tribune*, February 26, 1866; McPherson, *Political History*, 60–62; Washington *Morning Chronicle*, February 27, 1866.

19. Ibid. 403–404.

20. *Cong. Globe*, 39 Cong., 1 Sess., 917, 943, 950, 1147; McPherson, *Political History*, 74; Welles, *Diary*, II, 436.

21. *Cong. Globe*, 39 Cong., 1 Sess., 1438.

22. George Julian Diary quoted in Bowers, *The Tragic Era*, 102; *Cong. Globe*, 39 Cong. 1 Sess., Appen., 124; Storey, *Charles Sumner*, 303.

23. Thorndike, *The Sherman Letters*, 263.

24. *Cong. Globe*, 39 Cong., 1 Sess., Appen., 124, et seq.

25. *New York Herald*, February 24, 1866; *New York Times*, February 24, 1866; Ellis Paxson Oberholtzer, *The History of the United States Since the Civil War*. 3 vols. (New York: Macmillan Company, 1922), I, 171.

26. *New York Herald*, February 28, 1866; Augustus Maverick, *Henry J. Raymond* (Hartford: 1870), 184.

27. Rhodes, *History of the United States*, V, 578, n. 1.

28. McPherson, *Political History*, 51.

29. Welles, *Diary*, II, 483.

Chapter 8

1. Blaine, *Twenty Years*, II, 172, 175; McPherson, *Political History*, 78–81; *Cong. Globe*, 39 Cong., 1 Sess., 1367.

2. Sumner, *Works of Sumner*, X, 400; Blaine, *Twenty Years*, II, 155–59; *Cong. Globe*, 39 Cong. 1 Sess., 1564–73, 1589–1602, 1635–48, 1666–79; McKitrick, *Andrew Johnson*, 319–22.

3. Richardson, *Messages and Papers*, VI, 406–9, 411.

4. Ibid. 412–13.

5. Dewitt, *Impeachment and Trial*, 77–83; Blaine, *Twenty Years*, II, 178.

6. Welles, *Diary*, II, 475, 477; McPherson, *Political History*, 82; Blaine, *Twenty Years*, II, 179; *Cong. Globe*, 39 Cong., 1 Sess., 1809.

7. Welles, *Diary*, II, 479, 482.

8. McPherson, *Political History*, 81; Richardson, *Messages and Papers*, VI, 415; Sumner, *Works of Sumner*, X, 367, 370–71.

9. Richardson, *Messages and Papers*, VI, 413–16. Ten years passed before Colorado became a state.

10. Howard K. Beale, *The Critical Year: A Study of Andrew Johnson and Reconstruction* (New York: Harcourt, Brace, 1930), 94; *Cong. Globe*, 39 Cong., 1 Sess., 10.

11. Quoted in Stryker, *Andrew Johnson*, 295. For a short, compact history of the Fourteenth Amendment, see McKitrick, *Andrew Johnson*, 326–63.

12. Sumner, *Works of Sumner*, X, 429; Blaine, *Twenty Years*, II, 193–94, 198–99; Fessenden, *Life and Services*, II, 25–26; Washington *Morning Chronicle*, May 1, 1866. See also *Report of the Joint Committee on Reconstruction at the First Session Thirty-ninth Congress* (Washington: Government Printing Office, 1866).

13. Blaine, *Twenty Years*, II, 205, 215; Stryker, *Andrew Johnson*, 300; Burgess, *Reconstruction*, 81; McPherson, *Political History*, 93.

14. McPherson, *Political History*, 94–95, 98.

15. Welles, *Diary*, II, 494.

16. McPherson, *Political History*, 51; Burgess, *Reconstruction*, 34; Blaine, *Twenty Years*, II, 211.

17. Dr. S. J. Quinvy Testimony, House Report, 39th Cong., 1st Sess., Report no. 101; Oberholzer, *History of the United States*, I, 379–80.

18. McPherson, *Political History*, 83–84.

19. Hilary A. Herbert, et al., *Why the Solid South? or Reconstruction and Its Results* (Baltimore: R. H. Woodward & Company, 1890), 184; McPherson, *Political History*, 89.

20. Welles, *Diary*, II, 554–55, 557; Herbert, *Why the Solid South*, 186–87.

21. Herbert, *Why the Solid South*, 187–88; Dewitt, *Impeachment and Trial*, 100; Blaine, *Twenty Years*, II, 213.

22. Welles, *Diary*, II, 558; McPherson, *Political History*, 152.

23. Richardson, *Messages and Papers*, VI, 395–97.

24. Rhodes, *History of the United States*, V, 598; Dewitt, *Impeachment and Trial*, 106; *Cong. Globe*, 39 Cong., 1 Sess., 4113.

25. Blaine, *Twenty Years*, II, 217.

26. Richardson, *Messages and Papers*, VI, 422–23.

27. Burgess, *Reconstruction*, 89–90; McPherson, *Political History*, 151.

28. Dewitt, *Impeachment and Trial*, 105; Pierce, *Memoir and Letters*, IV, 286; *Cong. Globe*, 39 Cong., 1 Sess., 4276.

29. Welles, *Diary*, II, 551–53; Rhodes, *History of the United States*, V, 611; William H. Rehnquist, *Grand Inquests: The Historic Impeachments of Justice Samuel Chase and President Andrew Johnson* (New York: William Morrow and Company, 1992), 245–46; Burgess, *Reconstruction*, 91.

30. Welles, *Diary*, II, 403 note 1.

31. Ibid. 558.

32. Welles, *Diary*, II, 570; Burgess, *Reconstruction*, 92–95; Richardson, *Messages and Papers*, VI, 590; Willie Malvin Caskey,

Secession and Restoration in Louisiana (Baton Rouge: University of Louisiana Press, 1938), 165–214 passim; R. K. Cutler Testimony, House Report, 39th Cong., 1st Sess., Report no. 16; Monroe to Baird, July 25, Baird to Monroe, July 26, 1866, Baird to Stanton, July 28, 1866, Johnson Papers, "Telegrams," LC.

33. Rhodes, *History of the United States*, V, 612.

34. Albert Voorhies and A. J. Herron to Johnson, and Johnson to Voorhies, July 28, 1866, Johnson to Wells, Wells to Johnson, July 28, 1866, Johnson Papers, "Telegrams," LC.

35. *House Report*, 39 Cong. 2 Sess., No. 16, "Report of the Select Committee on the New Orleans Riots," 12–16; Burgess, *Reconstruction*, 97.

36. Richardson, *Messages and Papers*, VI, 591; Welles, *Diary*, II, 569–70.

37. Welles, *Diary*, II, 570–71; "Report of the Select Committee on the New Orleans Riots," 443–44, 546; Johnson to Herron, July 30, 1868, Johnson Papers, Telegrams, LC.

Chapter 9

1. Rhodes, *History of the United States*, V, 614; Blaine, *Twenty Years*, II, 223; Welles, *Diary*, II, 574; Oberholtzer, *History of the United States*, I, 389.

2. Welles, *Diary*, II, 555; Oberholtzer, *History of the United States*, I, 386–88.

3. Welles, *Diary*, II, 555–56.

4. McPherson, *Political History*, 241, 251.

5. Burgess, *Reconstruction*, 99–100; Pierce, *Memoir and Letters*, IV, 297, 298.

6. Welles, *Diary*, II, 581–83; U. S. Congress. Senate. *Trial of Andrew Johnson, President of the United States, on Impeachment by the House of Representatives for High Crimes and Misdemeanors*. 3 vols. 40 Cong., 2 Sess., 1868 (Washington: Government Printing Office, 1868), I, 9, 66–67, hereinafter *Trial*; McPherson, *Political History*, 127–28.

7. Welles, *Diary*, II, 425 note.

8. Bowers, *The Tragic Era*, 39–40.

9. Rhodes, *History of the United States*, V, 617.

10. Welles, *Diary*, II, 587.

11. McCulloch, *Men and Measures*, 377.

12. Welles, *Diary*, II, 587–89.

13. Ibid. 647.

14. Oberholtzer, *History of the United States*, I, 397; *New York Herald*, August 30, 1866.

15. McPherson, *Political History*, 129–34, passim.

16. Welles, *Diary*, II, 588; Oberholtzer, *History of the United States*, I, 401.

17. Welles, *Diary*, II, 589–90.

18. *Cleveland Herald*, September 4, 1866; *Cleveland Plain Dealer*, September 4, 1866.

19. Welles, *Diary*, II, 593; *Trial*, I, 316–18, 326, 328; Rhodes, *History of the United States*, V, 618; Oberholtzer, *History of the United States*, I, 404; McPherson, *Political History*, 134–35; *Cleveland Herald*, September 4, 1866.

20. *Trial*, I, 316–18; McPherson, *Political History*, 134–36; Welles, *Diary*, II, 593; *Cleveland Herald*, September 4, 1866.

21. Rhodes, *History of the United States*, V, 618; Welles, *Diary*, II, 594, 648; Burgess, *Reconstruction*, 102; Stryker, *Andrew Johnson*, 359; Doolittle to Johnson, August 28, 1866, Johnson Papers, LC.

22. McPherson, *Political History*, 124; Blaine, *Twenty Years*, II, 228.

23. Rhodes, *History of the United States*, V, 449, 621.

24. Blaine, *Twenty Years*, II, 225–27; McPherson, *Political History*, 241–42.

25. *New York Herald*, September 9, 1866.

26. Oberholtzer, *History of the United States*, I, 405; Grant to Julia Dent Grant, September 4, 1866, Grant Papers, LC; James H. Wilson to Orville E. Babcock, September 11, 1866, Babcock Papers, Newberry Library, Chicago; Milton, *The Age of Hate*, 367, 728 n. 56; *New York Tribune*, September 11, 12, 1866.

27. Welles, *Diary*, II, 594; Oberholtzer, *History of the United States*, I, 405.

28. Oberholtzer, *History of the United States*, I, 399; Welles, *Diary*, II. 594; *New York Herald*, September 12, 1866; *Trial*, I, 9, 341, 344, 637–40; McPherson, *Political History*, 136–41; *Chicago Tribune*, September 11, 1866.

29. *Age of Hate*, 369; McCulloch, *Men and Measures*, 372; Welles, *Diary*, II, 594.

30. Oberholtzer, *History of the United States*, I, 407; Lothrop, *William Seward*, 397.

31. Welles, *Diary*, II, 592, 594; Grant to Julia D. Grant, September 9, 1866, Grant Papers, LC.

32. Welles, *Diary*, II, 595.

33. Ibid. 595; Milton, *The Age of Hate*, 369.

34. Welles, *Diary*, II, 590; Donald, *Charles Sumner*, 269; Gregg Phifer, "Andrew Johnson Delivers His Arguments," *Tennessee Historical Quarterly*, vol. 11 (Spring 1952), 213, 214, 227, 232, 234; Crook, *Through Five Administrations*, 112.

35. Brian Steel Wills, *A Battle from the Start: The Life of Nathan Bedford Forrest* (New York: HarperCollins Publishers, 1992), 322–23, 333; Blaine, *Twenty Years*, II, 229–30.

36. John Bigelow, ed. *The Writings and Speeches of Samuel J. Tilden*, 2 vols. (New York: Harper & Sons, 1885), I, 344.

Chapter 10

1. Welles, *Diary*, II, 616–17.

2. Quoted from Bowers, *The Tragic Era*, 141–42.

3. Welles, *Diary*, II, 619–20; Benjamin F. Butler, *Autobiography and Personal Reminiscences: Butler's Book* (Boston: A. M. Thayer, 1892), 919; Stryker, *Andrew Johnson*, 395; Ashley letters to F. M. Case printed in *New York World*, January 12, 19, 1867.

4. Faust, *HTI*, 98–99; Blaine, *Twenty Years*, II, 289; McPherson, *Political History*, 243; *New York World*, October 9, 1866; *The Nation*, October 11, 1866.

5. Oberholtzer, *History of the United States*, I, 419; Rhodes, *History of the United States*, V, 625; J. G. de Roulhac Hamilton, ed., *The Papers of Thomas Ruffin* (Raleigh: North Carolina Historical Commission, 1920), 123.

6. Welles, *Diary*, II, 617; Fessenden to McCulloch, September 11, 15, 17, 1866, McCulloch Papers, LC; Alfred E. Burr to Welles, April 27, 1866, Welles Papers, LC; Weed, *Life of Weed*, I, 630–31.

7. Welles, *Diary*, II, 626–27.

8. Trefousse, *Andrew Johnson*, 268.

9. Richardson, *Messages and Papers*, VI, 445, 446, 448, 459; *New York Tribune*, December 4, 1866; Greeley to Amos Lawrence, December 16, 1866, Horace Greeley Papers, NYPL; *New York World*, November 24, December 4, 1866.

10. Welles, *Diary*, II, 631; *Cong. Globe*, 39 Cong., 2 Sess., 2, 107; McPherson, *Political History*, 159; Sumner, *Works of Sumner*, XI, 49.

11. Richardson, *Messages and Papers*, VI, 472; McPherson, *Political History*, 154–60; Welles, *Diary*, II, 640.

12. Welles, *Diary*, III, 4–5; *New York World*, October 13, November 21, 1866.

13. Richardson, *Messages and Papers*, VI, 473, 474, 476, 477, 478; McPherson, *Political History*, 160; *Cong. Globe*, 39 Cong., 2 Sess., 319–21; Orville Hickman Browning, *The Diary of Orville Hickman Browning*, James G. Randall and Theodore C. Pease, eds., 2 vols. (Springfield: Illinois, State Historical Library, 1933), II, 122.

14. *Cong. Globe*, 39 Cong., 2 Sess., 127, 335–36, 357; Trefousse, *Benjamin F. Wade*, 270–71.

15. Richardson, *Messages and Papers*, VI, 483, 489; Faust, *HTI*, 522; Trefousse, *Benjamin F. Wade*, 277–78.

16. *Cong. Globe*, 39 Cong., 2 Sess., 6–7.

17. Boutwell, *Reminiscences*, II, 107–108.

18. Thomas and Hyman, *Stanton*, 515; Blaine, *Twenty Years*, II, 270; Tyler Dennett, ed., *Lincoln and the Civil War in the Diaries and Letters of John Hay* (New York: Dodd, Mead, 1939), 267.

19. Rhodes, *History of the United States*, V, 621; Bigelow, *Writings and Speeches*, I, 270.

20. U. S. Constitution, Article 2, Section 2; Myers vs. U. S. Supreme Court, October Term, 1926, 5–20 passim, quoted in Stryker, *Andrew Johnson*, 403–4.

21. Charles Warren, *The Supreme Court in United States History*, 3 vols. (Boston, Little, Brown & Company, 1922), III, 144; James Bryce, *The American Commonwealth*, 2 vols. (New York, Macmillan Company, 1924), I, 276.

22. Rhodes, *History of the United States*, V, 317–18, 327; Stryker, *Andrew Johnson*, 407–8.

23. Warren, *Supreme Court*, III, 144–48; Welles, *Diary*, II, 476, III, 7–8; Thomas and Hyman, *Stanton*, 477–78; W. P. Phillips to Johnson, November 8, 1866, Johnson Papers, LC; Richardson, *Messages and Papers*, VI, 431–32, 440–41. For the Milligan case, see Charles Fairman, *Reconstruction and Reunion, 1864–88* (New York: 1971), 192–237.

24. Secret Circular to Military Commanders in the South, RG 108, Box 102, NA.

25. Warren, *Supreme Court*, III, 146, 149; S. Klaus, ed., *The Milligan Case* (New York: 1929), 43–47.

26. Warren, *Supreme Court*, III, 167, 151–54; Stryker, *Andrew Johnson*, 412; *Diary and Correspondence of Salmon P. Chase, Annual Report of the American Historical Society for the Year 1902*, vol. II (Washington, Government Printing Office, 1903), 519.

27. Warren, *Supreme Court*, III, 167–68, 169.

28. *Cong. Globe*, 39 Cong., 2 Sess., 319–21; Charles S. Ashley, "Governor Ashley's Biography and Messages," *Contributions to the Historical Society of Montana*, 6 (1907), 189.

29. *Cong. Globe*, 39 Cong., 2 Sess., 320–21; McPherson, *Political History*, 187; William Salter, *The Life of James W. Grimes* (New York: Appleton & Company, 1876), 323.

30. *Cong. Globe*, 39 Cong., 2 Sess., 323.

31. Hans L. Trefousse, *Thaddeus Stevens, Nineteenth Century Egalitarian* (Chapel Hill: University of North Carolina Press, 1997), 223.

Chapter 11

1. Benjamin F. Kendrick, *The Journal of the Joint Committee of Fifteen on Reconstruction, 39th Congress, 1865–1867* (New York: Columbia University Press, 1915), 121. Other House members were Henry Grider, Roscoe Conkling, Henry T. Blow, and Andrew J. Rogers.

2. Welles, *Diary*, III, 9–10.

3. Ibid. 11, 49–54, 736; Boutwell, *Reminiscences of Sixty Years*, II, 107–108; Browning, *Diary*, II, 132.

4. Welles, *Diary*, III, 17; William A. Dunning, *Reconstruction, Political and Economic 1865–1877* (New York: Harper and Bros., 1907), 91.

5. Stryker, *Andrew Johnson*, 425–26.

6. Warren, *Supreme Court*, III, 173–74.

7. *Cong. Globe*, 39 Cong., 2 Sess., 443–46; Welles, *Diary*, III, 12, 23–24; *New York World*, January 7, 12, 24, 1867.

8. McPherson, *Political History*, 194.

9. Sumner, *Works of Sumner*, XI, 66–67; Blaine, *Twenty Years*, II, 271; *Cong. Globe*, 39 Cong. 2 Sess, 544.

10. Blaine, *Twenty Years*, II, 272.

11. *Cong. Globe*, 39 Cong., 2 Sess., 1039–40, 1046.

12. Blaine, *Twenty Years*, II, 272; William Roscoe Thayer, *John Hay*, 2 vols. (Boston and New York: Houghton Mifflin Company, 1908), I, 260–61; Dennet, *Lincoln and the Civil War*, 267.

13. McPherson, *Political History*, 173–766; Blaine, *Twenty Years*, II, 267–74; Browning, *Diary*, II, 132.

14. *Trail*, III, 52–53; McPherson, *Political History*, 177; Sumner, *Works of Sumner*, XI, 70–80.

15. Richardson, *Message and Papers*, VI, 492–98, 587; Welles, *Diary*, III, 50–51, 158; William G. Moore, "Notes of Colonel W. G. Moore, Private Secretary to President Johnson, 1866–1888," edited by St. George L. Sioussat, *American Historical Review*, 19 (October 1913), 110.

16. Richardson, *Messages and Papers*, VI, 494–97, 588. The Supreme Court decision of October 1926 involved the removal without Senate approval of a postmaster in Oregon by Woodrow Wilson. The postmaster sued, claiming protection under the Tenure of Office Act. After hearing the case, Chief Justice William H. Taft wrote an opinion that upheld Andrew Johnson's interpretation of the act in 1867. See Rehnquist, *Grand Inquests*, 265–69.

17. McPherson, *Political History*, 177.

18. Rhodes, *History of the United States*, VI, 14–15.

19. Woodburn, *Life of Thaddeus Stevens*, 456, 461; *Cong. Globe*, 39 Cong., 2 Sess., 1073–80, 1099; Blaine, *Twenty Years*, II, 251; Benedict, *A Compromise of Principle*, 223–24.

20. Blaine, *Twenty Years*, II, 252, 256; Woodburn, *Life of Stevens*, 471; Daniel E. Sickles to Johnson, January 25, 1867, *AJP*, II, 628.

21. *Cong. Globe*, 39 Cong., 2 Sess., 1206–17, 1334–40, 1399–1400.

22. McPherson, *Political History*, 191–92; Burgess, *Reconstruction*, 116.

23. McPherson, *Political History*, 173.

24. Welles, *Diary*, III, 42–44.

25. Ibid. 45–46, 49, 50; Stryker, *Andrew Johnson*, 444.

26. Richardson, *Messages and Papers*, VI, 498, 507.

27. Ibid. 498–99; Welles, *Diary*, III, 42.

28. Richardson, *Messages and Papers*, VI, 500–501.

29. Ibid. 508–11.

30. Woodburn, *Life of Stevens*, 481–83; Blaine, *Twenty Years*, II, 262.

31. McPherson, *Political History*, 178; Boutwell, *Reminiscences*, II, 107–8; George S. Boutwell, "Johnson's Plot and Motives," *North American Review* 141 (December 1886), 570–79; Ralph Korngold, *Thaddeus Stevens, A Being Darkly Wise and Rudely Great* (New York: Harcourt, Brace & Company, 1955), 126; Richardson, *Messages and Papers*, VI, 472; William G. Moore Diary, March 4,1867, 28–29, Johnson Papers, LC.

32. Welles, *Diary*, III, 51; Burgess, *Reconstruction*, 126; *New York World*, March 6, 1867.

Chapter 12

1. Oberholtzer, *History of the United States*, I, 451.

2. Welles, *Diary*, III, 56–57.

3. Oberholtzer, *History of the United States*, I, 452; *Cong. Globe*, 40 Cong., 1 Sess., 18, 26; *New York Herald*, March 7, 1867.

4. *Cong. Globe*, 39 Cong., 2 Sess., 2003; DeWitt, *Impeachment and Trial*, 179; Oberholtzer, *History of the United States*, I, 452.

5. Boatner, *CWD*, 115; Faust, *HTI*, 159, 340, 424, 513–14.

6. Blaine, *Twenty Years*, II, 284–89; Bowers, *The Tragic Era*, 159.

7. *Cong. Globe*, 40 Cong., 1 Sess., 18–25.

8. Welles, *Diary*, III, 62.

9. Rehnquist, *Grand Inquests*, 58–107; Welles, *Diary*, III, 60–61.

10. Welles, *Diary*, III, 61; Sumner, *Works of Sumner*, XI, 150–52, 168–70, 175; *Senate Bill no. 7*, 40 Cong., 1 Sess.; *Cong. Globe*, 40 Cong., 1 Sess., 245, 280, 407.

11. Richardson, *Messages and Papers*, VI, 551, 552; Welles, *Diary*, III, 62, 65.

12. *Cong. Globe*, 40 Cong., 1 Sess., 203–208.

13. Welles, *Diary*, III, 17, 62; McPherson, *Political History*, 180, 192–94; John Paxton to Stevens, March 16, 1867, Stevens Papers, LC; *Cong. Globe*, 40 Cong., 1 Sess., 167; Sumner, *Works of Sumner*, XI, 146–47.

14. Richardson, *Messages and Papers*, VI, 534; *Cong. Globe*, 40 Cong., 1 Sess., 314.

15. Burgess, *Reconstruction*, 147, 245.

16. Storey, *Charles Sumner*, 337; Richardson, *Messages and Papers*, VI, 517.

17. Oberholtzer, *History of the United States*, I, 542, 549; Rhodes, *History of the United States*, VI, 212; Welles, *Diary*, III, 75, 83–84; Albert A. Woldman, *Lincoln and the Russians* (Cleveland and New York: World Publishing Company, 1952), 288–89.

18. Boatner, *CWD*, 417–18; Warren, *Supreme Court*, III, 177–78; James P. Shenton, *Robert John Walker: A Politician from Jackson to Lincoln* (New York: Columbia University Press, 1961), 209.

19. Warren, *Supreme Court*, III, 177–79, 181.

20. Ibid. 183–84; Shenton, *Robert John Walker*, 209–10.

21. Warren, *Supreme Court*, III, 186, n. 1.

22. Rhodes, *History of the United States*, V, 521–22, VI, 56–57; Burke Davis, *The Long Surrender* (New York: Random House, 1985), 211–14; 218–23; Varina Howell Davis, *Jefferson Davis Ex-President of the Confederate States of America*, 2 vols. (New York: Belford & Company, 1890), II, 777, 790–97.

23. DeWitt, *Impeachment*, 234–35; Welles, *Diary*, III, 102.

24. Richardson, *Messages and Papers*, VI, 551; Rhodes, *History of the United States*, VI, 78; Cox, *Three Decades*, 544–45.

25. Welles, *Diary*, 93–110; Oberholtzer, *History of the United States*, I, 458.

26. Richardson, *Messages and Papers*, VI, 552–56; Welles, *Diary*, III, 117; Rhodes, *History of the United States*, VI, 63; Cox, *Three Decades*, 546.

27. *Cong. Globe*, 40 Cong., 1 Sess., 500; DeWitt, *Impeachment*, 237.

28. Blaine, *Twenty Years*, II, 294; Burgess, *Reconstruction*, 138–39.

29. Richardson, *Messages and Papers*, VI, 537, 539–40.

30. Ibid. 544; Blaine, *Twenty Years*, II, 295–96.

31. Blaine, *Twenty Years*, II, 296; Sumner, *Works of Sumner*, XI, 421–22, 424.

32. Blaine, *Twenty Years*, II, 296; Welles, *Diary*, III, 123.

Chapter 13

1. Welles, *Diary*, III, 127, 146, 150–52: Richardson, *Messages and Papers*, VI, 584.

2. Rhodes, *History of the United States,* V, 159; Welles,*Diary,* III, 143–44, 157; De-Witt, *Impeachment,* 279–81.

3. Richardson, *Messages and Papers,* VI, 584; Welles, *Diary,* III, 157.

4. Welles, *Diary,* III, 167.

5. McPherson, *Political History,* 307; *Trial,* III, 53; Grant to Johnson, August 1, 1867, Johnson Papers, LC.

6. Welles, *Diary,* III, 155–56; William S. McFeely, *Grant: A Biography* (New York: W. W. Norton & Company, 1981), 262.

7. Richardson, *Messages and Papers,* VI, 583–84; McPherson, *Political History,* 261–62; William G. Moore, "Notes of Colonel Moore," *American Historical Review,* 19 (October, 1913), 107–9; Browning, *Diary,* II, 154–56; Moore Diary, August 11, 12, 1867, 39–45, Johnson Papers, LC.

8. Welles, *Diary,* III, 167; Rhodes, *History of the United States,* VI, 66, 384; Horace White to E. B. Washburne, August 13, 1867, Washburne Papers, LC.

9. Welles, *Diary,* III, 177, 180–81.

10. Cox, *Three Decades,* 547; Richardson, *Messages and Papers,* VI, 556, 557; Welles, *Diary,* III, 187: Moore Diary, August 17–29, 1867, Johnson Papers, LC.

11. Welles, *Diary,* III, 188; Moore Diary, August 24, 1867, 48, Johnson Papers, LC; Moore, "Notes of Colonel Moore," 111–12.

12. Richardson, *Messages and Papers,* VI., 557; Welles, *Diary,* III, 182, 185; Chase to Garfield, August 7, 1867, Garfield Papers, LC.

13. Welles, *Diary,* III, 186.

14. Welles, *Diary,* III, 234, 235.

15. Ibid. 234–35.

16. *New York World,* September 24, 1867.

17. McPherson, *Political History,* 373; Rhodes, *History of the United States,* VI, 95; Thorndike, *Sherman Letters,* 299.

18. Myrta Lockett Avary, *Dixie After the War* (New York: Doubleday Page & Company, 1906), 253–55.

19. H. H. Jacobs to John Sherman, October 9, 1867, Sherman Papers, LC; J. Glancey Jones to Thaddeus Stevens, November 26, 1867, Stevens Papers, LC; Colfax to Garfield, September 11, 1867, Garfield Papers, LC; Fessenden to McCulloch, September 2, 1867, McCulloch Papers, LC.

20. Blaine, *Twenty Years,* II, 343, 345; Welles, *Diary,* III, 238–39; DeWitt, *Impeach-ment,* 290–91; *New York World,* November 22, 1867.

21. *Impeachment Investigation,* House Reports, 40th Cong., 1st Sess., no. 7, 1166–1208: Blaine, *Twenty Years,* II, 345; DeWitt, *Impeachment,* 298, 303–8.

22. Moore, "Notes of Colonel Moore," *American Historical Review,* 19 (October 1913), 113; John Tyler to Johnson, November 26, 1867, Johnson Papers, LC; Benedict, *Impeachment and Trial,* 73–74.

23. Welles, *Diary,* III, 237–38; Browning, *Diary,* II, 167–68; Moore Diary, November 30, 1867, Johnson Papers, LC.

24. Richardson, *Messages and Papers,* VI, 559–60.

25. Ibid. 563–64.

26. Ibid. 568.

27. Ibid. 568–69.

28. Ibid. 569.

29. DeWitt, *Impeachment,* 311–12.

30. Theodore Clarke Smith, ed. *Life and Letters of James Abram Garfield,* 2 vols. (New Haven: Yale University Press, 1925), I, 423; *New York Herald,* July 8, 1867; Blaine, *Twenty Years,* II, 346; *Cong. Globe,* 40 Cong., 2 Sess., 1560.

31. Blaine, *Twenty Years,* II, 349.

32. Moore, "Notes of Colonel Moore," 113–14; Thomas Ewing to Johnson, November 28, 1867, Johnson Papers, LC; *The New Orleans Riot,* House Exec. Doc. 68, 39th Cong., 2nd Sess., 4–5; Richardson, *Messages and Papers* VI, 588–94; Welles, *Diary,* III, 240.

33. Blaine, *Twenty Years,* II, 349; George C. Gorham, *Life and Public Services of Edwin M. Stanton.* 2 vols. (Boston: Houghton Mifflin Company, 1899), II, 412–26; Stanton to E. L. Stanton, December 26, 27, 1867, Pratt Collection, Columbia University; DeWitt, *Impeachment,* 315.

34. John Binney to Fessenden, December 30, 1867, Fessenden Papers, LC.

Chapter 14

1. Welles, *Diary,* III, 158, 246–49; *Intelligencer,* January 11, 1868; Gorham, *Stanton,* II, 413–26; Grant to Fessenden, December 30, 1867, Fessenden Papers, LC. See also documents in *Removal of Hon. E. M. Stanton and Others,* House Exec. Doc. 57, 40th Cong., 2d Sess.

2. Moore, "Notes of Colonel Moore," 114–15; McPherson, *Political History*, 284.

3. McPherson, *Political History*, 285.

4. DeWitt, *Reconstruction*, 321; *Trial*, I. 155; Moore, "Notes of Colonel Moore," 114–15; McPherson, Political History, 262, 284–86; Sherman, *Memoirs*, II, 421–26; Sherman to Grant, January 27, 1868, James G. Blaine Papers, LC.

5. Sherman, *Memoirs*, II, 420; McPherson, *Political History*, 262; William G. Moore Diary, January 14, 1868, 69; Johnson Papers, LC; Thomas and Hyman, *Stanton*, 569–70.

6. Welles, *Diary*, III, 259–61; McPherson, *Political History*, 289–91; Moore Diary, January 14, 1868, 69–70, Johnson Papers, LC; Browning, *Diary*, II, 173–75.

7. Moore Diary, January 15, 1868, 70–71; Johnson Papers, LC; *New York World*, January 16, 1868; Browning, *Diary*, II, 175–76; Sherman, *Home Letters*, 371; Sherman, *Memoirs*, II, 423–24.

8. Sherman, *Memoirs*, II, 425–26; McPherson, *Political History*, II, 286; Welles, *Diary*, III, 263.

9. Moore Diary, 117, Johnson Papers, LC; McPherson, *Political History*, 283–84, 286; John M. Schofield, *Forty-Six Years in the Army* (New York: Century Company, 1897), 413; Blaine, *Twenty Years*, II,351–52.

10. Donn Piatt, *Memories of the Men Who Saved the Union* (New York: Bedford Clarke & Company, 1887), 78, 83, 85; Thomas and Hyman, *Stanton*, 66.

11. McPherson, *Political History*, 283–84; Grant to Johnson, January 24, 28, 1868, and Moore Diary, 74–76, Johnson Papers, LC.

12. Moore Diary, 73, Johnson Papers, LC; Moore, *Notes of Colonel Moore*, 117.

13. Moore Diary, 77–78; Johnson Papers, LC; McPherson, *Political History*, 284.

14. *Cong. Globe*, 40 Cong. 2 Sess., 977; Stanton to Colfax, February 4, 1868, Sec. War, Reports to Congress, XI, 105, RG 107, NA.

15. Moore Diary, 79–89, Johnson Papers, LC; *Correspondence — Grant and the President*, House Exec. Doc. 149, 40 Cong., 2d Sess.; Richardson, *Messages and Papers*, VI, 602–20; Welles, *Diary*, III, 269–73, 282; McPherson, *Political History*, 282–86; *New York World*, February 12, 1868.

16. Johnson to Grant, February 10, 1868, Johnson Papers, LC.

17. *New York World*, February 18, 1868.

18. William S. Hillyer to Johnson, January 14, 1868, Johnson Papers, LC; Lloyd Lewis, *Sherman, Fighting Prophet* (New York: Harcourt, Brace & Company), 1932, 592–93.

19. Moore, "Notes of Colonel Moore," 114–15; Sherman to Johnson, January 27, 29, 31, February 14, 1868, Johnson to Sherman, February 18, 1868, Johnson Papers, LC; *Trial*, I, 529; Sherman, *Home Letters*, 361, 368–70.

20. Sherman, *Home Letters*, 361.

21. Welles, *Diary*, III, 276–77; McPherson., *Political History*, 282.

22. Welles, *Diary*, III, 279–80; Faust, *HTI*, 754; *Trial*, I, 248, 415–16, 433–35.

23. *Trial*, I, 248, II, 334, 337; *Constitution*, Article II, Section 2.

24. *Trial*, I, 418–19.

25. Ibid. 419, 675; Welles, *Diary*, III, 284.

26. Richardson, *Messages and Papers*, VI, 621; Welles, *Diary*, III, 53, 285; *Cong. Globe*, 40 Cong. 2 Sess., 1329–30; *Trial*, I 156–57.

27. Welles, *Diary*, III, 290; *Trial*, I, 159, 210.

28. *Trial*, I, 625.

29. Ibid. 159, 663, 704–706; Welles, *Diary*, III, 289.

30. *Trial*, I, 509, 515–16; Welles, *Diary*, III, 286.

31. *Trial*, I, 427–28, 516, 617.

32. Ibid. 232–33, 428; Rhodes, *History of the United States*, VI, 112.

33. *Trial*, I, 429.

34. Welles, *Diary*, III, 289; Stryker, *Andrew Johnson*, 569.

35. Welles, *Diary*, III, 289; *Trial*, I, 234–35, 249–52.

36. *Trial*, I, 619–20.

37. Ibid. 605.

38. Ibid. 537, 556–57, 625.

Chapter 15

1. Rhodes, *History of the United States*, VI, 96; Thomas and Hyman, *Stanton*, 566; Horace White, *The Life of Lyman Trumball* (Boston: Houghton Mifflin Company, 1913), 327.

2. White, *Life of Trumball*, 327.

3. Warren, *Supreme Court*, III, 187.

4. Ibid. 189; See exchanges on the Mc-Cardle case between Grant, Ord, Stanton, and Stanbery, December 31, 1867, to January 30, 1868, in Adjutant General's Office, File 670220, NA; Browning, *Diary*, II, 169; Welles, *Diary*, III, 255–57.

5. DeWitt, *Impeachment*, 358: Oberholtzer, *History of the United States*, II, 72.

6. DeWitt, *Impeachment*, 359; Georges Clemenceau, *American Reconstruction, 1865–1870*, Fernand Baldensperger, ed. (New York: DaCapo, 1969), 153–54; *Cong. Globe*, 40 Cong., 2 Sess., 1336.

7. *Cong. Globe*, 40 Cong., 2 Sess., 1336–69, 1382–84, Appen, 247; Milton Lomask, *Andrew Johnson, President on Trial* (New York: Farrar, Strauss and Cudahy, 1960), 270–74.

8. *Cong. Globe*, 40 Cong., 2 Sess., 1400; Welles, *Diary*, III, 300. Seventeen House members did not vote.

9. *Trial* I, 2, 3, 5; *New York Tribune*, February 26, 1868.

10. *Cong. Globe*, 40 Cong., 2 Sess., 1542–68, 1612–13; *Trial*, II, 362; Stevens to Butler, February 28, 1868, Butler Papers, LC; DeWitt, *Impeachment*, 379–86; Rhodes, *History of the United States*, VI, 116. For all eleven articles, see *Trial*, I, 6–10.

11. *Trial*, I, 4; *Cong. Globe*, 40 Cong., 2 Sess., 1618–19, 1638–42; *Chicago Tribune*, March 5, 1862.

12. *Trial*, II, 11–16; *New York Tribune*, March 7, 1868.

13. *Trial*, I, 5; *New York Tribune*, March 5, 1868.

14. Welles, *Diary*, III, 301.

15. *Trial*, I, 606, 609; Welles, *Diary*, III, 293; Rehnquist, *Grand Inquests*, 265–68.

16. Gorham, *Life of Stanton*, II, 442–44; Grant, *Memoirs*, II, 537; Welles, *Diary*, III, 297.

17. Welles, *Diary*, III, 297.

18. See dozens of letters to Johnson dated from February 25 to March 20 in Johnson Papers, LC.

19. John Sherman, *Recollections of Forty Years in the House, Senate and Cabinet, an Autobiography*. 2 vols. (Chicago: Werner Company, 1895), I, 423–24; W. T. Sherman to John Sherman, February 25, John Sherman to W. T. Sherman, March 1, 1868, John Sherman Papers, LC.

20. *Trial*, I, 6; *New York Tribune*, March 5, 6, 1868.

21. Welles, *Diary*, III, 239; Oberholtzer, *History of the United States*, II, 92–93; Warren, *Supreme Court*, 170–71; *Cong. Globe*, 40 Cong., 2 Sess., 1353, 1387; Rhodes, *History of the United States*, VI, 113.

22. *Trial*, I, 6; *New York Tribune*, March 5, 1868.

23. Warren, *Impeachment*, III, 195.

24. *New York Tribune*, March 6, 1868; *Trial*, I, 11.

25. *Trial*, I, 12; Lord Macauley, *Miscellaneous Works of Lord Macauley*, Lady Trevelyan, ed. 5 vols. (New York: Harper & Brothers, 1879), III, 257.

26. *Trial*, III, 360–401.

27. Welles, *Diary*, III, 302–3.

28. Ibid. 303; Moore, "Notes of Colonel Moore," 124.

29. Stryker, *Andrew Johnson*, 597.

30. Welles, *Diary*, III, 51, 205.

31. Rhodes, *History of the United States*, VI, 135; Oberholtzer, *History of the United States*, II, 90.

32. Oberholtzer, *History of the United States*, II, 90.

33. *Trial*, I, 10.

34. Moore, "Diary of Colonel Moore," 123, 125–26.

35. Warren, *Supreme Court*, III, 195, 198–99, 203 n.2; *New York Herald*, March 14, 1868.

36. *Trial*, I, 363, 555; Welles, *Diary*, III, 311.

Chapter 16

1. *New York Tribune*, March 14, 1868.

2. *Cong. Globe*, 40 Cong., 2 Sess., 2897; Sumner, *Works of Sumner*, XII, 349–50, 383; Milton, *Age of Hate*, 471.

3. *New York Tribune*, March 14, 1868; *Trial*, I, 18.

4. *Trial*, I, 18; *New York Tribune*, March 14, 1868.

5. *Trial*, I, 19–20.

6. Ibid. 20–24; *New York Tribune*, March 14, 1868.

7. *Trial*, I, 25–34; Welles, *Diary*, III, 313–14; Butler, *Butler's Book*, 929.

8. Rhodes, *History of the United States*, VI, 95–96.

9. *Trial*, II, 144–45; Welles, *Diary*, III, 305, 316.

10. Stryker, *Andrew Johnson*, 829–30; *Trial*, II, 266; White, *Life of Trumball*, 327.

11. Welles, *Diary*, III, 302 n.1; *Trial*, I, 34.

12. *Trial*, I, 37–53.

13. Ibid. 69–86.

14. Welles, *Diary*, III, 324.

15. Richardson, *Messages and Papers*, VI, 647–48; McPherson, *Political History*, 351.

16. *Trial*, I, 87–88.

17. *Trial*, I, 88–89.

18. Ibid. 89–90.

19. Ibid. 96–97.

20. Ibid. I, 103, III, 53.

21. Ibid. I, 110–11, III, 346.

22. DeWitt, *Impeachment*, 414–15; *Trial*, I, 116–17.

23. Welles, *Diary*, III, 81–82.

24. *Trial*, I, 121–22.

25. Ibid. 147–48, 154–55.

26. Oberholtzer, *History of the United States*, II, 98 n.2; Welles, *Diary*, III, 326.

27. *Trial*, I, 155–58.

28. *Trial*, I, 185.

29. *Trial*, I, 186–87.

30. Ibid. 206, 228–30; DeWitt, *Impeachment*, 394.

31. *New York Tribune*, April 3, 1868.

32. *Trial*, I, 233–39.

33. Ibid. 241–47.

34. Ibid. 253–68.

35. Ibid. I, 271–76.

36. Welles, *Diary*, III, 320; *New York Tribune*, April 3, 1868.

37. *Trial*, I, 278–369 passim.

38. *Trial*, I, 367, 371.

Chapter 17

1. *Trial*, I, 372; *New York Tribune*, April 10, 1868.

2. *Trial*, I 377.

3. Ibid. 379–84.

4. Ibid. 386–87.

5. Ibid. 390.

6. Ibid. 396–97.

7. Ibid. 401–3.

8. Ibid. 405–6.

9. Ibid. 406–8.

10. Ibid. 409–13.

11. Both quoted in Stryker, *Andrew Johnson*, 652.

12. *Trial*, I, 414–62.

13. Ibid. 462–81.

14. Ibid. 485, 487, 488, 489–90, 493–501.

15. Ibid. 510–17.

16. Ibid. 517–29.

17. *New York Tribune*, April 15, 1868; Welles, *Diary*, III, 331, 332.

18. *Trial*, I, 537–38, 545; Richardson, *Messages and Papers*, VI, 622–27.

19. *Trial*, I, 595–628.

20. Ibid. I, 628–34; Welles, *Diary*, III, 333.

21. *Trial*, I, 634–53.

22. Ibid. 663–701; Rhodes, *History of the United States*, VI, 125; Warden, *Salmon Chase*, 684–85; Welles, *Diary*, III, 333.

23. *Trial*, III, 304.

24. William H. Crook, *Memoirs of the White House*. Henry Rood, ed. (Boston: Little, Brown & Company, 1911), 45, 48–49; William H. Crook, "Andrew Johnson in the White House, being the Reminiscences of Col. W. H. Crook," compiled and written by Margarita S. Gerry, *Century Magazine*, vol. 76, no. 5 (September 1908), 655, 659.

25. Moore, "Diary of Colonel Moore," 127, 130; Crook, "Andrew Johnson Reminiscences," 655.

26. Rhodes, *History of the United States*, VI, 145; Cox, *Three Decades*, 592; Welles, *Diary*, III, 336–37; John B. Henderson, "Emancipation and Impeachment," *Century Magazine*, vol. 95, no. 2 (December 1922), 205, 207.

27. Smith, *Life and Letters of Garfield*, I, 425.

28. Schofield, *Forty-Six Years*, 413–14.

29. Ibid. 415–18.

Chapter 18

1. *New York Tribune*, April 20, 21, 22, 1868; *Trial*, II,14–66.

2. *Trial*, II, 67–81.

3. Ibid. 81–116.

4. *Trial*, II, 119–21.

5. Ibid. 124–27.

6. Ibid. 146–87.

7. Welles, *Diary*, III, 337; *New York Tribune*, April 25, 1868.

8. *Trial*, II, 192, 206–7.

9. Ibid. 214–15.

10. Ibid. 216.

11. Ibid. 217.

12. Oberholtzer, *History of the United States*, II, 111–12; Welles, *Diary*, III, 338; De-Witt, *Impeachment*, 480–81; *New York Tribune*, April 15, 1868.

13. Schofield, *Forty-Six Years*, 418.

14. *Trial*, I, 634; *New York Tribune*, April 25, 1868.

15. *Trial*, II, 219; Welles, *Diary*, III, 340–41; *New York Herald*, May 17, 1868.

16. *Trial*, II, 219, 223, 225; Sumner, *Works of Sumner*, XII, 320–23.

17. Ibid. 249–62; Welles, *Diary*, III, 239.

18. *New York Tribune*, April 30, 1868; *Trial*, II, 144–45, 263–68.

19. Rhodes, *History of the United States*, VI, 135.

20. *Trial*, II, 273–78; Sumner, *Works of Sumner*, XII, 320–23.

21. *Trial*, II, 264, 280–84.

22. *Trial*, II, 304.

23. Ibid. 306–7.

24. Ibid. 308–28.

25. Ibid. 355–59: Welles, *Diary*, III, 342.

26. *Trial*, II, 389; Welles, *Diary*, III, 274; *New York Tribune*, May 5, 1868; *New York World*, May 4, 1868.

27. Oberholtzer, *History of the United States*, II, 120–21; *Trial*, II, 390–91; Rhodes, *History of the United States*, VI, 139.

28. *Trial*, II, 468–73.

29. Ibid. II, 479, III, 11, 247; DeWitt, *Impeachment*, 482; Welles, *Diary*, III, 351.

30. *Trial*, III, 16–31, 319–28, 328–40; Welles, *Diary*, III, 351; Morrill to Fessenden, May 10, 1868, Fessenden Papers, LC; Parker, *Life and Public Services of Morrill*, 211.

Chapter 19

1. *New York Tribune*, May 6, 7, 1868.

2. Donald, *Charles Sumner*, 334; Rhodes, *History of the United States*, VI, 174; DeWitt, *Impeachment*, 518.

3. DeWitt, *Impeachment*, 521.

4. Ibid. 525–26; John B. Henderson to Carl Schurz, May 1, 1868, Schurz Papers. LC.

5. Trefousse, *Andrew Johnson*, 332.

6. *Trial*, II, 482–84.

7. Welles, *Diary*, III, 357; DeWitt, *Impeachment*, 528–30.

8. McCulloch, *Men and Measures*, 403; DeWitt, *Impeachment*, 531–33.

9. *New York Tribune*, May 13, 1868; Welles, *Diary*, III, 353.

10. DeWitt, *Impeachment*, 537, 539–40.

11. Ibid. 541, 543–44.

12. *New York Tribune*, May 15, 1868.

13. *New York World*, May 12, 1868.

14. Welles, *Diary*, III, 357; Schuckers, *Life of Chase*, 559 n.1.

15. DeWitt, *Impeachment*, 544–45.

16. *Trial*, II, 484–85.

17. Ibid. 485; Salter, *Life of Grimes*, 357; Oberholtzer, *History of the United States*, II, 131.

18. *Trial*, II, 486; Julian, *Political Recollections*, 316; Crook, *Memoirs*, 67.

19. *Trial*, II, 486.

20. *Trial*, II, 486–7; Blaine, *Twenty Years*, II, 374; Julian, *Political Recollections*, 317.

21. *Trial*, II, 486–87.

22. Crook, "Andrew Johnson in the White House," *Century Magazine*, vol. 76, no. 6 (October 1908), 870; Crook, *Memoirs*, 66–67.

23. *Trial*, II, 487–89.

24. *New York Tribune*, May 18, 1868.

25. Stanwood, *History of the Presidency*, I, 319; Donald, *Charles Sumner*, 338, 339; *New York Tribune*, May 22, 1868.

26. Stanwood, *History of the Presidency*, I, 318–19; Blaine, *Twenty Years*, II, 388.

27. Blaine, *Twenty Years*, II, 389–90; Stanwood, *History of the Presidency*, I, 321; Rhodes, *History of the United States*, V, 13–15.

28. DeWitt, *Impeachment*, 567; Welles, *Diary*, III, 362–66.

29. DeWitt, *Impeachment*, 560–62, 569.

30. Ibid. 571; Welles, *Diary*, III, 367–69; *New York Tribune*, May 25, 1868.

31. *Trial*, II, 495; Welles, *Diary*, III, 368.

32. *Trial*, II, 491, 495–97.

33. Ibid. 497.

34. Welles, *Diary*, III, 353. 394; Oberholtzer, *History of the United States*, II, 133, 136; White, *Life of Trumbull*, 315, 322, 326; Salter, *Life of Grimes*, 358.

35. Julian, *Political Recollections*, 318; Blaine, *Twenty Years*, II, 376; Henderson, "Emancipation and Impeachment," *Century Magazine*, vol. 95, no. 2 (December, 1922), 209; Sherman, *Recollections of Forty Years*, I, 432; Parker, *Life and Public Services of Morrill*, 213.

36. White, *Life of Trumbull*, 321.

37. Gorham, *Life of Stanton*, II, 456–57; Schofield, *Forty-Six Years*, 418; McPherson, *Political History*, 350.

38. Blaine, *Twenty Years*, II, 384.

Chapter 20

1. Rhodes, *History of the United States*, VI, 162–63; Stryker, *Andrew Johnson*, 737; Robert B. Warden, *An Account of the Private Life and Public Services of Samuel Portland Chase* (Cincinnati: Wilstach, Baldwin & Company, 1874), 677–7, 683; Schukers, *Life of Chase*, 586.

2. Welles, *Diary*, III, 394.

3. Blaine, *Twenty Years*, II, 392; Oberholtzer, *History of the United States*, II, 165; Rhodes, *History of the United States*, IV, 283, V, 571, 585, 626; *Trial*, III, 361–401; Stanwood, *History of the Presidency*, I, 325.

4. Blaine, *Twenty Years*, II, 397; Richardson, *Messages and Papers*, VI, 655–56; Burgess, *Reconstruction*, 213; Stanwood, *History of the Presidency*, I, 322–25.

5. Oberholtzer, *History of the United States*, II, 166, 173–75; Welles, *Diary*, III, 397.

6. *New York Tribune*, July 8, 1868; Stanwood, *History of the Presidency*, I, 325; Welles, *Diary*, III, 397.

7. Blaine, *Twenty Years*, II, 402; Rhodes, *History of the United States*, VI, 167; Stanwood, *History of the Presidency*, I, 325; Welles, *Diary*, III, 400.

8. Rhodes, *History of the United States*, IV, 325, VI, 167; Oberholtzer, *History of the United States*, 179–80.

9. Blaine, *Twenty Years*, II, 404.

10. Ibid. 406; Rhodes, *History of the United States*, VI, 175–77; McPherson, *Political History*, 336–37; Trefousse, *Thaddeus Stevens*, 236.

11. Richardson, *Messages and Papers*, VI, 648; Burgess, *Reconstruction*, 202.

12. Burgess, *Reconstruction*, 197, 202; Grant, *Memoirs*, II, 491–92; McPherson, *Political History*, 380; Cox, *Three Decades*, 257.

13. Richardson, *Messages and Papers*, VI, 651–52; McPherson, *Political History*, 379.

14. Rhodes, *History of the United States*, VI, 178–79.

15. Pierce, *Memoir and Letters*, IV, 360, 361; *Cong. Globe*, 40 Cong., 2 Sess., 3786,

4473–74; Julian, *Political Recollections*, 313–14; Crook, "Reminiscences," *Century Magazine*, vol. 76, no. 6 (October 1908), 871; Forney, *Anecdotes*, I, 37; Woodburn, *Life of Stevens*, 586; Trefousse, *Thaddeus Stevens*, 239–41.

16. Welles, *Diary*, III, 403, 405, 411; James Schouler, *History of the United States Under the Constitution*. 7 vols. (New York: Dodd, Mead & Company, 1880–1913), VII, 125–26.

17. Rhodes, *History of the United States*, VI, 180, 181, 185, 190–92.

18. Ibid. 194; Oberholtzer, *History of the United States*, II, 184–85, 194.

19. Benjamin C. Truman, "Anecdotes of Andrew Johnson," *Century Magazine*, vol. 81, no. 1 (January 1913), 439, 440.

20. Welles, *Diary*, III, 440, 445.

21. Oberholtzer, *History of the United States*, II, 191–92; *New York World*, October 15, 1868; Blaine, *Twenty Years*, II, 405; Welles, *Diary*, III, 455, 457, 459.

22. Stanwood, *History of the Presidency*, II, 328; Burgess, *Reconstruction*, 212.

23. Richardson, *Messages and Papers*, VI, 672–91; Archelaus N. Hughes, "Remarkable Career of Andrew Johnson," *Nashville Banner*, December 18, 1927.

24. Oberholtzer, *History of the United States*, II, 200; *New York Tribune*, December 10, 1868.

25. Richardson, *Messages and Papers*, VI, 708; McPherson, *Political History*, 420.

26. Crook, *Memoirs*, 70–71; Frank Cowan, *Andrew Johnson, President of the United States, Reminiscences of his Private Life and Character* (Greensburgh, PA: Oliver Publishing House, 1894), 6.

27. Welles, *Diary*, III, 496–97; Crook, *Through Five Administrations*, 97.

28. Welles, *Diary*, III, 503–4; Oberholtzer, *History of the United States*, II, 204; Blaine, *Twenty Years*, II, 455; Hoar, *Autobiography*, II, 137–38.

29. Rhodes, *History of the United States*, VI, 202.

30. Welles, *Diary*, III, 536, 538; Burgess, *Reconstruction*, 218.

31. Welles, *Diary*, III, 537, 542.

32. Ibid. 540–42.

33. Ibid. 542.

34. Ibid. 544; Richardson, *Messages and Papers*, VII, 6.

35. Oberholtzer, *History of the United States*, II, 209; Welles, *Diary*, III, 542.

Chapter 21

1. Crook, *Memoirs*, 73; Jones, *Life of Johnson*, 334–35; Truman, "Anecdotes of Andrew Johnson," *Century Magazine*, vol. 81, no. 1 (January 1913), 440.

2. Oberholtzer, *History of the United States*, II, 215–18; Richardson, *Messages and Papers*, VII, 8; Blaine, *Twenty Years*, II, 426; Adams, *Education of Henry Adams*, 263; White, *Life of Trumbull*, 333; McCulloch, *Men and Measures*, 351.

3. Rhodes, *History of the United States*, IV, 302, VI, 240; Charles A. Dana, *Recollections of the Civil War* (New York: D. Appleton & Company, 1899), 62, 72–73.

4. McCulloch, *Men and Measures*, 349–50; Welles, *Diary*, III, 543; Oberholtzer, *History of the United States*, II, 216.

5. Jones, *Life of Johnson*, 335–46.

6. Herbert, *Why the Solid South?*, 193, 198.

7. Ibid. 195–96.

8. Ibid. 190, 195, 199.

9. Ibid. 214–15; Temple, *Notable Men*, 183, 441–42; DeWitt, *Impeachment*, 616–17.

10. Milton, *Age of Hate*, 660; E. C. Reeves Statement, Johnson Papers, TSLA; *New York Times*, October 20, 22, 23, 1869; Trefousse, *Andrew Johnson*, 357–58.

11. McPherson, *Political History*, 408–9; Rhodes, *History of the United States*, VI, 286; Blaine, *Twenty Years*, II, 447–48; Sumner, *Works of Sumner*, XIII, 336–38.

12. Rhodes, *History of the United States*, VII, 156; Cox, *Three Decades*, 625; Walter L. Fleming, *The Sequel of Appomattox* (New Haven: Yale University Press, 1920), 236–37.

13. Fleming, *Sequel of Appomattox*, 240; Rhodes, *History of the United States*, VI, 390; E. C. Reeves Statement, Johnson Papers, TSLA; Stanwood, *History of the Presidency*, I, 341–42.

14. Rhodes, *History of the United States*, VI, 412; Stanwood, *History of the Presidency*, I, 345, 349; Blaine, *Twenty Years*, II, 528; Oberholtzer, *History of the United States*, III, 51; Pierce, *Memoir and Letters*, IV, 423.

15. Blaine, *Twenty Years*, 535; Julian, *Political Recollections*, 352.

16. E. C. Reeves Statement in Johnson Papers, TSLA; Stryker, *Andrew Johnson*, 804; Jones, *Life of Johnson*, 348; Harriet S. Turner, "Recollections of Andrew Johnson," *Harper's Monthly*, no. 120 (January 1910), 168–76.

17. Rhodes, *History of the United States*, VII, 2–17; Hoar, *Autobiography*, I, 314–23. For a history of the Credit Mobilier, see Edward Winslow Martin, *Behind the Scenes in Washington, Being a Complete and Graphic Account of the Credit Mobilier Investigation* (Washington: Continental Publishing Company, 1873).

18. *New York Times*, July 24, 1873; Johnson's Statement, June 23, 1873, and Johnson to Dr. Basil Norris, July 12, 1874, Johnson Papers, LC.

19. Trefousse, *Andrew Johnson*, 364–65. In the 1866 elections, Cooke had supported the Radicals, hopeful that money could be obtained from Congress to support the bank's private enterprises.

20. Rhodes, *History of the United States*, VII, 68.

21. Temple, *Notable Men*, 440–41; E. C. Reeves Statement in Johnson Papers, TSLA.

22. *Journal of the House of Representatives of Tennessee*, 1st Sess., 39th General Assembly (Nashville: 1875), 106, 115–37, 142–83; Temple, *Notable Men*, 440–42; *New York Herald*, January 26, 27, 1875.

23. Temple, *Notable Men*, 447; *New York Times*, January 27, 1875, Johnson Papers, LC.

24. E. C. Reeves Statement in Johnson Papers, TSLA; Temple, *Notable Men*, 442; *Journal of the House of Representatives of Tennessee*, 1st Sess., 39th Gen. Assy., 188–93, 199–201; Stryker, *Andrew Johnson*, 834.

25. E. C. Reeves Statement in Johnson Papers, LC; Trefousse, *Andrew Johnson*, 372; Temple, *Notable Men*, 442; Stryker, *Andrew Johnson*, 807–8, 834; *New York Times*, January 27, 1875.

26. *New York Herald*, January 27, 1875; Jones, *Life of Johnson*, 353; Welles to Johnson, January 25, 1875, Johnson Papers, LC.

27. *New York Herald*, January 27, 1875; Truman, "Anecdotes," *Century Magazine*, vol. 81, no. 1 (January 1913), 440.

28. *Trial*, III, 218; Crook, "Andrew Johnson in the White House," *Century Magazine*, vol. 76, no. 6, (October 1908), 877; Hamlin, *Life of Hamlin*, 509–10; *Cong. Record*,

44 Cong., Special Session, 4; New York *Herald*, March 8, 1875.

29. *New York Tribune*, March 5, 6, 1875; E. C. Reeves Statement in Johnson Papers, LC.

30. Boutwell, *Reminiscences*, II, 106; *New York Tribune*, March 6, 1875.

31. *New York Tribune*, March 8, 1875; *New York Herald*, March 8, 1875; Crook, "Andrew Johnson in the White House," *Century Magazine*, vol. 76, no. 6, (October 1908), 877; Donald, *Charles Sumner*, 585–86; Salter, *Life of Grimes*, 387.

32. Herbert, *Why the Solid South?*, 397, 401, 429; Oberholtzer, *History of the United States*, III, 230; Rhodes, *History of the United States*, VII, 105.

33. Oberholtzer, *History of the United States*, III, 230–32; Burgess, *Reconstruction*, 269–71; Rhodes, *History of the United States*, VII, 109–11, 232–33; Herbert, *Why the Solid South?*, 414.

34. Richardson, *Messages and Papers*, VII, 212, 221, 224; Rhodes, *History of the United States*, VII, 112–13.

35. Oberholtzer, *History of the United States*, III, 235–38; Richardson, *Messages and Papers*, VII, 276, 309.

36. Rhodes, *History of the United States*, VII, 119–22; Oberholtzer, *History of the United States*, III, 240.

37. Richardson, *Messages and Papers*, VII, 307; *Cong. Record*, 44 Cong., Special Session, 121–27.

Chapter 22

1. DeWitt, *Impeachment*, 628.

2. Ibid. 629; Jones, *Life of Johnson*, 371; Stryker, *Andrew Johnson*, 823–24, 836; Richardson, *Messages and Papers*, VII, 330–31.

3. Statement of E. C. Reeves, Johnson Papers, TSLA; Trefousse, *Andrew Johnson*, 378; Johnson to Dr. Basil Norris, July 12, 1874, Johnson Papers, LC.

4. *New York Herald*, May 25, 1865; Winston, *Andrew Johnson*, 239; McCulloch, *Men and Measures*, 377.

5. Dunning, *Reconstruction*, 19; Crook, *Through Five Administrations*, 84, 85; Adams, *Education of Henry Adams*, 24–25.

6. Cox, *Three Decades*, 240.

Bibliography

Columbia University Library, Special Collections, Edwin M. Stanton Papers in the Pratt Collection

Historical Society of Pennsylvania, Philadelphia, Salmon P. Chase Papers, Thaddeus Stevens Papers

Huntington Library, Harvard University, Cambridge, Mass., William T. Sherman Papers

Indiana Historical Society, Indianapolis, George W. Julian Papers

Library of Congress, Washington, DC, Jeremiah S. Black Papers, James G. Blaine Papers, Benjamin F. Butler Papers, Salmon P. Chase Papers, William Pitt Fessenden Papers, James A. Garfield Papers, Herndon-Weik Papers, Ulysses S. Grant Papers, Andrew Johnson Papers, Abraham Lincoln Papers, Robert T. Lincoln Collection, Hugh McCulloch Papers, Edward McPherson Papers, William G. Moore Diary in Andrew Johnson Papers, Carl Schurz Papers, John Sherman Papers, William T. Sherman Papers, Edwin M. Stanton Papers, Thaddeus Stevens Papers, Charles Sumner Papers, Lyman Trumbull Papers, Benjamin F. Wade Papers, Elihu B. Washburne Papers, Gideon Welles Papers

National Archives, Washington, DC, Record Group 37, Select Commission on Impeachment Papers; Record Group 59, Andrew Johnson Impeachment, Pardons; Record Group 60, Andrew Johnson Letters, Abraham Lincoln Letters; Record Group 94, Adjutant General's Office, File 670220; Record Group 107, Secretary of War Reports to Congress, Vol. 11; Record Group 108, Secret Circular in Box 102 Issued by Grant and Stanton to Military Commanders in the South; Record Group 132, Andrew Johnson Papers, Abraham Lincoln Papers; Record Group 233, Andrew Johnson Impeachment

New York Historical Society, New York, NY, Salmon P. Chase "Diary"

New York Public Library, New York, NY, Horace Greeley Papers

Newberry Library, Chicago, Illinois, Orville E. Babcock Papers

Tennessee State Library and Archives, Nashville, Andrew Johnson Papers

Official Documents and Records

Journal of the House of Representatives of the State of Tennessee at the 21st General Assembly. Knoxville: 1836.

Journal of the House of Representatives of Tennessee, 1st Sess., 39th General Assembly. Nashville: 1875.

"Report of Carl Schurz on the States of South Carolina, Georgia, Alabama, Mississippi, and Louisiana," *Sen. Exec. Doc. No. 2, 39 Cong., 1 Sess., 2-105.*

U. S. Congress. *Congressional Globe.*

U. S. Congress. *Congressional Record.*

U. S. Congress. House. *Correspondence — Grant and the President,* House Exec. Doc. 149, 40 Cong., 2d Sess.

U. S. Congress, House Exec. Doc., 39 Cong., 1 Sess., no. 70.

U. S. Congress. House. *Impeachment Investigation,* 40th Cong., 1st Sess., Exec. Doc. 7.

U. S. Congress. House. *The New Orleans Riot,* 39th Cong., 2nd Sess., Exec. Doc. 68.

U. S. Congress. House. *Removal of Hon. E. M. Stanton and Others,* 40th Cong., 2d Sess., Exec. Doc. 57, 1868.

U. S. Congress. House. *Report of the Joint Committee on Reconstruction at the First Session Thirty-ninth Congress.* Washington: Government Printing Office, 1866.

U. S. Congress. House. 39 Cong. 2 Sess., no. 16, "Report of the Select Committee on the New Orleans Riots."

U. S. Congress. House. R. K. Cutler Testimony, House Report, 39th Cong., 1st Sess., Report no. 16.

U. S. Congress. House. Dr. S. J. Quinvy Testimony, House Report, 39th Cong., 1st Sess., Report no. 101.

U. S. Congress. Senate. Ulysses S. Grant Report, Senate ex. Doc., 39 Cong., 1st Sess., no. 2.

U. S. Congress. Senate. Benjamin C. Truman's Report, Senate Ex. Doc., 39 Cong., 1 Sess., no. 43.

U. S. Congress. Senate. *Proceedings of the Senate Sitting for the Trial of Andrew Johnson, President of the United States.* Washington, D.C.: F. & J. Rives & George A. Bailey, 1868.

U. S. Congress. Senate. *Trial of Andrew Johnson, President of the United States, on Impeachment by the House of Representatives for High Crimes and Misdemeanors.* 3 vols. 40th Cong., 2nd Sess., 1868. Washington, DC: Government Printing Office, 1868.

U. S. Constitution.

War of the Rebellion: A Compilation of the Official Records of the Union and Confederate Armies. 128 vols. Harrisburg: National Historical Society, 1971. *(OR)*

Newspapers

Chicago Tribune
Cleveland Herald
Cleveland Plain Dealer
Nashville Banner
Nashville Union
Nashville Union and American
The Nation
New York Herald
New York Times
New York Tribune
New York World
Washington Daily National Intelligencer
Washington Morning Chronicle

Primary Sources

Adams, Henry. *The Education of Henry Adams, an Autobiography.* Boston: Houghton Mifflin Company, 1918.

Baker, G. E., ed. *The Works of William H. Seward.* 5 vols. Boston: Houghton Mifflin Company, 1884.

Barnes, John S. "With Lincoln from Washington to Richmond in 1865," *Appleton's Magazine,* vol. 11 (June 1907), 742–51.

Basler, Roy P., ed. *The Collected Works of Abraham Lincoln,* 9 vols. New Brunswick: Rutgers University Press, 1953–55.

Bigelow, John, ed. *The Writings and Speeches of Samuel J. Tilden,* 2 vols. New York: Harper & Sons, 1885.

Blaine, James G. *Twenty Years in Congress, 1861–1881,* 2 vols. Norwich, Conn.: Henry Bill Publishing Company, 1884.

Boutwell, George S. *Reminiscences of Sixty Years in Public Affairs.* 2 vols. New York: McClure Phillips & Company, 1902.

_____. "Johnson's Plot and Motives," *North American Review* 141 (December 1886), 570–79.

Browning, Orville Hickman. *The Diary of Orville Hickman Browning.* Edited by James G. Randall and Theodore C. Pease. 2 vols. Springfield: Illinois State Historical Library, 1933.

Butler, Benjamin F. *Autobiography and Personal Reminiscences: Butler's Book.* Boston: A. M. Thayer, 1892.

_____. *Private and Official Correspondence of General Benjamin F. Butler.* Edited by Jessie Ames Marshall. 5 vols. Norwood, Mass.: Plimpton Press, 1917.

Cowan, Frank. *Andrew Johnson, President of the United States, Reminiscences of his Private Life and Character.* Greensburgh, PA: Oliver Publishing House, 1894.

Cox, Jacob D. *Military Reminiscences of the Civil War.* 2 vols. New York: Scribner's, 1900.

Cox, Samuel S. *Three Decades of Federal Legislation.* Providence: J. A. and R. H. Reid, 1885.

Craven, John J. *Prison Life of Jefferson Davis.* New York: Carleton Publisher, 1866.

Crook, William H. "Andrew Johnson in the White House, Being the Reminiscences of Col. W. H. Crook," compiled and written by Margarita S. Gerry. *Century Magazine,* vol. 76, no. 5 (September 1908), 654–69; no. 6 (October 1908), 865–78.

_____. "Lincoln's Last Day; new facts now told for the first time. Compiled and written down by Margarita S. Gerry." *Harper's Monthly Magazine,* vol. 115, pt. 1 (September 1907), 519–30.

_____. *Memoirs of the White House.* Henry Rood, ed. Boston: Little, Brown & Company, 1911.

_____. *Through Five Administrations: Reminiscences of Colonel William H. Crook, Body-guard to President Lincoln.* Margarita Spalding Gerry, ed. New York: Harper's Brothers, 1910.

Dana, Charles A. *Recollections of the Civil War.* New York: D. Appleton & Company, 1899.

Davis, Varina Howell. *Jefferson Davis Ex-President of the Confederate States of America,* 2 vols. New York: Belford & Company, 1890.

Dennett, Tyler, ed. *Lincoln and the Civil War in the Diaries and Letters of John Hay.* New York: Dodd, Mead, 1939.

Depew, Chauncey M. *My Memories of Eighty Years.* New York: Macmillan Company, 1922.

DeWitt, David Miller. *The Impeachment and Trial of Andrew Johnson.* New York: Macmillan Company, 1903.

Diary and Correspondence of Salmon P. Chase: Annual Report of the American Historical Society for the Year 1902. vol. 2. Washington: Government Printing Office, 1903.

Donald, David H. *Inside Lincoln's Cabinet: The Civil War Diaries of Salmon P. Chase.* New York: Longmans Green & Company, 1954.

Fessenden, Francis. *Life and Public Services of William Pitt Fessenden.* Boston: Houghton Mifflin Company, 2 vols. 1907.

Field, Maunsell B. *Memories of Many Men and Some Women.* New York: Harper's Brothers, 1874.

Forney, John W. *Anecdotes of Public Men,* 2 vols. New York: Harper's Brothers., 1873–1881.

Graf, LeRoy P. and Haskins, Ralph W. et al., eds. *The Papers of Andrew Johnson.* 14 vols. Knoxville: University of Tennessee Press, 1967–97.

Grant, Ulysses S. *Personal Memoirs of Ulysses S. Grant.* 2 vols. New York: Charles L. Webster & Company, 1885.

Greeley, Horace. *Proceedings of the First Three Republican National Conventions, 1856, 1860, and 1864.* Minneapolis: 1893.

Hamilton, J. G. de Roulhac, ed. *The Papers of Thomas Ruffin.* Raleigh: North Carolina Historical Commission, 1920.

Henderson, John B. "Emancipation and Impeachment," *Century Magazine,* vol. 95, no. 2 (December 1922), 200–215.

Herndon, William H. and Jesse W. Weik. *Abraham Lincoln.* 2 vols. New York: D. Appleton and Company, 1896.

Hoar, George F. *Autobiography of Seventy Years.* 2 vols., New York: Scribner's Sons, 1903.

Howe, M. A. DeWolfe, ed. *Home Letters of General Sherman.* New York: Charles Scribner's Sons, 1909.

Julian, George W. *Political Recollections, 1840–1872.* Chicago: Jansen McClurg & Co., 1884.

Kendrick, Benjamin F. *The Journal of the Joint Committee of Fifteen on Reconstruction, 39th Congress, 1865–1867.* New York: Columbia University Press, 1915.

McClure, Alexander K. *Abraham Lincoln and Men of War-Times.* Philadelphia: Times Publishing Company, 1892.

McCulloch, Hugh. *Men and Measures of Half a Century.* New York: DaCapo Press, 1970.

McPherson, Edward. *The Political History of the United States of America During the Period of Reconstruction.* Chicago: James J. Chapman, 1880.

_____. *The Great Rebellion.* New York: D. Appleton & Company, 1864.

Moore, Frank, Comp. *Speeches of Andrew Johnson.* Boston: Little Brown & Company, 1866.

Moore, John Bassett, ed. *The Works of James Buchanan, Comprising His Speeches, State Papers, and Private Correspondence.* New York: Antiquarian Press, 1960.

Moore, William G. "Notes of Colonel W. G. Moore, Private Secretary to President Johnson, 1866–1888," edited by St. George L. Sioussat, *American Historical Review,* 19 (October 1913), 98–132.

Morgan, James Morris. *Recollections of a Rebel Reefer*. Boston: Houghton Mifflin Company, 1917.

Nicolay, John G. and John Hay. *Abraham Lincoln, A History*, 10 vols. New York: Century Company, 1894–1905.

Palmer, Beverly, ed. *The Selected Letters of Charles Sumner*, 2 vols. Boston: Little, Brown & Company, 1990.

Palmer, John M. *Personal Recollections of John M. Palmer; The Story of an Earnest Life*. Cincinnati: R. Clarke Company, 1901.

Phillips, Wendell. *Speeches, Lectures and Letters*. Boston: James Redpath, 1867.

Piatt, Donn. *Memories of the Men Who Saved the Union*. New York: Bedford Clarke & Company, 1887.

Pierce, Edward L. *Memoir and Letters of Charles Sumner*. 4 vols. Boston: Roberts Brothers, 1893.

Reid, Whitelaw. *After the War: A Southern Tour, May 1, 1865 to May 1, 1866*. London: Sampson Low, Son, & Marston, 1866.

Richardson, James D. *A Compilation of the Messages and Papers of the Presidents, 1789–1897*. 11 vols. Washington: Bureau of National Literature and Art, 1897–1907.

_____. *A Compilation of the Messages and Papers of the Confederacy*. 2 vols. Washington: Bureau of National Literature and Art, 1896–99.

Ross, Edmund G. *Impeachment of Andrew Johnson*. Santa Fe: New Mexican Printing Company, 1896.

Schofield, John M. *Forty-Six Years in the Army*. New York: Century Company, 1897.

Schurz, Carl. *The Reminiscences of Carl Schurz*. 3 vols. New York: Doubleday, Page & Company, 1908.

Seward, Frederick W. *Reminiscences of a War-Time Statesman and Diplomat, 1830–1915*. New York and London: G. P. Putnam's Sons, 1916.

Sherman, John. *Recollections of Forty Years in the House, Senate and Cabinet, an Autobiography*. 2 vols. Chicago: Werner Company, 1895.

Sherman, William T. *Memoirs of General William T. Sherman, by Himself*. 2 vols. New York: D. Appleton & Company, 1875.

Sherman, William T. *Home Letters of General Sherman*. M. A. DeWolfe Howe, ed. New York: Charles Scribner's Sons, 1909.

Simpson, Brooks D. et al. *Advice After Appomattox: Letters to Andrew Johnson, 1865–1866*. Knoxville: University of Tennessee Press, 1987.

Smith, Theodore Clarke, ed. *Life and Letters of James Abram Garfield*. 2 vols. New Haven: Yale University Press, 1925.

Stephens, Alexander H. *A Constitutional View of the Late War Between the States*. 2 vols. Philadelphia: National Publishing Company, 1868–1870.

Stewart, William M. *Reminiscences*. George Rothwell Brown, ed. Washington, D.C.: Neale, 1908.

Sumner, Charles. *The Works of Charles Sumner*, 15 vols. Boston: Lee and Shephard, 1870–1883.

Thorndike, Rachel Sherman, ed. *The Sherman Letters: Correspondence Between General and Senator Sherman from 1837 to 1891*. New York: Charles Scribner's Sons, 1894.

Truman, Benjamin C., "Anecdotes of Andrew Johnson," *Century Magazine*, vol. 81, no. 1 (January 1913).

Turner, Harriet S. "Recollections of Andrew Johnson," *Harper's Monthly*, no. 120 (January 1910), 168–76.

Turner, Justin G. and Turner, Linda Levitt. *Mary Todd Lincoln, Her Life and Letters*. New York: Alfred P. Knopf, 1972.

Villard, Henry. *Memoirs of Henry Villard, Journalist and Financier, 1835–1900*. 2 vols. Boston: Houghton Mifflin, 1904.

Weed, Harriet A., ed. *The Life of Thurlow Weed*. 2 vols. Boston: Houghton Mifflin Company, 1884.

Welles, Gideon. *Diary of Gideon Welles, Secretary of the Navy under Lincoln and Johnson*. 3 vols. Boston and New York, Houghton Mifflin Company, 1960.

Secondary Sources

Ashley, Charles S. "Governor Ashley's Biography and Messages," *Contributions to the Historical Society of Montana*, 6 (1907), 143–289.

Avary, Myrta Lockett. *Dixie After the War*.

New York: Doubleday Page & Company, 1906.

Bancroft, Frederic. *Life of William H. Seward.* 2 vols. New York: Harper & Brothers, 1900.

Barnes, William H. *History of the Thirty-ninth Congress.* New York: Harper & Brothers, 1868.

Beale, Howard K. *The Critical Year: A Study of Andrew Johnson and Reconstruction.* New York: Harcourt, Brace, 1930.

Benedict, Michael Les. *The Impeachment and Trial of Andrew Johnson.* New York: W. W. Norton and Company, 1973.

_____. *A Compromise of Principle: Congressional Republicans and Reconstruction, 1863–1869.* New York: W. W. Norton, 1974.

Blue, Frederick J. *Salmon P. Chase: A Life in Politics.* Kent, Ohio: Kent State University Press, 1987.

Boatner, Mark M., III, *The Civil War Dictionary.* New York: David McKay Company, Inc., 1959.

Bowers, Claude. *The Tragic Era: The Revolution After Lincoln.* Cambridge: Houghton Mifflin Company, 1929.

Brabson, Fay W. *Andrew Johnson: A Life in Pursuit of the Right Course, 1808–1875.* Durham, NC: Duke University Press, 1972.

Bradbury, Erwin Stanley. *Simon Cameron, Lincoln's Secretary of War.* Philadelphia: University of Pennsylvania Press, 1966

Bradford, Gamaliel. *Confederate Portraits.* Boston: Houghton Mifflin Company, 1912.

_____. *Union Portraits.* Boston: Houghton Mifflin & Company, 1916.

Brock, William R. *An American Crisis: Congress and Reconstruction, 1865–1867.* New York: St. Martin's Press, 1963.

Bryce, James. *The American Commonwealth.* 2 vols. New York: Macmillan Company, 1924.

Burdick, Charles K. *The Law of the Constitution.* New York: C. P. Putnam's Sons, 1922.

Burgess, John W. *Reconstruction and the Constitution, 1866–1876.* New York: Da-Capo Press, 1970.

Callender, Edward Belcher. *Thaddeus Stevens, Commoner.* Boston: Houghton Mifflin, 1882.

Caskey, Willie Malvin. *Secession and Restoration in Louisiana.* Baton Rouge: University of Louisiana Press, 1938.

Castel, Albert. *The Presidency of Andrew Johnson.* Lawrence: Regents Press of Kansas, 1979.

Chadsey, Charles Ernest. *The Struggle Between President Johnson and Congress Over Reconstruction.* New York: Columbia University Press, 1896.

Charnwood, Lord. *Abraham Lincoln.* New York: Henry Holt and Company, 1917.

Clemenceau, Georges. *American Reconstruction, 1865-1870.* Fernand Baldensperger, ed. New York: Da Capo, 1969.

Cox, LaWanda and John Cox. *Politics, Principle and Prejudice, 1865–1866.* New York: Free Press, 1963.

Craven, Amory. *Reconstruction: the Ending of the Civil War.* New York: Holt, Rinehart and Winston, Inc., 1969.

Current, Richard N. *Old Thad Stevens.* Madison: University of Wisconsin Press, 1942.

Curtis, George Ticknor. *Life of James Buchanan,* 2 vols. New York: Harper & Brothers, 1883.

Davis, Burke. *The Long Surrender,* New York: Random House, 1985.

Donald, David. *Charles Sumner and the Rights of Man.* New York: Alfred P. Knopf, 1970.

_____. *The Politics of Reconstruction 1863–1869.* Baton Rouge: Louisiana State University Press, 1965.

_____. *Charles Sumner and the Coming of the Civil War.* New York: Alfred A. Knopf, 1967.

Dunning, William A. *Reconstruction, Political and Economic 1865–1877.* New York: Harper and Bros., 1907.

_____. *Essays on the Civil War and Reconstruction.* New York: Macmillan Company, 1898.

Eisenschmil, Otto. *In the Shadow of Lincoln's Death.* New York: Funk and Wagnels, 1940.

Fairman, Charles. *Reconstruction and Reunion, 1864–88.* New York: Macmillan Company, 1971.

Faust, Patricia L., ed. *Historical Times Illustrated Encyclopedia of the Civil War.* New York: Harper and Row, 1986.

Fleming, Walter L. *The Sequel of Appomat-*

tox. New Haven: Yale University Press, 1920.

Flower, Frank Abial. *Edwin McMaster's Stanton, The Autocrat of Rebellion, Emancipation, and Reconstruction.* Akron: Saalfield Publishing Company, 1905.

Foner, Eric. *A Short History of Reconstruction 1863–1867.* New York: Harper & Row, Publishers, 1990.

Gorham, George C. *Life and Public Services of Edwin M. Stanton.* 2 vols. Boston: Houghton Mifflin Company, 1899.

Hall, Clifton R. *Andrew Johnson, Military Governor of Tennessee.* Princeton: Princeton University Press, 1916.

Hamlin, Charles Eugene. *Life and Times of Hannibal Hamlin.* Cambridge: Riverside Press, 1899.

Hanchett, William. *The Lincoln Murder Conspiracies.* Urbana, Ill.: University of Illinois Press, 1983.

Hart, Albert Bushnell. *Salmon Portland Chase.* New York: Chelsea House, 1980.

Herbert, Hilary A. et al. *Why the Solid South? or Reconstruction and Its Results.* Baltimore: R. H. Woodward & Company, 1890.

Herndon, William H. and Weik, Jesse W. *Herndon's Lincoln: The True Story of a Great Life, The History and Personal Recollections of Abraham Lincoln.* 3 vols. Chicago: Belford, Clarke, & Co., 1889.

Hesseltine, William B. *Lincoln's Plan of Reconstruction.* Chicago: Quadrangle Books, 1967.

Hollister, C. J. *Life of Schuyler Colfax.* New York: G. P. Putnam's, 1886.

Hyman, Harold M. ed. *The Radical Republicans and Reconstruction 1861–1870.* Indianapolis: Bobbs Merrill, 1967.

James, Joseph B. *The Framing of the Fourteenth Amendment.* Urbana, Ill., University of Illinois Press, 1956.

Jellison, Charles J. *Fessenden of Maine: Civil War Senator.* Syracuse: Syracuse University Press, 1962.

Jones, James S. *Life of Andrew Johnson.* Greeneville, TN: Greeneville Publishing Company, 1901.

Klaus, S. ed. *The Milligan Case.* New York: Harcourt, Brace & Company, 1929.

Korngold, Ralph. *Thaddeus Stevens, A Being Darkly Wise and Rudely Great.* New York: Harcourt, Brace & Company, 1955.

Lewis, Lloyd. *Sherman, Fighting Prophet.* New York: Harcourt, Brace & Company, 1932.

Lomask, Milton. *Andrew Johnson, President on Trial.* New York: Farrar, Strauss and Cudahy, 1960.

Lothrop, Thornton K. *William Henry Seward.* Boston and New York: Houghton Mifflin & Co., 1896.

Macauley, Lord. *Miscellaneous Works of Lord Macauley.* Lady Trevelyan, ed. 5 vols. New York: Harper & Brothers, 1879.

Martin, Edward Winslow. *Behind the Scenes in Washington, Being a Complete and Graphic Account of the Credit Mobilier Investigation.* Washington: Continental Publishing Company, 1873.

Maverick, Augustus. *Henry J. Raymond.* Hartford: 1870.

McCall, Samuel W. *Thaddeus Stevens.* Boston: Houghton Mifflin Company, 1899.

McCarthy, Charles H. *Lincoln's Plan of Reconstruction.* New York: AMS Press, Inc., 1966.

McFeely, William S. *Yankee Stepfather: General O. O. Howard and the Freedmen.* New Haven: Yale University Press, 1968.

_____. *Grant: A Biography.* New York: W. W. Norton & Company, 1981.

McKitrick, Eric L. *Andrew Johnson and Reconstruction.* New York: Oxford University Press, 1960.

Metzger, Milton. *Thaddeus Stevens and the Fight for Negro Rights.* New York: Thomas Y. Crowell, 1967.

Milton, George Fort. *The Age of Hate: Andrew Johnson and the Radicals.* New York: Coward McCann, 1930.

Morse, John T., Jr. *Abraham Lincoln,* 2 vols. Boston: Houghton Mifflin & Co., 1893.

Nelson, William E. *The Fourteenth Amendment: From Political Principle to Judicial Doctrine.* Cambridge: Harvard University Press, 1988.

Niven, John. *Gideon Welles, Lincoln's Secretary of the Navy.* New York: Oxford University Press, 1973.

_____. *Salmon P. Chase, A Biography.* New York: Oxford University Press, 1995.

Oberholtzer, Ellis Paxson. *The History of the United States Since the Civil War.* 5 vols. New York: Macmillan Company, 1917–37.

Oubre, Claude F. *Forty Acres and a Mule: The*

Freedmen's Bureau and Black Landownership. Baton Rouge: Louisiana State University Press, 1978.

Parker, William Belmont. *The Life and Public Services of Justin Smith Morrill*. Boston: Houghton Mifflin Company, 1924.

Pearson, Henry Greenleaf. *Life of John A. Andrew, Governor of Massachusetts, 1861–1865*. 2 vols. Boston: Houghton Mifflin Company, 1904.

Phifer, Gregg. "Andrew Johnson Delivers His Arguments," *Tennessee Historical Quarterly*, vol. XI (spring 1952), 212–34.

Randall, J. G. *The Civil War and Reconstruction*. Boston: D. C. Heath & Company, 1937.

Randall, J. G. *Lincoln the President*. 4 vols. New York: Dodd, Mead & Co., 1945–55.

Rehnquist, William H. *Grand Inquests: The Historic Impeachments of Justice Samuel Chase and President Andrew Johnson*. New York: William Morrow & Co., Inc., 1992.

Rhodes, James Ford. *History of the United States from the Compromise of 1850 to the Final Restoration of Home Rule in the South in 1877*, 7 vols. New York, Macmillan Company, 1910.

Riddleberger, Patrick W. *George Washington Julian: Radical Republican*. Indianapolis: Bobbs Merrill, 1966.

Salter, William. *The Life of James W. Grimes*. New York: D. Appleton & Company, 1876.

Savage, John. *Life and Public Services of Andrew Johnson*. New York: Derby & Miller Publishers, 1866.

Schouler, James. *History of the United States Under the Constitution*. 7 vols. New York: Dodd, Mead & Company, 1880–1913.

Schuckers, J. W. *The Life and Public Services of Salmon Portland Chase*. New York: D. Appleton and Company, 1874.

Sefton, James E. *Andrew Johnson and the Uses of Constitutional Power*. Boston: Little, Brown and Co., 1980.

Shenton, James P. *Robert John Walker: A Politician from Jackson to Lincoln*. New York: Columbia University Press, 1961.

Sioussat, St. George L. "Andrew Johnson and the Early Phases of the Homestead Bill," *Tennessee Historical Magazine*, VI (1920), 14–75.

Stampp, Kenneth M. *The Era of Reconstruction, 1865–1877*. New York: Alfred A. Knopf, 1965.

Stanwood, Edward. *A History of the Presidency from 1788 to 1897*. 2 vols. Boston: Houghton Mifflin Company, 1916.

Stoddard, William O. *Abraham Lincoln and Andrew Johnson*. New York: Frederick A. Stokes & Brother, 1888.

Storey, Moorfield. *Charles Sumner*. Boston: Houghton Mifflin Company, 1900.

Stryker, Lloyd Paul. *Andrew Johnson, A Study in Courage*. New York: Macmillan Company, 1929.

Tarbell, Ida. *The Life of Abraham Lincoln*. 4 vols. New York: Lincoln History Society, 1904.

Temple, Oliver P. *Notable Men of Tennessee, from 1833–1875*. New York: Cosmopolitan Press, 1912.

Thayer, William Roscoe. *John Hay*. 2 vols. Boston and New York: Houghton Mifflin Company, 1908.

Thomas, Benjamin, and Harold M. Hyman. *Stanton: The Life and Times of Lincoln's Secretary of War*. New York: Alfred A. Knopf, 1962.

Trefousse, Hans L. *Andrew Johnson*. New York: W. W. Norton & Co., 1989.

_____. *Benjamin Franklin Wade: Radical Republican from Ohio*. New York: Twayne Publishers, Inc., 1963.

_____. *Impeachment of a President*. Knoxville: University of Tennessee Press, 1975.

_____. *Thaddeus Stevens, Nineteenth Century Egalitarian*. Chapel Hill: University of North Carolina Press, 1997.

Van Deusen, Glyndon G. *William Henry Seward: Lincoln's Secretary of State*. New York: Oxford University Press, 1967.

Warden, Robert B. *An Account of the Private Life and Public Services of Samuel Portland Chase*. Cincinnati: Wilstach, Baldwin & Company, 1874.

Warren, Charles. *The Supreme Court in United States History*. 3 vols. Boston: Little, Brown & Company, 1922.

White, Horace. *The Life of Lyman Trumball*. Boston: Houghton Mifflin Company, 1913.

Williams, T. Harry. *Lincoln and the Radicals*. Madison: University of Wisconsin Press, 1941.

Wills, Brian Steel, *A Battle from the Start: The*

Life of Nathan Bedford Forrest. New York: Harper Collins Publishers, 1992.

Wilson, Woodrow. *Division and Reunion*. New York: Longmans Green & Company, 1925.

Winston, Robert W. *Andrew Johnson: Plebian and Patriot*. New York: Henry Holt, 1928.

Woldman, Albert A. *Lincoln and the Russians*. Cleveland and New York: World Publishing Company, 1952.

Woodburn, James Albert. *The Life of Thaddeus Stevens: A Study in American Political History, Especially in the Period of the Civil War and Reconstruction*. Indianapolis: Bobbs, Merrill Company, 1913.

Woodley, Thomas Frederick. *Thadeus Stevens*. Harrisburg: Telegraph Press, 1934.

Zornow, William Frank. *Lincoln & the Party Divided*. Norman: University of Oklahoma Press, 1954.

Index